MASTERING THE
OLD TESTAMENT

THE COMMUNICATOR'S COMMENTARY SERIES
OLD TESTAMENT

MASTERING THE OLD TESTAMENT

MICAH, NAHUM, HABAKKUK, ZEPHANIAH, HAGGAI, ZECHARIAH, MALACHI

WALTER KAISER

LLOYD J. OGILVIE, GENERAL EDITOR

WORD PUBLISHING
Dallas•London•Vancouver•Melbourne

To:
Robert Duncan Culver,
My first Mentor in the Minor Prophets,
and to the memory of
Arlene Culver
Friends, Colleagues, Fellow Servants of Christ

Library of Congress Cataloging in Publication Data
Main entry under title:

Mastering the Old Testament
[The Communicator's commentary.]
   Bibliography: p.
   Contents: OT21. Micah-Malachi/by Walter C. Kaiser
   1. Bible. O.T.—Commentaries. I. Ogilvie, Lloyd
John. II. Kaiser, Walter C.
BS1151.2.C66   1993   221.7′7   93-39330
ISBN 0–8499–3559–8 (v. OT21) [pbk]
ISBN 0–8499–0427–7 (v. OT21) [hd]

Printed in the United States of America

349   AGF   987654321

Contents

Section Four: The Book of Zephaniah

Section Five: The Book of Haggai

Section Six: The Book of Zechariah

Contents

Editor's Preface

God has called all of His people to be communicators. Everyone who is in Christ is called into ministry. As ministers of "the manifold grace of God," all of us—clergy and laity—are commissioned with a challenge to communicate our faith to individuals and groups, classes and congregations.

The Bible, God's Word, is the objective basis of the truth of His love and power that we seek to communicate. In response to urgent, unexpressed needs of pastors, teachers, Bible study leaders, church school teachers, small group enablers, and individual Christians, the Communicator's Commentary is offered as a penetrating search of the Scriptures of the Old and New Testament to enable vital personal and practical communication of the abundant life.

Many current commentaries and Bible study guides provide only some aspects of a communicator's needs. Some offer in-depth scholarship but no application to daily life. Others are so popular in approach that biblical roots are left unexplained. Few offer impelling illustrations that open windows for the reader to see the exciting application for today's struggles. And most of all, seldom have the expositors given the valuable outlines of passages so needed to help the preacher or teacher in his or her busy life to prepare for communicating the Word to congregations or classes.

This Communicator's Commentary series brings all of these elements together. The authors are scholar-preachers and teachers outstanding in their ability to make the Scriptures come alive for individuals and groups. They are noted for bringing together excellence in biblical scholarship, knowledge of the original Hebrew and Greek, sensitivity to people's needs, vivid illustrative material from biblical, classical, and contemporary sources, and lucid communication by the use of clear outlines of thought. Each has been selected to contribute to this series because of his Spirit-empowered ability to help people live in the skins of biblical characters and provide a "you-are-there" intensity to the drama of events of the Bible which have so much to say about our relationships and responsibilities today.

The design for the Communicator's Commentary gives the reader an overall outline of each book of the Bible. Following the introduction, which reveals the author's approach and salient background on the book, each chapter of the commentary provides the Scripture to be exposited. The New King James Bible has been chosen for the Communicator's Commentary because it combines with integrity the beauty of language, underlying Hebrew and Greek textual basis, and thought-flow of the 1611 King James Version, while replacing obsolete verb forms and other archaisms with their everyday contemporary counterparts for greater readability. Reverence for God is preserved in the capitalization of all pronouns referring to the Father, Son, or Holy Spirit. Readers who are more comfortable with another translation can readily find the parallel passage by means of the chapter and verse reference at the end of each passage being exposited. The paragraphs of exposition combine fresh insights to the Scripture, application, rich illustrative material, and innovative ways of utilizing the vibrant truth for his or her own life and for the challenge of communicating it with vigor and vitality.

It has been gratifying to me as editor of this series to receive enthusiastic progress reports from each contributor. As they worked, all were gripped with new truths from Scripture—God-given insights into passages, previously not written in the literature of biblical explanation. A prime objective of this series is for each user to find the same awareness: that God speaks with newness through the Scriptures when we approach them with a ready mind and a willingness to communicate what He has given; that God delights to give communicators of His Word "I-never-saw-that-in-that-verse-before" intellectual insights so that our listeners and readers can have "I-never-realized-all-that-was-in-that-verse" spiritual experiences.

The thrust of the commentary series unequivocally affirms that God speaks through the Scriptures today to engender faith, enable adventuresome living of the abundant life, and establish the basis of obedient discipleship. The Bible, the unique Word of God, is unlimited as a resource for Christians in communicating our hope to others. It is our weapon in the battle for truth, the guide for ministry, and the irresistible force for introducing others to God.

12

A biblically rooted communication of the Gospel holds in unity and oneness what divergent movements have wrought asunder. This commentary series courageously presents personal faith, caring for individuals, and social responsibility as essential, inseparable dimensions of biblical Christianity. It seeks to present the quadrilateral Gospel in its fulness which calls us to unreserved commitment to Christ, unrestricted self-esteem in His grace, unqualified love for others in personal evangelism, and undying efforts to work for justice and righteousness in a sick and suffering world.

A growing renaissance in the church today is being led by clergy and laity who are biblically rooted, Christ-centered, and Holy Spirit-empowered. They have dared to listen to people's most urgent questions and deepest needs and then to God as He speaks throughout the Bible. Biblical preaching is the secret of growing churches. Bible study classes and small groups are equipping the laity for ministry in the world. Dynamic Christians are finding that daily study of God's Word allows the Spirit to do in them what He wishes to communicate through them to others. These days are the most exciting time since Pentecost. The Communicator's Commentary is offered to be a primary resource of new life for this renaissance.

It has been very encouraging to receive the enthusiastic responses of pastors and teachers to the twelve New Testament volumes of the Communicator's Commentary series. The letters from communicators on the firing line in pulpits, classes, study groups, and Bible fellowship clusters across the nation, as well as the reviews of scholars and publication analysts, have indicated that we have been on target meeting a need for a distinctly different kind of commentary on the Scriptures, a commentary that is primarily aimed at helping interpreters of the Bible to equip the laity for ministry.

This positive response has led the publisher to press on with an additional twenty-one volumes covering the books of the Old Testament. These new volumes rest upon the same goals and guidelines that undergird the New Testament volumes. Scholar-preachers with facility in Hebrew as well as vivid contemporary exposition have been selected as authors. The purpose throughout is to aid the preacher and teacher in the challenge and adventure of Old Testament exposition in communication. In each volume you will meet Yahweh, the "I AM" Lord who is Creator, Sustainer, and Redeemer in the unfolding drama of His call and care of Israel. He is the Lord who acts, intervenes, judges, and presses His people into the immense challenges and privileges of being a chosen people, a holy nation. And in the descriptive exposition of each passage, the implications of the ultimate revelation of Yahweh in Jesus Christ, His Son, our Lord, are carefully spelled out to maintain unity and oneness in the preaching and teaching of the Gospel.

I am pleased to introduce to you the author of this volume, Dr. Walter C. Kaiser, Jr. For most readers Dr. Kaiser needs no introduction, for he has distinguished himself over the years as an outstanding scholar, teacher, and writer. It is a privilege to include him among the authors of the Communicator's Commentary.

Walter Kaiser began his academic pilgrimage at Wheaton, where he received the A.B. and the B.D. degrees. He continued his studies at Brandeis University, earning the M.A. and Ph.D. degrees. After beginning his teaching career at Wheaton, Dr. Kaiser joined the faculty of Trinity Evangelical Divinity School in 1966. There he has served in many roles, including Professor of Old Testament and Semitic Languages, Academic Dean, and Senior Vice President of Education. At Trinity, Dr. Kaiser has trained hundreds of outstanding pastors and Christian leaders.

Those of us who have not had the privilege of studying directly under Walter Kaiser have known him through his prolific writings. He is the author of numerous articles in both scholarly journals and popular magazines. This commentary will be Dr. Kaiser's seventeenth book. His writings have helped a generation of Christians to understand the Old Testament and its relevance to today's world.

This commentary covers the last seven books of the minor prophets, Micah through Malachi. It features a thoroughgoing exegesis of all biblical passages, with an eye to the needs of the contemporary interpreter. As you use this commentary, you will no doubt be impressed with Dr. Kaiser's breadth of learning and able skill as an exegete. You will also appreciate his application of the text to our challenges today. This volume will help the modern communicator of the Bible to understand and to convey the message of the last seven minor prophets.

Surveys tell us that Americans are becoming less and less familiar with the Bible. Such is especially true of the Old Testament, and even more so, of the minor prophets. Yet as Christians and as a nation we desperately need to hear afresh God's call to righteousness, justice, and faith as found in the latter books of the Old Testament. This commentary will help us to hear again the fullness of God's word. I thank Walter Kaiser for his valuable contribution to the Communicator's Commentary, and commend it to you with confidence.

LLOYD OGILVIE

Author's Preface

If we are ever going to bridge the gap between the "then" of the B.C. message of the Old Testament and the "now" of the contemporary audience of readers of and listeners to the Scripture, it is going to take a different type of commentary than what we have generally come to expect.

This volume is one attempt to fill the need for that different type of commentary. It is consistently concerned with two questions: what *did* a text mean when it was first written and, just as significant, what *is* the Lord saying to His readers in these modern days? The outlines for the seven books discussed here are not the traditional descriptive surveys of the books' contents. Instead, they are modern declarations of how the books can continue to speak to us in our involvement with modernity. (The notes on Malachi are a loose rewrite of a volume I wrote for Baker Book House entitled *Malachi: God's Unchanging Love.* That copyright has now been returned to me.) This has not always been an easy assignment, for there are practically no guides available. We found ourselves continually pioneering. But our prayer is that lay students, Bible study leaders, college and seminary teachers, and pastors will all find our results both stimulating and time-saving in bridging the enormous chasm between the "then" and the "now" of these texts.

I have been amazed once again, as I have studied these texts, at how powerfully and poignantly they speak to many of the issues I have heard many raise in these days—issues for which precious few have directed us to any authoritative answers. These seven prophets (Micah, Nahum, Habakkuk, Zephaniah, Haggai, Zechariah and Malachi) have a mighty contribution to make.

My New Testament teacher, Dr. Merrill Tenney (now with the Lord), observed in an off-hand manner one day in class, "If you want a heresy to grow, simply neglect one area of God's Word or a particular doctrine and the next generation will, in all likelihood, fill that vacuum with an exaggeration that either verges on heresy or is indeed just that!"

Could that not be the situation with regard to the teaching and preaching of the Minor Prophets? Where could one find a more neglected part of God's Word? The designation "minor" seems to imply that the prophets are not all that significant. However, the term indicates the books' length, not their significance. The twelve books that come at the end of our English canons are much shorter than those of the "major prophets" like Isaiah, Jeremiah, and Ezekiel. The text of each of those three prophets extends for almost 100 pages, whereas the texts of all the Minor Prophets together hardly fill seventy-five pages. But all of that says nothing about the significance of the books.

So, we conclude with the same challenge the apostle Paul gave when he noted in Acts 20:27 that he had "not shunned to declare [to his generation] the whole counsel of God." I wonder what will be said of our Bible study patterns, the balance of our teaching and the breadth of our preaching? Will we be able to say that we have covered the whole of the biblical canon? It is sad to consider that all too many teachers and pastors hardly turn to the text these days for more than a "jump start" for what *they* want to say. One used to be able to follow a person who carried a Bible on a Sunday morning and find a sound, Bible-preaching church. Unfortunately, all too few carry their Bibles to church anymore. No longer it is not only the fad; it simply is a waste of time—one hardly needs to refer to it for more than a peek at a slogan or two. Great exposition of the Bible is getting rarer and rarer. Would that there were a holy clamor for its return!

If someone were to err in serving a meal with too many calories, too much fat or foods that were carcinogenic, we would be emotionally upset and raise as strong a protest as we could. But there is an even greater danger of junk theology, of carcinogenic religious pep talks that are being accepted and well received in almost any secular setting. Who is raising a cry of despair over these abuses? It will be a sad day when the lectern and the pulpit capitulate to every fad and eddy of the day—responding to society's changes and playing a "me too" game—instead of boldly setting the trends and announcing the powerful word of God. Our teachers and preachers must expect the word of God to effect changes in society.

These seven Minor Prophets are not for those who are timid in their Christian faith. Their boldness will initially shock most, but will ultimately bring an amazing amount of insight, light and great hope to both our present and future ministry and service.

It has been a pleasure to work with Lloyd J. Ogilvie, the General Editor of the *Communicator's Commentary*, and with the publisher, Word Books.

May our Lord be magnified as He is set forth in all of His majestic magnificence in these seven Minor Prophets. I pray that our Lord's church may be unusually strengthened, challenged, and moved to greater endeavors because of her response to the mighty declaration of our Lord in His Word!

WALTER C. KAISER, JR.

SECTION ONE:

The Book of Micah

Micah 1:1–7:10

Introduction to Micah

One of the great ages of prophecy was the eighth century B.C., the century when Amos, Hosea, Isaiah, Jonah and Micah were ministering. Micah, who lived in the last quarter of the 700s (c. 735–690 B.C.), is not as well known today as are his contemporaries. We do know that in his lifetime he made a strong impression because we have direct evidence that Micah's words were still being recalled a century later by the prophet Jeremiah (Jer. 26:18–19, quoting Mic. 3:12).

THE AUTHOR

Although Micah was a prophet primarily to the southern kingdom and lived between c. 735–690 B.C., he is sometimes confused with another prophet who bears the longer form of his name, Micaiah ben Imlah (1 Kings 22:8–28; 2 Chron. 18:3–27), a prophet to the northern kingdom almost 100 years earlier during the reign of King Ahab (c. 874–852 B.C.). The confusion arises not only out of the prophets' similar names; so similar are these prophets in some respects that several scholars have suggested that the eighth century Micah deliberately patterned himself after the ministry and characteristics of Micaiah ben Imlah. The similarities are these:

Micaiah ben Imlah (1 Kings 22):	Micah of Moresheth (Mic.):
1. Each had a contest with false prophets (22:6–12, 19–25)	Micah 2:6,11
2. Each mentions the horn of iron (22:11)	Micah 4:13
3. Each mentions the smiting on the cheek (22:24)	Micah 5:1
4. They introduce their messages similarly: "Take heed all you people" (22:28)	Micah 1:2; 3:1; 6:1 "Hear, all you people"

These similarities, however, are better understood to be coincidental and circumstantial rather than evidence of deliberate patterning.

Both Micaiah and Micah mean "Who is like Yahweh?" Micah has even left his calling card within his prophecy by artfully including his name in one of the most important questions posed in his book: "Who is a God like You, pardoning iniquity and passing over the transgression of the remnant of His heritage?" (Mic. 7:18).

Micah was a native of a somewhat obscure village in Judah, Moresheth-gath. Moresheth was about twenty miles southwest of Jerusalem, not far from the Philistine city of Gath. The site today is unoccupied and is a rather large tell with a commanding view of the lowlands (also called the "Shephelah"). Since he was known as "Micah of Moresheth," many suppose that he was a resident of Jerusalem. Had the prophet continued to live in Moresheth, many reason, he would not have been known as the one who *came* from Moresheth. More likely, since Micah was as common a name then as our English derivatives of Michael, Michelle, and Micky are today, his place of origin may merely have distinguished him from the several other Micahs of his time. Certainly it is concluding too much to allege, as many have, that including his place of origin implied that he was an outsider to Jerusalem and to the other professional prophets in that capital city, as he functioned as a bold shaper of national and spiritual policy for the southern kingdom of Judah.

Micah ministered during the reigns of Jotham, Ahaz and Hezekiah (c. 750–686 B.C.). Initially, at least, he also ministered to the northern kingdom and to its capital, Samaria. It was not long, however, before Samaria fell, in 722 B.C., to the Assyrians.

BACKGROUND TO THE BOOK

The death of the Judean king Uzziah in 740/739 B.C. is an event in history that closes one era and introduces another. The unprecedented prosperity, peace, and enlargement of the boundaries that Israel and Judah had experienced during the days of Jeroboam II in the North and Uzziah in the South came to an abrupt end in 745 B.C. as Tiglath-pileser III of Assyria came to the throne in Nineveh. What followed was an almost unbroken century of Assyrian imperialism, from 745 to 609 B.C., over most of the Near East.

During that Assyrian-dominated period, every nation east of the

Euphrates River lived in mortal fear of most of the Assyrian rulers. As for Tiglath-pileser III, he directed his incursion into Palestine in 734 B.C. over the Philistine Plain, including Ashdod, Ashkelon, Ekron and Gath; but Gaza he conquered. The following year he entered northern Israel, completely destroying Hazor (stratum V), Megiddo (stratum IV) and parts of Galilee and Transjordanian Gilead. He returned again in 732 B.C. to conquer Damascus, the capital of Syria. Before his death in 727 B.C., he reorganized the whole of Syria into an Assyrian province. Through his military campaigns, he had succeeded in reducing Philistia, Israel, Ammon, Moab, Edom and Judah to vassal territories which paid enormous tribute to him and his expensive war machine in Assyria.

At about the same time that Uzziah was completing his golden era and the times were drastically changing down south, Jeroboam II, the greatest king of the Jehu dynasty, was completing his forty-year reign over Israel, in 753 B.C. The moral and spiritual decay that had set in during the reigns of Uzziah (of Judah) and Jeroboam II (of Israel) came to fruition in the next decades; judgment came particularly fast to the northern kingdom, since it was less responsive to the call of the prophets to "turn" back to the Lord. King Hezekiah (and what must have been a small number of Judeans) did, however, respond to Micah's preaching, as we learn from Jeremiah 26:18–19. Israel did not.

Jeroboam II's son, Zachariah, ruled for a mere six months in 753 B.C. before he was assassinated by Shallum. Thus the Jehu dynasty came to an abrupt end, ironically in the same manner as it had begun. Shallum, in turn, was murdered by Menahem after only a one month rule, but Menahem had to pay heavy tribute to Tiglath-pileser III in order to stay in power (c. 752–742 B.C.). His son, Pekahiah, ruled from 742–740 B.C., and he too was assassinated, by Pekah (c. 752–732 B.C.). Pekah made the mistake of leading an anti-Assyrian coalition with Syria's King Rezin, supported by Tyre and Philistia. To reprimand Judah's King Ahaz, who refused to join with them (Isa. 7:1–15), Pekah and Rezin attempted to replace the Davidic King with the son of a certain Tabeel, but the venture failed and so did the coalition's attempt to throw off Assyria's yoke. Pekah was murdered (by now it was becoming a rather routine way to leave office in Israel) by Hoshea, who had the somewhat dubious honor of being the last king of Israel before the capital was taken by Shalmaneser V (727–722 B.C.) of Assyria in 721 B.C. Shalmaneser V's successor, Sargon II (722–705

B.C.), completed the siege of Samaria begun by his predecessor and boasted over the gates of his palace in Khorsabad (a site unknown to moderns for many years, since Sargon II broke with the tradition of having Nineveh as his palace, choosing instead a site thirteen miles northeast) that he was the conqueror of Samaria.

THE UNITY AND STRUCTURE OF MICAH

The literary style of the prophets is quite unusual for most modern readers. Martin Luther commented on it, saying: "They have a queer way of talking, like people who, instead of proceeding in an orderly manner, ramble off from one thing to the next, so that you cannot make head or tail of them or see what they are getting at."[1] Admittedly, there are a number of abrupt transitions from one section to the next, but understanding the prophets is not as hopeless a task as Luther portrayed it to be.

Over the years, there have been four basic proposals as to how Micah was structured. They are:

   I. 1–3 / 4–5 / 6–7
  II. 1–3 / 4–5 / 6:1–7:6(7) / 7:7(8) –20
 III. 1–5 / 6–7
 IV. 1–2 / 3–5 / 6–7

Of the four, the last two have been favored by the greater number of recent scholars. Our preference is for the fourth proposal because each section suggested begins with an imperative "Hear" (šemʾû) followed by a judgment message and concludes with a salvation oracle.[2]

The key to interpreting and structuring the book of Micah certainly must be found in Micah 2:12–13. If these verses are read as a salvation message of hope—as they invariably are by most scholars—then 2:12–13 concludes the judgment section just as chapters 4–5 and 7:7–20 conclude the other two sections of the threefold structure in proposal IV. But so controversial are these two verses that some regard them as intrusive, or read them as a judgment oracle. Others suppose they have been erroneously placed, or even allege that they are unnecessary and hence should be deleted (just like that!). But the text must be dealt with as it stands, for no evidence in the manuscript warrants us doing otherwise. Even Rabbi David Kimchi interpreted 2:12–13 messianically.

So why do some still hesitate to adopt the threefold division based on the literary sigla of "Hear?" Simply because there are two places in addition to Micah 1:2, 3:1 and 6:1 where "hear" appears: Micah 3:9 and 6:9. Since Micah 3:9–12 in many ways is a summary oracle, perhaps it merely echos Micah 3:1, for the addressees of 3:1 and 3:9 are the same. Thus chapter 3 has an A B A structure (vv. 1–4/5–8/9–12). At least in the view of Hagstrom,[3] however, Micah 6:9 can not be treated as an echo of 6:1. But once again the repetition of the word "hear" seems to be a further outworking of the charges made against Judah in Micah 6:1–6, for in Micah 6:9 the sentencing is announced. In that sense, then, we view 6:9 as a continuation of the "hear" in 6:1. In fact, the Hebrew verb "to hear" (*šama'*) appears in the prophets in the imperative form of the basic stem ninety-three times. But it functions as a structural form frequently: e.g., Isaiah 1:2, Amos 3:1; 4:1; 5:1 (note that in chapters 3–6 Amos introduces each of his three discourses with "hear"), Hosea 4:1 and Jeremiah 2:4.

In contrast to Isaiah's long sustained arguments, Micah's style is desultory. His transitions are abrupt as he moves speedily from threatening judgment to promising deliverance (e.g., 2:12–13; 4–5; 7:7–20), and he frequently changes topics just as abruptly (e.g., 7:1–7; 7:11–13). He even switches from one personal pronoun to another and from one number and gender to another (1:10; 6:16; 7:15–19). But most of Micah's abruptness can be attributed to the boldness of his style, the excited nature of his proclamation, and the dynamic nature of his personality; it is hardly fair to attribute Micah's difficult style to a lack of culture.

Micah also uses an abundance of figures of speech, such as similes (1:8,16; 2:12,13; 4:9) and, especially, paronomasia, or "plays on words." In his first chapter alone, almost every one of the cities cited becomes a vehicle for a satirical play on words (often difficult to reproduce in English) (e.g., "Tell it not in 'Tell Town'," v. 1:10 [here I have rendered Gath as "Tell Town" because the Hebrew spelling of the city is similar to the verb "to tell or declare"]).

Citing these factors and more, scholars have generally concluded that Micah lacks any structural unity or coherence of message. Fortunately, this conclusion is beginning to be challenged, particularly in two recent works.[4] The organized structure of the book creates a framework for a coherent message. Within this framework are common themes, recurring motifs, repeated uses of similar rhetorical devices and linking words from one section to the next that bear a family resemblance. Examples of these literary devices will be given in the exposition of the book to follow.

An Outline of Micah

I. What Is the Transgression of My People?   1: 1–16
   A. The Response of Nature to the Appearance of God   1:2–4
   B. The Response of Samaria to the Appearance of God   1:5–7
   C. The Response of Judah to the Appearance of God   1:8–16
   D. Conclusion
II. Is the Spirit of the Lord Restricted?   2: 1–13
   A. The Evil of Coveting   2:1–5
   B. The Evil of Placebo Preaching   2:6–11
   C. Conclusion   2:12–13
III. Is There No Word From the Lord?   3: 1–12
   A. Answers for the Abuse of Position   3:1–4
   B. Answers for the Abuse of Proclamation   3:5–8
   C. Answers for the Abuse of Privilege   3:9–12
   D. Conclusion
IV. Will God's King Not Come and Reign?   4:1–5:15
   A. The Prominence of the Mountain of the Lord   4:1–8
   B. The Working of the Counsel of the Lord   4:9–5:1
   C. The Birth of the Davidic King   5:2–9
   D. The Cleansing of the Land   5:10–15
   E. Conclusion
V. What Does the Lord Require of Us?   6:1–16
   A. Have I Mistreated You?   6:1–3
   B. Have I Required Too Much From You?   6:4–8
   C. Have I Approved of Your Exploiting One Another?   6:9–12
   D. Have I Blessed Your Get–Rich–Quick Schemes?   6:13–16
   E. Conclusion
VI. Where Is the Lord Our God?   7:1–10
   A. When We Look for Just One Righteous Person   7:1–4
   B. When We Look for Just One Friend   7:5–7
   C. When We Look for Just One Adjudicator   7:8–10
   D. Conclusion

VII. Who Is a Pardoning God Like Ours?   7: 11–20
    A. In the Rebuilding of His People   7:11–13
        1. Their Walls—11a
        2. Their New Boundaries—11b
        3. Their Population—12–13
    B. In the Resumption of His Marvelous Deeds   7:14–17
        1. Of Shepherding—14
        2. Of Working Miracles—15
        3. Of Conquering Nations—16–17
    C. In the Remission of Our Sins   7:18–20
        1. Based on Who He Is—18
        2. Based on What He Will Do—19–20
    D. Conclusion

CHAPTER ONE

What Is the Transgression of My People?

Micah 1:1–16

1:1 The word of the LORD that came to Micah of
Moresheth in the days of Jotham, Ahaz, and
Hezekiah, kings of Judah, which he saw concerning
Samaria and Jerusalem.
   2 Hear, all you peoples!
     Listen, O earth, and all that is in it!
     Let the Lord GOD be a witness against you,
     The Lord from His holy temple.
   3 For behold, the LORD is coming out of His place;
     He will come down
     And tread on the high places of the earth.
   4 The mountains will melt under him,
     And the valleys will split
     Like wax before the fire,
     Like waters poured down a steep place.
   5 All this is for the transgression of Jacob
     And for the sins of the house of Israel.
     What is the transgression of Jacob?
     Is it not Samaria?
     And what are the high places of Judah?
     Are they not Jerusalem?
   6 "Therefore I will make Samaria a heap of ruins
      in the field,
     Places for planting a vineyard;
     I will pour down her stones into the valley,
     And I will uncover her foundations.
   7 All her carved images shall be beaten to pieces,

And all her pay as a harlot shall be burned
  with the fire;
All her idols I will lay desolate,
For she gathered it from the pay of a harlot,
And they shall return to the pay of a harlot."

8 Therefore I will wail and howl,
  I will go stripped and naked;
  I will make a wailing like the jackals
  And a mourning like the ostriches,

9 For her wounds are incurable.
  For it has come to Judah;
  It has come to the gate of My people,
  even to Jerusalem.

10 Tell it not in Gath,
   Weep not at all in Beth Aphrah,
   Roll yourself in the dust.

11 Pass by in naked shame, you inhabitant of
     Shaphir;
   The inhabitant of Zaanan does not go out.
   Beth Ezel mourns;
   Its place to stand is taken away from you.

12 For the inhabitant of Maroth pined for good,
   But disaster came down from the LORD
   To the gate of Jerusalem.

13 O inhabitant of Lachish,
   Harness the chariot to the swift steeds
   (She was the beginning of sin to the daughter
     of Zion),
   For the transgressions of Israel were
     found in you.

14 Therefore you shall give presents to
     Moresheth Gath;
   The houses of Achzib shall be a lie
     to the kings of Israel.

15 I will yet bring an heir to you,
     O inhabitant of Mareshah;
   The glory of Israel shall come to Adullam.

16 Make yourself bald and cut off your hair,
   Because of your precious children;
   Enlarge your baldness like an eagle,
   For they shall go from you into captivity.

Micah 1:1–16

The divine origin of this prophecy is immediately stated in verse 1 as *"The word of the LORD."* Micah's calling is both the source of and the authority for what he is to record here; they are to be found in the Living God. The revelation *"came"* (or *"happened"*) to Micah, a man who was filled with the Holy Spirit (Mic. 3:8) and emboldened to declare to his people both their sin and God's willingness to forgive their sin.

This first message has three main parts to it, each answering the questions posed in verse 5—*"What is the transgression of Jacob? Is it not Samaria? And what are the high places of Judah? Are they not Jerusalem?"* Three answers are given, in verses 2–4, 5–7 and 8–16:

A. The Response of Nature to the Appearance of God   1:2–4
B. The Response of Samaria to the Appearance of God   1:5–7
C. The Response of Judah to the Appearance of God   1:8–16

THE RESPONSE OF NATURE TO THE APPEARANCE OF GOD (1:2–4)

The announcement of God's forthcoming judgment for the sin of His people is set against the background of world judgment. Micah does not summon just Israel or Judah, but *"all you peoples"* and *"O earth,"* to pay attention to what is going to be said. The God of the Old Testament is no local provincial deity, but is the Lord over all nations and history. Even if Israel will not function in her priestly role as a "light to the nations" (Isa. 42:6), she will nonetheless function as an involuntary witness to judgment from the hand of God to all nations (cf. Lev. 18:28). So, let the whole earth witness what Yahweh is now going to do in the imminent judgment.

God, as transcendent, is *"The LORD from His holy temple"* (v. 2b). But He is also immanent, *"For behold, the LORD is coming out of His place"* (v. 3a). Accordingly, those who depict our God as someone who is way off in space and far-removed from the daily events of our world are incorrect. Here is the great Old Testament theme of theophany, the appearance of God. It depicts our Lord suddenly coming in all His power and majesty to help His beleaguered people or to dispense justice regardless of the persons upon whom that judgment must come. So awesome is His presence that even nature itself threatens to come apart as it responds to Him.

Micah 7:18–20 says God will also manifest Himself in mercy and compassion, but this chapter says only that He will show His power and presence in chastising sin. Even so, all of creation acknowledges the Creator's presence as *"the mountains . . . melt under Him,"* and *"the valleys . . . split"* (v. 4; cf. Judg. 5:4; Ps. 18:7–10; 68:8; 65:9–13; 114:3–8; Isa. 64:1–2; Hab. 3:5). The scene is very similar to when the Lord touched down on Sinai: there were earthquakes, volcanic eruptions and other similar examples of the infinite power of God (Exod. 20:18–21).

Nature's response to the mighty presence of God strikes one with a terrifying realization of who He is. He moves like a mighty giant across the landscape, causing the mountains to melt with the intense heat of His wrath and the valleys to skid away into yawning chasms.

If God's inanimate creations are this responsive, why is it that we who are created in the image of God, and in some cases are also redeemed, are more recalcitrant and slower to perceive the coming of our Lord? This Lord of all the nations will indeed come and manifest His power among the nations as He has in nature.

THE RESPONSE OF SAMARIA TO THE APPEARANCE OF GOD (1:5–7)

The reason for the coming of God in judgment must now be given: *"All this is for the transgression of Jacob"* (v. 5). "The time has come for judgment to begin at the house of God" (1 Pet. 4:17). And the first to feel the impact of that action will be the northern ten tribes, here called "Jacob," a deliberately ambiguous term that could refer either to the north or the south, or to both nations. But while it is clear from the explanation given in the parallel line—*"for the sins of the house of Israel"* (v. 5b)—that Micah pointed first to the northern ten tribes, Judah will not escape judgment. Judgment will culminate in *"Judah"* and *"Jerusalem"* (v. 5b). The capitals of both nations were seats of corruption. The high places, where altars had been erected to worship and offer sacrifices to idols (2 Kings 12:3;14:4), would be consumed by the approach of the only God and King of the whole universe. But so would the lovely city of Samaria (v. 6). So heinous were the northern nation's crimes that nothing less would do than the total eradication of the capital Samaria.

Some scholars have questioned Micah's credibility because he predicted, inaccurately, that Sargon II would demolish Samaria (*"a heap of ruins"* and *"places for planting a vineyard"* with *"her stones . . . [poured down] into the valley"* [v. 6]). However, Sargon II did deport Samaria's citizens in order to make room for the foreign elements he introduced into Samaria in an attempt to prevent the people from uniting against him in revolt.

The total destruction of Samaria came at the hand of John Hyrcanus in 107 B.C. Josephus recorded the devastation of Samaria:

> And when Hyrcanus had taken that city, which was not done til after a year's siege, he was not contented with doing that only, but he demolished it entirely, and brought rivulets to it to drown it, for he dug such hollows as might let the water run under it; nay, he took away the very marks that there had ever been such a city there. [5]

Thus what Sargon began, Hyrcanus completed years after the 721 B.C. fall of Samaria. Samaria the beautiful became nothing more than a heap of stones and a site for vineyards. And lest Judah should think she had escaped the same fate, Micah warns that the same devastation was in store for her (Mic. 3:12) if she too refused to repent and turn back to God.

The overthrow of Samaria included the destruction of her idols (v. 7), which often employed prostitutes in the service of the pagan deity. *"All her pay as a harlot"* (v. 7) referred to Samaria hiring herself out for sacred prostitution (cf. Deut. 23:18; Isa. 23:17; Hos. 9:1). Just as the prophet Hosea had earlier censured the people of the northern kingdom for their abominable syncretism in worshipping Baal along with Yahweh, so Micah once again calls the nation to its senses. The appeal of the Canaanite fertility religions was so strong that Israel willingly exchanged its worship of the One and only true God for the orgies of religious prostitution. No wonder the Great God of Glory would now come in judgment!

Even more pathetic was the fact that the images and idols the Samarians worshipped were paid for from the wages of the cult prostitutes (cf. v. 7 NIV). Repeating the cycle, their conquerors would destroy these golden images in order to use the precious metal to make new idols from the "pay of a harlot." All too often evil is like a treadmill that keeps on repeating itself apart from the dramatic intervention of the Spirit of God.

THE RESPONSE OF JUDAH TO THE APPEARANCE OF GOD (1:8–16)

What do we learn from history? Anything? It must have been clear by now that because Samaria had not responded to God's final call, she went off into captivity and suffered the loss of almost everything. Surely Judah would wise up and would not follow in Samaria's footsteps. But alas, she did not repent!

Micah begins this text with a lament (vv. 8–9). He then lists twelve cities, no doubt towns of his childhood experience, on which Sennacherib V did finally come and wreak his vengeance (vv. 10–15). Jerusalem narrowly escaped because of a last-minute intervention of God in 701 B.C. The text closes in verse 16 with an invitation for the people of Judah to begin the mourning rites over their own pending captivity.

Understandably, the prophet mourns for Samaria. As a sign of his grief, he goes about naked (v. 8). His wail is like the banshee cries of jackals and the gruesome screech of the ostrich (v. 8). The jackals and ostriches embody wildness and desolation. Jackals are scavengers that live in packs near human settlements. These greyish-brown animals, about the size of an average dog, move about in the night, howling and evoking feelings of desolation and fear. The ostrich, on the other hand, is a two-toed flightless runner, the largest of the birds. Weighing around three hundred pounds and standing six to eight feet tall, it exhibits both cruelty and uncleanness. It is easily frightened and stupid. Micah uses these animals to symbolize his mourning and wailing for a nation that could have been saved if she had listened to the repeated warnings from God's prophets.

Adding to Micah's sorrow was the surprising announcement that *"it has come to Judah"* (v. 9). The funeral dirge might just as well begin for Jerusalem too, for we are told, beginning in verse 9, about the results that will come from the invasion of Sennacherib, King of Assyria, on Judah and his siege on Jerusalem.

Sennacherib attacked Philistia and Judah in 701 B.C. He advanced along the Phoenician coast, dethroned the king of Tyre, dealt the Egyptian army a severe blow in the Valley of Eltekeh in the Sorek River area, accepted the surrender of Ashkelon and Ekron, and headed for his great encounter with the Judean city of Lachish. So significant and so thorough was his conquest of the great city of Lachish that he celebrated by having huge murals drawn on his palace walls in Nineveh (now housed in the British Museum). Proudly Sennacherib announced that he was triumphant:

> But as for Hezekiah of Judah, who did not submit to my yoke, I
> laid siege to 46 of his strong cities, walled forts and to countless

> small villages in their vicinity, and conquered them. . . . I drove
> out 200,150 people. . . . He [i.e., Hezekiah] himself I shut up
> like a caged bird within Jerusalem, his royal city. . . . and
> turned back to his disaster any who went out of its city gate.[6]

Seven of the twelve towns listed can now be identified with known archaeological sites. Each is located southwest of Jerusalem and most are within a ten-mile radius of Micah's birthplace, Moresheth-gath.[7]

In verses 10–15, Micah indulges in a number of puns, word-plays and alliterations. Because some of these are now lost on us, being so removed in time and culture, some assert that the text of 1:10–15 is poorly preserved. But the name of each city listed appears to have an omen of some tragic consequences attached to it. Peter Craigie brilliantly illustrated how a Scottish preacher might have imitated Micah's style had he been speaking to a Scottish audience about towns in Scotland:

> Crieff will know grief. Forfar will forfeit. Craill will be frail. Wick
> will be burned. Stornoway will be blown away. Edinburgh will
> be no Eden. For Tain, there will only be pain.[8]

Accordingly, *"Tell it not in Gath"* (v. 10) heads the list of cities in Micah. Gath was the border town of Philistia and one of the famous pentapolises in that country. "Gath" means "winepress," but it also may function here as a shortened form of the verb "to announce" or "to tell." Hence, "tell it not in tell-town."

"Weep not at all in Beth Aphrah, roll yourself in the dust" (v. 10). Beth-le-aphrah is "house of dust"; thus "rolling in the dust" was a sign of grief and mourning (cf. Jos. 7:6; 1 Sam. 4:12; Job 16:15; Jer. 6:26, for examples of this sign of expressing grief or a humiliating defeat).

The inhabitants of *"Shaphir"* (v. 11), meaning "beauty-town," were to *"pass by in naked shame."* They must be stripped naked and marched past their conquerors. *"Zaanan,"* meaning "Going forth town," will crouch behind its wall hoping it will not have to "go forth" with the long line of captives already taken.

Likewise, *"Beth Ezel,"* reflecting the meaning "House of taking away," will have *"its place [of] stand[ing] taken away from you"* (v. 11). It, too, was one of the forty-six towns that were "taken away" from King Hezekiah and Judah by Sennacherib.

"Bitter town" is the image connected to *"Maroth"* (v. 12). But while she *"pined for good," "disaster came down from the* LORD*."* Thus the "good" or "relief" (NIV) expected from one quarter never came. Instead the Assyrians marched right up to the *"gate of Jerusalem"* (v. 12). Indeed, Sennacherib boasts that he "shut up [Hezekiah] like a caged bird" so that "any who went out of its city gate" were "turned back to [their] disaster."

"Lachish" sounds like the Hebrew *lārekeš,* "to the steeds": for its people were instructed to harness the horses to the war chariots. Micah singles out Lachish since *"she was the beginning of sin to the daughter of Zion"* (v. 13). Lachish must have been our Reno, Atlantic City, and Hollywood all rolled into one town; the place, Micah explained, was where sin got its foothold—and eventually affected all of Judah. Both physical and spiritual adultery emanated from Lachish, following the sinful practices of the northern kingdom.

The prophet's own hometown of Moresheth-gath (v. 14) sounds like the Hebrew *me°ōrešet,* "betrothed," suggesting that this city was promised like an engaged girl to another, in this case to an enemy invader from Nineveh.

"The houses of Achzib shall be a lie to the kings of Israel" (v. 14b), promised Micah. Achzib means "deception," or "disappointment," and the city would indeed prove deceptive to the kings of Israel. A similar Hebrew form of *achzib* is used in Jeremiah 15:18 to describe the disappointment of dry wadis to the thirsty traveler.

"Mareshah" (v. 15) is associated with the similar sounding Hebrew words for "heir," "conqueror" and "the one who dispossesses another from his property." Mareshah will be possessed by the Assyrian conqueror and the nobility will be forced to flee to *"Adullam"* (v. 15b). Just as David had to flee to Adullam in 1 Samuel 22:1 and 23:13, so would the Judean nobles be driven into exile by the conquering Assyrian. *"The glory of Israel"* (v. 15b) were the men of position and standing within the Judean community (cf. 2 Sam. 1:19–20; Isa. 5:13). (Note that the Judeans are now being called men of Israel, perhaps indicating that they are now imitating the northern kingdom—from whom they had learned many of the sins assailed by Micah.)

CONCLUSION

After listing the twelve cities of the Shephelah, Micah urges the people of Judah to *"make [themselves] bald and cut off [their] hair"* (v. 16) as a sign of deep mourning. Even though the custom of shaving one's head was prohibited in Leviticus 21:5 and Deuteronomy 14:1, the mourning should begin, for the judgment was certain if no one repented (cf. Isa. 15:2; Jer. 16:6; Amos 8:10). *"Enlarge your baldness like an eagle"* (v. 16b) or a vulture, advises Micah. Since both of these birds have white down covering their heads and necks, they give the impression of being bald. It was certain—*"they shall go from you into captivity."* The prophet uses the prophetic perfect tense, indicating that the northern captivity is so certain that it is as good as complete—"they have gone from you into exile" (NRSV). And so they did go into exile in 721 B.C. under Sargon II. But Sargon's successor Sennacherib came and captured 200,150 Judeans, young and old, male and female, in 701 B.C.

In retrospect, I wonder if the sins of Israel and Judah were worth all the trouble that resulted? This chapter is not a happy one, for it contains ten expressions of mourning and distress. But neither is Micah a dispassionate observer, steeled against the terrors that he predicts for both nations. Instead, he is so torn apart by the grief that was to come that he wails like a banshee and howls like the jackals as he goes about naked in a state of deep despair.

This ought to teach us something about the spirit and attitude of the announcer of God's judgments. Should we not mourn over the sins of our own nation? Wouldn't it be heartless to withhold the offer of grace and mercy to even the vilest of offenders in the midst of our proclamations of pending doom? And will not our listeners discern that we care what is going to happen to them, even if the message distresses them? Sometimes we love the truth so much we do not care about the people that it affects. That was not the heart of this servant of God, and therefore it ought never to be ours.

CHAPTER TWO

Is the Spirit of the Lord Restricted?

Micah 2:1–13

2:1 Woe to those who devise iniquity, And work
out evil on their beds! At morning light they practice
it, Because it is in the power of their hand.

2 They covet fields and take them by violence,
Also houses, and seize them.
So they oppress a man and his house,
A man and his inheritance.

3 Therefore thus says the LORD:
"Behold, against this family I am
devising disaster,
From which you cannot remove your necks;
Nor shall you walk haughtily,
For this is an evil time.

4 In that day one shall take up a proverb
against you,
And lament with a bitter lamentation, and say:
'We are utterly destroyed!
He has changed the heritage of my people;
How He has removed it from me!
To a turncoat He has divided our fields.'"

5 Therefore you will have no one to determine
boundaries by lot
In the congregation of the LORD.

6 "Do not prattle," you say to those who prophesy.
So they shall not prophesy to you;
They shall not return insult for insult.

7 You who are named the house of Jacob:
"Is the Spirit of the LORD restricted?
Are these His doings?

Do not My words do good
To him who walks uprightly?
8 "Lately My people have risen up as an enemy—
You pull off the robe with the garment
From those who trust you, as they pass by,
Like men returned from war.
9 The women of My people you cast out
From their pleasant houses;
From their children
You have taken away My glory forever.
10 "Arise and depart,
For this is not your rest;
Because it is defiled, it shall destroy you,
Even with utter destruction.
11 If a man should walk in a false spirit
And speak a lie, saying,
'I will prophesy to you of wine and drink,'
Even he would be the prattler of this people.
12 "I will surely assemble all of you, O Jacob,
I will surely gather the remnant of Israel;
I will put them together like sheep of the fold,
Like a flock in the midst of their pasture;
They shall make a loud noise because of so
many men.
13 The one who breaks open will come up before
them;
They will break out,
Pass through the gate,
And go out by it;
Their king will pass before them,
With the LORD at their head."

Micah 2:1–13

Whereas in chapter one Micah denounces the sins of the people against the Lord, in chapter two he rebukes the people for their sins against each other. The whole situation was beginning to get out of hand: did the people really think that God's reach was shortened so that He was unable to do anything against them for all their rebellion and oppression? Did their freedom of election mean that they were untouchable?

Before concluding with a promise of hope, salvation and the coming of the Messiah (2:12–13), Micah conveys God's impatience with people engaging in two types of sin: perverting the sanctity of property (2:1–5) and distorting the sanctity of God's revelation through His true prophets (2:6–11). Let us examine these two types of sin.

A. The Evil of Coveting   2:1–5
B. The Evil of Placebo Preaching   2:6–11

THE EVIL OF COVETING (2:1–5)

Landgrabbing had historically been a serious offense in Israel and Judah. Who can ever forget the lessons learned from Ahab and Jezebel's wicked scheme whereby they unlawfully gained control of Naboth's vineyard (1 Kings 21)? Had not Isaiah warned in the same century, "Woe to those who join house to house; they add field to field, till there is no place where they may dwell alone in the midst of the land" (Isa. 5:8; cf. Deut. 27:17; 1 Sam. 8:11, 14–17; Neh. 5:1–3; Prov. 23:10–11). Now Micah must deal with the problem as well.

Coveting is at the heart of this sin. The tenth commandment warns against coveting a neighbor's wife, his house, his field, his man-servant or maidservant, his ox, his ass or anything else that belongs to him. Deuteronomy 27:17 places landgrabbing at the head of a list of sins involving property, immediately following sins against God and against one's own family.

There is a theological reason for prohibiting landgrabbing. Not only was it a form of the sin of coveting, but land was considered one of God's gifts to His people (Gen. 12:7). The real owner of the land was God, not the landlord (Lev. 25:23) and, as such, the land was to remain in a family in perpetuity as a sacred trust. If anyone lost their land in the agricultural society of biblical times, they would have suffered enormous economic grief. Accordingly, a parcel of land could never be out of the hands of a family for a period longer than seven years; it reverted back to its original owners every seven years in the Sabbatical cycle (Lev. 25).

But, alas, the wealthy landowners illegally appropriated land that should not have been taken under any conditions, and, after identifying the people's transgression in verses 1–2, Micah prescribes an appropriate punishment in verses 3–5.

"*Woe*," cries the prophet (v. 1), for so certain and sure is the punishment of God on these landgrabbers that one might just as well have begun their funeral dirge. So intent were they on defrauding their neighbors that they stayed awake at night devising new ways to extract more property for their own empires (v. 1b).

The people's vices are laid out in verse 2—"*they covet fields*," "*take them by violence*," "*seize . . . houses*," and "*oppress . . . a man and his inheritance*." Coveting is prohibited in the Decalogue (Exod. 20:17; Deut. 5:21; cf. Rom. 7:8). No better is the bold seizure of property, under any pretense. Likewise, all fraudulent methods—whereby the land is taken by extortion, naked force, manipulation of the legal system or some other form of dishonesty (cf. Isa. 52:4; Jer. 50:33; Lev. 6:2,4; 19:13; Deut. 1:17; 17:8–13)—are condemned.

I am reminded of two unfortunate experiences that illustrate what this text condemns. The first took place during the Depression on a Pennsylvania farm. Our neighbor had never been to more than two or three years of school, but he had an uncanny gift of wisdom. So when the order came down from President Roosevelt that the only way to straighten out the country's economic problems was to plow under the crops and kill off the hogs, our neighbor was ready. A dozen or more state police with a number of dogs, workmen, tools and guns showed up at all our farms and systematically killed off the hogs. But not on our neighbor's property. Mr. Baxter stood his ground. He met this awesome retinue at the entrance to his property and warned everyone out of concern for their safety that they should not step one foot on his property. When asked if he was going to get his gun and shoot someone, he replied, "I don't know what I'm liable to do, for I've never been in this situation before. I'm warning all of you: I'm worried for your safety." Mr. Baxter's pigs were the only ones in our part of suburban Philadelphia to make it through the Depression. He knew better than to threaten an officer, but they knew better than to fool with that old timer. As he had said, there was no telling what he was liable to do. In his case, his property was preserved.

In the case of my father, the ending was not so happy. I returned from college to learn that our farm was the subject of a pending eminent domain proceeding by the county. With knowledge of the pending proceeding, a real estate agent pressured my father to sign a listing agreement entitling the agent to a five percent commission upon any sale of the property—including the "sale" to the county by eminent domain. I urged my father not to sign the realtor's agreement unless the realtor agreed that he would not be entitled to his commission if the county appropriated the property through eminent domain. It would be unfair, I argued, for the realtor to benefit from a sale pending before the listing agreement was signed—a sale for which the realtor would not have done any work. My father signed the agreement notwithstanding my arguments, and when his farm was deeded to the county the overreaching realtor cashed in on an easy deal. This story can be repeated again and again. What makes this story particularly tragic is that the realtor was a Christian friend who should have known better than to accept this easy money. He took advantage of my father's trust in his Christian ethics—ethics which, unfortunately, vanished in the moment of truth!

As in 1:14, the word *"Therefore"* that begins 2:3 signals the beginning of God's sentence for the people's sins. God would visit *"this family"* (here denoting the nation bound together into one large family) with *"disaster"* (v. 3). (Interestingly, the Hebrew word used here for "disaster" is virtually the same as the Hebrew word for the "evil" that the landgrabbers had committed.) All the property stolen by the nouveau riche would be ruthlessly snatched out of their hands by an invader. The time for self-satisfaction was over and *"an evil time"* had begun (v. 3b).

"In that day," declared the Lord, *"a proverb,"* or a taunt song, would be sung to these greedy men (v. 4a). It would mock the rich: *"We are utterly destroyed,"* they would wail. Ironically, the words of the taunt sound just like the Hebrew word for the "fields" the people had stolen. The fields would now be divided among the *"turncoat,"* meaning here the "rebellious," "obstinate," or just plain "willful" Assyrians (Isa. 10). The lesson here is clear: it is God who divides up the real estate of the earth and gives it to whomever He wishes (Acts 17:26; Dan. 4:34–5).

To emphasize the conclusion to this discussion, Micah begins verse 5 with a second *"Therefore."* The rich will not determine the boundaries *"in the congregation of the LORD"* (v. 5b). Only the meek will ultimately inherit the earth, taught our Lord in the Sermon on the Mount. In that eschatological assembly, the general land reform prescribed in the Sabbatical and Jubilee years would find its consummation. Then it would finally be true of all the poor in spirit that "The lines have fallen to [us] in pleasant places; Yes, [we] have a good inheritance" (Ps. 16:6).

THE EVIL OF PLACEBO PREACHING (2:6–11)

Micah now turns to the false prophets who had allied themselves with the rich and powerful and were proclaiming their voices rather than the voice of God. The true prophets of God, in contrast, were put on the defensive and treated contemptuously by an audience that cared little for any word from God.

The Hebrew verb *nataph* is key to our understanding of this text, for among its various meanings are: "drop," "drip," "let fall" (presumably prophetic declarations), "flow," "pour," "speak," "preach," and "prophesy" (vv. 6, 11). *"Do not prattle,"* Micah's listener's jeered; we don't need any prophecies from the Lord around here. Since the listeners used the plural form of the verb commanding the true prophets of God to stop, they must have regarded Micah as being in the same class as his colleagues Hosea, Amos and Isaiah.

The last part of verse 6 is probably rendered best by: "One should not preach of such things; disgrace will not overtake us" (NRSV; cf. NIV). What a frightening state of affairs, especially since it all sounds so contemporary! All too many in Micah's day, and our own, prefer to hear what they wish to hear. Any cheery bromide will do, such as: "disgrace will not overtake us." But this is like whistling in a graveyard. Saying it does not make it so. Later, Jeremiah's audience would prefer the same placebo: "The prophets prophesy falsely . . . and My people love to have it so" (Jer. 5:31). Micah's contemporary heard the same refrain: "Who say to the seers, 'Do not see,' and to the prophets, 'do not prophesy to us right things; speak to us smooth things, prophesy deceits'" (Isa. 30:10; cf. Amos 2:12; 7:16).

Apparently Micah's preaching against the land barons struck home and they would have none of it. The robber barons and their false prophets were more than confident that they were right because, in their view, God was forever and unconditionally on their side. So how could any disaster overtake them? For God to curse Jacob, He would have to retract His covenantal promises, they reasoned, so there was no reason to worry.

But their theology was only a half truth. The whole story is that God will keep His covenantal promises to Israel but may nevertheless withhold benefits from a disobedient generation. Members of the disobedient generation transmit the promise to the next generation even if they do not participate in it, just as members of David's royal family who did not personally believe transmitted the promise but failed to benefit from it.

Yes, our Lord could be counted on to *"do good to him who walks uprightly"* (v. 7b). But the "upright" was the one who believed God's word and responded to what He said, not the one who demanded silence from the true prophets of God or who rejected those whose message challenged him.

Micah now quotes his religious antagonists at length then responds in turn. God has seen how Israel's rulers have disregarded His Word. Our Lord has seen the enemy, and it is most of us (v. 8a)! The political leadership, supported by the renegade false prophets, have become merciless creditors, apparently urging hoodlums to rob debtors of their cloaks. Or were these acts committed by baliffs who were sent to collect unpaid debts? *"You pull off the robe with the garment,"* *"like men returned from war"* (v. 8b). Whatever happened to the teaching of the Law in Exodus 22:26–27?

Women, presumably widows, were tossed out of their homes and their children suffered the indignities of being sold as slaves, all in order to finance the lifestyles of the rich and powerful (v. 9). (Amos, a contemporary of Micah, also decried slave trade [Amos 1:6,9].)

Verse 10 contains God's judgment on the insensitive creditors and all who share their mentality. As they evicted others, God has evicted them from their land. No longer would the promised land be a place of *"rest"* (v. 10) (Deut. 12:9; Ps. 95:11).[9] Just as the Canaanites were dispossessed of the land, for moral and ethical reasons, before Israel entered it, so now would Israel herself be put out of the land for a period of time (Lev. 18:24–28). What was needed was pure and undefiled religion—a religion described by James in James 1:27. Only one standard of morality is acceptable in the divine ordering of things for mankind.

Still critical of his detractors, Micah describes their favorite prophets as those who promise them health, wealth and happiness (v. 11). But such prophets are filled with hot air; they are liars for hire! They exalt the benefits of God's promises, but do not tell God's people that there are conditions to receiving those benefits or that the people should walk faithfully with their Lord. It was all so much drivel! This extreme example of antinomianism was tolerated—and indeed encouraged—by the rich and powerful because it did not challenge their lifestyles.

CONCLUSION (VS: 12–13)

The last two verses of this chapter shift abruptly from the judgment theme that dominated the first section of this prophecy to the theme of salvation. Although God must now deliver His threatened judgment on an unrepentant and disobedient people, those people are assured here that God gathers His scattered sheep: they are His *"remnant"* (v. 12).

There is some debate among theologians as to when this oracle of salvation would become effective: was it Jerusalem's deliverance from Sennacherib's siege (2 Kings 18:32–36), Judah's return from the Babylonian captivity, or an eschatological salvation? Fortunately, we do not need to decide conclusively, for each of these deliverances was but an "earnest" or "downpayment" on the great return of the remnant in the final day when Christ returns.[10]

The best part of this message of hope is to be found in verse 13, *"The One who breaks open."* If the remnant of the flock are to be gathered and brought back to their land, they will need a leader. And what better leader is there than the One who is called here "the Breaker." Just as the Lord went before His people in the pillar of fire and the cloud through the wilderness, so three times in verse 13 we are told He will go before His people to guide them (cf. Exod. 13:21; Deut. 1:30,33; Isa. 52:12).

This Breaker can be none other than the Messiah Himself. It is He who will clear the way for the people to break out of their enemies' cities, passing through as if there were no gates. This messianic interpretation can be confirmed by the fact that "the Breaker" is also referred to in verse 13 as *"their king"* and *"the LORD."* All of Israel's blessings will be realized in the Messiah, our Lord Jesus Christ.

God is still calling that remnant during these days of grace (Rom. 11:5). He is not finished with Israel, as some have prematurely concluded. He who has broken out for His people so frequently will do so again in that final day of His second coming. No wonder this word was in such stark contrast to the deeds of the robber barons and the wrong-headed teaching of the false prophets who presumed upon the unconditional nature of the promises of God.

CHAPTER THREE

Is There No Word From the Lord?

Micah 3:1–12

3:1 And I said:
　　"Hear now, O heads of Jacob,
　　And you rulers of the house of Israel:
　　Is it not for you to know justice?
　2 You who hate good and love evil;
　　Who strip the skin from My people,
　　And the flesh from their bones;
　3 Who also eat the flesh of My people,
　　Flay their skin from them,
　　Break their bones,
　　And chop them in pieces
　　Like meat for the pot,
　　Like flesh in the caldron."
　4 Then they will cry to the LORD,
　　But He will not hear them;
　　He will even hide His face from them
　　　at that time,
　　Because they have been evil in their deeds.
　5 Thus says the LORD concerning the prophets
　　Who make my people stray;
　　Who chant "Peace"
　　While they chew with their teeth,
　　But who prepare war against him
　　Who puts nothing into their mouths:
　6 "Therefore you shall have night
　　　without vision,
　　And you shall have darkness without divination;
　　The sun shall go down on the prophets,
　　And the day shall be dark for them.

7 So the seers shall be ashamed,
   And the diviners abashed;
   Indeed they shall all cover their lips;
   For there is no answer from God."
8 But truly I am full of power
      by the Spirit of the LORD,
   And of justice and might,
   To declare to Jacob his transgression
   And to Israel his sin.
9 Now hear this,
   You heads of the house of Jacob
   And rulers of the house of Israel,
   Who abhor justice
   And pervert all equity,
10 Who build up Zion with bloodshed
   And Jerusalem with iniquity:
11 Her heads judge for a bribe,
   Her priests teach for pay,
   And her prophets divine for money.
   Yet they lean on the LORD, and say,
   "Is not the LORD among us?
      No harm can come upon us."
12 Therefore because of you
   Zion shall be plowed like a field,
   Jerusalem shall become heaps of ruins,
   And the mountain of the temple
   Like the bare hills of the forest.

Micah 3:1–12

Chapters 3–5 form the second main section of the book of Micah. Chapter 3 continues the theme begun in chapter 2:1–2 of the judgment that will befall Israel. Its three paragraphs contain four verses each. Verses 1–4 challenge the nation's rulers and verses 5–8 rebuke its false prophets. Verses 9–12 charge as a group the nation's rulers, priests and prophets who, since they have judged others, now await even greater judgment for their evil deeds. (The same principle is asserted in Romans 2:1.)

Not only are the three paragraphs of chapter 3 of equal length (4 verses), but they exhibit a common format, including: the address (3:1, 5, 9); the accusation introduced by *"who"* (3:2, 5, 9); and the sentence of judgment introduced by *"then"* (3:5), or *"therefore"* (3: 6,12). Each group censured in chapter 3 is guilty of attempting to rationalize their acts of evil, casting over them a biblical aura of legitimacy (3:11). Three times they search for "answers" from God, but there are none for those whose deeds are evil: The nation's rulers cry out, *"But he will not hear* [or, more literally, "answer"] *them"* (3:4); the false prophets will feel shame, *"For there is no answer from God"* (3:7); and by implication in 3:11 *"Is not the* LORD *among us? No harm can come upon us?"* Only Micah had the answers they were looking for. These answers suggest the following outline:

A. Answers for the Abuse of Position   3:1–4
B. Answers for the Abuse of Proclamation   3:5–8
C. Answers for the Abuse of Privilege   3:9–12

ANSWERS FOR THE ABUSE OF POSITION (3:1–4)

Each of the three paragraphs in chapter 3 focuses on the word *"justice"* (vv. 1, 8, 9). "Justice," [Benjamin Disraeli said in a speech to the House of Commons (1851),] "is truth in action."[11]

In contrast to the Shepherd of 2:12, the rulers of Micah's day exhibited a total disrespect for God, His Law and the justice they were to dispense to people who sought relief through their courts. The very persons who should have known better and been guided by a respect for God, His Law, and ideals of justice hated what was good and loved what was evil (vv. 1b–2a).

In effect, Micah says, these rulers became nothing more than brutal butchers who cannibalized God's people and skinned them alive (vv. 2–3). They were concerned only for themselves; everyone else could fend for themselves!

Unrighteousness in the halls of government is one of the inequities of life that Solomon pondered in the book of Ecclesiastes. When wickedness takes the place of justice, then it is time to appeal to heaven. That is why God instituted human tribunals in the first place: to grant some form of immediate relief for the more egregious wrongs in this life. Therefore, wronging the innocent and pardoning the guilty are dangerous business from the divine point of view. All who practice injustice will face the Judge of all judges both now and in that final judgment before Him.

Exodus 18:21 lists the qualifications of leaders. They are to be persons with an aptitude ("able men") for governing themselves and others well. They are also to be God-fearing, trustworthy men, and men who hate a bribe. The leadership course prescribed for these potential leaders includes teaching them God's statutes, helping them to know the way they ought to live, and teaching them what their jobs are and how to make decisions (Exod. 18:20).

Leaders fail, however, when they place personal preferences, evil, unfairness, and corrupt practices ahead of what God has ordained. In the name of healthy competition and charging what the market will bear in order to "get ahead," such leaders "Eat up my people as [if] they [were] eat[ing] bread" (Ps. 14:4). Again, "There is a generation whose teeth are like swords, and whose fangs are like knives, to devour the poor from off the earth, and the needy from among men" (Prov. 30:14).

God's "answer" to all of this is found in verse 4. Those who abuse their position of leadership will find themselves alone and without any help at a time when they cry out to God for relief. The word for "*cry*" (v. 4) is usually a technical term for an appeal to a judge. Thus it will happen that when business goes bad and the times get tough, these leaders too will plead in desparation to God, but He will not answer them because of their sinful deeds. God will "*hide His face from them at that time*" (v. 4b); His favor, goodness, and mercy will desert them. Here is the inverse of the famous Aaronic benediction: God will not cause His face to shine upon them; they will, instead, see His back as He hides from them.

There is a certain degree of poetic justice in all of this. Solomon taught: "Whoever shuts his ears to the cry of the poor will also cry himself and not be heard" (Prov. 21:13). But the point of privilege for the righteous is just the opposite of the destiny of these wicked rulers:

> Hear, O LORD, when I cry with my voice!
> Have mercy also upon me, and answer me.
> When You said, "Seek My face,"
> My heart said to You, "Your face, LORD, I will seek."
> Do not hide Your face from me;
> Do not turn Your servant away in anger;
> You have been my help;
> Do not leave me nor forsake me,
> O God of my salvation.
>
> *Psalm 27: 7–9*

ANSWERS FOR THE ABUSE OF PROCLAMATION (3:5–8)

For those who could pay the false prophet's fee, there was the soothing word *"Peace"* (v. 5), while the poor, unable to meet the financial requirements of the greedy prophets, were met with angry and abusive words (v. 5b). These prophets prostituted a divine gift in order to profit personally.

Three judgments are pronounced on these popular prophets: darkness, disgrace, and desertion of any answers from God (vv. 6–7). The word *"Therefore"* in verse 6 signals the commencement of the sentencing upon those who had violated the sacred and public trust given to them.

"Darkness" meant the false prophets would be *"without vision,"* so that they would speak without the benefit of any revelation from God. Proverbs 29:18 describes the consequence of living in darkness—"Where there is no revelation [or "vision"], the people cast off all restraint." The Hebrew verb *pāraʿ* [no restraint], was used earlier in Exodus 32:25 when Moses saw that the people at the golden calf "were running wild" [or "were unrestrained"] and no doubt influenced its use here. The point is this: abandon the revelation or word of God, even for forty days, as Israel did at the mount, and people become ungovernable and cast off all restraint! The absence of God's word is fatal to any people.

The second calamity that would visit the false prophets is disgrace. Once it was clear that they had been inaccurate in their predictions and that they had not lived according to what they taught, shame would surely supplant any glory previously gained. Was this not the case with Edgar C. Whisenant's booklet *88 Reasons Why the Rapture is in 1988: The Feast of Trumpets, September 11–12–13?*[12] Unfortunately, September 11–13, 1988 came and went; all that remained was Whisenandt's disgrace! Like unclean lepers, these disgraced prophets would go about with *"their lips"* *"cover[ed]"* (v. 7). Thus, the prophets would disguise their lips—the focal point of their gift—with moustaches (cf. Lev. 13:45) or even with a covering over the lower parts of their faces.

Finally, such prophets would be devoid of any answers (v. 7). These shalom prophets had "healed the hurt of My people slightly, saying, 'Peace, peace!' when there is no peace" (Jer. 6:14). They were now speechless and without any answers.

God's answer is found with Micah, for verse 8 begins with a strong adversative. God gave to him, as He does to all true proclaimers of

His message, the ministry of the Holy Spirit, power, justice and might. Instead of delivering cheery bromides and placebos of peace, happiness, wealth and health, Micah warned about Israel's sin and transgression (v. 8b). The Holy Spirit empowered Micah to declare in an impartial way God's holy judgment and gave him a holy boldness and the moral courage to say what others did not have the fortitude to say. Here was the God-given standard against which all who speak for our Lord must measure themselves. Here, too, was the source of justice—that scarce commodity that everyone longed for, but few found. Micah does not boast about his own aptitudes, but focuses instead on the Lord who sent him and on the four gifts that God gave him in order to do the job he was sent to do: power, justice, might and the Holy Spirit. That "might" is quite similar to the "boldness" that was so frequently exhibited in the book of Acts—for example, Peter and John's boldness referred to in Acts 4:13.

Placebo preachers are never in high demand when the times turn tough and the issues become critical. Surely it is possible to pay any proclaimer of the word to say what we wish to hear, but we should not expect any power or boldness, any sense of what is just or right, or any evidence of the presence and convicting power of the Holy Spirit to attend their anemic prattle. Their empty talk, lacking dynamic power, fails to call the nation to its senses or to hold forth God's standards of truth, righteousness and justice.

ANSWERS FOR THE ABUSE OF PRIVILEGE (3:9–12)

In a sweeping indictment of all three ruling classes—rulers, priests and prophets—Micah summarizes the chief sins of each. The rulers as magistrates would render the desired decision for an acceptable bribe. This practice violated every decent person's conscience and the teaching of God's word in Exodus 23:8 and Deuteronomy 16:19. Little better than the magistrates, the priests too would accept a fee to teach what folks wanted to hear. They, like the priests of a later day (Mal. 2:7–9), would turn many aside from the way and the teaching of the Lord. Finally, the sins of the prophets were right in step with the rest of that prurient and evil culture: they too would *"divine"* (v. 11) for money. The word "to divine" is used here, as it usually is in the Bible, in a negative sense; the prophets rendered favorable pronouncements in return for an appropriate price from their patrons.

The rulers, priests, and prophets all played the game "the price is right." What massive abuse of high privilege! Yet the prophets proclaimed the half truth that *"they lean on the LORD."* In their view, God would never abandon His holy city or His people; they relied on the promises of God like a talisman to protect them from all punishment. *"Is not the LORD among us? No harm can come upon us"* (v. 11b) they chanted to each other—hoping it was so. But it was not! Just as the people of Jeremiah's day chanted "The temple of the LORD, the temple of the LORD, the temple of the LORD" (Jer. 7:4, 8–11), so those in the previous century of Micah had done.

I'm afraid many in our day feel the same way. They believe that America is so specially favored by the Lord that no trouble will ever befall us. Surely, God would not touch the center of most missionary giving, the headquarters for so many evangelical works, schools and institutions. We tend to chant, "Evangelicalism, evangelicalism, evangelicalism." "If conservative Americans are judged, then who will defend inerrancy, missions, and the biblical concept of the family?" we ask, all the while hoping that our assertions alone will make such a difference that no matter how evil our nation grows we will never have to face the consequences. What are we doing but claiming that God will bless us in our wicked ways? Will He?

The sentencing comes in verse 12, beginning once again with *"Therefore." "Zion shall be plowed like a field, Jerusalem shall become heaps of ruins, and the mountain of the temple like the bare hills of the forest."*

What a shock to be told that the holy city, inviolable as it was in the theology of Scripture, would experience what apostate Samaria experienced (cf. 1:6)! This message made such a stir that it was still being remembered and quoted a century later in Jeremiah's day (Jer. 26:18). But the important point is that the people repented and the judgment did not come immediately. When Jerusalem finally fell in 586 B.C., for exactly the same reasons warned about here, Jeremiah lamented "Because of Mount Zion which is desolate" (Lam. 5:18; cf. Neh. 2:17; 4:2). Micah's prophecy had finally come true!

CONCLUSION

Is there no word from the Lord? There surely is! He has answered the abuses of position, proclamation, and privilege. Therefore, all cannabalistic leaders and greedy magistrates, disgraced prophets, and priests ought to recognize the contrast between themselves and a prophet like Micah who is full of power, might, justice and the Spirit of God. What comparison has chaff to wheat or placebos of false preachers to the mighty word of God? None!

It is time to introduce the hope of the good news, and that will occur in chapters 4–5.

CHAPTER FOUR

Will God's King Not Come and Reign?

Micah 4:1–5:15

4:1 Now it shall come to pass in the latter days
That the mountain of the LORD's house
Shall be established on the top of the mountains,
And shall be exalted above the hills;
And peoples shall flow to it.
2 Many nations shall come and say,
"Come, and let us go up to the
    mountain of the LORD,
To the house of the God of Jacob;
He will teach us His ways,
And we shall walk in His paths."
For out of Zion the law shall go forth,
And the word of the LORD from Jerusalem.
3 He shall judge between many peoples,
And rebuke strong nations afar off;
They shall beat their swords into plowshares,
And their spears into pruning hooks;
Nation shall not lift up sword against nation,
Neither shall they learn war any more.
4 But everyone shall sit under his vine and under
    his fig tree,
And no one shall make them afraid;
For the mouth of the LORD of hosts has spoken.
5 For all people walk each in the name of his god,
But we will walk in the name
    of the LORD our God
Forever and ever.
6 "In that day," says the LORD,
"I will assemble the lame,

I will gather the outcast
And those whom I have afflicted;
7 I will make the lame a remnant,
And the outcast a strong nation;
So the LORD will reign over them
      in Mount Zion
From now on, even forever.
8 And you, O tower of the flock,
The stronghold of the daughter of Zion,
To you shall it come,
Even the former dominion shall come,
The kingdom of the daughter of Jerusalem."
9 Now why do you cry aloud?
Is there no king in your midst?
Has your counselor perished?
For pangs have seized you like a
      woman in labor.
10 Be in pain, and labor to bring forth,
O daughter of Zion,
Like a woman in birth pangs.
For now you shall go forth from the city,
You shall dwell in the field,
And you shall go even to Babylon.
There you shall be delivered;
There the LORD will redeem you
From the hand of your enemies.
11 Now also many nations have gathered
      against you,
Who say, "Let her be defiled,
And let our eye look upon Zion."
12 But they do not know the thoughts of the LORD,
Nor do they understand His counsel;
For He will gather them like sheaves to the
      threshing floor.
13 "Arise and thresh, O daughter of Zion;
For I will make your horn iron,
And I will make your hooves bronze;
You shall beat in pieces many peoples;
I will consecrate their gain to the LORD,
And their substance to the LORD
      of the whole earth."
5:1 Now gather yourself in troops,

O daughter of troops;
He has laid siege against us;
They will strike the judge of Israel with a rod
   on the cheek.
2 "But you, Bethlehem Ephrathah,
Though you are little among the
   thousands of Judah,
Yet out of you shall come forth to Me
The One to be ruler in Israel,
Whose goings forth have been from of old,
From everlasting."
3 Therefore He shall give them up,
Until the time that she who is in labor has
   given birth;
Then the remnant of His brethren
Shall return to the children of Israel.
4 And He shall stand and feed His flock
In the strength of the LORD,
In the majesty of the name of the
   LORD His God;
And they shall abide,
For now He shall be great
To the ends of the earth;
5 And this One shall be peace.
When the Assyrian comes into our land,
And when he treads in our palaces,
Then we will raise against him
Seven shepherds and eight princely men.
6 They shall waste with the sword the
   land of Assyria,
And the land of Nimrod at its entrances;
Thus He shall deliver us from the Assyrian,
When he comes into our land
And when he treads within our borders.
7 Then the remnant of Jacob
Shall be in the midst of many peoples,
Like dew from the LORD,
Like showers on the grass,
That tarry for no man
Nor wait for the sons of men.
8 And the remnant of Jacob
Shall be among the Gentiles,

In the midst of many peoples,
Like a lion among the beasts of the forest,
Like a young lion among flocks of sheep,
Who, if he passes through,
Both treads down and tears in pieces,
And none can deliver.
9 Your hand shall be lifted against
  your adversaries,
And all your enemies shall be cut off.
10 "And it shall be in that day," says the LORD,
  "That I will cut off your horses from your midst
  And destroy your chariots.
11 I will cut off the cities of your land
  And throw down all your strongholds.
12 I will cut off sorceries from your hand,
  And you shall have no soothsayers.
13 Your carved images I will also cut off,
  And your sacred pillars from your midst;
  You shall no more worship the work
  of your hands;
14 I will pluck your wooden images from
  your midst;
  Thus I will destroy your cities.
15 And I will execute vengeance in anger and fury
  On the nations that have not heard."
Micah 4:1–5:15

In the second section of Micah's prophecy, begun in chapter 3, the judgment portion of the message (Mic. 3) is much briefer than it is in the first section of the prophecy (Mic. 1–2). In this section the dominating theme of the prophecy is the great hope and salvation pronounced by God in chapters 4–5.

Micah 4:1–8 contains the converse of the judgment announced in Micah 3:12. The blessing and majesty of the city of Zion *"in the latter days"* will exceed every sovereign and all reigns this planet will have seen to that point.

Just as Micah 4:1–8 is antithetically related to Micah 3:12, so Micah 4:9–14 is antithetically related to Micah 4:8. While the impending ruin of the kingdom signals doom and the collapse of all that had been built to that time (vv. 9–14 [Hebrew 4:14-English 5:1]), Micah 4:8 emphasizes the fact that the royal house of David, here called "O *tower of the flock,"* will be restored much like Micah 4:1–7 speaks of the exaltation of the mountain of the Lord.

Thus there is a startling contrast between the grand vision in Micah 4:1–8 of the future glory of God in Israel, with Jerusalem at the center of all the activities, and the deep humiliation experienced by God's people in 4:9–5:1. The salvation oracle of hope and blessing does not stop at the end of chapter 4, though, but continues into chapter 5. God's kingdom is enriched and furthered by the birth of a king (Mic. 5:2–9) and by the cleansing of the land (Mic. 5:10–15). Here, then, is one of the truly magnificent portions of Scripture that takes us deep into the doctrine of the coming Messiah and His kingdom.

These two chapters may be conveniently divided into four main paragraphs: 4:1–8 / 4:9–5:1 / 5:2–9 / 5:10–15. Each contributes to the question, "Is there no king in our midst?" (Mic. 4:9) by giving us four evidences of the king's presence. These evidences are:

A. The Prominence of the Mountain of the Lord   4:1–8
B. The Working of the Counsel of the Lord   4:9–5:1
C. The Birth of the Davidic King   5:2–9
D. The Cleansing of the Land   5:10–15

Thus we begin our study of the glorious hope of the magnificent reign of Yahweh, from David's royal line, over the capital of Israel.

THE PROMINENCE OF THE MOUNTAIN OF THE LORD (4:1–8)

Since the first three verses of Micah 4 are practically identical to Isaiah 2:2–4, a question about the identity of their original author is always raised. Unfortunately, it is difficult to make a declaration with any degree of finality. The contextual linkages, the fact that Micah 4:4 has no parallel in Isaiah 2, and the vocabulary all seem to suggest Micah is the author, but since both prophets wrote in the same century (at most twenty to forty years apart) it hardly makes too much difference which one is ultimately declared the original author—indeed there may even be a third, unnamed, author.[13]

The time for the actualization of Micah's prophecy is *"in the latter days."* This is the phrase often used in the biblical text to indicate those events connected with the future coming of our Lord. The entire prophecy is dominated by a mountain on which is located *"the LORD's house"* (v. 1). Its exalted position—it *"shall be established on the*

58

top of the mountains and . . . exalted above the hills" (v. 1b)—has more to do with its prominence in the thoughts and actions of the nations than with its physical prominence. However, there may be a secondary allusion to this physical aspect as well, since the post-exilic prophet Zechariah will note that seismic activity, in connection with the second coming of our Lord, will cause a drastic uplifting of the city of Jerusalem, even exceeding its present 2500 feet above sea level (Zech. 14:9–10).

So steady will be the stream of people from all nations to the house of God that it is figuratively described as a flowing river (v. 1b). Thus the pilgrims will come, for the invitation to go up to the mountain of the Lord will be on the lips of everyone (cf. Ps. 122:1,4). And what these pilgrims will long for—more than the thrill of travel, local trinkets or shopping deals—will be instruction in *tôrâh,* the "law" of God, and *"The word of the LORD"* (v. 2). Imagine the *tôrâh* as the featured attraction at the house of God for all the nations of the earth in that coming day of the Lord!

Messiah will not only be King and Teacher in Zion in that day, but He will be the final Arbiter of all disputes. That will effectively antiquate the need for the United Nations Security Council (v. 3a). No nation will be exempt from the sphere of His rule and arbitration, for even the *"strong nations afar off"* (v. 3a) will submit to His edicts. Then it will be possible to totally disarm the nations and convert their implements of war into instruments of agriculture and peace. This is what every commencement speech and politician has dreamily hoped for—but has never been able to guarantee or effect.

Agrarian images continue to accumulate in verse 4. A repeated sign of tranquility, relaxation, security and prosperity is represented by each person comfortably seated at their home under their own vine and fig tree (which form natural arbors) (cf. 1 Kings 4:25; 2 Kings 18:31; Isa. 36:16; Hos. 2:12; Joel 1:12; 2:22; 3:10; Zech. 3:10). What is this but a return to the paradisiacal conditions that existed in the Garden of Eden (Isa. 65:20–25; Ezk. 36:25; Hos. 2:18). Micah adds, *"And no one shall make them afraid"* (v. 4b), for the threats of war, violence, crime and injustice will have passed with the presence of the King, Teacher and Final Arbiter. So certain is this promise that it concludes with what is tantamount to a personal signature: *"For the mouth of the LORD of hosts has spoken."* You just can not get any more assurance than that!

The fifth verse is a bit more difficult, but it appears to give a "before and after" contrastive picture. Previously, *"all people walk each in the name of his god."* Nevertheless, the believing remnant affirms *"But we will walk in the name of the* LORD *our God forever and ever."* The idiom "to walk in the name" means to give allegiance to and to be guided by that which the name represents; the believing remnant will be guided by the nature and character of God as the standard of justice and of right living.

But before the blessing of the coming millennial rule and reign of the Messiah can be enjoyed, Israel must be reassembled in her own land (v. 6). The scattered flock of Micah 2:12–13 must be tended to, for they currently are *"lame"* (v. 7) and in a somewhat pitiful state due to the fact that the Lord has allowed them to be afflicted (v. 6b). But the Lord will transform these *"outcast[s]"* (v. 7a) into *"a strong nation"* (v. 7b). After He has done that, the Lord will reign over them from Mount Zion (v. 7c; cf. Isa. 9:6–7; Dan. 7:14, 27; Luke 1:33; Rev. 11:15).

The prophet interposes the pivotal verse 8 in the middle of this section. Verse 8 serves as a transition between verses 4:1–7 and 4:9–5:1 and, further, anticipates the contrasting theme proclaimed in verses 4:9–5:1. In verse 8 Micah addresses the people at two sites: *"O tower of the flock"* and *"stronghold [or, literally, "Ophel"] of the daughter of Zion."* To understand the allusion to the tower of the flock, it is necessary to go back to Genesis 35:16 ff. There the patriarch Jacob was on his way south from Bethel to Bethlehem when his wife Rachel died giving birth to Benjamin. Jacob buried his wife north of Jerusalem (1 Sam. 10:2) and continued south where he camped just south of "Tower of the Flock" or "Migdal Ader." According to the Church Father Jerome, who lived in Bethlehem in the fourth century A.D., this Tower of Ader was about a mile from Bethlehem. Assuming that is true, the "Tower of the Flock" refers to David's birthplace, marked by a tower out in the field amidst the flock.

The second site is the well-known "Ophel," or "stronghold," that formed the acropolis on the eastern slope of the old city of Jerusalem (cf. 2 Kings 5:24). A reference to this part of the city stands for the whole of it. Since the city is referred to in the feminine case in verse 8, *"the daughter of Zion"* becomes the new terminology for this primitive city of David.

Both Bethlehem and Jerusalem are then put on notice that their former dominion and prominence, having served, respectively, as the birthplace and the seat of the royal government, will now be restored to them. Micah christens the "Tower of the Flock" as the emblem of the future kingdom of Messiah, He who is the new David. It is also the symbol of the royal house of David, since he was a native of Bethlehem and "kept the flock." Once again, Zion would turn to the flock to find her king. Jerusalem would turn to David's heir and the nations of the earth would turn to Jerusalem.

Alas, however, as Amos prophesied, in the interim the royal house of David will crumble and the kingdom will disintegrate (Amos 9:11 ff.). But, as Amos also promised, that grand dynasty, or "house," which is now nothing more than a "booth," or a "hut," will be restored in the latter days.

Parallel to the reference to the Tower of the Flock is the allusion to the birth pangs of Rachel in Genesis 35, which appear also in Micah 4:9. Micah uses that incident in Jacob and Rachel's lives to symbolize the progress of the nation toward its final deliverance in the Tower of the Flock. The nation will be filled with distress before the Messiah is born amidst the deadly birth-pangs, as Micah 5:2–3 would seem to indicate.

THE WORKING OF THE COUNSEL OF THE LORD (4:9–5:1)

Other nations, of course, had lost their leaders—to death, assassination, or political *coup de etats*. Israel though, lost her leader mainly through her own rebellious sinfulness. And since so many of the divine promises in the plan and counsel of God were intertwined with the Davidic kingdom, it is no wonder that the removal of the visible representative of all of God's promises was a sign of divine wrath against the nation.

With the approach of the Assyrian conqueror, there is an outcry from the people of Israel, who know they will lose their king and counselor (v. 9). Thus a period of suffering must occur in the nation between a time of lost glory and a time of restoration. The people's cries—*"like a woman in labor"* (v. 9)—are reminiscent of Rachel's birth pangs.

Not only would the Assyrians come, but so would the Babylonians (v. 10). The oracle describing these events is developed in three parts, each commencing with the word *"Now"*: verses 9–10; 11–13; and 5:1. The plan of God called for an exile, but the first part of the oracle describes a liberation from exile. God's plan also called for an invasion of Jerusalem by many nations, but that invasion would be soundly defeated, as described in the second part of the oracle. The third "now" in 5:1 begins a reference to the distress of Sennacherib's siege in 701 B.C., but the contrast will come with the strong adversative of 5:2.

It is necessary, then, for Israel to experience a time of trials before the kingdom of God can come. However, the emphasis of these verses is not on the trials and suffering of Israel, but, as the repetition of the word *"there"* in verse 10c signifies, it is on the release of God's people. Even the curse of being exiled from the land will be reversed.

Verse 11 introduces the theme of *"many nations"* being gathered against Israel. "Many nations" probably does not refer to either the Babylonians or the Assyrians, for, while there were different national groups in each of those imperial armies, they did not form several nations. No, this is a different siege from any that Sennacherib mounted in 701 B.C. or that Nebuchadnezzar led, culminating in the fall of Jerusalem in 586 B.C. This appears to be that last great attack by the nations of the earth as they attempt to settle "the Jewish Question" once and for all. Whether it will be sparked by pressures from the oil producing nations or by some other world-wide incident, we cannot say. But it parallels events predicted in Joel 3, Ezekiel 38–39, and Zechariah 12 and 14. The purpose of this international gathering of all nations against the single nation of Israel is described in verse 11: *"Let her be defiled."* As though Israel were a virgin daughter, the nations will lustfully slaughter her people and attempt to seize her land in an act of international genocide. The nations will stare insultingly at her (v. 11c) as she experiences the pain and shame of her rape and the desecration of her holy places.

Should it be thought impossible to summon all the nations of the earth so quickly, let us recall August 1990 and the phenomenal response that followed the United Nation's call for the world to deal with Saddam Hussein's takeover of the country of Kuwait. Over thirty nations representing all seven continents gathered, trained, and were battle-ready by the middle of January 1991! Nothing like that had ever been witnessed in human history. The summons of verse 11 suddenly became much more believable to our privileged generation. Many passages in the Psalms and prophets tell how the nations will attack Jerusalem in the end day. They include: Psalms 46:6; 48:4–5;

76:3–6; Isaiah 17:12–14; 29:5–8; Ezekiel 38–39; Joel 3:1–3, 9–12; and Zechariah 14:1–3, 12–15.

What the nations fail to realize is that God is still working His plan (v. 12). Even with the prophecy available in almost every one of their languages, they still fail to understand it—either because they are ignorant or because they have been educated by unbelieving scholars who expressly deny the very possibility of predictive prophecy. The love, grace and mercy of God will turn Israel's darkest moment into His finest hour on earth. When the nations lie broken and beaten *"like sheaves [on] the threshing floor"* (v. 12c; cf. Isa. 21:10; 41:15–6; Jer. 51:33), God will suddenly revive His people with an order that they should *"Arise and thresh"* (v. 13).

At that moment Israel will become like the beast that treads out the grain, trampling her enemies as if she had a horn of iron and hooves of bronze. Only the hooves are needed for threshing; the horn is the proverbial symbol of strength and power.

Following the custom of setting aside a portion of one's spoils to the deity that secured the victory for the nation, victorious Israel sets aside a portion of her gain for the temple of the Lord (v. 13c; cf. Isa. 60:1–9).

In verse 5:1 Micah returns to the difficulties to be expected in the future (the Hebrew text makes this verse 14, which is a better arrangement of the text since this verse returns to the thought of Micah 4:9.) Zion is urged to *"gather yourself in troops"* so that she can withstand the enemy's attack. Already Micah can envision the siege against Jerusalem. The first line of this verse is difficult to render, for it can be translated as "You are walled around with a wall" (NRSV; based on the LXX) or "You are slashing yourself." Since self-laceration was associated with the Canaanite culture, the first translation is probably to be preferred. Note also the parallel line *"He has laid siege against us."* But it can be read as "troops" just as well. The Hebrew root *gdd* is to be preferred over the Greek Septuagint which must have read *gdr* "wall."

The *"judge"* referred to here is no doubt the king. To smite someone on the cheek was considered a great insult. But this cannot refer to the humiliation of Jesus Christ, since He was not smitten in connection with any siege, past or future, and He was not smitten by a rod, as described here. The most plausible referent is the awful treatment that King Zedekiah received at the hands of Nebuchadnezzar during the Babylonian invasion. No greater reproach could have been suffered by the people of Israel than to have their king as ill-treated as Nebuchadnezzar was when the capital of Judah fell in 586 B.C.

THE BIRTH OF THE DAVIDIC KING (5:2–9)

If the last Davidic King of Judah suffered such humiliation and degradation, watch what God is going to do now as He makes amends. For soon Jerusalem will have labored and the birth pangs will have ended; God will have given a son to the Davidic family that comes from *"Bethlehem Ephrathah."* All this will be done by God's power (5:2).

Bethlehem means "house of bread," and the district in which it was located was Ephrathah, meaning "fruitful" (Ps. 132:6). The deliverer of Judah would not come from Zion, but from the rather unpretentious town of Bethlehem. Bethlehem was not even deemed important enough to appear in the list of conquered cities in the book of Joshua. *"Though you are little,"* prophesied Micah, the results of what would come to pass would not be "despised" or judged to be "weak" (one definition of "little" found in other contexts [Judg. 6:15; Ps 119:141]).

Out of lowly Bethlehem would come a *"ruler"* *"whose goings forth have been from of old, from everlasting"* (v. 2c). The prophets usually avoided the word "king" because of its pagan connotations. Thus the Messiah was called a "Ruler." *"To me"* (in the emphatic position [v. 2b]) He was to come. In other words, the Messiah was to be first of all for the Lord's benefit and His plans, and only secondarily in response to Israel and her distress. But this Ruler was not a recent creation, for even though He would be born in Bethlehem, He had existed from eternity. When the Hebrew word for "everlasting," ꜥôlam, is used in connection with God, it can only mean "from eternity on" (cf. Pss. 25:6; 90:2). That can be its only meaning here if the Ruler is none other than the Son of God, the Messiah.

But for a period of unspecified duration, *"He shall give them up, until the time that she who is in labor has given birth"* (v. 3). From the Babylonian exile to the present day, God has abandoned Israel and will continue to do so "until" the one in labor has given birth (cf. the virgin birth in Isa. 7:14 and the national birth in Rev. 12:1–6). Thus all the births in the line of Eve, Shem, Abraham, Isaac, Jacob and David, since the earliest announcement of the promise doctrine, are one with the final and ultimate promised Seed that is to come. The women who give birth, then, are in one sense the mothers of the next heir in the promised line, while in another sense they are the people of Judah predicted in Genesis 49:10. Rachel must continue to groan, as it were, until the Tower of the Flock is born (see v. 8).

Verses 4–6 focus on the second coming of the Messiah. He will take His stand as Governor and supreme Ruler. He will carry the name of His father, "mighty God" (Isa. 9:6; 10:21), and He will abide and dwell in peace (vv. 4b–5a). There can be no doubt about who He is, for *"He shall be great to the ends of the earth"* (v. 4; cf. Ps. 72:8; Mic. 4:1–4).

Meanwhile, the kingdoms of this world, with all their antagonism toward Him, will be destroyed. The *"seven shepherds and eight princely men"* (v. 5c) are not to be taken literally, but are an example of the "x" + 1 (i.e. 7, yea 8) factor; therefore an indefinite but adequate number of leaders will be available to withstand any resistance against Messiah and His Kingdom.

The Messiah will empower Israel to overcome her enemies (vv. 7–9). References to the *"Assyrian"* (vv. 5 and 6) and *"the land of Nimrod"* (v. 6) foretell events both in the near and distant future; not in a double sense or double meaning, but in the sense that the invasions of the Assyrian Sennacherib and the Babylonian Nebuchadnezzar are only "earnests" or "downpayments" for what is to come in the final day. They functioned in a typical and representative way of the nations, doubtlessly from the same area and territory, who would come in a future day to threaten Israel in the same way some had in Micah's day. The "land of Nimrod," of course, refers to Babylonia, as it did in Genesis 10:8–12 and 1 Chronicles 1:10. This prediction was elaborated upon in Isaiah 13–14 and Jeremiah 50–51. But the outcome was assured in Micah: *"He shall deliver us from the Assyrian, when he comes into our land and when he treads within our borders"* (v. 6c).

The revitalizing effect of Messiah's reign will be like that of dew on the land in the heat of summer, and like showers on the dry land (v. 7b). Thus empowered, the *"remnant of Jacob"* (v. 8a) will be *"like a lion among the beasts of the forest"* (v. 8b). Now that Israel is in the center of the will of God, she will be unbeatable and unconquerable (v. 9).

THE CLEANSING OF THE LAND (5:10–15)

If Israel is to be a usable instrument once again in the hands of the Lord, she must cast off every form of support that has been or could be raised to the same or higher level as her trust in the Living God.

Micah singles out four sources of self-reliance upon which Israel (and perhaps we too) had vainly relied in the past. They are: self-help (v. 10); self-defense (v. 11); self-deception (v. 12); and self-worship (vv. 13–14a). Each one proved to be nothing but a broken reed on which no one could lean.

How many times had Israel and Judah put more trust in their military armaments, such as *"horses"* and *"chariots"* (v. 10), than in the Lord? But that evil had to be uprooted if they were to be victorious and used by God in that day to come. This form of self-help was simply another subtle idolatry in the life of that ancient nation—and, unfortunately, it is in the lives of modern nations still. Whenever a people trust more in their systems of defense and military preparedness than they do in the Lord of the universe, they are in for trouble. This is not to disparage adequate military preparation, but all the technology in the world will be to no avail if it is not matched—and indeed exceeded—by a strong faith and trust in our Lord!

The perversion of trusting in one's defense systems more than in God also resulted in demeaning the greatness of God and failing to trust Him wholeheartedly. The walled *"cities"* and *"strongholds"* (v. 11) became a form of obsession just as the military armaments did, although these could do little more than create a false sense of security. Again, it was not the existence of the defense systems that was being condemned, but the inappropriate trust in these things in place of, or more than, a trust in the Living God.

This misplaced trust could even be carried to the extreme of consulting *"sorceries"* or *"soothsayers"* (v. 12) in lieu of seeking God's face and trusting His revelations. But mark it down: whenever the word of God is scarcely heard because of a widespread disregard for it, or boredom with it, humans will suddenly find that they need a word from above; then they will seek out the netherworld, for they now fear that they have offended God—and they probably have! But He is merciful and gracious and He will hear. There is no reason to go to the demonic for a word of perspective from above, or beyond, ourselves. That is what both Leviticus 19:26 and Deuteronomy 18:9–14 warned against. Instead, we are to depend on God's prophets who deliver His word.

Finally, self–worship often takes over as we start being more impressed with the work of our hands than we are with the fact that we are the work of God's hands. *"Carved images," "sacred pillars"* and *"wooden images"* (vv. 13–14a) were the stock and trade of pagan religions. They represented an attempt to manipulate spiritual forces by getting in touch with what is magically represented by these man-made products. Along with all the theological distortions, self–worship had overtones of sexual perversion since the "sacred pillars" probably referred to Baal and to male reproduction, just as the "wooden images" were associated with Asherah and with female reproduction. These images were to be rejected and destroyed (Exod. 34:13; Deut. 16:21). Yet how frequently worshipping these images had been the occasion for the downfall of Israel (2 Kings 13:6; 23:6).

But if Israel would discard all these false sources of self reliance, Messiah would execute His vengeance on the nations that refused to be reconciled to God and that insisted on opposing the Living God, His people, and His purposes (v. 15). God's *"vengeance"* would not be vindictive, or, as our English word suggests, be filled with envy and jealousy; He would merely act zealously for His own name and plan. He would vindicate all wrongs lest the righteous should despair that right would never be done in any sphere.

CONCLUSION

The day of our Lord Jesus Christ will be a most remarkable day. It will be filled with some of the most awesome displays of God's power of all time, as every form of opposition that the gospel or God's people have ever faced go down in smoking defeat. And at the center of this whole spectacle will stand our Messiah, the promised One of God. And miracle of miracles, the people of Israel shall once again turn to Him with all their hearts and souls as they see that He indeed is the expected One who has saved them just in the nick of time from the whole world, gone crazy in attacking them with the single intent of eradicating all traces of their existence from planet earth.

God indeed was in the midst of His people; and He will come yet again with the most dramatic demonstration of power this world has ever seen.

CHAPTER FIVE

What Does the Lord Require of Us?

Micah 6:1–16

6:1 Hear now what the LORD says:
"Arise, plead your case before the mountains,
And let the hills hear your voice.
2 Hear, O you mountains, the LORD's complaint,
And you strong foundations of the earth;
For the LORD has a complaint against
His people,
And He will contend with Israel.
3 "O My people, what have I done to you?
And how have I wearied you?
Testify against Me.
4 For I brought you up from the land of Egypt,
I redeemed you from the house of bondage;
And I sent before you Moses, Aaron,
and Miriam.
5 O My people, remember now
What Balak king of Moab counseled,
And what Balaam the son of Beor answered him,
From Acacia Grove to Gilgal,
That you may know the righteousness
of the LORD."
6 With what shall I come before the LORD,
And bow myself before the High God?
Shall I come before Him with burnt offerings,
With calves a year old?
7 Will the LORD be pleased with
thousands of rams,
Or ten thousand rivers of oil?
Shall I give my firstborn for my transgression,

The fruit of my body for the sin of my soul?

8 He has shown you, O man, what is good;
And what does the LORD require of you
But to do justly,
To love mercy,
And to walk humbly with your God?

9 The LORD's voice cries to the city—
Wisdom shall see Your name:
"Hear the rod!
Who has appointed it?

10 Are there yet the treasures of wickedness
In the house of the wicked,
And the short measure that is an abomination?

11 Shall I count pure those with the wicked balances,
And with the bag of deceitful weights?

12 For her rich men are full of violence,
Her inhabitants have spoken lies,
And their tongue is deceitful in their mouth.

13 "Therefore I will also make you sick
by striking you,
By making you desolate because of your sins.

14 You shall eat, but not be satisfied;
Hunger shall be in your midst.
You may carry some away,
but shall not save them;
And what you do rescue I will give
over to the sword.

15 "You shall sow, but not reap;
You shall tread the olives, but not anoint
yourselves with oil;
And make sweet wine, but not drink wine.

16 For the statutes of Omri are kept;
All the works of Ahab's house are done;
And you walk in their counsels,
That I may make you a desolation,
And your inhabitants a hissing.
Therefore you shall bear the reproach
of My people."

Micah 6:1–16

The third and final section of this book moves, as did the two preceeding sections, from judgment (6:1–7:10) to salvation (7:11–20).

There are two parts to the judgment message (6:1–16 and 7:1–10) and one part to the salvation message (7:11–20).

Micah begins this remarkable section in chapter six with a lawsuit. But this is no ordinary courtroom case, for God sits as the judge, with the prophet Micah as His counsel. The jury on this case is a rather unusual assemblage as well, for the ancient hills and mountains are called to hear the complaint that God has raised against the defendants, His people Israel.

The scene shifts from the courtroom to the street on a busy market day where the local commerce is in full swing (6:9–16). It appears that Micah has juxtaposed these two scenes in order to show precisely what God means when He gives His famous answer in verse 8 to the defendant's almost whimsical question in verse 6. Judah asked, *"With what shall I come before the LORD?"* (v. 6). The answer in verse 8 is, *"And what does the LORD require of you but to do justly, to love mercy, and to walk humbly with your God?"* It is this justice, mercy and humble walk that Micah illustrates in 6:9–16 as he condemns the wicked commercial practices of his people.

The text cites four indictments against the people of Israel as it answers the key question, "What does God require of us?" Each of these indictments, which we now pose in the form of a question, has such an obvious answer that it almost seems as if it needs no answer; nevertheless, the questions must be posed and answered since the actions of the people belie their ability to answer properly. Four indictments arise out of these four questions:

A. Have I Mistreated You?   6:1–3
B. Have I Required Too Much From You?   6:4–8
C. Have I Approved of Your Exploiting One Another?   6:9–12
D. Have I Blessed Your Get–Rich–Quick Schemes?   6:13–16

Let us go, then, to the trial.

HAVE I MISTREATED YOU? (6:1–3)

The first half of this chapter, especially Micah 6:6–8, has become known as one of the great passages of the Bible. Along with Hosea 6:6 and Amos 5:24, it epitomizes the teaching of the eighth century prophets.

The use of questions and answers in the lawsuit format of verses 1–8 has confused the literary purists who have decreed, by their own canons of what should and should not be, that each text arises from a specially recurring sociological or cultic "setting in life" (*Sitz im Leben*)—each with its own distinctive literary form. However, it is not necessary for those who accept the claim of revelation to confine the question and answer pattern solely to a cultic entrance liturgy, a prophetic sermon, or a wisdom teaching situation. The question and answer pattern may also have been used in a lawsuit format and the passage may be regarded as a whole unit, without hypothesizing a fusion of different sources and disparate units welded by a somewhat clumsy redactor doing a rather poor scissors-and-paste job of putting together diverse lines.

The lawsuit opens with the word *"Hear"* (6:1), the word used previously in two major sections (Mic. 1:2; 3:1) to mark and divide the sections. The mountains and the hills will serve as the jury, since they were present when Yahweh ratified His covenant with His people (Deut. 4:26; 30:19; 31:28) and served as witnesses to that covenant (Deut. 32:1; Ps. 50:4; Isa. 1:2). In the Near East literature, mountains serve as witnesses in other treaties, so it is not unusual here. Obviously, however, to appeal in this way to the mountains in the context of a lawsuit is a gripping rhetorical device that emphasizes how serious the situation is and how solemnly Judah—and we who read this text—should take these proceedings.

"The Lord has a complaint against His people, and He will contend with Israel" (6:2b). But rather than charge them directly, the Lord asks two questions to determine if His people likewise have something they feel they should charge God with. The Lord's two questions are: *"What have I done to you?"* and *"How have I wearied you?"* (v. 3).

The defendants are addressed as *"O My people"* (v. 3a, 5). Even as God renders judgment against the people of Judah, He does not suggest a distance in His relationship with them, as He does in the book of Haggai, where He calls them "this people" (Hag. 1:2). Nevertheless, this is clearly a picture of an outraged love, as in Isaiah 5 and Hosea 11. Or, to quote Isaiah 1:2, "I have nourished and brought up children, and they have rebelled against Me."

Have I Required Too Much From You? (6:4–8)

With what irony our Lord now invites His people to bring any and all charges they may have against Him! God is willing to set all things right. God has not been unjust to the people of Judah; nor has He asked too much from them. Any suggestion that He has constitutes sheer ingratitude on the part of the nation.

"I brought you up from the land of Egypt" (v. 4) is the first rebuttal that God makes to any inference that He has been unfair or unjust, or that He requires too much from His people. This statement appears 125 times in the Old Testament. Micah, ever the punster and one who played with words, warns that instead of God "wearying" them (*hel᾽ētîkā*, v. 3), he "brought" them "up" (*he᾽elitîkā*, v. 4) out of Egypt. It was this very environment of grace that laid the foundations for the requirements of the Law in Exodus 20:1. Notice how tenderly and compassionately God addresses His erring people. He continues, *"I redeemed you from the house of bondage"* and I gave you spiritual leaders: Moses the lawgiver to instruct them, Aaron the High Priest to offer atonement for their sins, and Miriam the prophetess and songleader to lead them in praising God.

God also turned the intended curse of King Balak by Balaam into a blessing (Num. 22–24). Thus the journeying Israelites were led safely from Shittim (also known as Acacia), east of the Jordan River, to Gilgal on the west side of the Jordan. But, alas, despite all the good that God had done, the people had not responded as expected, and the list of the acts of God's salvation became the basis for the present indictment.

God had bound Himself to fulfill what He had promised to do out of His free grace. In fact, each act was an evidence of *"the righteousness of the LORD"* (v. 5b). The word "righteousness" is a plural word in the Hebrew text. This is extremely rare, happening only five times (Judg. 5:11 *[bis]*; 1 Sam. 12:7; Ps. 103:6; Dan. 9:16) in the Old Testament. It points to the righteous *results* that have come from all of God's works on His people's behalf. These results were to have had the purpose of demonstrating that God's word was "correct, straight, faithful," i.e., "righteous."

The people, upon hearing this word of grace, burst into a barrage of questions. Their questions were meant to excuse their failures, but, instead, only betrayed the fact that the people did not really understand how serious the case against them was. In a spurt of false religious fervor they asked, *"With what shall I come before the LORD?"* (v. 6). The fact that they used the word "what" indicates that they still did not understand; they thought the solution was ritual activity!

"With what [thing] must I come?" they were asking, as if God could be bought off by substitutes for genuine piety. But God always inspects the heart of the giver before He looks at the gift itself.

The people also attempted to substitute quantity for quality, suggesting as an offering *"thousands of rams"* and *"ten thousand rivers of oil"* (v. 7). In their ignorance, they even suggested as a human offering to God *"[their] firstborn for [their] transgression"* (v. 7b). Only Molech-worship in Moab required such an awful sacrifice—that's how theologically unaware the nation was!

In the background of verses 6–8 is the informing theology of Deuteronomy 10:12. In the Deuteronomy text, God announced himself ready to destroy Israel because of her worship of the golden calf (Exod. 32:10, 14), but God accepted Moses's prayer on Israel's behalf and turned from His threatened judgment. After the people had been forgiven because of Moses's intercession with God for forty days and forty nights, Moses said, "And now, Israel, what does the LORD your God require of you, but to fear the LORD your God, to walk in all His ways and to love Him, to serve the LORD your God with all your heart and with all your soul" (Deut. 10:12).

Some might aver that Moses appears to be more merciful and gracious than God, for Moses was the one who intervened and, in effect, saved the people from God's threatened doom. But they would be incorrect, for the God that Israel had provoked to wrath and to judgment was the same God who had prepared Moses and had given to him the responsibility for interceding on behalf of the nation Israel. It was this same Lord who had taught Moses how to pray. The connection between forgiveness and obedience is this: since Israel had experienced so gracious a remission of her sin of worshipping the golden calf, what sort of people ought her people to be now? Was not the next logical question: "What does the LORD our God require of us?" That is the question in Micah 6:8.

The requirements of God had already been revealed; the nation had only to listen. *"He has shown you, O man, what is good; And what does the LORD require of you but to do justly, to love mercy, and to walk humbly with your God?"* (v. 8). Jesus referred to this passage in Matthew 23:23 as representing the "weightier matters of the law." In other words, since justice, mercy, and humility are based on the character and nature of God, it pointed to that aspect of the Mosaic law that would never go out of vogue!

The Law is epitomized in verse 8a as being *"good"* while the latter part of the verse captures its essence with three terms. *"To do justly"* is to act with equity, fairness and deference to those who are in a weaker social position—the opposite of the violence, oppression, fraud, lying and injustice described in Micah 6:10–12. Thus "justice" is a comprehensive term for a way of life that finds its expression in the covenant of God. *"To love mercy"* adds the spirit of generosity, loyalty and graciousness to all acts of justice and assistance. The Hebrew word *ḥesed* occurs 250 times in the Old Testament and is at once one of the most beautiful and the most difficult words to render by a single English term. It is the faithful, loyal love, mercy, and grace that binds a man to his Lord and to his neighbor or friend.

The third essential element of doing "good" is *"to walk humbly with your God."* Walking, of course, is the Hebrew idiom for what we call one's "lifestyle." And "to walk humbly" is simply to live by faith, for faith is the antithesis of pride. Pride alone insists on taking first place, but faith seeks to give God first place. Humility is that virtue required of those who are faithful followers of our Lord (Ps. 131:1). Living a circumspect lifestyle will bring one's life into conformity with God's will. Adam, Noah and Abraham serve as examples of people who "walked with God" (Gen. 3:8; 6:9).

For those who believe that Micah totally abrogated ceremonial obedience in order to make way for moral obedience, we must stress the fact that the word *"but"* in verse 8 refers to the need for setting moral obedience as a priority and precondition for carrying out ceremonial obedience.[14] God requires more than outward performance; He requires certain qualities of the heart: righteousness, love, humility, and faith. It is impossible to fulfill the requirements of the Law as an unregenerate person. Only the Spirit of God can enable us to fulfill the righteousness of the Law, whether in Old or New Testament times (Rom. 8:3–4).

HAVE I APPROVED OF YOUR EXPLOITING ONE ANOTHER? (6:9–12)

In verse 9 we learn that the *"city"* of Jerusalem (cf. Mic. 3:10–12; 4:2, 7–13) is accused in the lawsuit. The word translated *"rod"* in verse 9 should probably be rendered as "tribe," meaning Judah; so Judah, too, was named in the suit.

But just as the resident merchants of Jerusalem were setting up their spaces for business, Micah delivers a scorching and withering condemnation of their shoddy practices. Obviously they did not know what it meant "to do justly" or "to love mercy."

Fortunes were being made, but they were *"treasures of wickedness"* (v. 10). The merchants employed every scheme conceivable to make a profit. A *"Short measure"* (v. 10) was a "short ephah" (NIV) or a "scant half bushel" (the ephah should have measured twenty-two liters, but it didn't). The merchants also used stone weights that were either underweight or overweight, depending on whether a merchant was buying or selling (v. 11). And the merchants would threaten *"violence"* (v. 12) against anyone who confronted them about their cheating. Truthfulness was exchanged for deceit and fraud.

Of course, that is why God gave government, the courts, and His servants the prophets—each group was to do its part to provide a series of checks and balances on a corrupt society. But when practices such as Micah describes persisted, it is clear that the government was not cracking down on the violators and that the courts were not providing relief. Only God's prophets decried the practices.

HAVE I BLESSED YOUR GET–RICH–QUICK SCHEMES? (6:13–16)

The *"Therefore"* of verse 13 introduces God's judgment on all the corrupt practices and those who foster them. Did not the Mosaic Law prohibit such dishonest business practices? (cf. Lev. 19:35–36; Deut. 25:13–16). Solomon collected proverbs censuring the same evils (cf. Prov. 11:1; 20:10, 23). Even Micah's colleagues had sounded an alarm against them (Hos. 12:7; Amos 8:5).

God's punishment would have a ring of poetic justice to it, perhaps to help the perpetrators of evil associate the punishment with the crime and thereby repent all the sooner. The royal family, the rich, and the land barons would suffer because of their abuse of the poor and the powerless. They would eat, but it would make them *"sick"* (v. 13). They would eat, but they would not feel satisfied (v. 14). The sentence in verse 14, *"Hunger shall be in your midst,"* is rendered by the NIV as "Your stomach will still be empty." Recently, A. Ehrman has defended the Syriac, which says that the evil-doers would be afflicted with "dysentery,"[15] as the proper correction of the difficult Hebrew.

Therefore, food and money acquired by illegal means will not last or satisfy. Savings will disappear; fields will be sown, but harvests will be small or nonexistent (v. 15). Olives will be squeezed in the olive press, but all the work will produce a negligible amount of, or even no, oil (v. 15). The grapes may be tramped in the wine press, but that will not be worth all the trouble either (v. 15).

These words remind us of the later message of Haggai 1:5–6. Haggai probes, "Are you sowing more and harvesting less? Are you eating more and feeling less satisfied? . . . Are you earning more only to put it into a bag with holes?" No one cheats God or man without badly cheating himself at the same time. God keeps very good books and knows when justice has been overlooked. He will finally act, so all who race on in their deceitful ways should take immediate notice that all their labors are bound to produce nothing in the end.

Micah's message closes in verse 16 with an allusion to Omri and Ahab; the once thriving city of Samaria is recalled here through two of its most infamous kings. Samaria had to be visited with judgment because its merchants, government, judges, priests, and prophets failed to do justly and to love mercy, much less to walk humbly with their God. If Samaria was a warning to Jerusalem, then Samaria, Jerusalem and a host of other cities, both ancient and modern, ought to be a lesson to us today.

The guilty of Micah's day had repeated the same evil practices of the Israelite Omride dynasty. That dynasty, in the northern kingdom, began when Omri assassinated Zimri and seized the throne of Israel. His son Ahab took over after he died and Ahab added child sacrifice (1 Kings 16:34) and widespread Baal worship to his father's list of sins (1 Kings 18). Ahab was the epitomy of greed and power as he seized Naboth's vineyard (1 Kings 21) and allowed the grossest of socioeconomic injustices to fester in his realm. After Ahab's death the entire house of Ahab, including his seventy sons, were violently killed by the next usurper, Jehu.

Micah declares that Judah has become like the Omride dynasty in her sins. If those sins led to the demise of the northern kingdom, what does the southern kingdom think will happen to her if she does not repent?

CONCLUSION

Before God requires anything of a person, He calls out to that person with His compassion, mercy, grace, and redemption. It is the environment of grace, then, that becomes the sole basis for urging men and women to do anything for God.

But even for redeemed persons, the order of first priority will always be the heart. The first priority, even for a redeemed person, will always be to have an acceptable attitude of the heart, since God requires this before He will notice or accept any work for Him—whether in the form of rituals, liturgy, or social involvement.

CHAPTER SIX

Where Is the Lord Our God?

Micah 7:1–10

7:1 Woe is me!
For I am like those who gather summer fruits,
Like those who glean vintage grapes;
There is no cluster to eat
Of the first-ripe fruit which my soul desires.
2 The faithful man has perished from the earth,
And there is no one upright among men.
They all lie in wait for blood;
Every man hunts his brother with a net.
3 That they may successfully do evil with
both hands—
The prince asks for gifts,
The judge seeks a bribe,
And the great man utters his evil desire;
So they scheme together.
4 The best of them is like a brier;
The most upright is sharper than a thorn hedge;
The day of your watchman and your
punishment comes;
Now shall be their perplexity.
5 Do not trust in a friend;
Do not put your confidence in a companion;
Guard the doors of your mouth
From her who lies in your bosom.
6 For son dishonors father,
Daughter rises against her mother,
Daughter-in-law against her mother-in-law;
A man's enemies are the men of his
own house.

7 Therefore I will look to the LORD;
  I will wait for the God of my salvation;
  My God will hear me.
8 Do not rejoice over me, my enemy;
  When I fall, I will arise;
  When I sit in darkness,
  The LORD will be a light to me.
9 I will bear the indignation of the LORD,
  Because I have sinned against Him,
  Until He pleads my case
  And executes justice for me;
  He will bring me forth to the light,
  And I will see His righteousness.
10 Then she who is my enemy will see,
  And shame will cover her who said to me,
  "Where is the LORD your God?"
  My eyes will see her;
  Now she will be trampled down
  Like mire in the streets.

Micah 7:1–10

Having heard the prophet Micah minister to the public officials and merchants in the public eye, we are now given an intimate picture of his private life. The literary form of this chapter is a lament in which Micah weeps over the sad state of affairs into which his nation has fallen by its sin. Those who heard him preach must have assumed that he possessed a hard interior that held very little compassion or concern for the impact his messages had on his hearers. But, as this chapter reveals, they would have been wrong; here Micah is exposed as a man deeply distressed and greatly moved by the moral condition into which his nation has slipped.

It is difficult to know just where to end the first unit of the lament. Is it correctly concluded at verse 7 or does it extend to verse 10, as we have proposed? Despite the fact that most scholars conclude the first unit at the end of verse 7, we assert that verses 8–10 belong with it because we view the second unit of the lament, the message of hope from the Lord, to begin in verse 11 and continue to the end of the chapter, verse 20. Our assertion is supported by the fact that the repeated use of a significant phrase in the message of hope, *"In that day,"* is first seen in verse 11. Admittedly, most scholars since

Hermann Gunkel regard verses 8–20 as a prophetic liturgy, with verses 8–10 making up the first moment of "acknowledgment of sin." Whether this is or is not so must be judged by each reader, but the eschatological unity of verses 11–20 just cannot be missed.

Once again we have chosen a question from the text as the focal point for the passage: *"Where is the LORD your God?"* (v. 10). This question, concerning the location and powerful presence of God, is most commonly asked on three different occasions:

    A. When We Look for Just One Righteous Person 7:1–4
    B. When We Look for Just One Friend 7:5–7
    C. When We Look for Just One Adjudicator 7:8–10

In many ways, this section of Micah's prophecy is very similar to the first chapter of Habakkuk. Habakkuk was so deeply moved by the sin of his people that he too cried out in a lament to God. Both prophets passionately regretted the fact that there were too few righteous people to be found.

Let us examine each of the three occasions when the question "Where is the LORD your God?" is most insistent.

WHEN WE LOOK FOR JUST ONE RIGHTEOUS PERSON (7:1–4)

The Greeks used to tell the story about one of their philosophers named Diogenes who searched all the land with a lantern looking for one honest man. Similarly, in the Bible, God's servants, who were in tune with His heart and mind, searched continually for that one righteous person. Abraham begged God to save the five cities of the plain if he could find in them ten righteous persons (Gen. 18:23–33). Some have thought that these must have been very small cities, but they were not. We have now uncovered the cemetary used by these five cities at Bab-ed-Dra, in modern Jordan. We have identified some 500,000 persons buried from 2000 to 1800 B.C. at Bab-ed-Dra, roughly the time when Abraham would have lived there. It would appear that ten righteous persons could have saved a population of something in excess of 500,000! Later, Jeremiah and Ezekiel would likewise, search for that one righteous person, but would have about the same success as Micah had in verse 7:2. The Lord instructed Jeremiah, "Run to and fro through the streets of Jerusalem; see now and know; and seek in her open places, if you can find a man, if there is anyone who executes judgment, who seeks the truth, and I will pardon her" (Jer. 5:1). Ezekiel sought a person who would "stand in the gap" before the Lord so that the Lord would not need to destroy Jerusalem, "but [Ezekiel] found no one" (Ezk. 22:30). In Micah's day and now, righteous people are hard to find, but are oh-so-necessary if those persons who richly deserve it are to be spared God's judgment.

"*Woe is me!*" (v. 1), cries the prophet, as he begins the personal part of his lament. The Hebrew word used here is not the normal word for "woe" (cf. Job 10:15), but is a heart-wrenching cry that initiates this personal portion of the lamentation. What misery, wretchedness and grief was the prophet's as he contemplated what was ahead for a people who persisted in their own wicked ways. Those wicked ways are described in verses 1b–6.

The search for one righteous person, Micah says, is very similar to the experience of the owner of an orchard or vineyard who goes to his fruit trees and vines hoping to find some fruit or grapes only to discover that there are none (v. 1b–c). After all his toil and labor, he is denied the enjoyment of the expected benefits. That must have been how God felt about His search for at least one who listened, one who trusted and obeyed; alas, there was not one!

Verses 2–4 describe a terrible litany of sins and faults that support the conclusion that "*The faithful man has perished from the earth, and there is no one upright among men*" (v. 2). All have gone astray; all are corrupt; all have turned to their own ways to do their own things (Ps. 14:3).

Moral standards are being totally disregarded. Everyone is lying in wait to pounce on another person, just as Cain murdered his brother (Gen. 4:9). The people trap one another like hunters going after animals (v. 2c). So adept are all the people in doing evil that they indulge in evil "*with both hands*" (v. 3a). What had been true primarily of the leadership appears now to have filtered down to the general populace.

Bribery was a way of life for princes and judges. Profit, not justice, was the new motivation for leaders. Once the powerful man had spoken, or revealed, the passion of his soul (v. 3b), a web was spun that captured all his friends, allies and neighbors. But this practice was not limited to ancient times. Just recently, in the summer of 1991 it was revealed that a Chicago lawyer had paid off a long list of judges, lawyers and officials, and even a suburban mayor, for twenty-five years in order to protect his guilty clients—twenty-five years this travesty of justice went on!

Even the best of the lot are as crooked and as likely as a *"brier"* bush to rip anyone going by them (v. 4a). Even the most upright in the city are like a *"thorn hedge"* (v. 4b) that will scratch and tear all who pass by. Once again, Micah employs his love of word-play to make his point: the *mesûkâ*, "thorn hedge," will result in *mebûkâ*, "perplexity" (v. 4b).

WHEN WE LOOK FOR JUST ONE FRIEND (7:5–7)

Micah turns from his analysis of the character of the whole of society to an investigation of his own immediate friends and neighbors. But he is not encouraged by any signs of hope here, for his friends and neighbors are bathed in the same dread effects of sin that are so prevalent in the culture.

Sin has ruptured the most basic of human relations. No one can be trusted any more, not even one's friends or neighbors. If some think this is strange, then listen to an illustration that comes from contemporary experiences. One family, in a very fine neighborhood in California, left home for a week, only to learn upon their return that their next-door neighbors had stolen everything in their house while they were gone! When this happens, the fabric of society has indeed thoroughly eroded.

One's enemies, in these sorts of times, are those who live in one's own household. Family members no longer trust one another; in fact, they dishonor one another and take up positions of hostility against each other (v. 5c–6). Jeremiah witnessed the same trouble in the next century: "Everyone take heed to his neighbor, and do not trust any brother; for every brother will utterly supplant, and every neighbor will walk with slanderers. Everyone will deceive his neighbor, and will not speak the truth; they have taught their tongue to speak lies" (Jer. 9:4–5b). It is a sad day indeed when *"A man's enemies are the men of his own house"* (v. 6b).

But there is a ray of hope in this dark lament. It comes in verse 7. The prophet declares, turning from all that is going on around him, *"Therefore I will look to the LORD; I will wait for the God of my salvation; My God will hear me."* That was exactly what Habakkuk concluded.

Though he did not like what he saw happening to his people—either their wicked sinfulness or their inevitable punishment—he took his stand on his watchtower and waited to see what God would do (see our comments on Hab. 2:1–6). Micah and Habakkuk could wait for their God because the faithful, whose trust is not in themselves or their times, but in their Lord, can really live and survive in moments as dark as these. Micah and Habakkuk waited patiently for the Lord and His deliverance, for the Lord has always been good to those who wait for Him (Lam. 3:25–26). God would intervene to deliver His people when the time was right—through appropriate judicial, military, and spiritual intervention.

The Hebrew words for to *"look to"* and to *"wait for"* are not passive verbs, as our English words suggest, but involve active participation through faith, prayer and certain hope. So while the whole society was coming apart, one man plus God was a majority!

WHEN WE LOOK FOR JUST ONE ADJUDICATOR (7:8–10)

The city of Jerusalem is personified as as prisoner of war, fallen and sitting in darkness (v. 8). Thus positioned, this city pleads that her *"enemy . . . not rejoice over [her]"* (v. 8).

This "enemy" cannot be firmly identified, for it could be any of several nations. The Hebrew text treats the word as feminine. We can only surmise that the enemy is the nation of Babylon that later captured Jerusalem after Samaria experienced a similar fate at the hands of the Assyrians.

The city and people resolve that, regardless of who the enemy is or what she will do to Jerusalem, *"The LORD will be [their] light"* (cf. Ps. 27:1).

At this point, finally, the people confess their sins. They realize that God has been just and fair in what He has done to them. They, like the prodigal son (Luke 15:18), will return to their Father, and they will be welcomed home. Only then will the nation again be able to see the light; that light will appear as the people begin walking in the light.

Those who had taunted the people of Israel by asking "Where is the LORD your God?" will see where He is when He becomes Israel's great vindicator and adjudicator in the final day. Then it will be that Jerusalem will trade places with the jeerers and mockers, who infer that Judah's God is either nonexistent or impotent. Shame will cover Jerusalem's enemy, not Jerusalem. Then it will be that the enemy will be vanquished and trodden down as, symbolically, the foot of the conqueror is placed upon the neck of the defeated adversary. And so will Micah's people's sins be trodden under foot (7:19).

CONCLUSION

It is a grave error to live and act as if God were not present or aware of our lifestyles. It is also dangerous to reason that, since so many could not be wrong, the majority's thoughts and actions should set the standards for everyone. Even if our search for one righteous person, or for one friend who would be different and follow God's standards, is unsuccessful, we are not justified in participating with the masses in their evil deeds.

God longs for those who will wait for Him in believing faith. He watches for those who will dare to hope in His salvation even when the times are evil and when there is no one else who seems to be following Him.

Fortunately, as Jeremiah 26:18–19 indicates, Micah's preaching woke up some of King Hezekiah's generation, because the King (and apparently some others) repented. Therefore God did not bring the threatened judgments on that generation, for Judah waited more than a century before the same hardness of heart had settled so firmly that there was no changing and no repentance. May our Lord grant our generation the good sense to turn to God before we too find it is too late to repent.

CHAPTER SEVEN

Who Is a Pardoning God Like Our God?

Micah 7:11–20

11 In the day when your walls are to be built,
   In that day the decree shall go far and wide.
12 In that day they shall come to you
   From Assyria and the fortified cities,
   From the fortress to the River,
   From sea to sea,
   And mountain to mountain.
13 Yet the land shall be desolate
   Because of those who dwell in it,
   And for the fruit of their deeds.
14 Shepherd Your people with Your staff,
   The flock of Your heritage,
   Who dwell solitarily in a woodland,
   In the midst of Carmel;
   Let them feed in Bashan and Gilead,
   As in days of old.
15 "As in the days when you came out of
      the land of Egypt,
   I will show them marvelous things."
16 The nations shall see and be ashamed of all
      their might;
   They shall put their hand over their mouth;
   Their ears shall be deaf.
17 They shall lick the dust like a serpent;
   They shall crawl from their holes like
      snakes of the earth.
   They shall be afraid of the LORD our God,

85

> And shall fear because of You.
> 18 Who is a God like You,
>   Pardoning iniquity
>   And passing over the transgression of the
>   remnant of His heritage?
>   He does not retain His anger forever,
>   Because He delights in mercy.
> 19 He will again have compassion on us,
>   And will subdue our iniquities.
>   You will cast all our sins
>   Into the depths of the sea.
> 20 You will give truth to Jacob
>   And mercy to Abraham,
>   Which You have sworn to our fathers
>   From days of old.

Micah 7:11–20

The period of dealing with Israel's sin has given way to that final glorious day when Israel will be rebuilt and expanded. This final message of Micah is one of the finest declarations of the grace of God, especially as it is seen in its act of free forgiveness. As in the previous two sections of Micah, this third section will conclude on a note of triumphant hope and deliverance.

The text sets forth three evidences of God's pardoning grace and power. These three evidences are found:

A.   In the Rebuilding of His People   7:11–13
1.   Their Walls   7:11a
2.   Their New Boundaries   7:11b
3.   Their Population   7:12–13
B.   In the Resumption of His Marvelous Deeds   7:14–17
1.   Of Shepherding   7:14
2.   Of Working Miracles   7:15
3.   Of Conquering Nations   7:16–17
C.   In The Remission of Our Sins   7:18–20
1.   Based on Who He Is   7:18
2.   Based on What He Will Do   7:19–20
    a.   He Will Love Us
    b.   He Will Tread Down Our Iniquities
    c.   He Will Hurl Our Sins into the Depths of the Sea
    d.   He Will Give Us Grace and Truth

IN THE REBUILDING OF HIS PEOPLE (7:11–13)

The echo of the question in 7:10, "Where is the LORD, your God?" can still be heard as a new day is announced that will silence the jeering and mocking crowd of unbelievers. Three times the text emphatically declares it will be God's act, *"In the day,"* . . . *"In that day,"* . . . *"In that day"* (vv. 11–12a). Thus this act of God is squarely set in an eschatological time. Both the intensity and the imminence of the act stir the excitement of all who long to see the full vindication of God's name and covenant.

Their Walls (7:11)

This is the promise of more than an urban renewal program for downtown Jerusalem. It is, in fact, that work of God, in the end day, that will remove all shame and frustration that Israel has experienced over the years because of her sin and failure to obey her Lord.

Of course the walls were rebuilt after the Babylonian exile, and most certainly under Nehemiah in 445 B.C. But the time of the rebuilding mentioned here was placed far into the future, "in that day." This expression is generally reserved in the prophets for eschatological use, and refers to the distant future when the Lord will come a second time. Thus the rebuilding of the walls is a symbol of being restored to God's favor and salvation (Ps. 51:18; Isa. 60:10; *see also* Jer. 31:38–40; Pss. 69:35; 102:16; 147:2). Note that the Hebrew word for "walls" is not the same as the word for "ramparts," but is the general word for walls that signifies enclosures for vineyards and flocks.

Their New Boundaries (7:11b)

The problem here is to identify what is meant by *"the decree"* (v. 11b). The Hebrew word is *hôq*, which can mean either a "law," "decree," "limit" or "boundary." Carl F. Keil understood this verse to mean that the law of Israel's exclusiveness will be abolished, while Carl P. Caspari concluded that the borders to the land of Israel will be extended way beyond their original compass. E. W. Hengstenberg's interpretation differed from both of these: these were the statutes imposed by heathen oppressors that would be removed. Finally, Charles Feinberg, and Kleinert in Lange, thought the correct meaning for this passage was the removal of the middle wall of partition between Jews and Gentiles.

While it is impossible to say conclusively which of these thoroughly diverse meanings is the correct one, it is safe to say that the nation will have new boundaries of some sort. Since the text has just mentioned "walls," enlarged territorial boundaries might be the preferred interpretation.

We do know, however, that God will remove every boundary that encumbers and limits His people, placing them far and away from where any thought they might have been. This passage, then, like the New Covenant passage of Jeremiah 31:31–34, looks forward to God's new work in that final day of the Lord.

Their Population (7:12–13)

There will be a movement of peoples from all over the earth. The people will come to Jerusalem, as Micah 4:1–5 promises. The geographical notations are only of a general sort—much like the points of a compass. Some, such as the Assyrians and those from "the cities of Egypt" (in NKJV, "the fortified cities"), symbolize the inveterate enemies of Israel. They too would join God's people in that final day (Isa. 19:23–25; Zech 10:11). They would come from one coast to the other, *"from sea to sea."*

The return of the Diaspora is one of the great themes of the prophets. All too many interpreters find themselves squeezed between the obvious teaching of the word of God and their prior theological commitments. Thus it is not easy for them to hear of a return of the remnant in the final day. But the language in Micah is similar to that of Isaiah 11:11–16; 27:12 and Zechariah 10:8–12. Not only will the Jews return to their homeland, but the Gentiles will come with them (Isa. 2:2ff; 60:3; Zech. 14:16).

Verse 13, beginning with an adversative that is best rendered "But," describes the punishment that must visit the earth in the meantime. Two reasons are given for this worldwide judgment: (1) the lifestyles of the earth's inhabitants, and (2) the fruit or results of their deeds (cf. Isa. 24:1,3).

IN THE RESUMPTION OF HIS MARVELOUS DEEDS (7:14–17)

Of Shepherding (7:14)

As Micah concludes his prophecy, he commits his people to the care of their Great Shepherd. The Shepherd imagery occurs in all three sections of hope in this book (2:12; 4:6f; 7:14). The Lord himself, of course, is that Good Shepherd who leads, guides, protects, and rules His flock. As Psalm 100:3b reminds us: "We are His people and the sheep of His pasture." We hear the theme again in Psalm 95:7: "For He is our God, and we are the people of His pasture, and the sheep of His hand."

Micah prays that God would *"Shepherd [His] people with [His] staff"* (v. 14), not the rod or staff of judgment referred to in Micah 6:9, but the staff of tender care and protection found in Psalm 23:4c: "Your rod and Your staff, they comfort me."

The people are called *"the flock of Your heritage"* (v. 14b). The metaphor designates the shepherd's people as a flock. Another metaphor sets high value on Israel, because she is God's special possession (Exod. 19:5–6). Moreover, the people of God *"dwell solitarily,"* i.e., they live separately and apart from the heathen nations all around them. (Num. 23:9—"There!" prophesied Balaam, "A people dwelling alone, not reckoning itself among the nations.")

The prophet's prayer is that this flock might find good grazing in those proverbial beauty spots in the Holy Land, viz., *"Carmel," "Bashan,"* and *"Gilead"* (v. 14c). At that time, however, these good grazing and farming areas were in the hands of others. Micah's prayer is that God would shortly change that by restoring these lands to Israel *"As in days of old"* (v. 14c). That would have been in the era of David and Solomon. In the next century, the prophet Jeremiah will make the same promise: "But I [the LORD] will bring back Israel to his habitation, and he shall feed on Carmel and Bashan; his soul shall be satisfied on Mount Ephraim and Gilead" (Jer. 50:19).

Of Working Miracles (7:15)

The answer to the prayer in verse 14 is found in verses 15–17. God will intervene on behalf of Israel just as He did when He took her by the hand to lead her out of Egypt. Once again, He will also show His power in "marvelous things," i.e., His miracles. Behind the word *"marvelous"* (v. 15c) is the Hebrew root *pele'*, similar to one of the names for the Messiah in Isaiah 9:6, "His name shall be called *Wonderful* Counselor"(NIV). The awesome and breathtaking splendor of the magnitude of His power had been demonstrated in the ten plagues of Egypt and the miracles at the Red Sea and along the wilderness journey. And God will once again show Himself mighty in the future return of Israel to the land in the end time. No miracles are recorded in connection with Judah's return from the Babylonian exile except a reference to "great things" in Psalm 126:1–3.

One day in the eschatological future, God will return His flock to their land from all over the earth. At that time His people will see His miracle-working powers once again.

Of Conquering Nations (7:16–17)

In that final day when the Lord once again pastures His people in their land, feeds them, and works His mighty miracles on their behalf as He did in the exodus, the nations that opposed God, including this conquering nation, will be defeated by the power of God. The rebellious nations, astounded at Israel's deliverance *"shall see and be ashamed."* (v. 16). No longer will they taunt Israel, as recorded in Micah 7:10 saying, "Where is the LORD your God?" Instead, *"they shall put their hand over their mouth; their ears shall be deaf"* (v. 16bc). They will be so humiliated that it will be best if they say nothing and no longer listen to the vain boasts of those to whom they should never have given the time of day in the first place (cf. Isa. 52:15).

So completely routed will Israel's enemies be that they will be best compared to Satan in that ancient prophecy in Genesis 3:14 ff which says that the enemy *"shall lick the dust like [the serpent"* (v. 17a). Since in the Hebrew the article precedes the word for "serpent," we have included it here. We have capitalized "Serpent" because it appears here to mean, as it does in Genesis, something other than a reptile form; it is the title of that evil one against whom we all struggle—Satan. We still use this figure of speech—"to bite the dust"—as a symbol of defeat. In biblical times and now it refers to a defeated opponent—on the football field or battlefield or in a spiritual contest (cf. Ps. 44:25; 75:9; Isa. 49:23). God will make all the rebellious heathen speechless as He turns the tables on them.

The nations will come trembling out of their hiding places before the Lord of Hosts. The Lord's victory at the climax of history will be deliberately patterned after David's earlier victory over his enemies, expressed in similar terms in Psalm 18:45: "The foreigners fade away, and they come frightened from their hideouts." Great will be the day of our Lord!

IN THE REMISSION OF OUR SINS (7:18–20)

The third and last movement of this poetic symphony is a choral piece that forms a magnificent doxology. It is much like Romans 11:33ff, Psalm 104:32ff and Psalm 68:30ff. What a tremendous climax to a book!

Based on Who He Is! (7:18)

Before concluding with this anthem of praise, the prophet asks, *"Who is a God like You?"* This question (which has embedded in it the very name of Micah, meaning "Who is like Yah[weh]?") asks all of us to focus on the incomparability of God. Can anyone or anything be compared to Him or be said to be His equal? This passage, which is so reminiscent of the magnificent chapter Isaiah 40:9–31, also recalls the question first asked at the Red Sea—"Who is like You, O LORD, among the gods? Who is like You, glorious in holiness, fearful in praises, doing wonders [miracles]?" (Exod. 15:11). The answer, of course, is that there is no one that even comes close to measuring up to who God is and to what He has done. So why, then, are we so intrigued by all the enticing sins of the times? And why are we so terrified by all the faces of the contemporary issues which are nothing but empty masks of our day? Should we not, instead, be encouraged by all the promises of God, if He so far exceeds every one else?

Not only is our God incomparably great, but with that greatness He will condescend in *"pardoning iniquity and passing over . . . transgression"* (v. 18). The formula for forgiveness given here is as ancient as Exodus 34:6–7. God will "lift up" (for that is the literal meaning of "pardon" in the Hebrew) the burden of sin from the shoulders of all who will confess their sin and ask for His forgiveness. He himself can forgive and "pass over" (an allusion to the Passover night in Egypt with its provision of the paschal lamb) the transgression because He became the paschal lamb and substitute for our sins and was thereby able to offer full release from them. *"He does not retain His anger forever, because He delights in mercy"* (v. 18c). God delights in "grace," "loving-kindness," and "mercy" (once again that beautiful Hebrew word *hesed*, meaning God's "grace"); He does not delight in holding a grudge, or in bottling up His anger over our sins. Psalm 103:9–10 celebrated the same truth—"Nor will He keep His anger forever. He has not dealt with us according to our sins, nor punished us according to our iniquities." Likewise Jeremiah marveled over the same graciousness of our God: "But let him who glories glory in this, that he understands and knows Me, that I am the LORD, exercising lovingkindness, judgment, and righteousness in the earth" (Jer. 9:24). What a wonderful and gracious Savior, who removes our sin and guilt and freely gives us His joy and satisfaction despite all the grief we have given to Him! That is unheard of!

Based on What He Will Do! (7:19–20)

God will love us, in spite of the fact that we, and Israel, should expect nothing but His anger (v. 18a). He will tread down our sins that rise up against us and threaten to overpower us, just as Psalm 65:3 announces.

And just as Pharaoh's chariots were "hurled into the sea" and sank into the depths like a stone or lead weight (Exod. 15:4, 5, 10), so God will "hurl," or *"cast all our sins into the depths of the sea"* (v. 19c).

The last three verses of this book are linked with the book of Jonah for the afternoon reading in the synagogue on Yom Kipper, the "Day of Atonement." Once every year, on Ros Hashanah, the Jewish New Year, the orthodox Jew goes to a stream or river and symbolically empties his sins from his pockets into the water as he recites Micah 7:18–20. This is the *Tashlich* service, named after the word *"You will cast."* It symbolizes the fact that God can and will take our sins, wash them down the streams of running water and bury them deep in the depths of the ocean. God not only forgives our sins, He also forgets them. If some object that God cannot forget our sins if He is omniscient, let it be remembered that what He does when He forgets our sins is remember them *against us no more!*

Micah concludes by recalling the whole promise-plan of God as it was originally given to Abraham and the fathers in *"days of old."* The content of that promise-plan was *"truth"* and *"mercy."* The combination of these two words is also found in John 1:17: "grace and truth." Literally John 1:17 says, "Law through Moses was given, grace and truth in Jesus happened." Both words, "grace and truth," were taken from Exodus 34:6.

God's promise is guaranteed both by His Word (in Genesis 12:2–3) and by His oath (in Genesis 22:16). Thus by God's indelible word and oath, in which it is impossible for God to lie, we have a strong assurance and a solid hope for the future (Heb. 6:18). God's promise is called His "everlasting covenant" in Psalm 105:8–11, "His word," and His "sworn promise." How excellent is the plan of God in its truthfulness, dependability and, especially, in its graciousness.

CONCLUSION

Only a God who exceeds every comparison, known and unknown, can pardon, forgive, and forget our iniquities, our sins, and our transgressions. Why should any mortal still choose to carry his or her load of guilt when that weight can be borne by our Lord? Why would we not want to have our sins forgiven and cast into the depths of the deepest sea?

Only this incomparably great God can also break down the barriers and walls that presently separate Israel and the nations. And one day that is exactly what God will do! He will do such marvelous miracles before the eyes of the watching world that all will be amazed. Even kings will exclaim, "Well shut my mouth!" For they will see what they had not even dared to believe, and they will be ashamed.

God is great! God is Great! Therefore, "Who is like our God?" We answer, with Micah, there is nothing and no one that even comes close. He exceeds them all!

NOTES

1. Martin Luther, *Works*, Weimar Edition, Vol. XIX, p. 350 (transl. Eido C. Mason), as cited by Leslie C. Allen, *The Books of Joel, Obadiah, Jonah and Micah* (Grand Rapids: Eerdmans, 1976), p. 257, n. 56.

2. *See* the definitive studies on these matters: John T. Willis, "The Structure, Setting, and Interrelationships of the Pericopes in the Book of Micah" (Ph.D. diss., Vanderbilt University, Nashville, Tn., 1966) and David Gerald Hagstrom, *The Coherence of the Book of Micah: A Literary Analysis* (Atlanta: Scholars Press, 1988).

3. Hagstrom, *The Coherence of the Book of Micah*, pp. 22–27.

4. *See* Willis, "Structure, Setting, and Interrelationships of Pericopes in Micah" and Hagstrom, *Coherence of Micah*.

5. Flavius Josephus, *The Works of Flavius Josephus*, tr. William Whiston (Philadelphia: The John C. Winston Co., n.d), *Antiquities of the Jews*, XIII, x, 3.

6. *Taylor Prism* (British Museum No. 91032) ii.34 – iii.41 (Plate 4). For another translation, *see* Thomas, Winton D. *Documents From Old Testament Times* (New York: Harper and Row, 1958), p. 67.

7. In order to make sense out of the sequence of the listing of the towns, *see* map number 154 in Yohanan Aharoni and Michael Avi-Yonah, *The Macmillan Bible Atlas* (New York: Macmillan Co., 1968), p. 99.

8. Peter C. Craigie, *Twelve Prophets* (Philadelphia: Westminster, 1985), II: 14.

9. *See* the development of this important theological theme in Walter C. Kaiser, Jr., "Experiencing the Old Testament 'Rest' of God: Hebrews 3:1–4," in *The Uses of the Old Testament in the New* (Chicago: Moody, 1985), pp. 153–75.

10. *See* the development of this concept of inaugurated eschatology in Walter C. Kaiser, Jr., *Back Toward the Future: Hints for Interpreting Biblical Prophecy* (Grand Rapids: Baker, 1989), pp. 117–24.

11. As cited by Craigie, *Twelve Prophets*, II:26.

12. This work was privately published in 1988 by Edger C. Whisenant. It created quite a stir and reportedly sold over 30,000 copies.

13. *See* the fine discussion on this issue and the matter of the alleged post-exilic dating of Micah 4:1–5 in Bruce Waltke, "Additional Note of the Date of Micah 4:1–5," in *Obadiah, Jonah, Micah: An Introduction and Commentary*, Desmond Alexander, David W. Baker and Bruce Waltke, ed. (Downers Grove, Il.: Inter-Varsity Press, 1988), pp. 170–74.

14. The Hebrew phrase *kî 'im* is equivalent to "nothing but," implying absolute and mutual exclusion only in those cases where there is a negative sentence or clause prior to its appearance. That is not the case here; therefore, it simply has a limiting sense indicating priority. *See* E. Kautzsch., ed., *Gesenius' Hebrew Grammar*, ed. 2nd ed. rev. (Oxford: Clarendon Press, 1910), p. 500. Cf. Gen. 15:4; 32:29; 47:18; Exod. 12:9; Deut. 7:5; 12:5; 16:6; Josh. 23:8; 1 Sam. 2:15; 8:19; 21:5; 2 Sam. 5:6; 1 Kings 18:18; 2 Kings 10:23; Ps. 1:2, 4; Prov. 23:17; Isa. 33:21; 55:10, 11; Jer. 3:10; 7:23; 16:15; 20:3; Ezk. 36:22; 44:10; Amos 8:11. *See* Rebecca Anne Krahn, "An Investigation of Micah 6:6–8 with a View to Examining Micah's Use of the Deuteronomic Ethic as a Timeless Basis for True Religion" (M.A. Thesis, Trinity Evangelical Divinity School, 1976), p. 45–46.

15. A. Ehrman, "A Note on Micah VI, 14," *Vetus Testamentum* 23 (1973): 103–4.

SECTION TWO:

The Book of Nahum

Nahum 1:1—3:19

Introduction to Nahum

In the Hebrew text, the Latin Vulgate and the Syriac Peshitta, Nahum is regularly placed as the seventh book in the list of the twelve Minor Prophets. Only in the Greek Septuagint does it follow the book of Jonah rather than Micah.

THE AUTHOR

Nahum's name appears only once in the Old Testament and that is in the superscription of his book, 1:1. The same name appears once in the New Testament, in the genealogy of Joseph in Luke 3:25. This name does show up in various inscriptions from the ancient Near East, such as the Northwest Inscriptions, a seventh century ostracon from Arad, the seventh century Lachish Letters and, often, the Mishnah (which, of course, is late into the Christian era). The name, therefore, is a genuine name.

Nahum means "comfort," or "consolation." His name is probably related to Menahem (2 Kings 15:14), Naham (1 Chron. 4:19), Nehemiah, and, in a shortened form, Noah (Gen. 5:29).

Nahum is described as an *"Elkoshite"* (1:1), a term generally taken to be the name of his hometown. Three sites contend for the honor of being the prophet's birthplace. Local Assyrian tradition identifies an Assyrian site, *Al-Qosh*, a little over twenty-five miles north of modern Mosul and just opposite the ancient site of Nineveh. Austen Henry Layard, writing in 1857, noted that there was a "large Christian village" in *Al-Qosh* and that local residents pointed to "the tomb of Nahum, the prophet," a site honored by Muslims and Christians.[1] There is no independent confirmation of this site, however, and its identification by local residents must be treated like other popular traditions.

A Galilean location was championed by Jerome, the translator of the Latin Vulgate. In the preface to his commentary on Nahum, he reports that he visited a Galilean village named "Elkesi" and was shown a house purported to be the home of the prophet Nahum. Another possible Galilean location is Capernaum, meaning "the village of Nahum." But neither Josephus nor Jerome connect the prophet's hometown with Jesus's own city. Nor was Capernaum ever called Elkosh, as far as we know.

The best candidate for the location of Elkosh is a southern town in Judah. This town is some twenty-five miles southwest of Jerusalem. The basis for this identification is Epiphanius's *Lives of the Prophets*, in which Epiphanius says "Nahum was of Elkosh beyond *Bet Gabre* of the tribe of Simeon."[2] The modern name of this Judean Elkosh is Beit-Jebrin, a town in the same vicinity as Micah's hometown, Moresheth. While we do not have enough evidence to identify this town as Elkosh with absolute certainty, it is the best identification based on the evidence at hand.

THE TIMES OF THE ASSYRIANS

The name "Assyria" is derived from "Asshur," the descendant of Shem (Gen. 10:22). Asshur and his descendants settled in the land between the Tigris and Euphrates rivers, north of Babylonia.

At first its capital city was located in Asshur, but later it was moved to Nineveh and the name Asshur was given to the chief god of Assyria. The earliest reference to this people occurs in Hammurapi's law code (IV, 60–62).

Whenever we find any records of this people, we are immediately startled by their savage cruelty and deep-seated desire to dominate as much territory as possible. Already in 1100 B.C. the Assyrian King Tiglath-pileser I described on victory monuments how he conquered eighty-three kings and littered the mountains with corpses. Two centuries later, Ashur-nasirpal II vaunted his deeds of flaying captive kings alive and wall-papering pillars with their skins, walling up other captives alive, impaling captives on stakes, putting out eyes, cutting off hands, feet, noses and ears and burning boys and girls alive. The atrocities and brutalities of the Assyrians became legendary in the ancient Near East.

The first contact Israel had with the Assyrians was during the reign of the Assyrian, Shalmaneser III (858–824 B.C.). In 854 B.C. King Ahab of Israel and King Benhadad II of Syria gathered nine other princes and tried unsuccessfully to put a check on this monarch; however, Shalmaneser boasted that he slew over 20,000 men in his victory. Twelve years later, King Jehu of Israel and King Hazael of Syria were defeated a second time and ended up paying tribute to Shalmaneser.

The Assyrians dominated the Near East for over a century, beginning in 745 B.C. with Tiglath-pileser II as king. From 645 to 612 B.C. six successive Assyrian monarchs (Tiglath-pileser II, Shalmaneser V, Sargon II, Sennacherib, Esarhaddon and Ashurbanipal) were invincible.

The last of these monarchs achieved a greatness that exceeded all the rest. Ashurbanipal began his reign in 668 B.C. and ruled for forty-two years. Only towards the end of his reign did his empire begin to decline as rebellion broke out all over his kingdom. Added to his headaches were the new challenges presented by the Medes and the Babylonians. Ashurbanipal's reign came to an end in 627 B.C. and was followed by weaker Assyrian monarchs. Cyaxares, King of the Medes, invaded Assyria in 614 B.C. Two years later, in 612 B.C., the capital of Assyria, Nineveh, fell to a combined force of Babylonians, Medes and Scythians.

THE DATE

Two events establish the range of dates for this seventh century B.C. prophecy of the destruction of Nineveh: the first is the Assyrian destruction of Thebes, Egypt (Nah. 3:8), to which the prophet refers in his argument that the coming destruction of Nineveh is certain (Nah. 2:8). The Assyrians conquered Egypt as far south as the capital city of Thebes in 663 B.C. under the leadership of Ashurbanipal, marking the zenith of the empire's dominion over land. The second is the actual destruction of Nineveh in 612 B.C.[3] at the hands of the combined armies of the Babylonians and Medes, just as Nahum had predicted. Most scholars favor a date closer to the events of 612 B.C. Given the vivid detail of the battles in Nahum 2 and 3, in particular the fact that Nineveh fell because the river gates were opened and the city was flooded (Nah. 2:6–8), a date closer to the actual fall of the city—when the details would have been fresh in Nahum's mind—seems most likely. Yet prophecy is hardly affected by such an argument, for God can reveal details quite distant in time.

Some have argued, though on very slight grounds, that Nahum 1:15 refers to the death of Ashurbanipal in 627 B.C., an event that marked the beginning of the weakening of the Assyrian empire. Others are concerned that the book does not reflect anything of King Josiah's reforms after he found the book of the Law in 621 B.C. But they must remember that the book focuses on Nineveh, not Judah. Walter A. Maier, in one of the most definitive studies on this book in modern times, argues that 654 B.C. is the only proper date for the prophecy. From 663 B.C., when Thebes (the capital of Egypt and Ethiopia) was sacked, to 654 B.C., Thebes was without political leadership. After that point, according to Maier, the rhetorical question in Nahum 3:8, *"Are you better than Amon [Thebes]?,"* would have lost its force.[4]

THE MESSAGE OF NAHUM

This small prophecy is unique in that the entire theme of its three chapters focuses on a single topic: the coming judgment of God against Assyria. Of course there are similar collections of prophecies against other nations in other Old Testament books. Twenty five chapters and 680 verses in three of the Major Prophets (Isa. 13–23; Jer. 46–51; Ezk. 25–32) focus on messages to foreign nations. That is more biblical material than all the Pauline prison epistles put together. There are also smaller Old Testament books and portions of books that deal with prophecies to a foreign nation: Obadiah, Habakkuk, Zephaniah, Amos 1–2, Joel 3 and Jonah.

So single-minded and so vivid are Nahum's word pictures that one called the book of Nahum "An unmitigated Hymn of Hate." But we search in vain for examples of this hate or what another called his "malicious joy" and exaltation over the prospect of Nineveh's defeat. What we do find is a moral basis for God's indictment of a nation that has been guilty of extensive bloodshed, brutality, atrocity and political tyranny. The first person singular is only used in this book to refer to God, never to Nahum or Israel; hence there is no room for human pride or hate for Nahum or Israel's enemies.

It is not as if Nahum ignored Israel's sin. Nahum 1:12 implies that Judah had to be comforted after God dealt with her for her sin (cf. 2:3). In fact, the whole section of 1:2–8 shows that God will not absolve or refuse to punish the guilty. No one, including Judah, could ever stand before God's anger over their sin.

The message of this small prophecy concerns the character of God and His relationship to the nations of this world. The hymn in 1:2–8 serves as the point of departure for the whole book. The zeal of God for justice and righteousness explains His judicial visits of vengeance though He is patient and slow to show His anger.

The words of Nahum may have been sent to Assyria, just as the prophet Jeremiah sent word to other nations through their ambassadors in Jerusalem (Jer. 27:3) and even sent a messenger to read a message aloud in the foreign capital of Babylon (Jer. 51:61). The effect these prophetic words were to have on the people of God is not what is commonly assumed. They were to reaffirm that God is in control of the universe, that might does not make right, and that God is able to make all things right. People who violate divine morality, through violence, oppression, greed for land, power or possessions, and any acts of inhumanity against any persons, since all are made in the image of God, have to answer directly and ultimately to God.

The book, then, is not about Nahum's personal hatred for Assyria or about Judah's lust for vengeance. It is about God's almighty rule over all peoples, nations and cultures. It is another affirmation that, since God created all persons in His image, a person cannot treat others inhumanely and hope to escape God's punishment. It also affirms that the law of God is based on His nature and personal character; therefore, holiness, righteousness, and justice are expected of all rulers, potentates, and nations, regardless of whether they believe in the Living God.

STRUCTURE OF THE BOOK

With remarkable unity and symmetry, the book of Nahum provides its own outline based on the two rhetorical devices known as inclusion (a type of bracketing or "bookends" that uses a similar beginning and ending for a section) and the use of a repeated colophon (or tail-piece to indicate the end of section). The inclusion appears in 1:11 and 3:19. The opening hymn in 1:2–11, which is the key to the whole book of Nahum, ends in verse 11 with *"From you comes forth one who plots evil [ra'ah] against the LORD. . . ."* The book ends with a judgment oracle in 3:14–19, where verse 19c forms an inclusion with 1:11 by saying, *"For upon whom has not your wickedness [ra'ah] passed continually?"* Thus the hymn and the judgment oracle form something akin to bookends that embrace the total prophecy.

In between, there are four judgment oracles against Nineveh (1:12–15; 2:1–13; 3:1–7; 3:8–13) each ending with the colophon *"Behold"* (1:15; 2:13; 3:5; 3:13 [translated in NKJV, for some odd reason, as *"Surely"*]).[5]

The book opens with two titles: (1) *"The Burden,"* or a threatening message against Nineveh, and (2) *"The book of the vision of Nahum the Elkoshite."* The Hebrew word for "vision" means a "prophecy" or "revelation." Interestingly, this prophecy takes the form of a "book" *(sepher)*, or, most likely, "a scroll" (cf. Jer. 36:2). It was to be preserved for future generations.

An Outline of Nahum

I. An Avenger Is Our Lord   1:1–11
   A. The Vengeance of God   1:2–3a
   B. The Power of God   1:3b-6
   C. The Goodness of God   1:7–8
   D. The Severity of God   1:9–11
   E. Conclusion
II. The Wicked One Shall Exist No More   1:12–15
   A. God Will Liberate the Afflicted   1:12–13
   B. God Will Judge the Oppressor   1:14
   C. God Will Announce Good News   1:15
   D. Conclusion
III. The Lion of Assyria Will Be Routed   2:1–13
   A. In Spite of Any Preparation   2:1
   B. In Order to Restore the Excellency of Israel   2:2
   C. In the Swift Advance of the Attack   2:3–5
   D. In the Collapse of Its Defenses   2:6–10
   E. In the Finality of God's Judgment   2:11–13
   F. Conclusion
IV. The Harlot Will Be Exposed and Disgraced   3:1–7
   A. Her Sins Exposed   3:1–4
   B. Her Unfaithfulness Revealed   3:5–7
   C. Conclusion
V. The Invincible Will Be Destroyed   3:8–13
   A. Now the Mighty Have Fallen   3:8–10
   B. Now the Strong Are Helpless   3:11–13
   C. Conclusion
VI. Free At Last; Thank God, We're Free At Last   3:14–19
   A. Fight, Fight, Fight for Nineveh   3:14–17
   B. Clap, Clap, Clap for Victory   3:18–19
   C. Conclusion

CHAPTER ONE

An Avenger Is Our Lord

Nahum 1:1–11

1:1 The burden against Nineveh. The book of the vision of Nahum the Elkoshite.

2 God is jealous, and the LORD avenges;
The LORD avenges and is furious.
The LORD will take vengeance on
    His adversaries,
And He reserves wrath for His enemies;

3 The LORD is slow to anger and great in power,
And will not at all acquit the wicked.
The LORD has His way
In the whirlwind and in the storm,
And the clouds are the dust of His feet.

4 He rebukes the sea and makes it dry,
And dries up all the rivers.
Bashan and Carmel wither,
And the flower of Lebanon wilts.

5 The mountains quake before Him,
The hills melt,
And the earth heaves at His presence,
Yes, the world and all who dwell in it.

6 Who can stand before His indignation?
And who can endure the fierceness of
    His anger?
His fury is poured out like fire,
And the rocks are thrown down by Him.

7 The LORD is good,
A stronghold in the day of trouble;
And He knows those who trust in Him.

8 But with an overflowing flood

He will make an utter end of its place,
And darkness will pursue His enemies.
9 What do you conspire against the LORD?
He will make an utter end of it.
Affliction will not rise up a second time.
10 For while tangled like thorns,
And while drunken like drunkards,
They shall be devoured like stubble fully dried.
11 From you comes forth one
Who plots evil against the LORD,
A wicked counselor.

Nahum 1:1–11

Nahum begins with a very beautiful description of God's character (1:2–11). His character guarantees that He will be a vindicator of the oppressed and the judge of the oppressor.

A. The Vengeance of God   1:2–3a
B. The Power of God   1:3b–6
C. The Goodness of God   1:7–8
D. The Severity of God   1:9–11

THE VENGEANCE OF GOD (1:2–3A)

The basis for the divine sentence of judgment against Nineveh, the capital city of Assyria, is laid in 1:2: "*God is jealous, and the LORD avenges.*" Too often our childhood picture of Jesus as a "gentle Jesus, meek and mild" depicts a God who is too small to match the revelation of His character in the Bible. In the grown-up world of violence and hideous evil, such malignacies invite divine rebuke and ultimate judgment.

The adjective "*jealous*" (*qannô'*) is used exclusively in reference to God, and is best rendered as "zealous." It does not connote "envy" or any aspect of the "green monster mentality" that wrongfully wishes to have what others possess. What do any of us have that God might wish He had?

In verse 2 alone, Yahweh is mentioned three times; and in the first chapter He is mentioned ten times. Thus, the book of Nahum was not written from the perspective of cultural relativism; Nahum did not measure the Assyrians against some Israelite norm. Rather, the character and nature of God were the standards against which Assyria was judged—as are all nations today.

The Lord also *"avenges"* and *"takes vengeance"* (*nāqām*). In fifty-one of the seventy-eight instances of the root of this word in the Old Testament, God, either directly or indirectly, is the source of the vengeance. The classical passage is Deuteronomy 32:35, 41, "Vengeance is Mine, . . . I will render vengeance to My enemies, and repay those who hate Me." God's vengeance takes two forms: (1) God becomes the champion of His people against a common enemy (Ps. 94), and (2) He punishes those who break a covenant with Him or who violate His Law or will (Lev. 26:24–5).[6] God is depicted here as the Judge of the whole earth bringing to justice those who have openly opposed His Laws. Unlike jealousy on the human plane, which unfortunately involves all the wrong attitudes (suspicion, distrust, rivalry), God's jealousy shows itself as an eager zealousness to maintain the integrity of His own character and truth.

Three times verse 2 uses the same word for "avenge," or to "take vengeance" (all from the Hebrew root *nāqām*). All three times the verbal form in Hebrew is a participle denoting that this is an ongoing process and that it is a characteristic attribute of Yahweh. Why, then, do God's enemies take Him so lightly? Will they never include in their thinking that God *"reserves wrath for His enemies"*? (v. 2c). Even though the Lord may refrain from using His wrath, since He does not will that people should perish, He "guards" it, or "reserves" it for the appropriate moment. Make no mistake about its certainty; if there is no repentance and change, judgment must come.

The vengeance of God is not without any qualification. His is not a fury that is liable to flare up and boil out of control over any, or even every, crisis. *"The LORD is slow to anger and great in power, and will not at all acquit the wicked"* (v. 3a). Ever since Exodus 34:6–7, the Bible has been stressing God's merciful patience. It appears at least ten times in the Old Testament. But God's slowness in exercising His wrath must not be interpreted as weakness or as an indication that He is not all that concerned about the deeds of the wicked. He is!

God will never acquit the wicked, so they must not plan on Him forgetting or being too distracted with more demanding duties to exercise His wrath. He merely wishes to give everyone more than enough time to come to their senses and to repent of their sin. He does not want any to perish (2 Pet. 3:9).

THE POWER OF GOD (1:3B–6)

No one should doubt God's ability to carry out His threats of judgment. The approach of God in a classic theophany, or "appearance of God," is given vivid testimony by Nahum. All of nature seems to go into convulsions at His approach. If He had the power necessary to create the world, then He surely has the power to throw all of creation into reverse. Therefore, it would be good for unbelieving Assyria, tied as it was to the non-entity god Asshur, to avoid the fury of God's terrifying approach, which can be like a deadly tornado. Just as God relented a century ago when the Ninevites repented at the preaching of Jonah, so God could relent again—even at this eleventh hour—if the Ninevites again repented. But if they choose not to repent, then they will know the punishment of God in all its devastating power. The *"whirlwind"* and *"the storm"* are often used to express God's coming judgment (Ps 83:15; Isa 29:6). Like persons stirring up clouds of dust on the dry earth, the Lord stirs up the clouds of an approaching storm as He strides across the heavens to execute His order for the commencement of judgment.

Appropriately, Robert Grant taught us to sing in "O Worship the King:"

> O Tell of His might,
> O sing of His grace,
> Whose robe is the light,
> Whose canopy space;
> His chariots of wrath the deep thunderclouds form,
> And dark is His path on the wings of the storm.

He had only to speak the word and His power dried up the Red Sea and the Jordan River (v. 4a; cf. Exod. 14:21ff; Josh. 3:7–17). That should be enough energy to carry out His threat against a truculent Assyria.

More than just the rivers and seas dried up at His command: the legendary green pastures of *"Bashan," "Carmel,"* and *"Lebanon"* withered and dried up as well (v. 4bc; cf. Mic. 7:14). These proverbial beauty spots were renowned for their lush, verdant growth, but they too could be affected when Yahweh spoke the word.

"At His presence" (v. 5) the mountains *"quake"* and the hills *"melt."* The footings and foundations of the earth rattle in seismic agitation

(cf. Ps. 97:3–5; Mic. 1:3–4) in recognition of who it is that comes with all His power. Yet intelligent mortals are by and large unaware of who it is that approaches. There is the irony of the whole situation. Even pagan nations should be smart enough to recognize that God is approaching! The implications should be caught, *"Yes, the world and all who dwell in it"* (v. 5c). No one, no nation, no thing, is outside the sphere of God's sovereignty.

The conclusion that Nineveh—and all who read Nahum's prophecy—should have come to is found in verse 6: *"Who can stand before His indignation? And who can endure the fierceness of His anger?"* Malachi repeats the same question in Malachi 3:2. No matter how brazen and defiant Nineveh was, no one can maintain such an impudent posture in the face of the terrifying presence and power of God's fierce anger. So hot would God's fury be that the Ninevites would be utterly consumed even in the attempt to resist Him. He would be as unstoppable as a raging fire and as shattering as splitting of rocks depicted the smashing of what appeared to be durable and fixed.

Yes, judgment would come to Nineveh, because the zeal of the Lord would execute it. The Lord's power to effect what He said He would do was unlimited, while His zeal was regulated by His absolute holiness and consistency to His own character.

THE GOODNESS OF GOD (1:7–8)

Seldom do the prophets announce the judgment of God without immediately reminding us of the wonderful grace of God. *"The LORD is good"* and He is *"a stronghold in the day of trouble"* (v. 7). All goodness and blessings find their source in God alone. "No one is good but One, that is, God" (Luke 18:19). What a gracious source of repose and security can be found in our Lord, who is goodness itself and a strong tower into which we may run in the time of trouble.

Martin Luther celebrated the fact that God is our refuge and strength, a very present help in the time of trouble (Ps. 46:1–2). Luther referred to our Lord when he declared: "A Mighty Fortress is our God, a bulwark never failing." Consequently, when it comes to a choice between having the walls of Nineveh or the "stronghold" of God Himself to defend us, we should choose God's defense. *"And He knows those who trust in Him"* (v. 7c). So intimate is our Lord's knowledge of us that He is acquainted with everything we do and say.

What tender, personal, intimate and loving care we experience as sons and daughters of the Living God. He especially knows whether we have trusted in Him or not. "Trusting," in this text, means simply relying on Him to do what He says He will do.

But the wicked must not think God's goodness eclipses His clear intention to deal with evil. We were told in verse 3b that God will never *"acquit the wicked."* He is an enemy of those who reject His sovereignty. His enemies will experience *"an overflowing flood"* and *"darkness"* (v. 8) instead of His goodness. Wrong cannot forever remain on the throne while right goes begging for vindication.

The word "flood" is used in a figurative as well as a literal sense, but it is of more than passing interest that the Greek historian Diodorus Siculus (*Bibliotheca Historica*, II, 27) says that the Euphrates River (he probably meant the Tigris River) flooded its banks and caused twenty-one furlongs of Nineveh's walls to collapse, leaving the city open for the enemy to enter (cf. Nah. 2:6, 8). This inundation will bring about *"an utter end of its place,"* prophesied Nahum (1:8); and so it did.

THE SEVERITY OF GOD (1:9-11)

The writer addresses Assyria directly. Since there has been no movement of the people towards repentance, as there was in response to Jonah's preaching a century earlier, the question is this: "What do you take God to be?" Can you continue to *"conspire against the LORD?"* and think that you will not be punished at all? (v. 9).

The punishment God will measure out for Assyria will be so severe that He will not need to repeat it: *"Affliction will not rise up a second time"* (v. 9c). Whereas Sennacherib was given a warning in 701 B.C. when he lost 185,000 troops one night at the hand of God (cf. Isa. 37), God will not give Nineveh mercy or periods of recovery in 612 B.C. Yes, Assyria had once been used against Israel as the rod of God's judgment, but the axe had no right to vaunt itself to the One who was wielding it (Isa. 10:13-15).

So defiant had Assyria become that the Assyrian commander Rabshakeh bragged, "Has any one of the gods of the nations delivered its land from the hand of the king of Assyria? Where are the gods of Hamath and Arpad? Where are the gods of Sepharvaim? Indeed, have they delivered Samaria from my hand? Who among all the gods of these lands have delivered their countries from my hand, that the LORD should deliver Jerusalem from my hand?" (Isa. 36:18b–20). What hubris! Rabshakeh was drunk with his own power.

Verse 10 is exceedingly difficult to interpret word-for-word, yet its general meaning is clear. Nineveh will be as combustible as dried thorns (a very popular fuel in Palestine) for the fire, and as helpless as any drunk ever was. The once highly regarded army of Assyria will be easily overcome, combustible to the flame and as weak as a drunk.

The ultimate reason for Nineveh's destruction is given in verse 11. Nineveh has plotted evil against the Lord. That is the final measure of all her years of brutality, cruelty, and inhumane treatment toward the nations she subjugated. Men and women today should likewise fear God's judgment of their nation, as the Last Judgment, more than they fear another nation's military or economic reprisals. The Nuremberg trials that followed World War II or the United Nations inspection team that visited Iraq after Desert Storm and the Gulf War in 1991 are not the final review that dictators, generals and potentates must face. Crimes against humanity are, in the final analysis, crimes against a holy God and His Law.

The *"wicked counselor"* of verse 11 is usually identified as Sennacherib, and is less frequently identified as all the kings of Assyria. The Hebrew uses a proper name for wicked counselor, "Belial," a name usually translated as "worthlessness," or "lawlessness." That was the appropriate title used for Satan in intertestamental times and in the New Testament (John 8:44; 2 Cor. 6:15; 2 Thess. 2:3; 1 John 3:4–12). In biblical eschatology there is an element of "already" and an element of "not yet." Thus, in the passage there is a present or near fulfillment (already) of prophecy in the destruction of the Assyrian kings, but the prophecy will "not yet" be fulfilled completely until the destruction of the final manifestation of evil in the last day when the lawless one shall appear—the one who embodies all the evil that the earth will have seen partially in bits and pieces. Thus Nineveh must now be destroyed because of her wicked assault on God and on His people Israel.

CONCLUSION

The vindication, power, goodness, and severity of God! How awesome are the qualities and attributes of God both to those who love

Him and to those who refuse to acknowledge His lordship. He is the sovereign who has yet to be discovered in most nations, and especially in the United Nations.

But there is more here than a mere history lesson. In effect, God has set before us a mirror to study ourselves and our times. If we do not cast ourselves down before God and repent of our pride, hubris, and sins against humanity and God, can we expect to fare any better than Nineveh?

The goodness, grace, mercy, and patience of God must never lull us into complacency about the danger placed before us in the opportunity offered in the grace of God. We must never forget that we will stand under sentence from above unless we too repent and ask God for His forgiveness. All else is nothing less than the spirit of lawlessness and the spirit of the "lawless one" who has come in many a tyrant, but who will still come in that final day.

CHAPTER TWO

The Wicked One Shall Exist No More

Nahum 1:12–15

12 Thus says the LORD:
"Though they are safe, and likewise many,
Yet in this manner they will be cut down
When he passes through.
Though I have afflicted you,
I will afflict you no more;

13 For now I will break off his yoke from you,
And burst your bonds apart."

14 The LORD has given a command
   concerning you:
"Your name shall be perpetuated no longer.
Out of the house of your gods
I will cut off the carved image
   and the molded image.
I will dig your grave,
For you are vile."

15 Behold, on the mountains
The feet of him who brings good tidings,
Who proclaims peace!
O Judah, keep your appointed feasts,
Perform your vows.
For the wicked one shall no more pass
   through you;
He is utterly cut off.

Nahum 1:12–15

The book of Nahum opened with a hymn that exalted the character and person of God (1:2–11). Now Nahum addresses the people of Judah with the assurance that God will liberate them. In other words, Judah will now see God's divine nature in full operation against Nineveh. This in turn will suggest what He is like in His ability to secure our total release and redemption.

A. God Will Liberate the Afflicted   1:12–13
B. God Will Judge the Oppressor   1:14
C. God Will Announce Good News   1:15

GOD WILL LIBERATE THE AFFLICTED (1:12–13)

Verse 12 begins with the only example in Nahum of the prophetic formula that appears so frequently in the other prophets: *"Thus says the LORD."* This formula serves both to alert us to the seriousness of what is about to be said and to vindicate the fact that it comes from God.

The great promise, addressed to Judah, is that even *"though they [Nineveh] are safe [at peace, secure], and likewise many, yet in this manner they will be cut down."* Nothing will save Nineveh now except God himself. Donald J. Wiseman translated the Hebrew word *šelēmîm* rendered here as "safe" as "allies."[7] Using Wiseman's translation, the text says that neither treaties with allies, vast numbers, nor anything else will save Nineveh from the hand of God.

God will "cut down" or "cut off" the Assyrians (v. 12). The same verb is used to describe shearing sheep. Assyria had been "cut down" once when 185,000 military men died in one night by the mysterious act of God during the 701 B.C. invasion by Sennacherib. Sennacherib had boasted through his commander Rabshakeh that not one god had been able to resist him and wondered how Hezekiah of Judah thought his Yahweh could match Assyria's military prowess. Sennacherib got an answer fairly quickly that very night. This time God will give Assyria His final answer.

This was news that brought a tremendous relief to the *"afflicted"* or humbled in Judah. They found great consolation in the fact that they would now be liberated from the beastly Assyrian nation that had terrorized them for so many decades. *"Though I have afflicted you, I will afflict you no more"* (v. 12d). The suffering of the previous decades was going to end. God's "no more" is His note of finality.

"His yoke" and *"your bonds"* (v. 13) will be abolished. Freedom had come at last. Judah's yoke had been severe—weighted in cruelty,

oppression, tribute, bondage and injustice. But that was all over now. God would see to that.

GOD WILL JUDGE THE OPPRESSOR (1:14)

Now Nineveh is addressed directly, and the word is most assuredly from God. *"Your name shall be perpetuated no longer,"* declares God. This was an especially bitter pill for the Assyrian kings to swallow since they went to such great lengths to preserve their names on building inscriptions and the like. Ashurbanipal placed a curse in his annals on anyone who removed his name, invoking the eleven most powerful gods in the Assyrian pantheon to deal with such culprits. But, alas, now God Himself would remove his name and the king would be without progeny or succession.

God would also desecrate the temples of Assyria—a people who had destroyed and desecrated so many temples of so many other lands. The contempt the people had shown for other gods, including the only true God, would now be shown to them (Isa. 36:18–20).

Finally, God declared, *"I will dig your grave, for you are vile"* (v. 14d). The Assyrians had themselves been experts at desecrating conquered shrines and burial places; they would now feel the same sting. Nahum had said in 1:8 that God would "make an utter end of its place," and he elaborates on that idea here. God will execute His judgment because Assyria is so "vile" or, literally, so "light," i.e., lacking in any moral weight or consciousness. Thus it would appear that more nations than Babylon (Dan. 5:27) were weighed in the balances and found wanting.

God will indeed judge all oppressors. When God says "that is enough," everything they have strived to build—a name, a fortune, security, a reputation, prowess, and fame—will disappear faster than anyone can imagine.

GOD WILL ANNOUNCE GOOD NEWS (1:15)

Thus the first of the middle four judgment sections concludes, as each of the others will, with a verse that begins *"Behold."* Why the Hebrew text makes the 15th verse of chapter 1 the first verse of chapter 2 is not clear since it is so closely tied to 1:12–14.

But in words reminiscent of Isaiah 40:9, where the prophet is told to get up on a high mountain and shout to the inhabitants of Judah and Jerusalem "Behold your God," so Nahum is to shout with joy the good news unfolded in verses 12–14. This is the ancient way to spell relief: *"the wicked one shall no more pass through you; he is utterly cut off"* (v. 15e). Assyria, who was the very embodiment of evil and oppression, is now "cut off." This echoes 1:12.

The herald of *"good tidings"* (a phrase reminiscent of the messianic passage in Isaiah 52:7) *"proclaims peace."* While Nahum must have in mind the cessation of hostilities, "peace" here must also signal spiritual peace with God, since Nahum deliberately uses Isaiah's language in Isaiah 52:7. (The apostle Paul used the Isaiah text in Romans 10:15 to speak both of Messiah's triumph and the spread of the gospel itself—the ultimate good tidings.) Note that Isaiah's promise is found in a section dealing with release from Babylonian captivity, indicating that Nahum finds in Judah's earlier release from Assyrian captivity an earnest, or pledge, of Messiah's total victory, a victory over more than just the immediate military threat that happens to be on the horizon.

Consequently, it's time to keep the feasts and perform the vows that have been made to God. In this way the people's gratitude to God can be better expressed. God has slain the dragon once more: Belial, *"the wicked one"*[8] (cf. 1 Sam. 25:25; 30:22; 2 Sam. 16:6), is just one more enemy in a whole line of enemies that Christ "must" put down before He hands over all things to the Father (1 Cor. 15:25–28).

CONCLUSION

Evil will not reign forever unchallenged and undefeated. In every one of its hideous forms, it will be confronted, judged, and totally vanquished by our conquering Lord Jesus. What is seen here, therefore, is no disparate piece of history left for us to ruminate and reminisce on as we will. Certainly not. It is, instead, another important part of God's systematic vanquishing of all the forces of hell as He marches on toward His final victory.

And just as men and women can be set free from their enslaving political and military bonds, so they can be set free from their spiritual shackles. This too is part of the *"good tidings."*

CHAPTER THREE

The Lion of Assyria Will Be Routed

Nahum 2:1–13

2:1 He who scatters has come up before your face.
Man the fort!
Watch the road!
Strengthen your flanks!
Fortify your power mightily.
2 For the LORD will restore the excellence of Jacob
Like the excellence of Israel,
For the emptiers have emptied them out
And ruined their vine branches.
3 The shields of his mighty men are made red,
The valiant men are in scarlet.
The chariots come with flaming torches
In the day of his preparation,
And the spears are brandished.
4 The chariots rage in the streets,
They jostle one another in the broad roads;
They seem like torches,
They run like lightning.
5 He remembers his worthies;
They stumble in their walk;
They make haste to her walls,
And the defense is prepared.
6 The gates of the rivers are opened,
And the palace is dissolved.
7 It is decreed:
She shall be led away captive,
She shall be brought up;
And her maidservants shall lead her as with
    the voice of doves,

Beating their breasts.
8 Though Nineveh of old was like a pool
 of water,
Now they flee away.
"Halt! Halt!" they cry;
But no one turns back.
9 Take spoil of silver!
Take spoil of gold!
There is no end of treasure,
Or wealth of every desirable prize.
10 She is empty, desolate, and waste!
The heart melts, and the knees shake;
Much pain is in every side,
And all their faces are drained of color.
11 Where is the dwelling of the lions,
And the feeding place of the young lions,
Where the lion walked,
 the lioness and lion's cub,
And no one made them afraid?
12 The lion tore in pieces enough for his cubs,
Killed for his lionesses,
Filled his caves with prey,
And his dens with flesh.
13 "Behold, I am against you," says the LORD of
hosts, "I will burn your chariots in smoke, and the
sword shall devour your young lions; I will cut off
your prey from the earth, and the voice of your
messengers shall be heard no more."

Nahum 2:1–13

Assyria represented herself in her sculptures and friezes as a
proud lion. But that majestic king of the veldt would endure as the
nation's symbol only in her archeological remains. The "lion" would
be routed from its high lair for all the wickedness and evil it had per-
petrated before the Lord of the universe.

 A. In Spite of Any Preparation 2:1
 B. In Order to Restore the Excellency of Israel 2:2
 C. In the Swift Advance of the Attack 2:3–5
 D. In the Collapse of Its Defenses 2:6–10
 E. In the Finality of God's Judgement 2:11–13

Assyria, the perennial aggressor, is now confronted by *"He who scatters."* This "scatterer" or "router of armies" (cf. 2 Sam. 22:15; Ps. 18:14; Isa. 24:1) had been raised up by God, as evidenced by the conclusion of this pericope: *"Behold, I am against you, says the LORD of hosts"* (v. 13). Thus, the long history of wicked practices and human atrocities eventually invited the unshakeable opposition of God. A military coalition of the Medes and Babylonians will now be used as an instrument in God's hands, as Assyria herself was once used (Isa. 10:5, 15).

Cyaxerxes, king of the Medes (c. 625–585 B.C.) had attacked Nineveh in 614 B.C., but was able to capture only a section of its suburbs. In 612 B.C., however, Cyaxerxes teamed up with Nabopolassar, king of the Babylonians and Umman Manda (Scythians?), and conquered Nineveh in the month of Ab [April/May].[9]

With biting satire, Nineveh is encouraged by the prophet to do everything she can to prepare herself for the coming conflict—for she will need much preparation. In sharp, clipped, staccato commands, like gasps from an exhausted, but frightened leader, come these pieces of advice: *"Man the fort! Watch the road! Strengthen your flanks! Fortify your power mightily"* (v. 1). But the truth of the matter is that all of this would have been too late and in vain. No amount of preparation could help Assyria, because she was up against divine power.

What makes the urging for more preparation at first seem ridiculous is that Sennacherib had already spent six years building an armory that covered forty acres in the city. Esarhaddon had enlarged it by adding more chariots, wagons, horses, mules, bows, quivers, arrows, and similar equipment. Even the royal road inside the city had been enlarged to a width of seventy-eight feet, facilitating troop movement. But when God is against a nation, no amount of material resources will avail or insure victory.

IN ORDER TO RESTORE THE EXCELLENCY OF ISRAEL (2:2)

The splendor of Nineveh must now give way to the excellency of God's people, Israel. Whereas Jacob had been plundered in times past, God's people will now be restored. The word *"excellence"* (*geʾôn*) implies an elevation or raising to exaltation. The ruined vine (a common figure for the nation of Israel in Isaiah 5:1–7; Ps. 80:8–16) will be recultivated by God and placed back in her land of ancient Canaan. In Psalm 47:4 and Amos 6:8, "excellency" signifies the land of Canaan as separate from all the other countries. Nothing less than the resurrection of the nation of Israel is being hinted at in this passage (cf. Ezk. 37), for God will once again graft onto the main trunk the olive branches that have been broken off (Rom. 11). God's judgment on Israel's enemies means deliverance for Israel.

Verse 2 is simply a development of 1:7, 12–13, and, especially, 1:15. Here is the good news. Here also is the theology of the passage.

IN THE SWIFT ADVANCE OF THE ATTACK (2:3–5)

Ancient seventh century B.C. Nineveh was one of the most notable cities of antiquity. Its ruins are still visible, just across the Tigris River from modern Mosul, about 250 miles north of Baghdad. The wall of the inner city stretched almost eight miles and rose to heights of twenty-five to sixty feet. Set off from the wall at some distance was a moat. Fifteen heavily fortified gates guarded access to the city. The Tigris River flowed close to its western walls, while two tributaries, the Khosr and the Tebiltu, passed through the city itself. (The Khosr flowed through gates in the city walls, entering at the city's east wall and exiting at the west wall, to join the Tigris River.)

The city is estimated to have been large enough to provide for a population of 300,000 people. It enclosed an area of some 1800 acres. Surely it must have been an extraordinary city for its time.

But it was too late now. The men in *"red"* shields and *"scarlet"* uniforms, the colors of the Medes (v. 3), were already at the gates. So certain is the prophet of the course of this battle, that he describes it with a vividness rare even for those who view actual battles. Nahum writes all of this in the "prophetic perfect tense," which means that it had not happened as yet; but so sure is Nahum of God's triumph, that, following the custom for Old Testament prophets, he uses a Hebrew verb tense that describes completed action.

The Neo-Assyrian chariots careened through the streets, flashing their metal fittings in the reflected sunlight, so that they appeared to be *"torches."*

So numerous were the fallen corpses that *"they [the invader] stumble in their walk"* (v. 5). The attacker picked out his *"worthies"* (v. 5), or better rendered: his "picked troops" formed a sort of shock troop that would make the first assault into the city of Nineveh under the "protective shield" (v. 5c; in place of the NKJV, *"the defense"*).

The scene depicts a swift and relentless pounding of the city into rapid submission. The end will come quickly.

IN THE COLLAPSE OF ITS DEFENSES (2:6–10)

Verse 6, along with Nahum 1:8, seems to corroborate the tradition of Diodorus Siculus (*Bibliotheca Historica*, II, 27; c. 20 B.C.) that the city's walls were breached initially by an unusually high flood on the rivers that came together at Nineveh. Diodorus (II, 27) put it this way:

> [I]n the third year, a succession of heavy downpours swelled the Euphrates [*sic*], flooded part of the city, and cast down the wall to a length of 20 stades. 2. Thereupon the king realised that the oracle had been fulfilled, and that the river had manifestly declared war upon the city. Despairing of his fate, but resolved not to fall into the hands of his enemies, he prepared a gigantic pyre in the royal precincts, heaped up all his gold and silver and his kingly rainment as well upon it, shut up his concubines and eunuchs in the chamber he had made in the midst of the pyre, and burnt himself and the palace together with all of them.

The Assyrian monarch at the time was Sinsharishkun. It is possible that the Khosr River had flooded in April/May and therefore had undermined the northeast section of the wall, allowing easy access to the city. Whether the invaders also redirected more water into the city through the system of sluices and gates outside the city cannot be determined. But there certainly is a strong association between flooding and the capture of the city both in the Bible and in external sources. That must be why Nahum says *"The gates of the rivers are opened, and the palace is dissolved"* (v. 6).

After the invading armies gained access to the city through the damaged walls, terror spread as the enormous wealth of Nineveh, pilfered from the nations of the Near East, was taken as booty. And this happened because *"It is decreed"* (v. 7) by God that Nineveh's turn to be exiled had arrived.

Assyria's troops were no longer effective, but were *"like a pool of water"* (v. 8); i.e., they were like irrigation waters that had escaped and were therefore useless. The conquest by the Assyrian forces had turned into a complete rout. Everyone had turned his heels and was running for all he was worth, not even turning back to see what was happening (v. 8c).

"There is no end of treasure" (v. 9), observes the prophet, still viewing the scene in the future—but a scene so real he could depict it as a *fait accompli*. Anything anyone could desire was available: silver, gold, wealth of all kinds.

Terror-stricken Assyria was thoroughly overcome with the emotional, psychological and physiological horror of what was happening (v. 10). The terse style of Nahum captures the mood well. With alliterate words in Hebrew (*bûqâh ûmebûqâh umebullāqâh*) and expressions that could only be interpreted as reflecting sheer dread and terror, God's judgment set in on the people. Four expressions in verse 10 describe the seriousness of the situation.

IN THE FINALITY OF GOD'S JUDGMENT (2:11–13)

"Where is the dwelling of the lions, and the feeding place of the young lions, where the lion walked, the lioness and lion's cub?" (v. 11), asks Nahum, in another set of rhetorical taunts meant to point out the contrast between the nation then and now. The kings and the nation that loved to show their valor by the way they fearlessly hunted lions and referred to themselves as lions (cf. Isa. 5:29–30; Jer. 50:17) were now anything but lions. That culture, like verse 12, was dominated by the theme of "killing." Like wild beasts, the Assyrians brutally flayed, walled up, impaled and dismembered their victims until their lairs were filled with the horrible catch of their hunts. No wonder they were overcome by such a ghastly terror when it was their turn to be on the receiving end!

Consequently, this second of four judgment cycles concludes as the others do with a verse that begins with "Behold" and contains a divine announcement (v. 13). *"I am against you, says the LORD of hosts,"* as He announces His direct involvement in what was happening. God was the one who was ultimately responsible for what was happening, not the military prowess of the Medes or Babylonians. Three times the first person pronoun is used in verse 13 to stress the Lord's personal involvement. When the predator is done away with (*"cut off"*), the act of taking prey will stop.

Once Rabshakeh had asked, "Where are you going to get any help that will be able to stop me and my armies?" (2 Kings 18:34). He and all Assyria now had their answer: help would come from Yahweh.

CONCLUSION

Those nations and individuals that choose to rule by fear and intimidation, rather than in the fear of the Lord, will have to experience His righteous indignation. Sovereignty is granted to nations as a trust from God in order to bring some measure of amelioration for those injustices suffered here on earth and best dealt with on this side of eternity. When nations subvert the divine institution of the state with less noble causes, they must face God's judgment. And they will likely face it on earth, since nations are judged, by and large, on this side of eternity.

Assyria made another major mistake in taking on Israel. God was for that nation, so who could be against it? (Romans 8:31). And if God is against a nation, who or what can be for it and save it?

The last lion to roar was the strong Son of God, the lion of Judah. That lion easily defanged the lion of Assyria and once again restored right, justice, and equity to its rightful place.

How similar the events of this chapter are to those of the recent Gulf War. Iraq, in spite of all her boasts and threats, was so suddenly stopped in her tracks that many felt it was evident that God had declared that He was against Iraq. Her brutality, tyranny, and ruthless behavior towards the Iranians, Kurds, and Kuwaitis could not go unnoticed or unanswered by God. Here in our own day the lesson Assyria had to learn was repeated: God is holy, righteous, and just. He will not tolerate a deliberate flaunting of His laws and character forever, but after much longsuffering will step in decisively. The lion of Assyria will be routed.

CHAPTER FOUR

The Harlot Will Be Exposed and Disgraced

Nahum 3:1–7

3:1 Woe to the bloody city!
   It is all full of lies and robbery.
   Its victim never departs.
  2 The noise of a whip
   And the noise of rattling wheels,
   Of galloping horses,
   Of clattering chariots!
  3 Horsemen charge with bright sword and
     glittering spear.
   There is a multitude of slain,
   A great number of bodies,
   Countless corpses—
   They stumble over the corpses—
  4 Because of the multitude of harlotries of the
     seductive harlot,
   The mistress of sorceries,
   Who sells nations through her harlotries,
   And families through her sorceries.
  5 "Behold, I am against you,"
     says the LORD of hosts;
   "I will lift your skirts over your face,
   I will show the nations your nakedness,
   And the kingdoms your shame.
  6 I will cast abominable filth upon you,
   Make you vile,
   And make you a spectacle.
  7 It shall come to pass that all who look
     upon you

> Will flee from you, and say,
> 'Nineveh is laid waste!
> Who will bemoan her?'
> Where shall I seek comforters for you?"
>
> *Nahum 3:1–7*

The third judgment oracle begins with *"Woe"* and again concludes with verses that begin *"Behold"* (vv. 5–7). Nahum recapitulates the reason for God's judgment of Nineveh, as the vivid portrayal begun in Nahum 2:3–10 of the siege, attack, invasion, and shame heaped on the city continues.

>   A.   Her Sins Exposed   3:1–4
>   B.   Her Unfaithfulness Revealed   3:5–7

HER SINS EXPOSED (3:1–4)

The prophets reserved the cry of *"Woe"* for use against those who had been doomed by God (Isa. 5:8–24; 10:1–3; Mic. 2:1–4; Amos 5:18–20; Hab. 2:9–19). Though the word was used against Israel (Ezk. 24:6, 9), it was employed more frequently against foreign nations (e.g., Isa. 33:1).

A "woe" oracle has two parts: (1) the accusation, in which the evil provoking the announcement of doom is stated, and (2) the declaration of punishment by God for such evil. It is made clear here that the declaration of God's punishment comes after He has patiently waited for some sign of repentance of a nation's long list of crimes against others and is finally triggered by particular deeds—the last straw, as it were. The force of the woe on nations to whom it was pronounced was like a dirge at a funeral, for the nations were as good as gone.

The vividness of the battle scene, begun in 2:3–10, is resumed in chapter 3. Many have praised Nahum's description of the siege and overthrow of Nineveh as being of such graphic quality that it is unexcelled in all of sacred and secular literature. One can still hear the crack of the whip, the rattle of the wheels, the whinnying of the horses as they rear back and leap high, and the bounding of the chariots over the litter of the corpses and implements of war discarded by the defenders of the city in the panic of their retreat. It is pandemonium in the extreme!

The reasons for all this bloodshed are soon revealed. Nineveh, capital of the nation, was a city *"full of lies and robbery"* (v. 1). She was unreliable, untrustworthy, fraudulent in business and a truce-breaker. If it did not serve her purposes, truth did not mean all that much to her. Promises made to other nations were made to be broken. Who would care? Who could do anything even if someone did object, thought Assyria. But God cared and He would now do something about it.

This *"bloody city"* was filled with *"robbery,"* denoting "rapine," or "plunder." These were acts of violence committed by the Assyrians against the peoples they conquered. The Assyrians took a ghoulish delight in torturing people, indiscriminately killing captives, flailing and impaling and placing dog-collars on conquered kings as though they were beasts worthy of no mercy.

Capital cities often embody what a whole country stands for, and reflect the direction in which that country is drifting because there is no protest or an outcry for change and righteousness. Our own Washington D.C. has become one of the drug centers and murder capitals of the world. Evil has taken hold so fiercely that many sections of the city are practically off-limits for most police officers. Is this not what makes a city "bloody?" The implications of this are terrifying, to say the least, for the whole United States.

Nineveh's sins also included greed, extortion and opposition to all that God is and stands for. *"Its victim [or prey] never departs"* (v. 1). The word for "victim" or "prey" denotes that which a wild animal rips, tears, or devours, much as a lion does to its victims (cf. 2:11). Thus, there was no end to Assyria's history of pillage, raping and bringing devastation of other nations.

Assyria's conduct can best be compared to *"the multitude of harlotries of the seductive harlot"* (v. 4). This figure is frequently used by the writers of Scripture to indicate infidelity and unfaithfulness to God on the part of Israel (Hos. 4:12; Ezk. 23:27) and other sinful nations and cities. Besides this religious connotation, the figure had a political meaning. To trust more in one's military and national strength than in the God of the universe was just another form of "whoredoms" (Hos. 7:7ff; Isa. 33:1–3). In time, this concept of harlotry was applied to the commercial realm as well (Isa. 23:17). As discussed below, that appears to be the usage here.[10]

Like a prostitute who peddles her favors for a fee, Nineveh had hired her powers out to many nations, but always with her own advantage clearly in mind. Assyria, like a common prostitute, had beguiled and captured peoples all over the ancient Near East, both with her charms and with the bitter dregs of her snares.

While Assyria was guilty of idolatry, having elevated gods like Asshur and goddesses like Ishtar to the place that belonged to Yahweh, the emphasis of verse 4 seems to be on the use of the world of the occult: *"The mistress of sorceries."* Nineveh sold *"nations through her harlotries, and families through her sorceries [witchcraft]."* Whatever the means, they involved sorcery and witchcraft as Assyria's way to allure and manipulate nations. Often these arcane arts were also used to determine the will of the gods (2 Kings 9:22; 2 Chron. 33:6; Mic. 5:12).

Thus Assyria used an ungodly mixture of harlotry and sorcery to entrap other nations. These sins were the basis for her downfall.

Her Unfaithfulness Revealed (3:5–7)

"Behold," begins God's announcement of judgment. Five times the first person pronoun is used in these three verses to emphasize God's divine intervention and displeasure with Assyria.

As in 2:13, God declares, *"I am against you, says the LORD of hosts"* (v. 5). God will requite Assyria for all her ungodliness, immoralities and atrocities. Both the seriousness and certainty of the threat are made most clear by the repetition of this divine declaration.

The international harlot would now receive a punishment fitting her disgusting action: God would *"lift [her] skirts over [her] face, [he would] show the nations [her] nakedness, and the kingdoms [her] shame"* (v. 5bc). This practice of exposing to the public those accused of unchastity (Hos. 2:3; Ezk. 16:35–39) is used by God in a graphic figure of speech for His public censure of this nation of violence. Proud and haughty Nineveh must now bear the disgrace and indignity that she had so often exposed others to, literally stripping them and forcing them to march into captivity naked.

Even though human agents were used, God—in the first person—is said to do each of the five acts listed in these three verses. Nineveh will receive, before the whole world, the treatment received by condemned prostitutes who, in ancient times, were subjected to public ridicule by having filth of all kinds tossed at them as they were made *"a spectacle"* (v. 6c).

So appalled will the whole world be that little sympathy or comfort will be left for Nineveh. People will just flee in disgust and amazement as they mutter to themselves, *"Nineveh is laid waste!"* How suddenly the fortunes are reversed and she who was so loathsome is now just a part of a bad memory. Payday came and Nineveh was paid in full.

CONCLUSION

How frequently we make incorrect assessments of others based on appearances of success, wealth, status, and power. Nineveh seemed to be invincible. But her day in God's court came.

The great harlot was judged; God's righteousness was restored; and all who cried out "How long?" were answered.

How are we to act, think, or pray in a situation such as this? John Calvin prayed:

> Grant, Almighty God, that as we have now heard of punishments so dreadful denounced on all tyrants and plunderers, this warning may keep us within the limits of justice, so that none of us may abuse our power to oppress the innocent, but, on the contrary, strive to benefit one another, and wholly regulate ourselves according to the rule of equity.[11]

CHAPTER FIVE

The Invincible Will Be Destroyed

Nahum 3:8–13

8 Are you better than No Amon
  That was situated by the River,
  That had the waters around her,
  Whose rampart was like the sea,
  Whose wall was like the sea?
9 Ethiopia and Egypt were her strength,
  And it was boundless;
  Put and Lubim were your helpers.
10 Yet she was carried away,
  She went into captivity;
  Her young children also were dashed to pieces
  At the head of every street;
  They cast lots for her honorable men,
  And all her great men were bound in chains.
11 You also will be drunk;
  You will be hidden;
  You also will seek refuge from the enemy.
12 All your strongholds are fig trees with ripened figs:
  If they are shaken,
  They fall into the mouth of the eater.
13 Surely, your people in your midst are women!
  The gates of your land are wide open
    for your enemies;
  Fire shall devour the bars of your gates.

Nahum 3:8–13

The fourth, and last, of the judgment oracles is a taunt song that pictures Nineveh as a drunk, too weak and helpless to do anything to hurt others, much less to save herself. Nineveh has been depicted as a lion, a harlot, and now a drunk. Nahum is certainly a graphic writer and a master of metaphor.

The section opens with Nahum's rhetorical question, *"Are you better than No Amon [Thebes]?"* and concludes for the fourth time in the book with a verse that begins *"Surely [Behold]"* (v. 13). The times have certainly changed in two important ways:

> A. Now the Mighty Have Fallen   3:8–10
> B. Now the Strong Are Helpless   3:11–13

NOW THE MIGHTY HAVE FALLEN (3:8–10)

Nineveh's seemingly impregnable position must have made Nahum's prophecy seem utterly ridiculous to a number of people. Who or what could have ever brought down a city that strong? She was armed to the teeth and no one around was any match for her armies. Nahum is dreaming. It could never happen.

But if it could not happen to Nineveh, argues Nahum, someone had better explain how it happened to Thebes (No-Amon), the seemingly impregnable capital city of Upper Egypt that was captured by Ashurbanipal in 663 B.C.

Thebes was beautifully located on the upper Nile River some 440 miles south of modern Cairo and 150 miles north of the present Aswan Dam, at the first cataract.

The city was located on both banks of the Nile. It was the first great monument city of the Near East and one of the most magnificent of all the ancient cities. The name "No" was derived from the Egyptian word for "city," *nwt*. "Amon" (or Amun), the sun god, was the chief god of the pantheon at that time, a god with a human body and a ram's head. The city of Thebes is mentioned five times in the Old Testament (Jer. 46:25; Ezk. 30:14, 15, 16; Nah. 3:8).

The famous temples of Karnak and Luxor were located on the eastern bank of the Nile. Ruins of this part of Thebes covered some 27 miles. The western bank contained Thebes proper and the ruins of Hatshepsut's temple and the tombs of the kings. So grand were these monuments that the Greeks called the western part of Thebes Diospolis, thinking that the counterpart of the Greek god Jupiter was worshipped and honored there.

But all of this led to the question at hand: Was Nineveh so high and mighty that she was untouchable? Wasn't Thebes even more impregnable? Yet she had been reduced. In spite of Thebes's natural water defences, similar to Nineveh's system of rivers and canals, she was captured. In addition, Thebes had allies in North Africa, *"Put and Lubim"* (v. 9); Nineveh did not even have these. Old Persian inscriptions identified "Put" with Libya in North Africa, calling it "Putya." Some have suggested "Put" is "Punt," modern Somaliland. The Lubim are the Libyans of North Africa. So: *"Are you better than No Amon that was situated by the [Nile] River?"* (v. 8). That was the haunting question for Nineveh, as it should be for all capitals in all times that have become too big in their own eyes to bow down before God, and worship their own power instead. The obvious answer to the question is "No!"

"Yet she was carried away, she went into captivity" (v. 10). Wealth, size, remoteness, alliances, defences, and divinities meant nothing. Thebes fell, and so would Nineveh.

The atrocities of war, though not condoned by God, were a fact of life and are recalled here to force Nineveh into calculating properly. *"Her young children also were dashed to pieces at the head of every street"* (v. 10b). The barbarity, sensationalism and despicable nature of all that happened to Thebes should have only increased Nineveh's revulsion. Even Thebes's honorable men were humiliated by being objects of a common raffle, later to be subjected to slavery and bound in chains. Perhaps it is understandable now why the psalmist uses some of the same expressions in Psalm 137:9—"Happy the one who takes and dashes your little ones against the rock." What Nineveh had done to Thebes would now be done to Nineveh. The psalmist's expression is metaphorical, since we know that there were no rocks in Babylon.[12] In our Lord's lament over Jerusalem, however, the same Greek verb is used in Luke 19:44 as appears in the Septuagint of Psalm 137:9. Our Lord wept! The very thought of children being "dashed to pieces!"

NOW THE STRONG ARE HELPLESS (3:11–13)

"You also will be drunk" (v. 11). Both literally (as her people engaged in a drunken orgy, reminiscent of the night Babylon fell in Daniel 5 and the Saturday night before the bombing of Pearl Harbor in the United States) and figuratively (as her people drank the cup of God's wrath) Assyria would fall into a drunken stupor. The cup of God's wrath is a frequent figure for judgment that God visits on a

130

people (Isa. 51:17, 21–23; Jer. 25:15–28; Lam. 4:21; Ezk. 23:33, 34; Obad. 16; Hab. 2:16).

Diodorus Siculus (c. 20 B.C.) records that the Assyrians were surprised during one of their drinking orgies and thus the city of Nineveh fell easily.

"You will be hidden," prophesies Nahum about the great city of Nineveh. And so it was. Nineveh disappeared from the public eye and is now an obscure ruin in the Near East. It was not until A.D. 1842, when the Frenchman Paul Emile Botta, the Englishman Austen Henry Layard, and the native Christian, Hormuzd Rassam (1849–51) excavated this site, that it received any attention at all.

What Nineveh had counted on so strongly, her *"strongholds"* (v. 12), were no more reliable than the first ripe figs on a tree. Shake the tree and the figs will drop into the mouths of their connoisseurs; these strongholds, ramparts and defences likewise would give way and fall just as easily.

The oracle of judgment begins in verse 13. Verse 13 opens with the word translated in the NKJV as *"Surely,"* though it is better translated as "Behold," as it was in 1:15, 2:13, and 3:5. Nineveh's troops would become as weak as women (a frequent metaphor for fear in situations like this: cf. Isa. 19:16 describing the fear of the Egyptians and Jer. 50:37 and 51:30 describing the fear of the Babylonians). The famous gates would be thrown wide open, apparently by the unexpected flood we discussed earlier. The rest of the destruction would come as the city was set on fire. Archeologists who have excavated the city attest to the presence of layers of ashes. Rawlinson concludes, "The recent excavations have shown that fire was a great instrument in the destruction of Nineveh palaces."[13]

CONCLUSION

How silly it is to trust in false securities. How unwise it is to presume that somehow we are less vulnerable than those before us who have been judged for exactly the same sins that we presently engage in—and refuse to repent of.

God is no respecter of persons or nations. He cannot be partial to any and still be true to His own holy character. No nation is invincible. If it has defied God and His laws, it will suffer judgment—unless it repents now!

CHAPTER SIX

Free at Last; Thank God, We're Free At Last

Nahum 3:14–19

14 Draw your water for the siege!
   Fortify your strongholds!
   Go into the clay and tread the mortar!
   Make strong the brick kiln!
15 There the fire will devour you,
   The sword will cut you off;
   It will eat you up like a locust.
   Make yourself many—like the locust!
   Make yourself many—like the swarming
      locusts!
16 You have multiplied your merchants more
      than the stars of heaven.
   The locust plunders and flies away.
17 Your commanders are like swarming locusts,
   And your captains like great grasshoppers,
   Which camp in the hedges on a cold day;
   But when the sun rises they flee away,
   And the place where they are is not known.
18 Your shepherds slumber, O king of Assyria;
   Your nobles rest in the dust.
   Your people are scattered on the mountains,
   And no one gathers them.
19 Your injury has no healing,
   Your wound is severe.
   All who hear news of you
   Will clap their hands over you,
   For upon whom has not your wickedness
      passed continually?

Nahum 3:14–19

Just as this book begins with a hymn (1:2–11) that celebrates God's character and His ability to avenge "evil" (1:11b), so the prophecy concludes with two taunt songs that assure Judah that "evil" (3:19b) will be overcome. Verses 14–17 form the first taunt and verses 18–19 form the second—the final funeral dirge.

The exhilarating aspect of this news is that everyone who hears of the collapse of Nineveh will "clap their hands." Feelings ran so high against the long-suffered atrocities that they must have matched the intensity of the Romanians' feelings on Christmas 1989 as news spread that the dictatorship of the Ceausescus family had finally ended. No Romanian mourned their sudden demise or death by a firing squad. Forty years of horrors had ended for the Romanians. In like manner, the nations clapped their hands when Nineveh fell.

    A. Fight, Fight, Fight for Nineveh   3:14–17
    B. Clap, Clap, Clap, for Victory   3:18–19

FIGHT, FIGHT, FIGHT FOR NINEVEH (3:14–17)

In imperatives filled with ironic overtones, Nahum urges the Assyrian defenders of the capital city—almost like a cheerleader—to spare no amount of effort in getting ready for the massive attack they are about to face.

Every precaution must be taken: (1) store up enough water, (2) reinforce every vulnerable spot in your defensive system, and (3) store up enough baked clay bricks so that you can easily repair any unexpected breach in the walls (v. 14).

Alas, however, all of this would be in vain, for *"the fire will devour you, the sword will cut you off; it will eat you up like a locust"* (v. 15). Both the fire and the sword would eat through the city like locusts devouring everything in their path, leaving only the scorched earth in their wake.

True, the city had a population that was about as numerous as a swarm of locusts (v. 15b). Locusts have an amazing ability to reproduce and Nineveh had an estimated population of around 300, 000—an enormous city in its time.

In addition to her military prowess, Assyria had a strong entrepreneurial spirit; she *"multiplied [her] merchants more than the stars of the heaven"* (v. 16a). What a lucrative trade Assyria carried on in her day!

Down the Tigris River her merchants would go to gain access to the sea, and link up with the Phoenicians. Nevertheless, Assyria's gains from an excellent trade balance—an enormous income and heaps of goods from all over the known world—would become the enemy's spoils to be carted off. The enemy would be as thorough in looting Assyria's goods as locusts which scour the land (v. 16b) and suddenly fly away. Assyria would go from riches to rags in a matter of hours.

Unfortunately, neither could her *"commanders"* or *"captains"* (v. 17) provide relief. They, too, took on characteristics of the locusts. (Nahum is really working this locust metaphor now, just like he worked the previous metaphors of the lion, the harlot, and the drunk.) The uncanny fact about locusts is that when their wings become cold in the evening, they grow stiff and lifeless. But when the warming rays of the sun come out and warm their wings up, their strength reappears and they become airborne once again. Consequently, there are two points of comparison between locusts and the Assyrian generals: (1) like cold locusts, the Assyrian generals were now inept, inert, and powerless to save the city; and (2) like locusts, which flee away as suddenly as they come, these generals would also fly away (v. 17bc).

Therefore, fight all you want to, O Assyria, derided Nahum, but it will not help you one ounce. You have been declared judged by God.

CLAP, CLAP, CLAP FOR VICTORY (3:18–19)

Nahum saves the best for the last. Now he addresses the Assyrian monarch directly with the grim words that all his *"shepherds"* and *"nobles"* have expired and are now dead (v. 18ab; cf. Ps. 76:6). Leaders of various sorts were called "shepherds" in the Old Testament (cf. Isa. 44:28; Jer 17:16; 23:1; Ezk. 34:2–23; 37:24; Zech. 10:2–3). It is not that these leaders were sleeping on the job; they were actually dead! Their *"rest"* was *"in the dust"* (v. 18b). No use looking for help in that direction. That was a cold trail.

But there were more troubles; without the leadership of their king, the Assyrian people were *"scattered on the mountains."* The scene here is reminiscent of the modern one after the Gulf War when the Kurds of northern Iraq fled to the mountains and refused to come down for fear of the humiliated Saddam Hussein and because they feared they had lost their leadership. In a similar way, the Assyrians fled to the remote hills and no leader was left to gather them (v. 18d). When the shepherd is taken, usually the sheep scatter. Nineveh had been wiped out for good.

Note the appropriate comment in the prestigious *Cambridge Ancient History*:

> The disappearance of the Assyrian people will always remain an unique and striking phenomenon in ancient history. Other, similar, kingdoms and empires have indeed passed away, but the people have lived on. Recent discoveries have, it is true, shown that poverty-stricken communities perpetuated the old Assyrian names at various places, for instance on the ruined site of Ashur, for many centuries, but the essential truth remains the same. A nation which had existed two thousand years and had ruled a wide area, lost its independent character. . . .[14]

Given the fact that Assyria's leaders were all gone and the city was lost, it was fitting that this judgment oracle—a funeral dirge to Assyria—should end with the words: *"Your injury has no healing, your wound is severe"* (v. 19a). Humpty Dumpty had had a great fall. All the king's horses and all the king's men could not put Humpty Dumpty together again, goes the nursery rhyme. And that is how it went for the king of Assyria. It is a fearful thing to fall into the hands of the Living God.

The surrounding nations that had been terrorized for decades now shouted in relief at the demise of so brutal a force. *"All who hear news of you will clap their hands over you"* (v. 19bc). Thus a thunderous roar of approval and relief ascended toward heaven.

The book of Nahum concludes with a theological note: *"for upon whom has not your wickedness passed continually?"* The effect of Assyria's sins was as universal as her empire; her wickedness had been exported all over the ancient world. The note here forms an inclusion with 1:11. Assyria's "evil" and "wickedness" were the central concerns of God and this book.

CONCLUSION

Martin Luther King, Jr.'s famous Washington D.C. speech will long be remembered for that famous line: "Free at last! Free at last! Thank God Almighty! Free at last!"[15] And that would sum it all up for Judah.

If some are offended by such a celebration, then let it be remembered that what is being celebrated is not a human victory, but a divine one. Nahum celebrates a vengeance that was not brought by human hands, but by God's hands. One cannot adequately evaluate the emotional impact of chapters 2 and 3 until he or she has adequately pondered the description of the character of God in chapter 1.

This is a celebration of a victory over evil and wickedness, which are offensive to God and all who love righteousness. Some of Assyria's neighbors doubtless clapped out of a bitter spirit and a vindictive heart, but God's people rejoiced in the Lord's vindication and in the reestablishment of justice, mercy and goodness.

The rejoicing here was no different from the rejoicing that will come as a result of the fall of Babylon in Revelation 18–19. It is the Lord who tries the hearts and assures that vengeance is done, because only He judges righteously (Jer. 11:20).

Like Kuwait in 1991 after the allied armies liberated her, Judah and the nations are now "Free at last!"

NOTES

1. Austen Henry Layard, *Popular Account of Discoveries at Nineveh* (1857), pp. 165–66.

2. This note is found in the Syriac version of the Old Testament by Paul of Tella, who inserted textual notes from Epiphanius and Pseudo-Epiphanius. George Adam Smith, *The Book of the Twelve Prophets* (1929) *See* Walter A. Maier, *The Book of Nahum: A Commentary* (St. Louis: Concordia, 1959), p. 25.

3. British Museum Tablet 21,901 has furnished 612 B.C. as the true date for Nineveh's collapse.

4. Maier, *Book of Nahum*, pp. 34–37.

5. I am indebted for the form of this outline and the significance of the word "Behold" to Elizabeth Achtemeier, *Nahum–Malachi; Interpretation—A Bible Commentary for Teaching and Preaching* (Atlanta: Knox, 1986), p. 6–7.

6. Elmer B. Smick, "*Nāqām,*" in *Theological Wordbook of the Old Testament,* ed. R. Laird Harris, Gleason L. Archer, Jr., and Bruce K. Waltke (Chicago: Moody, 1980), II: 598–99. *Also see* George E. Mendenhall, *The Tenth Generation: The Origins of the Biblical Tradition,* Chapter III, "The 'Vengeance' of Yahweh," (Baltimore: Johns Hopkins, 1973), pp. 69–104.

7. Donald J. Wiseman, "'Is it Peace?'—Covenant and Diplomacy," *Vetus Testamentum*, 32 (1982): 311–26.

8. In the pseudepigraphal books of the *Testament of the Twelve Patriarchs, The Ascension of Isaiah,* and the *Jubilees,* Belial becomes a proper name for Satan. Paul follows this usage in 2 Corinthians 6:15. In the *Sybilline Oracles,* the title of Belial is given to Nero. That is a continuation of the same process we have argued for here. The name may be connected with Belili, a Babylonian goddess of the underworld, a form that seems to suggest the connection in 2 Samuels 22:5. *See* Achtemeier, *Nahum–Malachi,* p. 16, for much of this documentation.

9. D. Winton Thomas, *Documents From Old Testament Times* (New York: Harper and Row, 1961), p. 76, for the text of British Museum 21901, 38–50. *See also* in ANET, pp. 304–5.

10. For a good discussion of this point, I have been indebted to T. Miles Bennett, *The Books of Nahum and Zephaniah* (Grand Rapids: Baker, 1968), p. 47.

11. John Calvin, *A Commentary on the Twelve Minor Prophets* (Edinburgh, 1948), III: 480, as cited by Achtemeier, *Nahum–Malachi,* p 25.

12. For a fuller discussion of the ethical problem of prayers of cursing, *see* Walter C. Kaiser, Jr., *Hard Sayings of the Old Testament* (Downers Grove, Il.: Inter-Varsity Press, 1988), pp. 171–75.

13. Sir Henry Rawlinson, *The History of Herodotus* (1862), p. 448. Quote as cited by Maier, *Book of Nahum,* p. 126.

14. *Cambridge Ancient History,* III: *The Assyrian Empire* (Cambridge: Cambridge University Press, 1970) p. 130, as cited by Carl E. Armerding, "Nahum," in *The Expositor's Bible Commentary,* ed. Frank E. Gaebelein (Grand Rapids: Zondervan, 1985), p. 489.

15. As recalled in Achtemeier, *Nahum–Malachi,* p. 28.

SECTION THREE :

The Book of Habakkuk

Habakkuk 1:1–3:19

Introduction To Habakkuk

Is it merely the love for the underdog, or is it some dreadful scholarly disease possibly known as "academic arcanism" that would prompt a series of messages on the Old Testament Minor Prophet named Habakkuk? Donald E. Gowan, in his slender but delightful volume entitled *The Triumph of Faith in Habukkuk*[1] also suggests that such an undertaking might be a manifestation of a type of "infracaninaphilia" (a made up word, meaning the "love of the underdog").

But I wish to assert, like Gowan, that there are a number of reasons why Habakkuk, obscure and small as it may be, should be lifted up to the attention of the Church at this time. The reasons are: pastoral, theological, apologetical, and spiritual. The pastoral reasons take us into the study and the prayer closet where we ask over and over again, "How long, O Lord? How long?" "Why? O Why?" As long as these questions continue to plague us, the need for Habakkuk's message will persist. As Gowan observes:

> Most people, even in the Bible, who have longed for the privilege
> of arguing with God, of questioning the way he does things, of
> seeking God's explanation of his ways, have not been given that
> opportunity. . . .What Habakkuk has recorded here is something
> rather extraordinary: a dialogue in which he twice complains to
> God about the world's injustice, and twice God answers him.[2]

The theological reasons for the study of Habakkuk become clear as soon as we recall that the central theme of this book is the principle that "The just shall live by faith" (Hab. 2:4). This theme appears three times in the New Testament, viz. Romans 1:17; Galatians 3:11 and Hebrews 10:38. Moreover, the principle became Luther's great rallying point and the watchword for the sixteenth century Reformation. These three words in the Hebrew text of Habakkuk 2:4 shook Europe and eventually the whole world! Habakkuk has much to teach us about the meaning of faith and righteousness, and about how, in the face of great difficulties, one can get on with the task of living now, enjoying the deep satisfaction of knowing who God is and that He is able to handle things, come what may!

The book of Habakkuk also wrestles with the problem of *theodicy*—the apologetical problem of squaring the goodness and justice of God with the presence of what seems like unbridled evil and wickedness among men and nations. Other passages in the Bible tackle this problem, but few come to as clear a resolution of many aspects of the problem as Habakkuk does.

But the most striking aspect of this compact manual is the way it places God in the center of history and of personal consciousness. The theme of a worshipping heart that has found its rest in the living God brings us to the spiritual reason for our study of this book. Habakkuk teaches us how to rejoice when the lid has blown off everything and nothing that we once counted on as a reference point remains fixed: everything is gone, including the food that we once took for granted. "What we will do then?" asks Habakkuk. He knows, for he has been there and has learned from the inner councils of revelation and the hard knocks of experience. Not that Habakkuk was a plaster saint or an unusually strong and courageous character; on the contrary, he was just as frightened as the next person, if not more. But balancing his outward fear and realistic assessment of the fact that his whole nation and its temple, army, and citizens, and all that he held dear, were to be lost to one of the most despicable, godless, and unmerciful conquerors known on earth to that time, he had a peace in his heart that passed all understanding. How he maintained a sense of peace in the face of such savagery, brutality and shocking demolition of everything he had held dear (not to mention everything that God had built up through the nation of Israel over the last millennia and a half) is a lesson worth learning in our own day.

Habakkuk, then, will teach us how to live by faith in a God who is alive and active in the current affairs of life, distasteful and unappealing as those affairs seem at times. His is a most succinct message for both good and bad times. As Raymond Calkins summarizes it:

> There is no Old Testament book that is able to do more for the burdened souls of men or to raise them to higher levels of hope

and confidence than the brief prophecy of Habakkuk. . . .
Hardly a book in the Bible is constructed on such simple and majestic lines. These three chapters stand like three august columns, side by side, each complete in itself, unparalleled in their power and appeal. . . . Search the Bible through and you will find nothing so matchless in concentrated power as these three chapters of the Book of Habakkuk. Of the outward circumstances of the prophet's life we know nothing. But here was a man with a soul sensitive to evil, yet firm in his faith in an omnipotent God. And this faith he has uttered with a force, an eloquence, a literary power which has caused his words to become a permanent part of the literature of the soul.[3]

THE AUTHOR

There is not that much to tell about the man Habakkuk. He is simply a "prophet" and he is given a "burden" (1:1), but we do not know who his parents were or under which reigns of which kings in Judah he ministered. Even his name is an enigma. Was it a nickname drawn from the Akkadian name of the plant *Hambakuku* or did it come from the Hebrew verb "to embrace?" Because the word for "embrace" occurs in the story of the Shunammite woman in 2 Kings 4:16, some have anachronistically identified Habakkuk as her son, for whom the prophet Elisha played a major role. But the association is most tenuous to say the least. Even the legendary story of *Bel and the Dragon* offers no help in identifying the prophet. This apocryphal addition to the story of Daniel reads:

> Now the prophet Habakkuk was in Judea. He had boiled pottage and had broken bread into a bowl, and was going into the field to take it to the reapers. But the angel of the Lord said to Habakkuk, "Take the dinner which you have to Babylon, to Daniel, in the lion's den." Habakkuk said, "Sir, I have never seen Babylon, and I know nothing about the den." Then the angel of the Lord took him by the crown of his head, and lifted him by his hair and set him down in Babylon, right over the den, with the rushing sound of the wind itself. Then Habakkuk shouted, "Daniel! Daniel! Take the dinner which God has sent you." And Daniel said, "Thou hast remembered me, O God, and hast not forsaken those who love thee." So Daniel arose and ate. And the angel of the God immediately returned Habakkuk to his own place.[4]

The Date and the Times

It is not the man, then, that is the significant point of the book of Habakkuk. The man was merely the messenger and the prayer warrior. More important were Habakkuk's God and the times during which his Lord worked. The clearest evidence for dating the book of Habakkuk is in 1:6, which mentions the "Chaldeans." This new world power had just destroyed the Assyrian capital of Nineveh, in 612 B.C. It then scored a decisive victory over Pharaoh Necho at Carchemish, in 605 B.C. It is likely that this book was written just before 605 B.C., for the prophet was told that God was going to do a work in his time of such magnitude that no one would believe it if they were told about it then (Hab. 1:5). God would use the Babylonians, a nation that was by no means a threat or a world empire at the time, to judge Judah's sin. This would be astonishing, to say the least.

An Outline of Habakkuk

I. Waiting for God's Intervention in History   1:1–2:1
   A. Our Distress Over Our Moral Condition   1:2–4
      1. In Our Sensitivity to Wrong   1:2–3a
      2. In Our Helplessness in the Presence of Wrong   1:3b
      3. In Our Frustration Over the Loss of Law and Justice   1:4
   B. Our Amazement Over the Divine Intervention   1:5–11
      1. In His Unbelievable Work   1:5
      2. In His Use of Such Unlikely Instruments   1:6–11
   C. Our Distress Over God's Use of the Wicked   1:12–17
      1. So Contrary to His Name   1:12a
      2. So Contrary to His Nature   1:12b–13
      3. So Contrary to His Justice   1:14–17
   D. Conclusion
II. Learning to Live by Faith   2:2–20
   A. The Proclamation of Faith   2:2
   B. The Implementation of Faith   2:3
   C. The Revelation of Faith   2:4–5
      1. The Scope of this Revelation
      2. The Principle of the Revelation
      3. The Contrast to this Principle
   D. The Vindication of Faith   2:6–20
      1. Inordinate Greed   2:6–8
      2. A Hunger to Dominate   2:9–11
      3. Atrocities   2:12–14
      4. Debauchery   2:15–17
      5. Idolatry   2:18–20
   E. Conclusion
III. Explaining God's Presence in History   3:3–15
   A. God's Past Actions Proclaim His Coming   3:3–7

145

1. The Theophany at Sinai   3:3a
2. The Theophany in all Creation   3:3b–4
3. The Theophany in the Plagues of Egypt   3:5
4. The Theophany Before the Nations   3:6
5. The Theophany in the Days of Othniel and Gideon   3:7

  B. God's Future Actions Foretell His Coming   3:8–15
  C. Conclusion

IV. Rejoicing in Tribulation   3:1–2, 16–19
  A. Let Us Begin Our Worship in Adoration   3:2a
  B. Let Us Focus Our Worship on the Kingdom of God   3:2b
  C. Let Us Confess Our Fears in Our Worship   3:16
  D. Let Us Celebrate the Joy of the Lord in Our Worship   3:17–19
  E. Conclusion

CHAPTER ONE

Waiting For God's Intervention in History

Habakkuk 1:1–2:1

1:1 The burden which the prophet Habakkuk saw.
2 O LORD, how long shall I cry,
And You will not hear?
Even cry out to You, "Violence!"
And You will not save.
3 Why do You show me iniquity,
And cause me to see trouble?
For plundering and violence are before me;
There is strife, and contention arises.
4 Therefore the law is powerless,
And justice never goes forth.
For the wicked surround the righteous;
Therefore perverse judgment proceeds.
5 "Look among the nations and watch—
Be utterly astounded!
For I will work a work in your days
Which you would not believe, though it were
told you.
6 For indeed I am raising up the Chaldeans,
A bitter and hasty nation
Which marches through the breadth
of the earth,
To possess dwelling places that are not theirs.
7 They are terrible and dreadful;
Their judgment and their dignity proceed
from themselves.
8 Their horses also are swifter than leopards,

And more fierce than evening wolves.
Their chargers charge ahead;
Their cavalry comes from afar;
They fly as the eagle that hastens to eat.
9 "They all come for violence;
Their faces are set like the east wind.
They gather captives like sand.
10 They scoff at kings,
And princes are scorned by them.
They deride every stronghold,
For they heap up mounds of earth and seize it.
11 Then his mind changes, and he transgresses;
He commits offense,
Imputing this power to his god."
12 Are You not from everlasting,
O LORD my God, my Holy One?
We shall not die.
O LORD, You have appointed them
    for judgment;
O Rock, You have marked them for correction.
13 You are of purer eyes than to behold evil,
And cannot look on wickedness.
Why do You look on those who
    deal treacherously,
And hold Your tongue when the
    wicked devours
One more rightous than he?
14 Why do You make men like fish of the sea,
Like creeping things that have
    no ruler over them?
15 They take up all of them with a hook,
They catch them in their net,
And gather them in their dragnet.
Therefore they rejoice and are glad.
16 Therefore they sacrifice to their net,
And burn incense to their dragnet;
Because by them their share is sumptuous
And their food plenteous.
17 Shall they therefore empty their net,
And continue to slay nations without pity?
2:1 I will stand my watch
And set myself on the rampart,

> And watch to see what He will say to me,
> And what I will answer when I am reproved.
> *Habakkuk 1:1–2:1*

"When the times get tough," goes a contemporary adage, "the tough get going." And the times were becoming tougher than this unknown prophet named Habakkuk could fathom. Clearly something was about to snap, for not only was violence on the rise, but so was the threat of the newest challengers to the balance of power in the Near East, known as the "Chaldeans" or "Babylonians" (Hab. 1:6).

But one man plus God is always a majority—even in a crisis situation such as the one Habakkuk faced. Therefore it was to God that the prophet carried his problems: Twice he bitterly complains to God and twice he is answered by the Lord. This dialogue with God takes the form of a "lament." Frequently the psalmist used the lament psalm as he poured out his complaint before the Almighty. Some psalms have a strong communal appeal, such as Psalm 74; others have an individualistic flavor, such as Psalm 13. The impassioned language of these laments cannot be missed. Psalm 13 is representative of their tone and theme:

> How long, O LORD? Will you forget me forever?
> How long will you hide your face from me?
> How long must I wrestle with my thoughts
> and every day have sorrow in my heart?
> How long will my enemy triumph over me?
> *Psalm 13:1–2* (NIV)

Not only does Habakkuk's interrogative "How long?" (v. 2) give us a major clue that we are dealing with a lament, so does his use of one of life's most persistent interrogatives—"Why?" (v. 3). The prophet Jeremiah also asked "Why?" He groaned: "Why does the way of the wicked prosper? Why do all who are treacherous thrive?" (Jer. 12:1b). Psalm 22:1b laments, "Why are you so far from saving me?" Clearly the man of God, in deep distress, had gone to the Lord for relief. Further, this is probably not the first time that Habakkuk had laid this plea before God, for the question "How long, O Lord?" implies that he had been doing so for some time.

Habakkuk's message is relevant to all times and peoples, as we are taught in the full scope of the canon (2 Tim. 3:16–17). But the problem is this: how can we contemporize his words without weakening the meaning they had in their original setting? It is all too easy to declare that we are under no obligation to discover the meaning Habakkuk's message had for its original author or first audience. But we do so at the risk of loosing the authority and any objective controls over what the text is saying. After all, it was the prophet who stood in the council of God, not we. And it is the author who must first state what he means to say if we are to gain any sense of what the Spirit of God is saying to our day and generation. What then is Habakkuk's message? Where do we begin if we are to be faithful to the original meaning of the text?

The book of Habakkuk is divided as follows:

	1:1	Title line
I.	1:2–4	The prophet's first complaint to God
II.	1:5–11	God's first response to the prophet's complaint
III.	1:12–17	The prophet's second complaint to God
IV.	2:1	The prophet's decision to wait for God to act
V.	2:2–5	God's second response to the prophet's complaint
VI.	2:6–20	God's five woes pronounced on Babylon
VII.	3:1–15	The prayer of Habakkuk
VIII.	3:16–19	Habakkuk's joy in the Lord.

The first four divisions of this book (vv. 1:2–2:1) comprise our first teaching or preaching block (a pericope) in that there are two prayers of complaint, the first followed by a divine response (vv. 1:5–11) and the second followed by a pause (2:1) while we await the decisive word from God that is both the central theme of and sole purpose for writing this book—"The just shall live by faith" (vv. 2:2–5).

Where is the "focal point," or heart, of this pericope? We believe it is at the top of our Lord's answer to Habakkuk in 1:5: "Look among the nations and watch—and be utterly astounded! For I will work a work in your days which you would not believe. . . ." From this center of what we will loosely call chapter one (indeed, the chapter break after 1:17 surely is ill-advised), we derive the title and subject for our message: "Waiting For God's Intervention in History."

The invitation in 1:5 to "look," "watch," and "be utterly amazed" was not directed only to the prophet, for the imperatives and the pronouns are all second person *plural* forms. The whole generation (and, apparently, each subsequent generation) was to watch international developments carefully, for God was about to intervene in a shocking and astonishing way. Note the irony in the use of the words "Look" (*rāʾâ*) and "watch" (*nābat*); those are the same words Habakkuk had used in his complaint in verse 3—"Why do you make me *look* at injustice? Why do you *tolerate [lit., "watch"]* wrong?" (NIV).

God will "work a work" "in your days" that will both frighten those who are unprepared and gladden those who have long awaited the dethronement of wrong and wickedness. The situation recalls the lines of James Russel Lowell:

> Careless seems the great Avenger;
> History's pages but record
> One death-grapple in the darkness 'twixt
> Old systems and the Word;
> *Truth forever on the scaffold,*
> *Wrong forever on the throne,—*
> Yet that scaffold sways the future,
> And, behind the dim unknown,
> Standeth God within the shadow,
> Keeping watch above his own.[5]

If Habakkuk 1:5 is the "focal point" that supplies us with the title and subject for our teaching and preaching from this pericope, what is the proper way to proceed with the exposition of this text? Notice that we called for an exposition. What our generation desperately needs is the faithful elucidation of the Word of God, line upon line, chapter upon chapter. All too frequently we offer topical sermons that use the Scriptures for little more than a springboard to launch us into what we want to say—something we have read elsewhere and felt was worth repeating for our people.

What we are commending here is called "textual exposition" of the Scriptures, or "expository preaching." Expository preaching is that method of preaching that allows the text of Scripture to supply both *the shape* and *the content* of the proclamation. The minimum block of text to consider is a single paragraph (or, in poetry, a strophe), for by definition a paragraph contains a single idea. Usually each paragraph in a pericope will supply one main point or roman numeral in our teaching or preaching outline. All the main points of the outline will center around the focal point of the pericope to provide unity to the sermon; the focal point is the common stance from which each of the main points is regarded.[6]

This first pericope of Habakkuk, in the form of a lament and a dialogue, suggests two homiletical keywords: "wrongs and works." The "wrongs" are those found in the prophet's complaints, while the "works" are God's responses to those complaints.

Our outline will be as follows:

A. Our Distress Over Our Moral Condition   1:2–4
1. In Our Sensitivity to Wrong   1:2–3a
2. In Our Helplessness in the Presence of Wrong   1:3b
3. In Our Frustration Over the Loss of Law and Justice   1:4
B. Our Amazement Over the Divine Intervention   1:5–11
1. In His Unbelievable Work   1:5
2. In His Use of Such Unlikely Instruments   1:6–11
C. Our Distress Over God's Use of the Wicked   1:12–17
1. So Contrary to His Name   1:12a
2. So Contrary to His Nature   1:12b–13
3. So Contrary to His Justice   1:14–17
D. Conclusion   2:1

Some years ago, Samuel Beckett produced his play "Waiting for Godot." The dialogue that takes place between two tramps, Estrogen and Vladimir, is tedious and repetitious; the essence of the dialogue is that the tramps are part of a waiting generation, although no one knows what it is they are waiting for. Who Godot is, and whether he even exists or will come to relieve the tramps' apprehensions, no one knows! Waiting—that is how that generation is described—as one that is just waiting!

Habakkuk 1:2–2:1 also gives us a sense of waiting, but it does not urge us to wait like Beckett's two tragic characters wait—for something they know nothing about. God would shortly—in an amazing and shocking way—work a work that all would see. Let us hear the "wrongs" that provoked the prophet's complaints and the "works" that constituted God's responses.

OUR DISTRESS OVER OUR MORAL CONDITION (1:2–4)

Habakkuk lived during Judah's final days. Despite King Josiah's remarkable revival that had taken place in 621 B.C. (2 Kings 22:8–20), probably not more than twelve years before this book was written, society was once again engaging in all sorts of social injustice and violence (Jer. 7:3–6; 22:13–17). Habakkuk uses six different words to describe this despicable situation: "violence," "injustice," "wrong," "destruction," "strife" and "conflict." The times were not good at all! Thus it was that the prophet continually lifted his prayer to God that something would be done about the unbearable amount of wrong he was experiencing in that society.

In Our Sensitivity to Wrong (1:2–3a)

Habakkuk puts four questions before God, two beginning with "How long?" (*ʾad ʾanah*) and two beginning with "Why?" (*lāmmâh*). As discussed above, these words establish the form as a lament, but the content of each complaint also makes plain the unspeakable corruption then present in Judah.

The prophet does not doubt God's ability to help; he just wonders why things have gone on for so long. Things are so bad that he can only cry, "Help!" In fact, it has gotten to the point where he wants to "scream," for the Hebrew word "cry out" means "to shout, to roar." The issue is "violence," for the fabric of society was beginning to come apart because of the prevalence of excessive violence. Five times in this brief book Habakkuk decries the overwhelming presence of violence (1:2, 3, 9; 2:8, 17). Noah used the same word to describe the society in his day, which God found necessary to destroy with the flood (Gen. 6:11). The violence was the manifestation of the meaner, baser, and more selfish instincts of the haughty persons against the weaker elements of their culture (cf. Amos 3:10; Jer. 6:7). Their deliberate oppression, exploitation, and terrorization called for an equally terrorizing intervention by God. Habakkuk wanted deliverance from above, for apparently no human help would be of any avail given the stage evil had reached.

In Our Helplessness in the Presence of Wrong (1:3b)

Habakkuk could not believe his eyes, for the violent deeds of humanity took place directly *"before [him]."* "Destruction" and "violence" were the order of the day and encouraged lawsuits (the Hebrew word, *rîb*, is translated in the NIV as "strife," but it was also the normative word for going to court against others). They also induced "wranglings," or "conflicts," over every sort of trivial detail.

"People devour each other, denounce one another to the authorities; everyone blames the other and in this way seeks to avert responsibility from himself. This description of moral corruption views it as a crisis on the horizontal plane, but the presentation on the vertical plane appears through an outlining of the ultimate outcome, which the prophet summons his fellows to regard as the real cause of the collapse."[7] Indeed, welcome to the litigious society of today.

In Our Frustration Over the Loss of Law and Justice (1:4)

"Therefore," begins verse 4, God's gracious teaching in His *Torah* is "paralyzed," "frozen," or just plain "chilled out." What could have helped the people with relationships that had gone awry no longer functioned because no one allowed it to do so. The "Law" that God had given "for [their and our] good" (Deut. 10:13) had been stripped of all its effectiveness. The very Law that King Josiah had rediscovered buried in the temple trash and rejoiced over so greatly was abandoned by his son Jehoiachin.

Since the Law was no longer consulted for moral or spiritual guidance, "true justice" could no longer come to light. Moreover, the wicked "hemmed in" or "trapped" the righteous like flies caught in a spider's web. There was a time when the wicked would have been more hesitant to challenge their victims so forthrightly, but now, encouraged by their own successes, they had placed a stranglehold on their victims—and on righteousness itself. Such is the price for neglecting the Law of God. As Proverbs 29:18 affirms, "Where there is no vision [i.e., no input from God's revelation], the people become unmanageable; but he who keeps the law, oh how truly blessed that one is"(author's trans.). Judah's people became their own enemy as they turned their back on Josiah's revival of 621 B.C., and especially as they turned away from their Lord.

OUR AMAZEMENT OVER THE DIVINE INTERVENTION (1:5–11)

God's challenge is for everyone (in verse 5, you will recall, the imperatives and pronouns are in the second person plural) to *"look,"* *"watch"* and *"be utterly astounded!"* He will work, but it will be a work of judgment first.

In His Unbelievable Work (1:5)

"[Y]ou would not believe [it], though it were told you," begins the Lord's answer to Habakkuk's complaint. In fact, you will become breathless with amazement at what I am going to do. Once again, God would perform one of His "wondrous works" that the Psalms often extolled (Ps. 30:5; 100:4; 106:1; 118:1, 29; 136:1; 147:7).

The community responsibility for what was going to happen is indicated not only by the plural verbs and pronouns in verse 5, but also by the form of the third verb, *"be utterly astounded"* (called a *Hithpael* in Hebrew), which stressed community involvement. So, this verse says, all of you had better watch out and be ready to be startled out of your skin when you see what God is going to do about the orgies of wickedness in full swing in this culture! You all are going to be mightily taken aback.

In His Use of Such Unlikely Instruments (1:6–11)

The most startling news of all is that God is *"raising up"* (or "arousing") the Babylonians to be His instrument to rectify the problems Habakkuk has noticed among his countrymen. A century earlier, the Assyrians had been used as "the rod of [God's] anger" (Isa. 10:5); now Judah must endure another pagan assault.

Habakkuk's characterization of the Babylonian power is graphic and discouraging. He describes this great power as *"bitter"* (v. 6), a word that connotes being bitter *(mar)*, savage, and merciless. The Babylonians were also "impetuous"; they would fall on Judah and devour her suddenly and speedily. As they swept over all the earth they would seize everything that was not their own (v. 6b).

The result of the Babylonians' campaign would be the spread of awful dread and fear (v. 7). The Babylonians were completely unprincipled and lawless, making up their own laws as they went. How ironical that lawless Judah should be confronted with a real taste of what it meant to be without the law of God or any vestige of its effects in society!

Nimble as leopards, passionately pursuing their prey like evening wolves, and as greedy as circling vultures or eagles, the Babylonians made a virtue out of violence. Once again, what irony for Judah to see its own *"violence"* (1:2, 3) played back by unprincipled pagans

(1:9). Had not God warned centuries earlier through Moses that if the people turned away from His Law, "The LORD will bring a nation against you from far away, from the ends of the earth, like an eagle [or vulture] swooping down, a nation whose language you will not understand" (Duet. 28:49 NIV). Is this warning relevant to modern nations or will we be exempt from God's judgment? We will not! It is so clear when we see other nations acting arrogantly, showing self-deification and acknowledging no authority other than their own. But how must it appear to our Lord when He sees the same tendencies showing up among His people and in His church? If the remnant—the faithful few—goes bad, what will the larger nation do in the day of adversity?

According to verses 10–11, the Babylonians scoffed at all forms of authority and power except their own. Nothing was impregnable to their mighty blows; fortified cities and palaces alike yielded to their military power. The whole mess is summarized in the last words of verse 11; the Babylonians are "guilty men, whose own strength is their god"(NIV). How frequently men and nations miss the point: they attribute their exalted positions in the world scene to their own doing (Isa. 47:8, 10; Zeph. 2:15). The old Descartian formula *Cogito ergo sum*, in the mouths of these scorners, becomes, "I am the greatest, therefore nothing else matters." But God who sits in the heavens will laugh at them (Ps. 2:4). They too shall pass away.

OUR DISTRESS OVER GOD'S USE OF THE WICKED (1:12–17)

So Contrary to His Name (1:12a)

In verse 12 Habakkuk cries, *"Are You not from everlasting, O LORD my God, my Holy One? We shall not die."*

The interrogative particle that begins verse 12—in Hebrew, *halo'*, ("Art Thou not")—marks its affinity with the laments in verses 2 and 3 ("How Long?" and "Why?"). In verses 2 and 3 Habakkuk expressed impatience; here he displays some perplexity over the sudden turn of events. But in all the laments his starting point in desperate moments is precisely what ours should be: calling on the name and character of our Lord.

God has existed from time immemorial. He is timeless; or, simply put, He is eternal! The One who has been active in space and time created both. It is comforting to know that He is the One who controls history (Deut. 33:27; Isa. 40:28; Ps. 90:2).

Habakkuk continues his personal confession of faith in his Lord. He repeatedly calls God "my" Lord. God is his *"Holy One."* This was the prophet Isaiah's favorite term for God, and appears also in the book of Acts. It refers to God's incomparability and purity. Leviticus 19:2 established God's holiness as the standard for all right acting, thinking, and living. It was this reassuring fact that kept Habakkuk from total despair when confronted by the problem of theodicy— reconciling the goodness and justice of God with the recent announcement of His intention to use the wicked Babylonians against Judah. For many in Habakkuk's time that would have been as hard to swallow as it would have been during the cold war for Americans to be told that God was going to use the Russians or the Red Chinese to punish the United States for its sins!

The prophet also reassured his soul by recalling that God is the "Rock." This name spoke of God's steadfastness and continuity. In Him could be found security, protection, refuge and constancy. The psalmists often used this name to evoke the same images (Ps. 19:15; 31:3; 62:8; 92:16) and the *"Rock"* appears as far back as Moses' speech in Deuteronomy 32:4. As unchanging and as enduring as the rocks, so was the Lord on whom the prophet cast all his cares.

So Contrary to His Nature (1:12b–13)

So secure was the prophet that he blurts out in verse 12b, *"we shall not die."* (One of the Rabbinic alterations of the text—the so-called *tiqqune sopherim*, "scribal changes"—was from "we shall not die" to "Thou doest not die." But there are no manuscripts that contain that reading, so it must be rejected.) Thus the prophet believed that God would protect His covenant people—breaking His covenant was not consistent with His promise—even though God's judgment of Judah was deserved and therefore inevitable.

Thus Judah was selected by God for judgment and ordained to be punished for her sin, even though, as was abundantly clear, God would never tolerate wrong nor look on what was impure. The prophet acknowledges God's divine prerogative to set up and carry out His royal decree, but the agonizing problem is this: How can God appear to stand by in silence as the wicked swallow up the righteous?

It seems as if God is tolerating all that He opposes. Habakkuk stops short of charging God with wrong-doing, but, nevertheless, he is unable to resolve the basic problem. We are likewise unable to resolve the problem in similar crisis situations in our day. But we may learn from this text how best to orient ourselves in the midst of these crisis situations.

So Contrary to His Justice (1:14–17)

Under Babylonian imperialism, human society seemed like one large gathering of fish and sea creatures—devoid of leadership and thoroughly exposed to the whims and wishes of fishermen. How helpless, defenseless and stranded were these fish exposed to the hooks, nets and dragnets of the monarch from Babylon.

How could any of this be in agreement with the justice of God? To make matters worse, the Babylonians would attribute the success of the draft of fish to their own skills and gods, not to the sovereign God who appointed them and ordained their activities.

But Habakkuk knows that God is in control of history. He knows that the outcome of the judgment on Judah will be in accord with the order God oversees. He just can't figure out how it all fits. God seems to have "zigzagged in his march towards his goal."[8] What can a mortal do in the face of such perplexing data?

CONCLUSION

No matter how great the prophet's perplexity (and it was great), he will wait patiently until he receives further revelation. He will continue to watch alertly from his tower on the city wall for the time when God will be pleased to answer his quandaries.

Thus we come to the end of our first study in this fascinating book. As we have seen, just at the point where the prophet complained that the morals of his society that were once fastened down seemed to be coming loose, God startled everyone with more than enough to think about.

But some will protest, "We are not prophets and we have no ability to predict the future. How can we be expected to distinguish what is just an ordinary occurrence from those events where God is doing something decisive in history?" The point is that we can't be expected to designate events at this level. In fact, even a prophet like Habakkuk, with all his gifts, still saw opaquely at key points.

What we are called upon to remember is that righteousness is not an optional feature of a believer's life. In that sense righteousness does exalt a nation, but sin is a reproach to any people (Proverbs 14:34). We are also called upon to know that the movements of men and nations are "His-story" just as much as they are part of our daily existence. God will deal fairly, with justice and love, for He is "from everlasting." He is the "Holy One" and He is the "Rock." Isn't that enough purity, stability, and longevity to fulfill more than all we could ask or think in times of crisis. Let us wait for our Lord, for He will surely demonstrate in the end that He alone is the Lord of history.

CHAPTER TWO

Learning to Live by Faith

Habakkuk 2:2–20

2 Then the Lord answered me and said:
"Write the vision
And make it plain on tablets,
That he may run who reads it.
3 For the vision is yet for an appointed time;
But at the end it will speak, and it will not lie.
Though it tarries, wait for it;
Because it will surely come,
It will not tarry.
4 "Behold the proud,
His soul is not upright in him;
But the just shall live by his faith.
5 "Indeed, because he transgresses by wine,
He is a proud man,
And he does not stay at home.
Because he enlarges his desire as hell,
And he is like death, and cannot be satisfied,
He gathers to himself all nations
And heaps up for himself all peoples.
6 "Shall not all these take up a proverb
against him,
And a taunting riddle against him, and say,
'Woe to him who increases
What is not his—how long?
And to him who loads himself with
many pledges'?
7 Will not your creditors rise up suddenly?
Will they not awaken who oppress you?
And you will become their booty.

8 Because you have plundered many nations,
All the remnant of the people shall
   plunder you,
Because of men's blood And the violence of the
   land and the city,
And of all who dwell in it.

9 "Woe to him who covets evil gain for
   his house,
That he may set his nest on high,
That he may be delivered from the power of
   disaster!

10 You give shameful counsel to your house,
Cutting off many peoples,
And sinned against your soul.

11 For the stone will cry out from the wall,
And the beam from the timbers will answer it.

12 "Woe to him who builds a town
   with bloodshed,
Who establishes a city by iniquity!

13 Behold, is it not of the LORD of hosts
That the peoples labor to feed the fire,
And nations weary themselves in vain?

14 For the earth will be filled
With the knowledge of the glory of the LORD,
As the waters cover the sea.

15 "Woe to him who gives drink to his neighbor,
Pressing him to your bottle,
Even to make him drunk,
That you may look on his nakedness!

16 You are filled with shame instead of glory.
You also—drink!
And be exposed as uncircumcised!
The cup of the LORD's right hand will be turned
   against you,
And utter shame will be on your glory.

17 For the violence done to Lebanon will
   cover you,
And the plunder of beasts which made
   them afraid,
Because of men's blood
And the violence of the land and the city,
And of all who dwell in it.

18 "What profit is the image, that its maker
   should carve it,
The molded image, a teacher of lies,
That the maker of its mold should trust in it,
To make mute idols?
19 Woe to him who says to wood, 'Awake!'
To silent stone, 'Arise! It shall teach!'
Behold, it is overlaid with gold and silver,
And in it there is no breath at all.
20 But the LORD is in His holy temple.
Let all the earth keep silence before Him."

Habakkuk 2:2–20

Before *"the just shall live by his faith"* (2:4b) became the battle cry for Martin Luther and the Reformation, it served as the central theme of the book of Habakkuk and as a summary of the biblical discussion of justification by faith that had begun with God's promise to Abraham in Genesis 15:6. One can hardly overstate the importance of this theme for the history of both Israel and the Church.

So central to the whole of Jewish thought was Habakkuk 2:4b that the *Talmud* records this famous remark made by Rabbi Simlai: "Moses gave Israel 613 commandments. David reduced them to eleven [Psalm 15], Micah to 3 [Micah 6:8], Isaiah to 2 [Isaiah 56:1], but Habakkuk to 1—*'the righteous shall live by his faith* [Hab. 2:4].'"[9] Jewish scholars felt that these words—only three words in the Hebrew text—fairly summarized the message of the whole Bible.

New Testament theology also builds on this text. S. Lewis Johnson, Jr., concludes: "'The just shall live by faith,'—it is without question, near the soul of Pauline theology. . . . Habakkuk's great text, with his son Paul's comments and additions, became the banner of the Protestant Reformation in the hands of Habakkuk's grandson, Martin Luther."[10] One can hardly find higher praise for any one single text in the whole Bible—Habakkuk 2:4b rates at the top.

But despite its high reputation, Habakkuk 2:4b has occasioned a host of critical studies. Indeed, almost every point in the text of Habakkuk 2:2–5 has been sharply debated. But the endeavor to understand will prove to be worth all the effort. Our treatment of this study in Old Testament Biblical Theology on Habakkuk 2:2–20 will take this form:

162

A. The Proclamation of Faith   2:2
B. The Implementation of Faith   2:3
C. The Revelation of Faith   2:4–5
    1. The Scope of this Revelation
    2. The Principle of the Revelation
    3. The Contrast to this Principle
D. The Vindication of Faith   2:6–20
    1. Inordinate Greed   2:6–8
    2. A Hunger to Dominate   2:9–11
    3. Atrocities   2:12–14
    4. Debauchery   2:15–17
    5. Idolatry   2:18–20
E. Conclusion

THE PROCLAMATION OF FAITH (2:2)

The long-awaited answer to the prophet's prayers of complaint comes in the surprising form of a "vision."

> "Then the LORD answer me and said:
> 'Write the vision
> And make it plain on tablets,
> That he may run who reads it.'"

The allusion to the Law of God cannot be missed in this passage, for the words to "inscribe" ("*write the vision*") and "*make it plain*" recall the inscribing of the ten commandments on tablets. In Deuteronomy 27:8, the text reads, "And you shall write very clearly [the same verb *ba᾽ēr* with *hêṭēb*] all the words of this law on these stones you have set up." (*See also* Exod. 31:18; 32:15–16; Deut. 9:10.)[11] Accordingly, Habakkuk's instructions were to write this vision up on tablets, thereby reflecting, as O. Palmer Robertson observes, "the long-established pattern of inscribing a fresh copy of covenant law as an essential step in covenant renewal. . . ."[12] The tablets might have been huge boards used for writing something in public, much as public notices are put on large bulletin boards in China and the Orient today.

It is curious that the word "tablets" is plural, since it does not appear that Habakkuk would need more than one tablet to record the vision in verses 4 and 5. Isaiah had been told to record his message on a "scroll" (Isa. 8:1; 30:8) and Jeremiah was told to put his message in a "book" (Jer. 30:2). The only possible explanation for the plural form "tablets" must be, as Robertson suggests, that "tablets" refers to the tablets of the covenant made at Sinai (Exod. 24:12; 31:18; 34:1, 28; Deut. 9:9–11; 10:2, 4; 2 Chron. 5:10). Thus this vision given to Habakkuk compares in importance with the original giving of the Law to Moses on Mt. Sinai.

What, then, we ask, is the meaning of that strange clause, *"That he may run who reads it?"* While it is true that the Lord is economical in how He expresses Himself, there can be no doubt what the subject and the main verb of this clause are. The subject, expressed by a participle both in the Hebrew and the Greek LXX, is "the one reading" ("or heralding"). The main Hebrew verb is "he may [or "will"] run." But the English translations invariably exchange syntactical places between the two verbs and come up with something like "so that he who runs may read it," making the syntactical error of transposing the main verb into the subject and shifting the participial subject into the main verb. But the original text has it the other way around: the vision was given to Habakkuk so that a reader might run, not so that the one running might be able to read it quickly.

The trouble in translating this text seems to have come from failing to understand what "run" means here. John Marshall Holt makes a good case for understanding "run" as a poetic device for "living one's life in obedience to God."[13] The prophets and wisdom writers freely used the metaphor of running or walking as a way of speaking about one's lifestyle and living in the right way. For example, Psalm 119:32 describes the godly person running in obedience to the Lord. Isaiah 40:31 depicts those who are waiting on God as being able to run and walk in the Master's service. This metaphor is also prevalent in the New Testament, where Paul uses the same language in 1 Corinthians 9:24–27 and in Philippians 3:13–14.

The demand, then, is that this "vision" not only be read, but acted on in obedience.

The subject of *"[the one] who reads it"* bears some investigation. Since the expression *qôrē'bô* can also mean to "proclaim," it would seem best to decide for the fact that God is calling on His messenger to proclaim this vision. Interestingly enough, Exodus 34:6 contains a similar command to "proclaim" the name of the Lord in connection with the delivering of the two tablets of the law.[14]

Thus the succinct statement in verses 4–5 calls for: (1) a permanent record of the vision that was to come, (2) a proclamation of the vision to all, and (3) a life that was marked by the obedience of faith. The command to preserve the vision on tablets and to proclaim it, presumably to all, suggests that the vision was intended to remain relevant for many a day and generation to come.

THE IMPLEMENTATION OF FAITH (2:3)

Like Abraham of old, who had to wait for his promised child for twenty-five years, Habakkuk is warned in this verse that God will fulfill His promises when He gets ready and not before. In other words, there may be a waiting period! The vision was for *"an appointed time"* and not one minute sooner.

The prophet (and we his readers) must remember, though, that God does not calculate time as we do. Habakkuk's original request for God's intervention had been triggered by God's perceived delay in dealing with Judah's sin (1:2; "O Lord, how long"). But the delay was not an indication that God was not going to do anything; it only meant that God would act in His appointed time. Other biblical writers would learn the same lesson:

> "The Lord is not slow in keeping his promise,
>   as some understand slowness.
> He is patient with you,
>   not wanting anyone to perish,
> but everyone to come to repentance."
>
> *2 Peter 3:9* (NIV)

Robertson reminds us of three earlier instances in which men of God had to "stand in waiting":

> *Moses* hid in the cleft of the rock while he "stood
> in waiting" for God's glory to pass by *(Exod. 33:21–3).*
>
> *Balaam* "stood in waiting" for God's revelation to come to him
> *(Num. 23:3).*
>
> *Elijah* was told to go "stand in waiting" on the mountain for God's revelation to come (*1 Kings 19:11*).[15]

Habakkuk's waiting, then, was not all that unusual.

165

God's assurance was that the vision would come and that it would not be late. The *"appointed time"* toward which this vision was moving was the time of the *"end."* By the "end" our Lord could hardly have meant merely "later on." In the Old Testament the word "end" regularly referred to some termination point (Gen. 4:3; 8:6; 41:1; Exod. 12:41; Ezk. 35:5). Especially by the time Daniel prophesied, the "appointed time" and the "end" possessed eschatological significance (Dan. 8:17, 19; 11:35, 40; 12:9). At a time when Judah was facing exile, it was quite appropriate for questions to be raised about the consummation of all things. The end would be the final stage of God's working out His redemptive purpose for all peoples.

In addition to its eschatological aspect, this vision was entirely dependable and certain; it *"will not lie."* When God predicts the future, or gives a revelation, He does not deceive or merely approximate the truth, for, as Balaam learned, "God is not a man that he should lie" (Num. 23:19).

Therefore, even though the vision *"tarries"* and lingers, God instructs Habakkuk to *"wait for it"* (v. 3b). Habakkuk would live "in the meantime" between that aspect of the vision that was *already* fulfilled and that which was *not yet* fulfilled. This inaugurated eschatology would become clearer in the New Testament in the progress of revelation (*see,* for example, Romans 8:23, "we . . . who have the firstfruits of the Spirit," and 2 Corinthians 6:2–9, "now is the day of salvation, . . . dying, yet we live on"), but hints of it were beginning to appear within the Old Testament.

In the last line of verse 3 our Lord once more emphasizes, *"it will surely come, It will not tarry."* Though this may seem to contradict the first line of verse 3 (that the vision "is yet for an appointed time"), the apparent conflict can be explained, as John Calvin suggested, in that the vision may appear to tarry from the human perspective while from the divine side its certainty is never in doubt and its fulfillment is never delayed.

Some have wondered whether the Septuagint translators did not modify this verse from its normal translation of "though it tarries, wait for it" to "If *he* tarry, wait for *him* [*autón*]." In fact, the Hebrew text may be read either way. Moreover, as O. Palmer Robertson notes, "[f]urther support for this rendering may be seen in the dependence of Hab. 2:3–4 on Gen. 15:6. Abraham's belief in God had a very specific focus in that ancient context. He believed God respecting the promise of a seed (Gen. 15:4–5), and so his faith was reckoned as righteousness. This blessing of a seed finds its full meaning only in term[s] of a salvation for God's people accomplished by a singular saving hero (cf. Gen. 3:15)."[16] The Greek translation must have been the one that the writer of Hebrews was following in Hebrews 10:37 when he affirmed that the righteousness by faith must wait for "the one who comes" (ho erchómenos). Thus, if Habakkuk had to be told to be patient and to wait, so must those who were living in stress under the new covenant. What the Greek translators did was to personify the hope of God's deliverance. This may not be what Habakkuk was told directly, but linking his revelation with the passage in Genesis 15:6—and we will shortly show that it must be so linked—shows that the Greek translators were entirely on the right track.

THE REVELATION OF FAITH (2:4–5)

The Scope of this Revelation

George J. Zemek, Jr., informs us that there are "Five separate viewpoints concerning the length of the inscription. . . ."[17] However, while some scholars restrict the placarded revelation to verse 4 alone, it seems best to link verses 4 and 5 together as a separate paragraph because the particle that begins verse 5, "indeed" in the NKJV and NIV (Hebrew, we'ap kî), is conjunctive and is best rendered here as "And furthermore," or "Moreover, in addition."[18]

The assertion that verses 4 and 5 should be read together is also supported by the argument from the context. Verse 6 refers, for the first time, to "all these" who will eventually "taunt," "ridicule" and "scorn" the Babylonians with the five-fold woes of verses 6–20; but who are "all these"? Their only possible identity is "all the nations" and "all the peoples" the Babylonian monarch has taken captive in verse 5. Thus verse 6 builds on verse 5, yet verse 5 is linked to verse 4 by a conjunction.

Accordingly, verses 4 and 5 both state the principle ("the just [righteous] shall live by [his] faith") along with the contrasting particular case of the ungodly Babylonians who stand in opposition to that principle.

The Principle of the Revelation.

In only three Hebrew words, one of the most triumphant notes of biblical revelation is sounded. The just person really lives and lives fantastically well; further, that righteous person lives solely by an active trust and faith in the God who has revealed himself in Scripture. Each of the three Hebrew words is worthy of minute examination.

a. *The Righteous or the Just.* Habakkuk emphasizes what a righteous or just person is *not* before he declares what he *is.* A righteous person is not "puffed up" or "lifted up" in his own conceits. Far from relying on himself or his personal resources to obtain or maintain his style of life, he trusts solely in the Living God. The contrast could not be sharper: the wicked rely on their might (1:11) and their savage plundering of others (1:16–17) to provide for themselves the good life, but such reliance results in a life that is crooked or curved, not *"upright"* (2:4a). Real living can only come from the hand of God, who gives daily to all who trust and believe in Him. Life apart from God—the only One who is able to grant it—proceeds to wither, shrivel, shrink, dry up, and eventually, ends.

The contrasts between the unrighteous and the righteous person are made strong by the parallelism seen in the Hebrew construction. Normally in Hebrew the verb is placed first in a sentence, but both clauses in verse 4 begin with the nouns that function as their subjects: "proud" or "the puffed up" versus "the just." In each clause, the subject is followed by an independent clause, including a pronoun suffix that refers back to the initial subject. As Robertson observes, the following parallelism develops:

a   The proud/puffed up—
   b   not [is] upright *his* soul
     c   in *him*
a   But the righteous/just
     c   by *his* faith
   b   he shall live[19]

The parallelism makes clear the startling contrast that is being set before Habakkuk in this vision. The prophet had worried about his nation's indulgence in sin only to be told that God would use a more sinful nation to punish Habakkuk's less sinful nation. When he asked how God could tolerate such an apparent aberration of His righteous ways, this vision was given to him as an answer. Clearly, says the vision, wicked persons are no match for righteous persons; nor do wicked persons "live" as God meant life to be lived. Habakkuk had asked whether less wicked Judahites should die while out-and-out cynical and arrogant blasphemers live? Now he is told: they do not live; only the righteous live.

The Hebrew word *sadîq*, sometimes rendered "the righteous," can more accurately be translated "the justified." John Skinner summarizes the forensic aspect of this term by noting that:

> [w]hat is meant is that questions of right and wrong were habitually regarded from a legal point of view as matters settled by a judge, and that this point of view is emphasized in the words derived from *sdq* ["*righteous*"]. This, indeed, is characteristic of the Hebrew conception of righteousness in all its developments: whether it be a moral quality or a religious status, it is apt to be looked on as in itself controvertible and incomplete until it has been confirmed by what is equivalent to a judicial sentence.[20]

This means that righteousness is first and foremost a religious, not an ethical, term in Israel. It "takes its origin in the forensic sphere and makes its home in the law of God."[21] Instances where this declarative or forensic aspect of the word "righteous" or "the justified" come to the fore are seen in Exodus 23:7 (where God will not "justify the wicked"), 2 Kings 10:9 (where Jehu exonerates the people from the blood guilt of the slaughter of Ahab's sons by saying, "You are righteous" or "innocent"), Job 40:8 (where God asks Job, "Would you condemn me that you may be justified? [justify yourself]?"), Job 13:18 (where Job is confident that he will be "declared righteous") and Isaiah 5:23 (where the wicked judge "makes the wicked righteous" for a bribe and turns aside the "righteousness of the righteous"). Clearly the righteous person is the one whom God has *declared* righteous and just; he is not one who has worked for such a status by ethical observances. It is God who acts as the judge that pronounces an Old Testament man or woman justified and free of all obligations to the law incurred by their sin and guilt!

b. *The Faith.* Of course the question arises as to just how a person can be declared by God to be righteous and justified before all of God's holy standards. The answer so many are ready to give on behalf of the Old Testament saint is that he or she had to remain an observant Jew by practicing all that the law commanded: "faithfulness" was the operational term in the Old Testament according to most interpreters.

But the phrase *"by his faith"* in Habakkuk 2:4b cannot be understood in that way. Exegetes have too quickly assumed that the Hebrew *ʾemûnâh* should be translated as "faithfulness" or "steadfastness." "Faith" or "trust" is the preferred rendering of *ʾemûnâh* in a number of passages in the Old Testament. This is particularly noticeable in those passages where the way of "falsehood" is being contrasted with the way of one who can be trusted to tell the truth (*see* Ps. 119:29–30; Prov. 12:17). Those who "trust" will tell the truth, for they believe that God will defend them.

But what really tips the scales in favor of translating *ʾemûnâh* as "faith" or "trust" within the context of the principle revealed in Habakkuk is the strong likelihood that God has deliberately made a connection between the revelation of this principle with the case of Abraham. Abraham "believed in Yahweh" and "he reckoned it to him for righteousness" (Gen. 15:6). Since there is no explicit antecedent for the feminine pronoun "it," "it" must refer back to the verb "he believed" (*heʾemîn*) and, thereby, to the corresponding feminine noun for the verb "believe," i.e., "belief" (*ʾemûnâh*). That, of course, was the precise word Habakkuk used in 2:4 to describe the life of the justified as contrasted to the life of the arrogant.

> The noun [in Habakkuk 2:4], like the corresponding verb of Gen. 15:6, affirms that *steadfast trust* is the way of receiving the gracious gift of life.
>
> As strange as it may seem, the Hebrew language does not abound in nouns that might be regarded as equivalent to the English term *faith*. As a matter of fact, *ʾemûnâ* would have been the most natural candidate if "faith" were the idea Habakkuk was intending to convey. Too quickly, it seems, have exegetes been ready to identify the meaning of the term (*ʾemûnâ*) exclusively with "faithfulness." But a careful consideration of the OT contexts in which the term occurs indicates that "trust" or "faith" may well explain its usage at several points.[22]

But the matter may be put even more strongly. As Donald Leggett notes, "the Old Testament does not conceive of faithfulness to God apart from trust and reliance upon God (Ps. 64:10)."[23] And added to this is the conclusion of Maria Eszenyei Szeles:

> The term *ʾemunah* is used here for "faith.". . . Its usage here is in the verbal form we know as active; deriving from it is its causative and reflexive forms, the Hiphil and the Niphal. . . . A line is to be drawn between an active and a passive feature of faith. It

is God who seizes a man and enables him (passive) to know the will of the LORD and to do it (active). . . . The verb thus brings together both the passive and the active aspects of human behavior toward God. . . .[24]

The point to remember, then, after studying all the evidence for translating ꞌemûnâh as "faith" or "trust," is best stated by H. S. Bryant: "It must be carefully maintained that neither the Old nor the New Testament separate faith from its fruits of faithfulness. The distinction between faith and faithfulness is somewhat artificial, for...in the long run they are the same thing. The Bible knows nothing of a true faith which does not hold fast its confidence to the end."[25]

c. *The Life.* The focal point of God's revelation to Habakkuk is that "the just *shall live* by his faith." It is clear from the structure of this clause in Hebrew that "by his faith" modifies "shall live" not "the just." Justified persons receive the gift of life by faith.

The life referred to here is primarily our day-to-day living. In chapter 3 of Habakkuk we shall see Habakkuk's joy and deep sense of peace even as he contemplated the imminent invasion of his nation by the ruthless Babylonians. Even as he faced certain national turbulence and terror, the joy in the Lord was as real to Habakkuk as it was for the apostle Paul, who wrote from prison, "Rejoice in the Lord always. Again I will say rejoice!" (Phil. 4:4).

Since the vision was to occur at "an appointed time," and spoke of "the end," "life" connotes eternal life as well. God is the sole source of eternal life as He is of "real" day-to-day living. How could anyone expect to share eternity with the Eternal God if they had not come to believe in Him personally and to be declared justified by Him?

The Contrast to this Principle

In contrast to the righteous and justified stand the proud. Verse 4a introduced the "proud," "puffed up," "bloated," and "tumorous" (ꞌuppelâ).[26] It is clear from the context that these arrogant ones are the Babylonians (1:7, 10–11).

The Babylonians violated every principle that faith set forth. They sought their own selfish ends and pridefully assured themselves that they could claim for themselves anything they wanted. One thing they could not have, however, was the benefit of God's abundant life. This is because they were "not upright." While this text refers primarily to God's imminent judgment on earth of the prideful Babylonians, it also hints at what is in store for the Babylonians in the final judgment.

Verse 5 continues to describe these puffed up, haughty persons who were so presumptuous in their grandiose concepts of themselves and their achievements. Now, deceived by the powers of wine, they were further blinded as to the real condition of their estates. To fully appreciate the deceptive powers of wine, one need only recall that drunkenness was responsible for the downfall of the Babylonian empire. Daniel 5 records how, on the night the empire fell, King Belshazzer sent for the gold and silver goblets that Nebuchadnezzar had taken from the Temple in Jerusalem and offered toasts to the gods of Babylon from these sacred goblets. It was then that the handwriting appeared on the wall and the sudden end to the Babylonian's arrogance came.

It is little wonder, then, that verse 5 says *he enlarges his desire as hell, and he is like death, and cannot be satisfied, He gathers to himself all nations and heaps up for himself all peoples.* Drunkenness engenders the same kind of boundless pride that was so characteristic of the spirit of this people. Like drunks, the Babylonians boasted of fantastic exploits. Their hubris was as boundless as death. Meanwhile, their lust for more kept growing until they had taken captive as many nations and peoples of the earth as possible. And all of this was for what? What shall man exchange his soul for? The whole world? In startling contrast to the wretched lives of the Babylonians, God offers these words, to serve as a beaconlight through the ages: "But the just shall live by his faith."

The Vindication of Faith (2:6–20)

God now pronounces that a five-fold woe will be taken up by the captured nations and peoples referred to in verse 5 against the Babylonian oppressors. The woe describes what will happen to the proud, arrogant, haughty, and boastful who reject God's principle of "the just shall live by faith." (Indeed, Israel herself had been warned that if she did not keep the commandments of God, she too would become the object of taunts among the nations [Deut. 28:37; 1 Kings 9:7].)

Those who question whether the Sovereign God would make use of such undignified taunting must remember that many of the righteous, such as Habakkuk, had cried out for a public vindication of God's name and righteousness. Could wrong forever remain on the throne and truth on the scaffold? The Babylonians' shame for their evil deeds must be equal in intensity to the injustice suffered by good men and women at the hands of the Babylonians—lest the good men and women begin to weary of waiting for vindication. The wealth the Babylonians accumulated by unjust means must be relinquished.

God condemns each of the excesses of Babylon in turn in the five woes that follow.

Inordinate Greed (2:6–8)

When a nation or people specializes in greed, robbery, and vandalism—as a means of acquiring whatever their hearts desire—they had better look out for the interest God will take from them when He rectifies the matter. After "putting the bite" on so many nations for so long, suddenly "the bite" will be put on them. (The words *"creditors"* and *"debtors"* derive from the Hebrew verb meaning "to bite.")

A Hunger to Dominate (2:9–11)

Like greed in the first woe, covetousness is blameworthy in the second woe. So power-hungry were the Babylonian conquerors that they stopped at nothing in order to exert their dominance and authority over other nations. In setting their own *"nest"* (v. 9) high out of reach like the eagle-nation they pretended to be, the Babylonian monarchs supposed they would be exempt from the ravages of conquest suffered by the rulers they had attacked. A high roost did not protect the Edomite king (Obad. 4) any better than it would this monarch. The very stones with which the Babylonian kings had built up their dynasty (*"house"*) would serve as plaintiffs against the Kings, witnessing against them in support of a verdict of "guilty."

Atrocities (2:12–14)

Nebuchadnezzar implemented his policy of beautifying Babylon at the expense of the blood, sweat, tears, and lives of his subjugated peoples. Such ruthlessness, whether at the hands of Hitler, Saddam Hussein, Idi Amin, Mao Tsi Tung or any other potentate, will necessarily be judged by God. The Lord had decreed judgment on Babylon, as recorded by Jeremiah (Jer. 51:58).

This dark discussion of Babylon's transgressions is relieved by a sudden ray of light. The oppressing, avaricious conquerors will be replaced by the knowledge of God that will fill the earth like the waters fill the seas. This slightly altered quotation of Isaiah 11:9 elevated Habakkuk's prophecy from a single reference of the defeat of the Babylonians to a new level of God's eschatological triumph over all evil.[27] God's triumph over all atrocities, ruthlessness, and unwarranted bloodshed would serve as His answer to all the prayers of those who pleaded with the Savior, "How long, O Lord?" and "Why?"

Debauchery (2:15–17)

When the Babylonians invaded a country, they stripped it of everything of value. They denuded its forests, pilfered the adornments from its buildings and desolated its land.

The Babylonians engaged in other forms of debauchery as well; they made their neighbors drink so they could indulge their prurient interests by gazing shamelessly on their neighbors' nakedness. Often in the Bible the sin of drunkenness is associated with the sin of sexual impurity and degradation of the body. Did not Noah become drunk on the night his son Ham made light of his father's naked condition? (Gen. 9:21). Did not Lot's daughters make him drunk before they committed incest with him? (Gen. 19:32–35).

God will, figuratively, make Babylon drink out of the cup of His wrath, not an actual drink like the Babylonians had given to others, but the judgment that God hands down. God held Babylon responsible not only for the violence done to Judah (1:9), but for the violence done to other nations, such as Lebanon (2:17). There are not two systems of morality and ethics in the world, one for the believing community and another for pagans; God requires justice, righteousness, and holiness of all nations regardless of their relationship to Him.

Idolatry (2:18–20)

People become like the things that they deeply admire and worship. The arrogant Babylonians "carved" and "cast" "worthless things" as their deities. But the deities were without life or breath, and could not offer guidance or direction for the future: so it was that the people likewise became cheap, valueless and worthless in their own eyes.

Once again, Habakkuk shines a contrasting scene across all this darkness by reminding us that "the LORD [was] in His holy temple." Consequently, "Let all the earth keep silence before Him."

CONCLUSION

It is not always possible to say where or when God will intervene and demonstrate that He is still Lord of history. But it is possible for all who are justified by faith to live—and that does not mean merely to "tough-it-out." Surely we see the judgments of God in fallen nations: a Saddam Hussein silenced in his bunker far beneath the surface of the earth, a Hitler ending his life in his bunker, a Mussolini strung up by his feet.

But God still warns all tyrants, dictators, presidents, and any who have authority over people to mark their step, for the five-fold woes are just samples of what awaits those who are not only bellicose in their threatenings against others, but also resistant to God's principle of life: trusting the only name that is above every other name for salvation (Acts 4:12). Just people live because they have been declared justified in that they have put their trust and faith in Him and Him alone. Is it any wonder that this theme became the rallying cry for the Reformation? May it be the rallying cry for a revived church once again as some continue to cry out "How Long, O Lord?" But God is in His heaven and He will mark iniquity. He will act decisively. And He will declare justified as many as trust in Him as Abraham did long ago and as Habakkuk urges in our passage.

CHAPTER THREE

Explaining God's Presence in History

Habakkuk 3:3–15

3:3 God came from Teman,
The Holy One from Mount Paran.   Selah
His glory covered the heavens,
And the earth was full of His praise.

4 His brightness was like the light;
He had rays flashing from His hand,
And there His power was hidden.

5 Before Him went pestilence,
And fever followed at His feet.

6 He stood and measured the earth;
He looked and startled the nations.
And the everlasting mountains were scattered,
The perpetual hills bowed.
  His ways are everlasting.

7 I saw the tents of Cushan in affliction;
The curtains of the land of Midian trembled.

8 O LORD, were You displeased with the rivers,
Was Your anger against the rivers,
Was Your wrath against the sea,
That You rode on Your horses,
Your chariots of salvation?

9 Your bow was made quite ready;
Oaths were sworn over Your arrows.   Selah
You divided the earth with rivers.

10 The mountains saw You and trembled;
The overflowing of the water passed by.
The deep uttered its voice,

And lifted its hands on high.
11 The sun and moon stood still
       in their habitation;
    At the light of Your arrows they went,
    At the shining of Your glittering spear.
12 You marched through the land in indignation;
    You trampled the nations in anger.
13 You went forth for the salvation of
       Your people,
    For salvation with Your Anointed.
    You struck the head from the house of
       the wicked,
    By laying bare from foundation to neck.   Selah
14 You thrust through with his own arrows
    The head of his villages.
    They came out like a whirlwind to scatter me;
    Their rejoicing was like feasting on the
       poor in secret.
15 You walked through the sea with Your horses,
    Through the heap of great waters.

Habakkuk 3:3–15

Habakkuk 3:3–15 is an awe-inspiring passage describing the majestic appearance of God in the midst of a stupendous storm and of earth-shattering disturbances in heaven and earth. George Adam Smith titled it "the Great Theophany."[28] And so it is, for now we will view the promise God made in Habakkuk 2:3 —"[the vision would] surely come, it will not tarry." So majestic is its theme and subject matter that the chapter is at once a prayer and a hymn of victory as 3:1 and 3:19d clearly indicate.

Habakkuk was given a picture of God's victory extending over the whole earth and of His kingdom being established over all. Elizabeth Achtemeier graphically depicts what was happening here:

Like Moses at the top of Mount Pisgah looking over into the promised land (Deut. 34:1–4), like Jeremiah inheriting a piece of property as a first fruit of the restoration (Jer. 32), like Christians being offered a foretaste of the new wine of the messianic banquet when they sit at the Lord's table (Mark 14:25 par.), or like Peter, James, and John being given that vision of the resurrected Lord on the Mount of Transfiguration (Mark 9:2–8), Habakkuk is

177

granted a foresight of God's purpose accomplished (3:3-15). The passage forms the most extensive and elaborate theophany to be found in the Old Testament.[29]

The pericope is best understood as composed of two major parts. Verse 3:3-7 is a theophany that proclaims God's past works, especially those done in connection with the Exodus. In 3:8-15 imagery of the Lord's conflicts and the Lord as a warrior predominate. The coming of the Lord is the dominant theme of both parts. In the second part Yahweh is addressed directly using the second person pronoun whereas in the first part Yahweh is spoken of in the third person. The historical actions of the Living God unfold in this manner:

    A.   God's Past Actions Proclaim His Coming   3:3-7
         1. The Theophany at Sinai   3:3a
         2. The Theophany in All Creation   3:3b-4
         3. The Theophany in the Plagues of Egypt   3:5
         4. The Theophany Before the Nations   3:6
         5. The Theophany in the Days of Othniel and Gideon   3:7
    B.   God's Future Actions Foretell His Coming   3:8-15.

GOD'S PAST ACTIONS PROCLAIM HIS COMING (3:3-7)

The prophet, turned psalmist and liturgist, looks back now over the mighty acts that have been performed for Israel at the Exodus and at Mount Sinai. Some significant religious scholars of the past, such as St. Augustine, have spiritualized every clause into a description of either the first or second coming.[30] Others, like John Calvin, viewed them as a picture of God's guidance of Israel from the time of the Egyptian plagues to the days of Joshua and Gideon. Calvin is more nearly correct, but Augustine's sensitivities were not altogether wrong.

The Theophany at Sinai (3:3a)

This text is either extremely archaic in its original form, or was deliberately cast in language reminiscent of an ancient usage. For example, the preferred word in this text for "God" is "Eloah" (ʾelôah), an ancient poetic form for the name of God. Eloah occurs forty-one times in the Book of Job and only sixteen times in the rest of the Old Testament (including one time in Habakkuk 1:11). The prophet is certainly comfortable with this word. He uses it in the third chapter through verse 8, where he begins to address his Lord as "Yahweh."

In verse 3 God is also called the *"Holy One,"* as He was in 1:12. He is the "Holy One" who comes "from Mount Paran." Associating the "Holy One" with Mount Paran is more than just coincidental. Deuteronomy 33:2 indicates that Mount Paran is another name for Mount Sinai (cf. Gen 21:21; 1 Kings 11:18). Thus the reference is to the giving of the Law where the aspect of God's nature that was emphasized was His holiness. At Sinai, Israel was told that she had to be holy because the Lord her God was holy (Lev. 11:44–45; 19:2). This meant that the nation had to be separate and distinct from all that was around it (Lev. 20:26). Here, then, Habakkuk has joined the quest for righteousness and holiness that had originally prompted his prayer to God in 1:2–4 with this reminder that God still desired for His people personal and national purity and sanctity. Holiness was still the order of the day then, as it is in our own day, for without holiness no one shall see God (Heb. 12:14).

The coming of God is traced from Teman and Paran. Teman is generally identified as a site in Edom or Seir territory (Obad. 9; Amos 1:12; Jer. 49:7). If Paran is Sinai, as we have pointed out above, then this hymn traces the steps over which God led Israel as she journeyed to take possession of the land of Canaan. We move from Sinai to Edom as Israel is poised to enter the Promised Land. Through this hymn we relive the far-reaching effects of the glory of God in times past.

The Theophany in all Creation (3:3b–4)

The prophet points to the boundless glory of God as it covers the heavens and the earth. He does not mean the glory that is reflected in the created order, as Psalm 19:1 does. Rather, he means the glory that has come as a result of God's appearances to His people throughout history. Those episodic points are enough to light up all of creation with His glory. For when He acted, as He did at the Exodus, the heavens and the earth were His main spectators, even if mortals were less appreciative of the magnitude of what they were witnessing.

Similar to the great theophany that Isaiah the prophet witnessed as he saw the heavenly temple (Isa. 6), wherein the glory of the LORD was being set forth in poignant and startling tones, here Habakkuk exalts God's great historic interventions. "Rays" or "horns" (v. 4b) proceeded from His hands, continues the prophet. But what can be the source of that strange allusion? The only possible source is the description given of Moses as he descended from Mount Sinai. That is the only other place in Scripture where *qeren*, "horn," (rays) is used in this manner. In Exodus 34:29–30, 35, Moses was unaware that his face "was radiant," i.e., literally, that it was "horned," or had "two horns." The association is made complete by the more detailed description in Deuteronomy 33:2. Moses declared: "The LORD came from Sinai and *dawned on* them from Seir; He shone forth from Mount Paran. And He came with ten thousands of saints. From his right hand [went] a fiery law for them."[31]

The Theophany in the Plagues of Egypt (3:5)

Now God is depicted as the King who has "pestilence" as His herald and *fever* coming after Him. The words translated "pestilence" (*rešep*) and *"fever"* (*deber*) were familiar words in the Canaanite repetoire, for both were names of deities they worshipped. Habakkuk probably is using them here as personifications, thereby demonstrating God's power over all the opposing forces just as he rescued Israel from Pharaoh in the Exodus.

God, as He reveals Himself in this theophany, was fully capable of handling all that resisted Him. The allusions to the pestilence and fever (plague) should not have surprised Judah, for she had been warned in the curses announced in the Law that God would send them in answer to her sin (Lev. 26:25; Deut. 28:21–22). The Hebrew word translated "pestilence" here in some renderings is referred to as God's fiery arrows in Deuteronomy 32:24 and as bolts of lightning in Psalms 78:48. The coming of the Lord was a coming in judgment just as much as it was a coming in salvation.

The Theophany Before the Nations (3:6)

Even the nations were frightened senseless by the manifestation of the approach of the Lord. His presence was so real and so powerful that He dominated the entire scene. The whole cosmos went into convulsions at the approach of the Lord who made it. For here now was the only One who was and is eternal; the mountains and the age-old hills collapsed in deference to His person and power.

What an amazing scene: God's inanimate creation seems to be more immediately responsive to His coming and presence than His rational creation made in His image! The disruptions in nature are the typical effects of the march of the divine warrior into battle. It is little wonder that the nations tremble before Him. Had they not done so at the Exodus (Exod. 15:14)? And they would do so again and again until the final glorious appearing of our Lord Jesus Christ (Titus 2:13).

The Theophany in the Days of Othniel and Gideon (3:7)

The prophet's hymn of joy moves from the stunned effect the appearance of God had on the nations to Israel's response to His coming on their behalf on two separate occasions.

The word *"Cushan"* could be a longer form of the nation Cush, "Ethiopia," or it could refer to a bedouin tribe in the Sinai peninsula. Indeed, Moses' wife from Midian, in the Arabian peninsula, is called a Cushite in Numbers 12:1 (NIV).

But it makes more sense that the name Cushan is the shortened form of the name "Cushan-Rishathaim" referred to in Judges 3:8–11. There it is said that Cushan was the first oppressor to rise up against Israel after she entered the Promised Land. God raised up the judge Othniel to deliver Israel from Cushan's oppression. Israel's problem in Judges parallels the very problem that Habakkuk was raising: the use of a foreign, godless, power to chastise Israel. Israel could be encouraged now by the recollection that the Lord had provided her relief from the ancient oppression of Cushan. He *"saw"* them; surely God would look now on the imminent affliction which His people must once again bear because of their sins. The parallel problems concerning Israel in Judges and Habakkuk and the encouragement provided to Israel here as she is reminded of God's prior intervention on her behalf at Cushan-Rishathaim underscore the appropriateness of identifying Cushan as the Cushan of Judges 3:8–11.

The *"curtains of the land of Midian"* is an allusion to the Midianites who invaded the land of Israel during the days of Gideon. Another uncertain servant of God—Gideon on this occasion—had to be reassured by overhearing a Midianite recounting a dream about a barley loaf (interpreted as Gideon and his troops) tumbling into the camp and striking the tents of Midian so that they collapsed (Judg. 7:13). This allusion underscores the point that any invading oppressor used by God against Judah—like the Midianites in Gideon's days—would itself be vulnerable. Any pain or grief such an oppressor caused would be as transitory as they were in Gideon's days.

By now it is clear that Habakkuk has reconciled himself to the fact that the Babylonians will be used by God to punish Judah for her sin. In the face of this terrifying prospect, however, Habakkuk has been given the vision that "the just shall live by his faith." This vision provided Habakkuk with a hope anchored in the Lord and His work. Moreover, the past experiences of God's people (at the Exodus and under the judges Othniel and Gideon) indicated that the God who would come in judgment would also come in deliverance and salvation. He had done so time and again in the past. Robertson beautifully concludes: "The structures of all oppressive kingdoms would quake and come *under distress*. But [Habakkuk] had citizenship in a kingdom that could not be shaken (cf. Heb. 10:29–30)."[32]

GOD'S FUTURE ACTIONS FORETELL HIS COMING (3:8–15)

The text turns from the third person used in verses 3–7 to the second person used in verses 8–15. Our psalmist now asks himself several rhetorical questions: *"O LORD were You displeased* [merely] *with the rivers? Was Your anger* [simply directed] *against the rivers? Was Your wrath* [solely] *against the sea, that You rode on Your horses, Your chariots of salvation?"* The ancient deeds of the rebuke of the Red Sea and the Jordan River (Josh. 4:23; Ps. 114:3b, 5b), and the coming of God in connection with the thunder storm (Ps. 29:3), especially at Sinai, serve here as models of what God will do in answer to Habakkuk's fears and in answer to all who wish to know what God will do as He brings all of history to a climax.

Verse 8 is filled with ancient Canaanite phraseology, used for its poetry, metaphors and allusions, without giving tacit approval to the pagan theology contained in the Ugaritic texts. Ugarit featured "Judge River," even "Prince Sea," as the one against whom Baal fought. Even the phrase "Rider of the Clouds" is one of Baal's favorite epithets. But that culture and pagan theology, which had thrived in

1200 B.C., had long since expired by the late 600s B.C. when Habakkuk was writing. Habakkuk found the terms most suitable for depicting the great historical interventions of God when He smote the Red Sea, the Jordan River, and the Kishon (Exod. 13:17–14:31; Josh. 3:13–17; 4:21–24). Whether this text also envisages a future divine smiting of the Euphrates River (Rev. 16:3–4) in God's wrath cannot be stated for certain. But it would not be inconsistent with God's character and past actions. If that thought brought comfort to the prophet as he faced a time of grief, is it not fair for us also to take comfort in the same kind of hope when we face difficult times?

In verse 9 God, using the thunder clouds as His personal chariotry, gets His arsenal of a *"bow"* and *"arrows."* This verse has been translated in over one hundred different ways owing mainly to the fact that it is in the form of poetry; even more disconcerting, each of the three Hebrew words in the second clause has more than one possible meaning. We believe the best translation is: "battle rods [arrows] are sworn by oath."[33] The "oath" is the oath of the covenant as recorded in Deuteronomy 32:40–43, where the Lord pledges by lifting up His hand to heaven that His sword and arrows would avenge the blood of His servants as they consumed His enemies. God had dramatically intervened at the critical hour on previous occasions, as He would in Habakkuk's day—and as He will in the days to come until all His enemies have been dealt with.

The warrior described in this text certainly is no ordinary soldier. His weapons and the scope of His battle are cosmic. No mortal or earthly power will be able to withstand His assaults.

As though in sheer terror, the mountains cringed and the torrents of water crashed as their waves acknowledged the presence of the divine warrior (v. 10). Even the *"deep"* (a reference to the "seas," *tehôm*) raised up its waves as though exalting over the Lord's appearance. There is no basis to argue that *tehôm* alludes to a myth about God struggling with a sea monster, for this is the same "deeps" that covered Pharaoh and his army in the Red Sea (Exod. 15:5). Indeed, *tehôm* is used to refer to a body of water in Ugaritic texts from Canaan dating from the twelfth to fourteenth century B.C. The usual comment by modern critical scholars that see some connection with the Babylonian goddess Tiamat, who was cut in two to form the heavens and earth, is completely absent here (and probably is without foundation in all of biblical studies).[34]

A dramatic reminder of how totally different a theophany is from the normal course of events can be seen in verses 11–12. An even greater response from nature than that described in verses 9–10 is the dramatic incident that took place one day when, in response to Joshua's prayer, the sun and moon were controlled to give relief to Joshua's weary army. At God's command the sun failed to appear for about a whole day (Josh. 10:12–14).

Such awesome descriptions of God's power over nature find close parallels with Psalm 77:16–20(NIV)

> The waters saw you, O God,
>   the waters saw you writhed;
>   the very depths were convulsed.
> The clouds poured down water,
>   the skies resounded with thunder;
>   your arrows flashed back and forth.
> Your thunder was heard in the whirlwind,
>   your lightning lit up the world;
>   the earth trembled and quaked.
> Your path led through the sea,
>   your way through the mighty waters,
>   though your footprints were not seen.
> You led your people like a flock
>   by the hand of Moses and Aaron.

Other similar Psalms are:

> Our God comes and will not be silent;
>   a fire devours before him,
>   and around him a tempest rages.
>   *Psalm 50:3* (NIV)
> When you went out before your people, O God,
>   When you marched through the wasteland, Selah
> The earth shook,
>   the heavens poured down rain,
> Before God, the One of Sinai,
>   before God, the God of Israel.
>   *Psalm 68:7–8* (NIV)
> Sing to God, O kingdoms of the earth,
>   sing praise to the LORD, Selah
> to him who rides the ancient skies above,
>   who thunders with mighty voice.
>   *Psalm 68:32–33* (NIV)

Finally the answer comes to the rhetorical questions asked in verse 8. No, God was not angry with the rivers or the sea, says verse 12. His anger is directed towards the wickedness of the nations of the earth. Try as the nations might, they could not throw off the sovereignty of God's reign over them. God would "thrash" the nations like Gideon thrashed the princes of Zebah and Zalmunna (Judg. 8:16). Then would Habakkuk's persistent question about God's use of a more wicked people to punish Judah finally be answered. All nations would be thrashed eventually under the fair, but certain, judgment of God.

But God would certainly deliver His people (v. 13). It is at this point in the text that the term *"Your anointed"* is suddenly introduced. To whom does it refer? The term *"your anointed [one]*," of course, means the "Messiah," or, in Greek, "Christ." Is this a promise of the Messiah's intervention? We think it is, for while the term customarily pointed to the anointing of a king or priest, it was not unknown as a prediction of the Promised One who was to come.[35]

And when Messiah comes, He will *"[strike] the head from the house of the wicked."* This text could be an allusion to the person God would specially anoint to punish the wicked nation. In fact, Cyrus the Persian had been so designated and called by Isaiah, God's "anointed" (Isa 45:1). But Cyrus is only a small example of what God will do in the days to come.

If this vision was for the "end" and "an appointed time" (Hab. 2:3), then verses 14–15 may indeed depict God's eschatological triumph over all His enemies. If it appears at that moment in history that there is no one on the scene who can take on the powers that confront righteousness, look again to God's coming in full splendor and power in the Last Day. He will allow the enemy to set his own trap. What he will devise for others will boomerang. Having dug a pit for others, he will promptly fall into it himself (Ps. 7:16). The destruction of the godless will be as severe and swift as the attack of a foreign nation.

But just as God had acted at the Red Sea, the Jordan River, on Joshua's long day, and when Othniel and Gideon were beseiged, so He would act in His great day of salvation. The Lord would go forth across the sea on His horses, churning up the waters once more as He had in that celebrated deliverance of Israel from Egypt. Once again, these examples of theophany could become benchmarks of all that is hoped for in His future coming in glory.

CONCLUSION

In James Joyce's *Ulysses*, his young hero represents the modern spirit of many. "History," Stephen said, "is a nightmare from which I am trying to awake." Henry Ford had a more down-to-earth way of putting the same thing: "History is bunk." These are, hopefully, the last cries of the Enlightenment, which viewed history as the worthless fabric of superstition and error.

Christians cannot afford to by-pass such knowledge of the past, for a nation or a society without a memory is not only a society devoid of a past, but a society with a detached present and no direction for the future.

The importance of acknowledging that the events recorded in the Bible actually happened is poignantly demonstrated in D. Martyn Lloyd-Jones's stern warning:

> If God did not actually do the things recorded in the Old Testament for Israel, then the whole Bible may be just a piece of psychology meant to keep me happy. The Bible, however, plainly shows that my comfort and consolation lie in facts—the fact that God has done certain things and that they have literally happened. The God in whom I believe is the God who could and *did* divide the Red Sea and the river Jordan. In reminding himself and us of these things, Habakkuk is not just comforting himself by playing with ideas; he is speaking of the things that God has *actually done*. The Christian faith is solidly based upon facts, not ideas. And if the facts recorded in the Bible are not true, then I have no hope and no comfort. For we are not saved by ideas; but by facts, by events.[36]

The theophany of this section of Habakkuk's message has brought us full circle from the prophet's first complaint at the beginning of this book. Now Yahweh stands face to face with the enemy, the "proud"; they were at the opposite end of the spectrum from the justified by faith! This great power, and, apparently, all haughty nations that take Babylon's path, will suffer smashing defeat and God's victorious conclusion. The victory over the wicked is described in a memorable picture. God will strike the head from the house of the wicked (v. 13). How reminiscent of Genesis 3:15 this is! The enemy may nip the heel of the coming Seed of the woman, but God will crush the head of Satan himself. Other scholars, however, link this victory with the act of Jael in the Song of Deborah (Judg. 5:24–27).

The prophet's vision is rooted in the historic past of Israel. Each of the themes Habakkuk chooses for his hymn-prayer comes from decisive chapters in the history of salvation. Thus the basic elements of theophany are woven together with remembrances of God's past acts, which serve to encourage Judah in desperate moments to keep on believing. There are elements from the Song of Deborah (Judg. 5), the song of Moses and Miriam (Exod. 15, Deut. 32), the wilderness wanderings (Exod. 16–17, Num. 21–25) and the motifs of several historical Psalms (Ps. 68, 95, 107, 136). All are prayers of praise and thanksgiving to God—responses to His bounteous acts of grace. Moreover, in this way the people not only called to mind with deep gratitude what God had done, but they expressed in a most vivid way that God is the One who truly lives. He is the sovereign Lord of history as well. Nothing takes place without His knowing it. History is not bunk; it is "His-story," and He will write its ending as well as its mission statement.

CHAPTER FOUR

Rejoicing In Tribulation

Habakkuk 3:1–2, 16–19

3:1 A prayer of Habakkuk the prophet,
    on Shigionoth.
  2 O LORD, I have heard your speech
    and was afraid;
    O LORD, revive Your work
    in the midst of the years!
    In the midst of the years make it known;
    In wrath remember mercy.
 16 When I heard, my body trembled;
    My lips quivered at the voice;
    Rottenness entered my bones;
    And I trembled in myself,
    That I might rest in the day of trouble.
    When he comes up to the people,
    He will invade them with his troops.
 17 Though the fig tree may not blossom,
    Nor fruit be on the vines;
    Though the labor of the olive may fail,
    And the fields yield no food;
    Though the flock may be cut off from the fold,
    And there be no herd in the stalls—
 18 Yet I will rejoice in the LORD,
    I will joy in the God of my salvation.
 19 The LORD God is my strength;
    He will make my feet like deer's feet,
    And He will make me walk on my high hills.
To the Chief Musician. With my stringed instruments.
Habakkuk 3:1–2, 16–19

Habakkuk's response to God's revelation of answers to the probing questions he had set before his Lord was to worship God with an exalted combination prayer and hymn. It was the prophet's "amen" to what he had been told, for now he could say, in effect, "Yes, Lord, do all those deeds that you have declared you would do." He had reoriented his thinking and at the center and pinnacle of all his thoughts stood the Living God.

The shift in this chapter from the dialogue format that characterized the first two chapters is highly noticeable. First of all, the chapter is called a "prayer." It is also said to be "on the *shigionoth*," a rare term that occurs in the Bible only here and in the singular form as a title for Psalm 7; its meaning it still unknown. Three times the poetic term "selah" appears (vv. 3, 9, 13). Its meaning too is still unknown, but undoubtedly it is some type of liturgical or musical instruction. The whole hymn and prayer must have been set to music, for verse 19 directs that it is to be played *"with my stringed instruments"* (presumably harps) and it is to be under the leadership of *"the Chief Musician,"* a notation that figures in fifty-five Psalm headings.

Habakkuk 3, therefore, has placed us in the framework of worship. How important it is for us to realize that the hard-probing questions of chapters 1 and 2 had not ended with fatalism, skepticism, or cynicism. The book of Habakkuk peaks with worship of the Living God and His deeds. Ending in worship was more than enough for the struggling heart and soul of the prophet. The sequence is much like that of Psalm 73. There the psalmist struggled with the problem of the prosperity of the wicked. So inflamed was he with the severity of the problem that he had almost gone over the jagged edge of orthodoxy. But then came the wonderful revelation of God Himself as the psalmist went into the house of God to worship. Psalm 73:16–17 records one of those mighty transitions in Scripture, as the psalmist declares, "When I tried to understand all this, it was oppressive to me *till* I entered the sanctuary of God; then I understood their final destiny" (NIV) (italics ours). So it was here.

When God becomes the all-consuming reality, our problems begin to take their proper perspective in relation to His greatness and ability to handle them. Thus Habakkuk could say, *"O LORD, I have heard your speech and was afraid"* (3:2a).

Although some scholars have denied that this chapter comes from the hand of the prophet Habakkuk, since it is not included in the commentary on Habakkuk found in the Dead Sea Scrolls, there are no compelling reasons why one should come to that conclusion. In fact, the Qumran scribes may have omitted chapter 3 from their commentary simply because that chapter did not suit their interests at the time.[37]

There is another reason to view chapter 3 as a continuation of the prophet's writings in chapters 1 and 2. Habakkuk 3 is the capstone to the book of Habakkuk in that it reveals how faith triumphs over the perplexities of sin, tyranny and destruction. It gives a fitting conclusion to a book that otherwise would be unresolved.

Let us, therefore, be led in the worship of our majestic Lord by Habakkuk's response to what he had heard. There are at least four responses that we can render in a similar act of worship to that of the prophet who has been our forerunner:

A.   Let Us Begin Our Worship in Adoration   3:2a
B.   Let Us Focus Our Worship on the Kingdom of God   3:2b
C.   Let Us Confess Our Fears in Our Worship   3:16
D.   Let Us Celebrate The Joy of the Lord in Our Worship   3:17–19

LET US BEGIN OUR WORSHIP IN ADORATION (3:2A)

Habakkuk now responds to the vision that was granted (2:4–5) and its corollaries (2:6–20). What a fantastic list of "deeds" that God has done or will shortly do. Whereas in 1:12–17 the prophet had brashly contested the first announcement of God's works, on hearing the whole case made by God, and especially being confronted by the reality of who and what He is, the prophet is awed and humbled before the King of kings and Lord of lords.

Neither contemplation nor worship of the Living God can take place while mortals are still proudly projecting themselves as equals or advisers to the Lord of the universe. So it is in tones of self-humility that the prophet confesses, *"O LORD, I have heard your speech and was afraid"* (3:2a). No longer is there any request that God should withdraw His threatened judgment or carry out His purposes in some other manner. Rather, there is a recognition that God is perfectly free to do what He wants to do and that in so doing He is absolutely in the right. Gone are all the attempts to defend his own nation vis-á-vis any pagan nation against which it might be compared.

How did Habakkuk arrive at this position after he had fought so hard for a different one? Apparently he changed the focus of his thinking. Instead of being centered on himself, his people, his nation, and his culture, he took one steady long look at God. Says Martyn Lloyd-Jones, "Our troubles can nearly all be traced to our persistence in looking at the immediate problems themselves, instead of looking at them in the light of God."[38] That is what Habakkuk learned as well.

Unfortunately, humility is a rare quality to find even in the present-day people of God. We complain about national and local tragedies and seldom, if ever, reflect quietly on whether it just might be possible that God is trying to say something to us through all these events. Again Lloyd-Jones is on the mark when he remarks:

> Herein lies the crux of the situation at the present time. Do we yet see our need of humiliation? Do we see it as members of the Christian Church? Do we see it as citizens of the nation? We are confronted by a world situation in which we do not know what is going to happen. Is there to be another war? If our attitude is still one of 'Why does God allow this?', 'What have we done to deserve this?', we have manifestly not learned the lesson Habakkuk learned. We did not truly humble ourselves in the last war or in the first world war. We failed to recognize that the two wars were the inevitable consequence of the godlessness that had been rampant for nearly a hundred years, all because of the pride and arrogance of man. Has the Christian Church realized that her present condition, and much of her suffering, may be the chastisement of the Lord for the infidelity and apostasy into which the Church herself has frequently fallen? For a century the Church, speaking generally, has been denying the supernatural and the miraculous, questioning the very deity of Christ and exalting philosophy over revelation. Is the Church therefore in a position to complain if she is having a hard time now? Has she humbled herself in sackcloth and ashes? Has she acknowledged and confessed her sin? . . . Has the world as a whole any right to complain? In spite of the judgments of God upon us, has there been a humbling? Is there a spirit of repentance? [39]

But Habakkuk did more than stand beneath the High Lord of the universe in humble contrition: he stood in adoration and awe for His person and work. Similarly, the same monarch who would conquer Jerusalem—the one Habakkuk dreaded when he heard that God would use the Babylonians against Judah—would eventually concede the greatness of God. After Nebuchadnezzar had gone mad and lived like an animal for seven years, he had his senses restored to him and he glorified God. Daniel 4:34–35 notes:

> At the end of that time, I Nebuchadnezzar, raised my eyes toward heaven, and my sanity was restored. Then I praised the Most High; I honored and glorified him who lives forever [because:] His dominion is an eternal dominion; his kingdom endures from generation to generation. All the peoples of the earth are regarded as nothing. He does as he pleases with the powers of heaven and the peoples of the earth. No one can hold back his hand or say to him: "What have you done?" (NIV)

Much later in history, it was King Louis XIV's turn to confess. This French monarch wanted to be known as the greatest king ever. Thus he requested that at his funeral in the great cathedral of Notre Dame all would be darkened except the one candle on his casket displayed at the front of the sanctuary. But when the great court preacher Masillon got up to give the funeral oration, he walked over to the casket and snuffed out the light. With that he commenced his message as he twice intoned the words: "Only God is great! Only God is great." And that truth is what every monarch, president, dictator, governor, pastor and parishoner must also come to realize and to live by. Only God is great. There is absolutely no one who competes with Him or is His equal. So important is this theme of the incomparability of God that Isaiah devotes a whole chapter to it (Isaiah 40). Repeatedly he asks, "To whom or to what shall we liken God?" What set of circumstances? What combination of world powers? What in all of creation will be equal to or exceed the knowledge, wisdom, power, grace and care of our loving heavenly Father? Of course the answer is: there is nothing; there is no one that compares with Him.

We must learn to picture God as seated in His holy temple above the world scene with total understanding of what is going on and with total ability to steer the world in the strategic direction for His purposes to be fulfilled and for righteousness to be vindicated.

Let Us Focus Our Worship on the Kingdom of God (3:2b)

Instead of praying selfishly that God might prosper his own work or vindicate his nation, Habakkuk now prays, *"Revive Your work in the midst of the years!"* (3:2b). Gone is the selfish desire to put himself, his people and his plans at the top. His concern now is with the kingdom of God.

Habakkuk prays: *"revive Your work in the midst of the years! In the midst of the years make it known."* The renewal that the prophet calls for is not primarily a spiritual renewal and revival, but a reviving of God's purpose and program. The works the prophet called for belonged to God's strange work of judgment (Isa. 28:21), but the prophet prays that the work of judgment may come quickly so that it might all the more quickly be replaced by God's saving work of restoring the nation. Thus what had previously been a source of perplexity is now seen as a prelude to God's grace.

The phrase *"in the midst of the years"* (or in the NIV, "in our day, In our time") seems to point to the in-between-time that will exist between the present time and the "appointed time" (2:3) that is to come. What is desired is that God might fill the tension between the appearance of delay and the certainty of what was sure to come. May this delay, prays the prophet, not be protracted more than it needs to be. Rather, may God's kingdom be the supreme concern and certainty in the midst of the crisis from another day.

The prophet only requests that *"in wrath [God would] remember mercy."* He could pray this way since he knew from previous revelation that God's nature was to be merciful, full of compassion and abundant in His loving-kindness (Exod. 34:6). In fact, the term "wrath of the LORD" is used 375 times in the Old Testament while the wrath of men is only referred to eighty times. "The consistent linking of nouns of wrath with Yahweh, the covenant God, is of supreme theological significance. It shows that the idea of wrath is closely bound up with belief in the covenant."[40]

The greatest cause in the world is the kingdom of God. As Martin Luther taught us to sing:

> Let goods and kindred go,
> This mortal life also;
> The body they may kill:
> God's truth abideth still;
> His kingdom is forever.   ("A Mighty Fortress is Our God")

Thus the question is not whether we have been vindicated or our plans salvaged; it is, instead, has God's rule and reign been furthered or has it been hindered? That is exactly how our Lord taught His disciples to pray: "Thy kingdom come, thy will be done, on earth as it is in heaven."

A self-centered generation moans about its own affliction, about particular issues such as communism, lawlessness, insensitivity to the poor and the homeless. Important as some of these issues are, few can see that our driving passion should be to bring glory to God. Our driving passion should not be the glorification of our schools, our denominations or our children—as good as some of these goals may be. If we would but remind ourselves of God's nature and His rule and reign, our priorities, perspectives, and programs would be more adequately fitted to the only lasting work in this universe: the kingdom of God. Then let that be our prayer as well: "O LORD, revive Your work in the midst of the years! In the midst of the years make [Your deeds] known."

While all the horrible things prophesied against Judah and Babylon were happening, Habakkuk prayed that in their midst God would preserve, correct, purify, and rectify what was needed among God's people and in the earth at large. Matthew Henry points out that the prophet did not just say, "O Lord, I do see that this punishment was necessary, but I would remind Thee that we have tried to be good and that there have been worse times in our history."[41] Habakkuk does not ask God to remember the people of Judah because of any of their merits, but he asks God to temper wrath with mercy.

LET US CONFESS OUR FEARS IN OUR WORSHIP (3:16)

The theophany described in verses 3–15 overwhelmed the prophet physically. He tells us frankly what his physical symptoms are: a trembling body, a heart that would not stop beating wildly, lips that trembled, teeth that chattered, and bones that felt brittle enough to crumble under their own weight. This is not the picture of some sort of super saint who can handle whatever comes his way. He understood all too well what was being told him. This revelation left as deep a mark on his physical being as the Word of God that came to Daniel in 7:28, where Daniel "was deeply troubled" and his "face turned pale." According to Daniel 8:27, that revelation caused Daniel to be "exhausted" so that he "lay ill for several days." Oh yes, they understood all too well what was being disclosed about the future. It left its mark on them—even in the form of temporary physical impairments!

All of this raises a question in relation to Christian worship and liturgy: What place do lament and confession of our fears have in public worship today? As Donald E. Gowan observes: "Christian worship tends to be all triumph, all good news (even the confession of sin is not a very awesome experience because we know the assurance of pardon is coming; it's printed in the bulletin). And what does that say to those who, at the moment, know nothing of triumph? That they've muffed it, somehow? That their faith hasn't been enough to grant them success? That the whole business is fraud?"[42]

No longer are the prophet's problems theological and philosophical; they are now physical and psychological. He must confess that he does not enjoy the future that he and the nation of Judah face. In spite of his confidence that God is in charge and in spite of the fact that he has been satisfactorily answered, he is impacted mightily by what he now knows—perhaps more than he had been by his original concerns. So what is he to do? What are we to do in the same situation?

The worst thing to be told in such a situation is what well-meaning friends sometimes say: "O, don't think about it." "It will be better if you just don't even give it another thought."

But there will be no "cheery bromides" here. Instead Habakkuk decides to face pain and to tell it like it is. Each and every pain is to be named just as the Book of Lamentations encouraged Judah to name everything, as we would say, from "A to Z."

Habakkuk would *rest in the day of trouble.* Behind the "strange work" of God he had been shown a loving Lord who cared for His people, His oath, and His covenant. He accepted God's answer even though he trembled at His word. But, let it be noted that "It is a mark of the godly to tremble at [his] word (Isa. 66:2b; Ps. 119:120)."[43]

Habakkuk was not the only one of God's past servants who experienced fear. Abraham, David, Jeremiah and many others similarly faced fear in their walk with God. No less susceptible to fear were John the Baptist in his great moment of crisis and the apostle Paul, who gave a long list of his fears and troubles in 2 Corinthians 6:4–10. The reality is that our fears are there; the question is, what will we do about them? This text urges that we voice them before our God in the context of worship.

LET US CELEBRATE THE JOY OF THE LORD IN OUR WORSHIP (3:17–19)

One of the most amazing pieces of biblical text now follows. In the face of the tragedies that were to ensue, Habakkuk states clearly and steadily, *"Yet I will rejoice in the LORD, I will joy in the God of my salvation"* (v. 18).

Again Lloyd-Jones is masterful on this point:

> It was not merely resignation or saying: 'Well, there is no use crying over spilt milk, or getting alarmed and excited, because we cannot do anything about it.' Nor was it just applying the principle of psychological detachment. It was not taking oneself in hand and saying: 'The best thing is not to think about it! Go to the pictures, read novels and don't think!'—a sort of escapism. Neither was it an attempt at being courageous. There is here no exhortation to courage. There is something infinitely greater than just making a mighty effort of the will and saying: 'I am not going to whimper or cry, I am going to be a man.' . . . Instead of mere resignation, or plucking up one's courage, the Scripture shows that it is possible even under such conditions to be in a state of actual rejoicing. . . .[44]

What would cause the conditions noted in verse 17? Why wouldn't the fig tree bud, grapes come on the vines, the olives form, the fields yield any produce, the pens be full of sheep or the stalls be filled with cattle? These may have been the result of the invasion of the Babylonians that was to come shortly (Jer. 5:17). But, ultimately, the reason can be traced to the failure of the people to maintain their covenantal relationship with the Lord. In fact, Moses had warned about such an eventuality in Leviticus 26:18–20 (NIV): "If after all this you will not listen to me, I will punish you for your sins seven times over. I will break down your stubborn pride and make the sky above you like iron and the ground beneath you like bronze. Your strength will be spent in vain, because your soil will not yield its crops, nor will the trees of the land yield their fruit."

Scripture makes a connection between the spiritual health of the inhabitants of a country and the health of the land they occupy. This nexus was taught early in Scripture when in the Garden of Eden a curse was put on the land because of the sin of Adam and Eve. Thus, every time there comes any sign of turning back to God on the part of a righteous remnant, or (if you will not confuse the saying) on the part of a moral *minority*, it is possible for God to send what we may call a substantial healing to the environment. Naturally, the whole created order itself awaits the final redemption that is to be realized at the time of the Second Coming of Christ (Rom. 8:19–21). But in the meantime, substantial healings may be realized in direct proportion to our experiencing the "times of refreshing" (Acts 3:19) from the Lord. Had not the prophet Amos declared that God had sent five separate judgments in order to get the people of Israel in the eighth century to repent, but they would not (Amos 4:6–12). In that same century, Micah had warned about the very real connection between the land's poor productivity and the people's poor spiritual state of health (Micah 6:15). But the lesson was not learned any faster by those generations than it is by our own. For even as late as the post-exilic times, Haggai the prophet had to ask, "Are you planting more and harvesting less? Are you eating more and feeling less satisfied? Are you drinking more and still feeling thirsty? Are you earning more only to watch it disappear, as if your wallets had holes in them?" (Haggai 1:5–6; 2:16–17, author's trans.).

Habakkuk understood. It was too late now to call for repentance and revival. Those opportunities had long since been squandered and expired. Had not Jeremiah preached his heart out? And how had the people of Judah responded? They mocked him and characterized him as a two-point preacher—his message always had two main points and they were always the same: "violence and destruction." But the people would have none of it. Jeremiah, they said, was a quisling, a fifth-columnist—a red-belly Babylonian!

So, come what may—violence and destruction—Habakkuk and those who had remained faithful would rejoice in the Lord and be joyful in God their Savior. The Lord would be Habakkuk's "strength." Just as Nehemiah taught his people in Nehemiah 8:10, "The joy of the LORD is your strength."

Donald G. Miller, in a sermon on this passage, recalled John Bunyan's experience in Bedford jail. Afraid of dying, yet even more afraid of bringing disgrace to the Lord and the gospel he preached, he wrote:

> I Thought with myself, if I should make a scrabbling shift to clamber up the Ladder, yet I should either with quaking, or other

symptoms of fainting, give occasion to the Enemy to reproach the Way of God and his People for their timorousness. This therefore lay with great trouble upon me, for methought I was ashamed to die with a pale Face and Tottering Knees, for such a cause as this.[45]

After grappling with his uncertainties, he finally concluded:

I am going on, and venturing my eternal state with Christ, whether I have comfort here or no. If God doth not come in, thought I, I will leap off the Ladder even blindfold into Eternity, sink or swim, come heaven, come hell. Lord Jesus, if thou wilt catch me, do; if not, I will venture for thy name.

What a commentary on what it means to *live*, and to live by faith. One could have wished that John Bunyon's assurance was greater, but let us be reticent to criticize him. He was in jail; very few of us have ever been in that kind of circumstance. No less affected was the imprisoned John the Baptist, yet our Lord did not lecture him for his moments of despair or his desire to be reassured by the same evidence (and more) of God's strength and joy in the midst of despair that he had given to so many others.

Let the words of the apostle Paul give us confidence:

Who shall separate us from the love of Christ? Shall trouble or hardship or persecution or famine or nakedness or danger or sword? . . . No, in all these things we are more than conquerors through him who loved us.

Romans 8:35, 37(NIV)

The final verses of Habakkuk 3 prompted William Cowper (1731–1800) to compose the poem "In Him Confiding," which became the Christian Hymn "Sometimes a Light Surprises," a hymn usually sung to the same tune as "The Church's One Foundation."

1   Sometimes a light surprises
        The Christian while he sings;
     It is the Lord who rises
        With healing in His wings:
     When comforts are declining,
        He grants the soul again

>   A season of clear shining,
>   To cheer it after rain.
> 2 In holy contemplation,
>   We sweetly then pursue
>   The theme of God's salvation,
>   And find it ever new.
>   Set free from present sorrow,
>   We cheerfully can say,
>   'E'en let the unknown morrow
>   Bring with it what it may:
> 3 'It can bring with it nothing
>   But He will bear us through;
>   Who gives the lilies clothing
>   Will clothe His people too.
>   Beneath the spreading heavens,
>   No creature but is fed;
>   And He who feeds the ravens
>   Will give His children bread.'
> 4 Though vine nor fig-tree neither
>   Their wonted fruit should bear,
>   Though all the fields should wither,
>   Nor flocks nor herds be there,
>   Yet, God the same abiding,
>   His praise shall tune my voice;
>   For, while in Him confiding,
>   I cannot but rejoice.

From Psalm 18:1 the prophet drew nourishment—"I love you, O LORD, my strength." David, the composer of that Psalm, knew straits similar to Habakkuk's. In Psalm 18:4–6a(NIV) David lamented, "The cords of death entangled me; the torrents of destruction overwhelmed me. The cords of the grave coiled around me; the snares of death confronted me. In my distress I called to the LORD." But David and Habakkuk knew the same way to spell relief; in 3:18 Habakkuk recites Psalm 18:33: "[The Lord] will make my feet like deer's feet, And He will make me walk on my high hills."

David's experience of finding "strength in God" came from his harrowing trials under the power-hungry Saul, who relentlessly pursued him as if he were an animal. Yet, Saul's son Jonathan came to David in the wilderness of Ziph and "helped [David] find strength in God" (1 Sam. 23:16).[46]

Thus, for those who are weary and feeling faint, the living God will supply His strength so that they can soar like the eagles, run and not be weary, walk and not faint (Isa. 40:31). He is our strength; that is why we can do everything through Christ who strengthens us (Phil. 4:13). Apart from Him, we can do nothing (John 15:5b). Accordingly, we may freely acknowledge our own weaknesses, for in that case, the power of Christ comes forth to its peak performance as it tabernacles with us (2 Cor. 12:9).[47]

CONCLUSION

Although Habakkuk is a rather small volume, its vision of the workings of God are on the grand scale of some of the later books, such as the book of Daniel's prophecies. Further, Habakkuk contains the best declaration of what it means for justified men and women to live by faith. That faith is an active trust in a Lord who is now working in the historic process as Lord of history. But it also includes God's working in the future eschaton: the two works are joined by a now-and-not-yet type of inaugurated eschatology.

Habakkuk's faith was not just salvific, redemptive and personal; it was practical and mundane in its implications. It could stand the test of total crop failure and the destruction of everything one held dear. It did not depend on God's promise that He would always supply health, wealth and prosperity in order to earn Habakkuk's trust, belief, and respect. He could still be loved and worshipped in the midst of tragedy. When the lid blew off everything, He was still the sole object of praise and adoration. The reason was simple: He was Lord; He was in charge; He would remain true to His word even at the end of the historic process when all else had come and gone. Thus in the face of all the extremities of life, we can go on because He goes on. Justified people really live! And they live by faith!

NOTES

1. Donald E. Gowan, *The Triumph of Faith in Habakkuk* (Atlanta: Knox, 1976), p. 9.

2. Gowan, *Triumph*, p. 20.

3. Raymond Calkins, *The Modern Message of the Minor Prophets* (New York: Harper, 1947), pp. 92–93. Also cited by Gowan, *Triumph*, p.10.

4. *Bel and the Dragon* vv. 33–39, as cited by Gowan, *Triumph*, pp. 12–13.

5. *The Complete Poetical Works of James Russell Lowell*, ed. H.E. Scudder (Boston: Houghton Mifflin, n.d.), p. 67, as cited by Cyril J. Barber, *Habakkuk and Zephaniah* (Chicago: Moody, 1985), p. 28.

6. For more detail and a fuller description of this method, *see* Walter C. Kaiser, Jr., *Toward an Exegetical Theology: Biblical Exegsis for Preaching and Teaching* (Grand Rapids: Baker, 1981).

7. Maria Eszenyei Szeles, *Wrath and Mercy: A Commentary on the Books of Habakkuk and Zephaniah*, trans. George A. F. Knight (Grand Rapids: Eerdmans, 1987), p. 18.

8. Elizabeth Achtemeier, *Nahum–Malachi, Interpretation: A Bible Commentary for Teaching and Preaching* (Atlanta: Knox, 1986), p. 41.

9. *The Babylonian Talmud: Seder Nizikin Makkoth* (New York: Rebecca Publications Inc., 1959) p. 23b–24a.

10. S. Lewis Johnson, Jr., "The Gospel That Paul Preached," *Bibliotheca Sacra* 128 (1971): 327, 328.

11. The word to "make it plain" (*ba'ar*) only occurs three times in the Old Testament: Deuteronomy 1:5; 27:8; and Habakkuk 2:2. In Deuteronomy 1:5, Moses begins to "explain" the Law.

12. O. Palmer Robertson, *The Books of Nahum, Habakkuk, and Zephaniah. The New International Commentaries on the Old Testament* (Grand Rapids: Eerdmans, 1990), p. 168.

13. John Marshall Holt, "'So He May Run Who Reads It,'" *Journal of Biblical Literature* 83 (1964): 301. (cf. 298–302)

14. As noted by Robertson, *Nahum, Habakkuk, and Zephaniah*, p. 170.

15. Robertson, "'The Justified (By Faith) Shall Live By His Steadfast Trust'—Habakkuk 2:4," *Presbyterion* 9 (1983): 52–71. esp. p. 53.

16. Robertson, *Nahum, Habakkuk, and Zephaniah*, p. 173.

17. George J. Zemek, Jr., "Interpretive Challenges Relating to Habakkuk 2:4b,"*Grace Theological Journal* 1 (1980): 56 (*see* pp. 43–69).

18. So concludes William H. Brownlee, "The Placarded Revelation of Habakkuk," *Journal of Biblical Literature* 82 (1963): 321, and Zemek, "Interpretative Challenges," p. 56. The other views on the scope of this revelation are not that important: one takes it to refer to the revelation of 1:5–11 and the other to the theophany of chapter 3.

19. Robertson, "'Justified (By Faith),'" p. 64.

20. John Skinner, "Righteousness in OT," in *A Dictionary of the Bible*, ed. James Hastings (New York: Charles Scribner's Sons, 1902), 4:273, as cited by Robertson, ibid., p. 62.

21. Leon Morris, *The Apostolic Preaching of the Cross* (Grand Rapids: Eerdmans, 1956), p. 235, as cited by Robertson, "'Justified (By Faith),'" p. 62.

22. Robertson, *Nahum, Habakkuk, and Zephaniah*, pp. 179–80. Note that I am following the argument laid down first by Robertson. Other passages

that Robertson lists where *ʾemûnâ* might mean "trust" or "faith" are Proverbs 28:20; Psalms 31:24 (Eng. 23); 37:3. He critiques, in part, Alfred Jepsen's article on "'*āman*" etc.," in *TDOT*, 1:317–8 for moving its central thrust too far into the abstract moral quality of "conscientiousness," even though he thought he was correct in finding an emphasis on "one's own inner attitude and the conduct it produces." Robertson correctly observes that "'Steadfastness' in relation to Yahweh lies at the heart of the concept."

23. Donald A. Leggett, *Loving God and Disturbing Men: Preaching From the Prophets* (Burlington, Ontario: Welch Publishing, 1990), p. 104.

24. Szeles, *Wrath and Mercy*, pp. 31–32.

25. H. S. Bryant, "The Meaning of Habakkuk 2:4" (Bachelor of Divinity thesis, Grace Theological Seminary, 1966), p. 49, as quoted by Zemek, "Interpretive Challenges," pp. 53–54.

26. This term is also used to refer to hemorroids. In 1 Samuel 5:6, 9, 12, it refers to tumors or raised pustules of skin.

27. David W. Baker, *Nahum, Habakkuk and Zephaniah: An Introduction and Commentary* (Downers Grove, Il.: Inter-Varsity, 1988), p. 65.

28. George Adam Smith, *The Book of the Twelve Prophets*, 2 vols. (London: Hodder and Stoughton, 1898), 2:150.

29. Achtemeier, *Nahum–Malachi*, p. 56.

30. St. Augustine, *De Civitate Dei*, XVIII. 32.

31. Robertson, *Nahum, Habukkuk, and Zephaniah*, pp. 224–25, corrects the last sentence in Deuteronomy 33:2 to what we have rendered it here. The Hebrew is indeed obscure, but perhaps the parallels of his "shining forth" in Habakkuk help make it clear that it alludes to the coming of the Lord. *See also* Richard D. Patterson, "The Psalm of Habakkuk," *Grace Theological Journal* 8 (1987): 168. Patterson suggests these translations for this *crux interpretum*: "And there is the covering of his power," or "The name of the covering is His Strength."

32. Robertson, *Nahum, Habakkuk, and Zephaniah*, p. 229.

33. J. H. Eaton, "The Origin and Meaning of Habakkuk 3," *ZAW* 76 (1964): 152, says that the conservative view of Delitzsch, which he "massively argued" for, is the best solution.

34. I refer the reader to the forthcoming discussion by Professor T. L. Fenton of Haifa, Israel. I attended a seminar he conducted on this topic entitled, "Do We Find Chaos in the Bible?" on May 15, 1991, at Sedgwick campus of Cambridge University, Cambridge, UK.

35. While the term *mešiah*, "anointed one," occurs thirty-nine times in the Old Testament, at least nine instances may well point to the Promised One who was to come, Christ. *See* Willis Judson Beecher, *The Prophets and the Promise* (Grand Rapids: Baker, 1975), pp. 299–304.

36. D. Martyn Lloyd-Jones, *From Fear to Faith: Studies in the Book of Habakkuk and the Problem of History* (London: Inter-Varsity, 1953), p. 71 (em-

phasis in the original).

37. That is the simple solution suggested by Gowan, *Triumph of Faith*, p. 68.

38. Lloyd-Jones, op. cit., pp. 57.

39. Lloyd-Jones, ibid., pp. 58–59.

40. Johannes Fichtner, "The Wrath of God," *Theological Dictionary of the New Testament*, ed. Gerhard Friedrich, trans. and ed. Geoffrey W. Bromiley, 10 vols. (Grand Rapids: Eerdmans, 1967), 5:395–96, n. 92.

41. As cited by Lloyd-Jones, op. cit., p. 63.

42. Gowan, *Triumph of Faith*, p. 38.

43. Leggett, *Loving God and Disturbing Men*, p. 114.

44. Lloyd-Jones, op. cit., pp. 68–69.

45. As reported by Gowan, op. cit., pp. 84–85.

46. This connection was pointed out by Leggett, *Loving God and Disturbing Men*, p. 116.

47. I am again grateful to Donald Leggett for calling these texts to my attention, ibid, pp. 116–17.

The Book of Zephaniah

Zephaniah 1:1–3:20

Introduction to Zephaniah

Zephaniah is the least known of all the twelve Minor Prophets. But it was he who broke the long period of silence that followed the famous eighth century B.C. prophets like Isaiah, Hosea, Amos and Micah. Central to his work is the most elaborate discussion by any of the prophets on the "day of Yahweh." Each of his three chapters is dominated by this theme; it is worldwide in its scope and portrays God's plans for the day of the Lord's fulfillment in the final event of history.

THE AUTHOR

Zephaniah means "the LORD has hidden," or "the LORD has caused to be hidden." The prophet's name is fairly common in Israel (1 Chron. 6:36; Jer. 21:1; 29:29; 52:24; Zech. 6:10, 14).

Since Zephaniah was born during the years of King Manasseh's oppressive reign (2 Kings 21:16), his name bears witness to God's might and to His power to preserve His servants and those faithful to Him during a period when much innocent bloodshed filled Jerusalem from one end to the other (2 Kings 21:16).

The author's unusual tracing of his genealogy for four generations has given rise to much speculation. The most plausible reason for the genealogy is that the author wanted to make clear that he was a Jew even though his father's name was "Cushi," meaning "Ethiopian." There is a strong chance that his father was a foreigner, but Jewish nevertheless, just as the thousands of recent Ethiopian immigrants to Israel are foreigners yet Jewish. As Moses prescribed in Deuteronomy 23:8, in Zephaniah's time if a Jewish woman married a foreigner, the offspring of that union could not be accepted into the Jewish community until a pure Jewish pedigree was established for at least three generations. Zephaniah demonstrated such a pedigree.

It has also been suggested on numerous occasions that Zephaniah carried his genealogy to the fourth generation in order to show his connections to King Hezekiah (1:1). While Hezekiah's name does appear in the genealogy, it is puzzling that Zephaniah did not specify that it was *King* Hezekiah. Why would he omit the title if showing his royal connections was the whole purpose of the exercise?

THE DATE

Zephaniah prophesied during *"the days of Josiah the son of Amon, King of Judah"* (1:1). Josiah was the sixteenth king of Judah, reigning from 640 to 609 B.C. (2 Kings 21:26–23:30; 2 Chron. 33:25–35:27). But when during that thirty-one year reign did Zephaniah proclaim his messages of this marvelously good king who came to the throne when he was only eight years of age?

Most place this book prior to the finding of the Book of the Law in the Temple in 621 B.C. (2 Kings 22:8–20) and the resulting revival and subsequent reform that Josiah carried out. The date that most favor is c. 630 B.C. The reasons usually cited in support of this date are: (1) Josiah's extremely young age when he came to the throne —and likely inability to rule with a firm hand—would have made it easy for the royal princes to practice the excesses condemned by the prophet in 1:8–9; (2) the extreme idolatrous practices that Zephaniah preached against (1:4–5) were the very ones abolished under Josiah's reform; (3) the words of 1:12, about searching out those who were complacent and who argued that the Lord would not do good or evil, fit the times prior to the reform of 621 B.C. better than they fit the times that followed; and (4) the threat against some of the nations—such as the Egyptian invasion of the Philistine plain (2:4–7) or the 611–612 B.C. fall of Nineveh, the capital of Assyria (2:13–14)—had not yet been fulfilled.

Commentaries on Zephaniah have traditionally supposed that the immediate threat to Judah came from the so-called Scythians, a group of barbarian tribes from what is the southern part of the former Soviet Union, covering the entire area between the Black and Caspian Seas. As early as 650 B.C., these tribes advanced, according to the Greek historian Herodotus, as far south as Syria, or even to Egypt. However, the extent of the Scythian activity in the Israelite-Philistine territory is not clear.[1]

Herodotus does report that the Egyptians were present in Philistia during Zephaniah's time. In one passage in his *History*,[2] Herodotus reports that the Pharaoh Psammetichus bribed the Scythians to leave the area after they had plundered the temple of Aphrodite at Ashkelon. In another, he claims that Psammetichus had conducted a twenty-nine year siege against Ashdod.[3] These attacks, it should be noted, were taking place during the early years of Josiah's reign. And if such a close neighbor as Philistia in the Gaza strip was under attack, what could Judah expect for her newly-announced independence?

BACKGROUND OF THE BOOK

In order to understand the background of this book, it is necessary to go back to the end of the eighth century B.C. King Hezekiah reigned at the end of that century and into the first part of the seventh century B.C. He had pleased the Lord with his work of reform, but his son Manasseh reversed literally all of his reforms. The "high places" that Hezekiah had pulled down (2 Kings 21:3) were reinstalled after his death by Manasseh. Altars were set up to worship Ashtoreth (the Canaanite goddess), Chemosh (the Moabite god), and Milcom (the Ammonite god), and numerous altars to local Baals were built all over Judah.

Manasseh's impudence knew no bounds, for he carried the abomination of heathen altars right into the Temple of Yahweh itself! There he installed altars to worship the sun, moon, and stars, which were worshiped in Nineveh.

Witchcraft and augury reappeared in Judah. Immorality, under the pretext of carrying out religious practices, was tolerated, and even condoned. But the most extreme example of Manasseh's decadence was his renewal of the horrible rite of child sacrifice (2 Kings 21). Though Manasseh professed a life-changing repentance after he was arrested by the Assyrians, it was too late then to reverse the impact he had made on Judah for well near half a century (2 Chron. 33:11–19).

So ecclectic had Manasseh become in his religious thought and practice that he even named his son after the Egyptian deity Amon. Amon ruled Judah for only two years before his eight-year-old son Josiah took the throne. In spite of having an evil grandfather and a wicked father, Josiah sought the Lord with all his heart and soul and walked in the ways of King David—all this while there was no extant copy of the word of God! (Josiah's reign began in 640 B.C., and a copy of the Word of God was not found until 621 B.C., almost twenty years prior to his inauguration as king.)

In the meantime, the Assyrian empire was beginning to crumble, even during the days of its greatest expansion under Asshurbanipal (668–626 B.C.). Asshurbanipal appeared on Israelite and Philistine soil for the last time in 645 B.C. He made no efforts to recapture Egypt when it revolted. In the wings of history stood Media and Babylon. In 611–612 B.C. Babylon would capture Nineveh and by 609 B.C. the last remnants of the Assyrian army would be defeated by Babylon at Carchemish.

King Josiah's one abiding fault was his vision to reunite the territory of the northern ten tribes, which had been repopulated with many nationalities after the fall of Samaria in 721 B.C. It was this vision that led him—in direct conflict with what God had ordered him to do (2 Chron. 35:21–23)—to attempt to stop Pharaoh Necho when he was going through the Megiddo Pass in 609 B.C. There it was that he lost his life; the nation's grief was beyond description—good king Josiah dead at the age of thirty-nine!

THE UNITY AND STRUCTURE OF ZEPHANIAH

The scholarly consensus is that Zephaniah is organized according to a tripartite division that served as a paradigm for many of the prophetic books, viz., (1) threats against Judah and Jerusalem (1:2—2:3), (2) threats against the Gentile nations (2:4–3:8) and (3) promises to Judah and the Gentile nations (3:9–20).

There are some ways, however, in which the book of Zephaniah does not fit neatly within this tripartite paradigm. The judgment against Jerusalem in 3:1–8, which would be included in the threats against the nations under the three-fold division, is not consistent with the pattern of threats against the nations. The judgment against Jerusalem (3:1–8) cannot be included with the promises described in 3:9–20 either, because it is inconsistent with the pattern of restoration for Judah and the nations.[4]

Although most modern critical analyses argue that Zephaniah is a collection of previously independent short speeches, better case can be made that the various themes of the book contribute to a central and coherent message for the book as a whole.

Sweeney cogently argues that a two-fold division provides better coherence to the argument and structure of the book. The two major sections of a two-fold division are: (1) the prophetic announcement of the "Day of the LORD," 1:2–18; and (2) the prophetic exhortation to seek the Lord, 2:1–3:20.[5] Taking such a view of the book, one sees well beyond the traditional estimate that the book focuses on judgment and ends briefly with a note about restoration. One sees, instead, that Zephaniah 2:1–3 is the pivitol text and that the purpose of Zephaniah's writing was to convince the audience to alter its behavior—to seek the Lord—in light of the announced judgments. Zephaniah thus prepared the way for King Josiah and, wittingly or unwittingly, the prophet and king acted in harmony with each other.

Zephaniah 2:3 is the fulcrum for the book's whole message: "*Seek the LORD, all you meek of the earth, who have upheld His justice. Seek righteousness, seek humility. It may be that you will be hidden in the day of the LORD's anger.*" Three times the prophet's audience is urged to "seek the Lord!" Perhaps in an attempt to drive home his message of deliverance and the promise of divine protection, the prophet incorporates here a synonym of his name: "It may be that you will be *hidden* in the day of the Lord's anger" (italics ours). (Modesty may have prevented him from using the Hebrew root *zāpan* [as in Zephaniah] meaning "to hide"; instead he uses another verb, *sātar*, meaning "to hide.") The promise, however, was the same.

An Outline of Zephaniah

CHAPTER ONE

The Announcement of the Day of the Lord

Zephaniah 1:1–18

1:1 The word of the LORD which came to
Zephaniah the son of Cushi, the son of Gedaliah, the
son of Amariah, the son of Hezekiah, in the days of
Josiah the son of Amon, king of Judah.

2 "I will utterly consume all things
From the face of the land,"
Says the LORD;
3 "I will consume man and beast;
I will consume the birds of the heavens,
The fish of the sea,
And the stumbling blocks along with
the wicked.
I will cut off man from the face of the land,"
Says the LORD.
4 "I will stretch out My hand against Judah,
And against all the inhabitants of Jerusalem.
I will cut off every trace of Baal from this place,
The names of the idolatrous priests with the
pagan priests—
5 Those who worship the host of heaven on the
housetops;
Those who worship and swear oaths
by the LORD,
But who also swear by Milcom;
6 Those who have turned back from following
the LORD,
And have not sought the LORD,
nor inquired of Him."

7 Be silent in the presence of the Lord GOD;
For the day of the LORD is at hand,
For the LORD has prepared a sacrifice;
He has invited His guests.
8 "And it shall be,
    In the day of the LORD's sacrifice,
That I will punish the princes
    and the king's children,
And all such as are clothed with
    foreign apparel.
9 In the same day I will punish
All those who leap over the threshold,
Who fill their masters' houses with violence
    and deceit.
10 "And there shall be on that day," says the LORD,
"The sound of a mournful cry from the
    Fish Gate,
A wailing from the Second Quarter,
And a loud crashing from the hills.
11 Wail, you inhabitants of Maktesh!
For all the merchant people are cut down;
All those who handle money are cut off.
12 "And it shall come to pass at that time
That I will search Jerusalem with lamps,
And punish the men
Who are settled in complacency,
Who say in their heart,
'The LORD will not do good,
Nor will He do evil.'
13 Therefore their goods shall become booty,
And their houses a desolation;
They shall build houses, but not inhabit them;
They shall plant vineyards,
    but not drink their wine."
14 The great day of the LORD is near;
It is near and hastens quickly.
The noise of the day of the LORD is bitter;
There the mighty men shall cry out.
15 That day is a day of wrath,
A day of trouble and distress,
A day of devastation and desolation,
A day of darkness and gloominess,

> A day of clouds and thick darkness,
> 16 A day of trumpet and alarm
> Against the fortified cities
> And against the high towers.
> 17 "I will bring distress upon men,
> And they shall walk like blind men,
> Because they have sinned against the LORD;
> Their blood shall be poured out like dust,
> And their flesh like refuse."
> 18 Neither their silver nor their gold
> Shall be able to deliver them
> In the day of the LORD's wrath;
> But the whole land shall be devoured
> By the fire of His jealousy,
> For He will make speedy riddance
> Of all those who dwell in the land.
>
> *Zephaniah 1:1–18*

Zephaniah was a no-nonsense, all-business writer and speaker. Many speakers will attempt to "warm up" their audiences with a certain amount of humor and various types of pleasantries; this prophet felt the times and the issues were far too serious for any "warm-up" period. Immediately he launches into the hard facts he had to deliver from God.

A. A Day of Universal Judgment 1:2–3
B. A Day of Judgment on Judah and Jerusalem 1:4–6
C. A Call for Silence 1:7
D. A Day of Judgment on God's People 1:8–13
E. A Day of Judgment on the World 1:14–18

A DAY OF UNIVERSAL JUDGMENT (1:2–3)

The temptation for modern readers is to tone down the harshness and horror of the judgment threatened in this text by juxtaposing against it the marvelous grace and mercy of our Lord. But their efforts cannot shield us from the seriousness or the certainty of these pronouncements for the future. An insipid view of the love of God should not obliterate an appreciation for the vigor of the wrath of God against all unrighteousness and ungodliness. In fact, Jesus alludes to Zephaniah 1:2–3 in his parable of the weeds in Matthew

13:41 where he says, "The Son of Man will send out His angels, and they will *gather out* of His kingdom all things that offend, and those who practice lawlessness" (italics ours). The concept of "utterly consuming," "gathering together," or "sweeping away" occurs four times in Zephaniah 1:2–3. The Hebrew *ʾāsap* means to "gather together," "sweep up," or "bundle together," as one would do in gathering a crop or in collecting troops. It is a comprehensive action strengthened by an emphatic form of the same verb. This gathering together will involve everything and will have a worldwide scope! Just as all creation had been corrupted since the Fall, so all creation would now be involved in the divine visitation: man, beasts of the land, birds of the air, and creatures of the sea. This would be a universal judgment.

Thus, like an overture to a symphony, these two verses announce the themes of the book of Zephaniah. They also warn that judgment is near. For the moment, no ray of hope or sign of mercy is apparent; instead, with drum-like rapidity come the verbs of destruction, overthrow, and cleansing of evil. "No hotter book lies in the Old Testament."[6]

As He did in the days of Noah, God will destroy the earth in order to deal with the wickedness of man. Along with the fire that will consume all else, God promised, *"I will consume. . . the stumbling blocks"* (v. 3). The words "stumbling blocks" were usually used to describe idols (e.g., Ezk. 14:3, 4, 7), but they have a wider application in this context. Not only will the wicked be judged, but so will the very instruments that were the occasions for their moral and spiritual failings.

A Day of Judgment on Judah and Jerusalem (1:4–6)

God's judgment is pronounced against Judah because her people *"have not sought the LORD"* (v. 6b). This is the basic problem addressed in this book and that triggers the most urgent appeal in Zephaniah's thrice-repeated invitation in 2:3 to *"Seek the LORD."* The key verb in this summons is "seek" (*bāgaš*).

Neither Judah nor Jerusalem will be exempt from this sweeping worldwide judgment. God *"will stretch out [His] hand against Judah"* (v. 4a); in other contexts stretching out God's hand is a metaphor for God's work of liberation and protection (e.g., Exod. 6:16; Deut. 4:34), but here it is an act of judgment (Exod. 15:12; Isa. 5:25; 14:26; 23:11; Jer. 21:5).

Four targets of divine visitation are selected by the prophet. First, God would *"cut off every trace of Baal from this place"* (v. 4c). The native

Canaanite fertility gods and goddesses had been a nettlesome affair ever since Israel set foot in Canaan. Their festivals of fertility, "sacred" prostitution, and sexual orgies had constantly tempted the people of Israel. Some translate what the NKJV renders "trace of Baal" as "remnant of Baal," and argue therefore that this "cutting off" indicates a time following Josiah's attempt to eradicate Baal worship in 621 B.C. But the NKJV translation is preferred. The Greek translation rendered the same Hebrew words "names of Baal" (as the phrase appears in Hos. 2:17).

God would also cut off *"the names of the idolatrous priests with the pagan priests"* (v. 4d). The Hebrew word meaning "idolatrous priests" appears to be a loan word from the Assyrian Akkadian *kumru,* "priest." The meaning of the root from which *kumru* comes is "to be black." It may be that the priests were so named because they wore long black robes.

Worship of the astrological bodies originated in Mesopotamia, but Judah also developed a taste for this type of worship. The people bowed down on top of their rooftops under the open sky in reverence to the major heavenly bodies.

With a syncretistic spirit that Elijah had condemned on Mount Carmel (1 Kings 18) with his query, "How long will you falter between two opinions?" the Judahites of King Manasseh's day were worshipping and swearing oaths by both the Lord and *"Milcom"* (v. 5). "Milcam," or *"Malkam"* in Hebrew, referred to the Ammonite cult (1 Kings 11:5, 33; 2 Kings 23:13). This god's name came from the Hebrew root *melek,* meaning "king," but the vowels of the Hebrew word *boshet,* "shame," were inserted between m-l-k, thereby stigmatizing the word from *melek* to *molek* to *molok* and then to *milkom* or *milcom.* Molok was also the Moabite god of fire, known in that land as Chemosh, to whom it was customary to offer one's children in human sacrifice—a practice thoroughly repudiated in Scripture (Lev. 18:21; 20:2–5; Deut. 12:31; 1 Kings 11:7; 2 Kings 3:27).

The people of Judah had no interest in *"following the LORD"* (v. 6); they wanted to desert Yahweh, to abandon His will, His law, and His ways. The people refused to seek Him or to inquire of Him.

A CALL FOR SILENCE (1:7)

Before describing the day of the Lord, Zephaniah calls for silence in the presence of the Lord. Everyone must now listen *"For the day of the LORD is at hand"* (v. 7).

The command *"Be silent"* (v. 7) is used by the prophets when the people should show awe and respect (Amos 6:10; 8:3; Hab. 2:20; Zech. 2:13).

This "Day of the LORD" is imminent, Zephaniah proclaims, just as four other prophets proclaimed in three other centuries (ninth century—Joel 1:15; 2:1; 3:14; Obad. 15; eighth century—Isa. 13:6; and sixth century—Ezk. 7:7; 30:3). Here in the seventh century, Zephaniah can see both the events pending in the immediate future as they were linked with God's action in the final day as being of one piece.

God has readied a sacrifice; ironically, His guests will serve as the sacrifice while He, the host, views the spectacle. Earlier in the eighth century, Isaiah described the Lord's sacrifice in Bozrah (Isa. 34:6) to punish the enemies of the Lord's people. Jeremiah, in this same seventh century, heralded the Lord's sacrifice in which the enemies of the Lord's people would be invited to witness their own destruction (Jer. 46:10, 27–28; cf. Ezk. 39:17–20).

A DAY OF JUDGMENT ON GOD'S PEOPLE (1:8–13)

Three sins of the leaders in Judah are listed as reasons for the invitation to the *"day of the LORD's sacrifice"* (v. 8):

(1)   Adopting new lifestyles, customs, and moral behavior, as symbolized by the use of *"foreign apparel"* (v. 8) for clothing. "A person is subject to him whose clothes he wears," counsels Maria Eszenyei Szeles.[7] Thus a person's inner being often is revealed by the clothes he chooses to wear.

(2)   Demonstrating respect for ancient religious superstitions. *"All those who leap over the threshold"* (v. 9) betrayed that they had as much, if not more, respect for the god Dagon and his insignia in the floor of the temple at Ashdod (1 Sam. 5:5) as they had for Yahweh.

(3)   Bringing all sorts of symbols from paganism in the royal palace, thereby filling *"their masters' houses with violence and deceit"* (v. 9c). The paraphernalia of pagan Assyria that graced the walls and floors of the royal palace were nothing more than frauds and perversions of all that is true and holy.

God's judgment against all rebellion on earth, in both Judah and the rest of the world, will begin in Jerusalem, just as judgment must begin with the household of faith (1 Pet. 4:17). It will begin at *"the Fish Gate"* (v. 10), where the fishermen (mostly from Tyre) from the seacoast would enter with their catch (Neh. 3:3; 12:39; 2 Chron. 33:14).

This gate opened westward toward the New City where the ancient gate intersected with the "second" city wall from Solomon's time and serviced the road that was the shortest route to the coast. Near the Fish Gate was *"the Second Quarter"* (v. 10), a suburb added to the city alongside Manasseh's wall, where the prophetess Huldah lived (2 Kings 22:14–20). Here is where the fashionable mansions of that day were built in Jerusalem.

The wail and cry of terror would also come from *"Maktesh,"* or "Morter," the business district or "Wall Street" of that day. "Maktesh," or "Mortar," means "hollow area"; the district was actually a quarry cut out of a hillside situated between Acra and Bezetha on the west side and the Spring of Shiloah on the east, usually known topographically as the Tyropean Valley. Josephus called it "the valley of the cheesemakers and of the fullers." The verb *kātaš*, meaning "to pound, smash, or shatter," is deliberately used by Zephaniah to depict what awaits the money-brokers and merchants of Maktesh in the "day of the LORD." The events of those days will grind them like a mill grinds grain. So wail, you pounded merchants. Behold He comes!

After beginning His day with judgment on that ancient Wall Street, God, like Diogenes of old with his lamp searching for truth, will *"search Jerusalem with lamps, and punish the men who are settled in complacency, who say in their heart, 'The LORD will not do good, nor will He do evil'"* (v. 12). As Jeremiah searched Jerusalem for one righteous person (Jer. 5:1), so God will comb every nook and cranny of Jerusalem until He has rooted out every individual who doesn't believe that He, the Lord, is in charge of His world. The comfortable, the well-to-do, the blasphemer, the idolater—all will be punished!

The complacent were those who had "thickened upon their lees" like wine left on its dregs. Jeremiah (48:11) had used this same figure as a picture of proverbial indifference to who God was and what He was doing in this world. In their boredom and apathy, the cynical citizens and leaders of Zephaniah's day doubted that God would do either good or bad; He was a paper tiger who frequently threatened, but never did anything.

But what a surprise was in store for those who thought this way. Everything they had saved would now become *"booty"* (verse 13). Their houses would become *"a desolation"* (verse 13). (Note that the last four lines of verse 13 contain the very curses described in Deuteronomy 28:30, 39—curses that would attend those who broke God's covenant.)

A DAY OF JUDGMENT ON THE WORLD (1:14–18)

"The great day of the LORD is near" (v. 14), announces Zephaniah. That "day" will not be a period of twenty-four hours, but a period of time encompassing the second coming of the Messiah. The character of that day may best be described in the following outline:

A. The Character of the Day of the Lord:
1. It is that time when God will come to judge the world with righteousness (Ps. 9:8; 96:13; 98:9).
2. On that day the Lord will become King over the whole earth and His name will be the only one (Zech. 14:9).
3. That day is always pending; it is near, because it has both a near and a distant aspect combined in one perspective (Joel 1:15; 2:1; 3:14; Obad. 15; Isa. 13:6; Zeph. 1:7, 14; Ezk. 7:7; 30:3).
4. It is the time of God's wrath against the wicked (Zeph. 1:15, 18; 2:2, 3; Jer. 4:8; 12:13; Ezk. 7:3, 8, 12, 14, 19).
5. It is a day of cosmic gloom and darkness (Amos 5:18; 8:9; Joel 2:2, 10, 31; Zeph. 1:15; Isa. 13:10).
6. It is a day of unprecedented battle when the Lord himself enters as a warrior (Zeph. 1:14; 3:17; Jer. 20:11; Ezk. 30:4–5; Zech. 12:2–3).

B. The Common Catchwords for that Day:
1. "Day of clouds and thick darkness" (Zeph. 1:15; Ezk. 34:12; Joel 2:2).
2. "Day of Trouble" (Nah. 1:7; Hab. 3:16; Zeph.1:15; Jer. 16:19; Obad. 12, 14; Zech. 10:11).
3. "Day of Vengeance" (Isa. 34:8; 63:4; Jer. 46:10).

C. The Blessings of that Day:
1. Protection of Jerusalem (Zech. 12:1ff)
2. Purification of Levi and others (Mal. 3:2)
3. Cleansing (Zech. 13:1f)
4. Endowment of the Spirit (Zech. 12:10; Joel 2:28–29)
5. Paradisean Waters for Jerusalem (Joel 3:18; Zech. 14:8).

D. Summary
The "Day of the Lord" is a term rich in content that denotes a divinely inaugurated period of time called "the days come," "in those days," or "at that time." It is not

always eschatological, for it may refer to specific conditions
that will befall the contemporaries of the prophets. But all
of these immediate fulfillments are but a sample of what
will take place in the grand climax of history when God
intervenes in such a way that His definitive answer to all
injustice, evil, and ungodliness will be observed in all the
earth. While it will be a day of horror and terror for the
wicked and the unbeliever, it will be a bright day for the
believer (John 6:39), a day when Christ will come for His
own (Matt. 16:27). He will spare His own just as He did on
the "day of Midian" (Isa. 9:4) when God gave the victory to
Gideon simply by ordering Gideon to stand still. But that
day will have awful consequences politically, historically,
cosmically, and soteriologically.

Zephaniah heaps one calamitous figure on another to describe the
awful events of the day of the Lord. The opening words of verse 15
were rendered in the Latin Vulgate as *Dies irae, dies illa,* "day of
wrath, that day." From the Vulgate has come the medieval hymn attributed to Thomas of Celano (c. 1190–1250), the biographer of St.
Francis of Assisi. The *"Dies Irae"* in translation reads:

> Day of wrath! O day of mourning!
> See fulfilled the prophets' warning,
> Heav'n and earth in ashes burning!

> O what fear man's bosom rendeth
> When from heav'n the Judge descendeth
> On whose sentence all dependeth!

> Wondrous sound the trumpet flingeth;
> Through earth's sepulchers it ringeth;
> All before the throne it bringeth.

> Death is struck, and nature quaking,
> All creation is awaking,
> To its Judge an answer making.[8]

In the fourteenth century, this poem was included in the sequence
of Requiem masses, but it was not officially adopted into the Roman Missal until 1570, where it stayed until 1969. Now it has fallen
into disuse. In the meantime, it was the basis for powerful requiems
by Mozart, Berlioz and Verdi, to mention just a few. Verses 15 and
16a contain five pairs of synonyms describing the effect that day

will have on humanity. Emotionally, it will be *"a day of trouble and distress"*; physically, it will be *"a day of devastation and desolation"*; psychologically, it will be *"a day of darkness and gloominess"*; cosmically, it will be *"a day of clouds and thick darkness"*; and militarily, it will be *"a day of trumpet and alarm."* God's judgment on that last day will exceed anything the world has ever experienced or imagined! His judgment will arrive like enemy forces storming a city (v. 16).

As verse 17 shows, peoples' outward distress will turn inward and men and women will grope like blind persons—symbolic of their helplessness and utter consternation (cf. Deut. 28:29; Isa. 49:10).

No longer was there any avenue of escape open to the people of Judah, *"because they have sinned against the LORD"* (v. 17c). This simple causal clause summarizes the entire history of the world to that point; what an indictment!

The blood of the slain and wounded will pour forth as if it were mere dust (v. 17d), and human carcasses will lie about the landscape as if they were little more than dung (v. 17e).

Nothing will save the people of Judah now: *"Neither their silver nor their gold shall be able to deliver them in the day of the LORD's wrath"* (v. 18a). The time when bribery may have worked is over. Verse 18b, as translated here, says *"the whole land shall be devoured,"* although the better translation is "the whole earth" (RSV), for God's judgment will be worldwide (1:2).

"By the fire of His jealousy" [or, better, "zealousness,"] God carries out His judgment. This is His answer to those who had complained all their lives, "How long, O Lord will it be before you step in and do something?" He will step in and all that rivals His person and work will be smashed and brought up short. The Lord is angry with the wicked everyday, but only on one day will He manifest just how angry He really is!

CONCLUSION

The unusually strong imagery of this section is enough to make us want to catch our breath and think all over again about how certain and how awesome the judgment of God is in the final day. It is foolhardy and senseless to offend God's moral laws and His holiness. For there is coming a day when all the ungodly will face intense wrath directly from the hand of God.

CHAPTER TWO

The Invitation to Seek the Lord

Zephaniah 2:1–3:20

2:1 Gather yourselves together, yes,
    gather together,
  O undesirable nation,
  2 Before the decree is issued,
    Before the day passes like chaff,
    Before the LORD's fierce anger comes upon you,
    Before the day of the LORD's anger
      comes upon you!
  3 Seek the LORD, all you meek of the earth,
    Who have upheld His justice.
    Seek righteousness, seek humility.
    It may be that you will be hidden
    In the day of the LORD's anger.
  4 For Gaza shall be forsaken,
    And Ashkelon desolate;
    They shall drive out Ashdod at noonday,
    And Ekron shall be uprooted.
  5 Woe to the inhabitants of the seacoast,
    The nation of the Cherethites!
    The word of the LORD is against you,
    O Canaan, land of the Philistines:
    "I will destroy you;
    So there shall be no inhabitant."
  6 The seacoast shall be pastures,
    With shelters for shepherds
      and folds for flocks.
  7 The coast shall be for the remnant of
      the house of Judah;
    They shall feed their flocks there;

In the houses of Ashkelon they shall lie down
  at evening.
For the LORD their God will intervene for them,
And return their captives.
8 "I have heard the reproach of Moab,
And the revilings of the people of Ammon,
With which they have reproached My people,
And made arrogant threats against
  their borders.
9 Therefore, as I live,"
Says the LORD of hosts, the God of Israel,
"Surely Moab shall be like Sodom,
And the people of Ammon like Gomorrah—
Overrun with weeds and saltpits,
And a perpetual desolation.
The residue of My people shall plunder them,
And the remnant of My people shall
  possess them."
10 This they shall have for their pride,
Because they have reproached and made
  arrogant threats
Against the people of the LORD of hosts.
11 The LORD will be awesome to them,
For He will reduce to nothing all the gods of
  the earth;
People shall worship Him,
Each one from his place,
Indeed all the shores of the nations.
12 "You Ethiopians also,
You shall be slain by My sword."
13 And He will stretch out His hand
  against the north,
Destroy Assyria,
And make Nineveh a desolation,
As dry as the wilderness.
14 The herds shall lie down in her midst,
Every beast of the nation.
Both the pelican and the bittern
Shall lodge on the capitals of her pillars;
Their voice shall sing in the windows;
Desolation shall be at the threshold;
For He will lay bare the cedar work.

15 This is the rejoicing city
That dwelt securely,
That said in her heart,
"I am it, and there is none besides me."
How has she become a desolation,
A place for beasts to lie down!
Everyone who passes by her
Shall hiss and shake his fist.

3:1 Woe to her who is rebellious and polluted,
To the oppressing city!

2 She has not obeyed His voice,
She has not received correction;
She has not trusted in the LORD,
She has not drawn near to her God.

3 Her princes in her midst are roaring lions;
Her judges are evening wolves
That leave not a bone till morning.

4 Her prophets are insolent, treacherous people;
Her priests have polluted the sanctuary,
They have done violence to the law.

5 The LORD is righteous,
He is in her midst,
He will do no unrighteousness.
Every morning He brings His justice to light;
He never fails,
But the unjust knows no shame.

6 "I have cut off nations,
Their fortresses are devastated;
I have made their streets desolate,
With none passing by.
Their cities are destroyed;
There is no one, no inhabitant.

7 I said, 'Surely you will fear Me,
You will receive instruction'—
So that her dwelling would not be cut off,
Despite everything for which I punished her.
But they rose early
and corrupted all their deeds.

8 "Therefore wait for Me," says the LORD,
"Until the day I rise up for plunder;
My determination is to gather the nations
To My assembly of kingdoms,

225

To pour on them My indignation,
All my fierce anger;
All the earth shall be devoured
With the fire of My jealousy.

9 "For then I will restore to the peoples
a pure language,
That they all may call on the name of the LORD,
To serve Him with one accord.

10 From beyond the rivers of Ethiopia
My worshipers,
The daughter of My dispersed ones,
Shall bring My offering.

11 In that day you shall not be shamed for any of
your deeds
In which you transgress against Me;
For then I will take away from your midst
Those who rejoice in your pride,
And you shall no longer be haughty
In My holy mountain.

12 I will leave in your midst
A meek and humble people,
And they shall trust in the name of the LORD.

13 The remnant of Israel shall do no
unrighteousness
And speak no lies,
Nor shall a deceitful tongue be found
in their mouth;
For they shall feed their flocks and lie down,
And no one shall make them afraid."

14 Sing, O daughter of Zion!
Shout, O Israel!
Be glad and rejoice with all your heart,
O daughter of Jerusalem!

15 The LORD has taken away your judgments,
He has cast out your enemy.
The King of Israel, the LORD, is in your midst;
You shall see disaster no more.

16 In that day it shall be said to Jerusalem:
"Do not fear;
Zion, let not your hands be weak.

17 The LORD your God in your midst,
The Mighty One, will save;

> He will rejoice over you with gladness,
> He will quiet you with His love,
> He will rejoice over you with singing."
> 18 "I will gather those who sorrow over the
>   appointed assembly,
> Who are among you,
> To whom its reproach is a burden.
> 19 Behold, at that time
> I will deal with all who afflict you;
> I will save the lame,
> And gather those who were driven out;
> I will appoint them for praise and fame
> In every land where they were put to shame.
> 20 At that time I will bring you back,
>   Even at the time I gather you;
> For I will give you fame and praise
> Among all the peoples of the earth,
> When I return your captives before your eyes,"
> Says the LORD.

Zephaniah 2:1–3:20

The heart of Zephaniah's message is found in the opening verses of the second, and final, division of the book. It is an earnest exhortation to "seek the LORD."

A. An Exhortation to Seek the Lord   2:1–3
B. The Lord's Purpose in Punishing the Nations   2:4–15
C. The Lord's Purpose in Punishing Judah   3:1–8
D. The Lord's Purpose in Restoration   3:9–20
   1. The Conversion of the Nations   3:9–10
   2. The Preservation of the Remnant   3:11–13
   3. A Psalm of Joy   3:14–17
   4. The Regathering of Israel   3:18–20

AN EXHORTATION TO SEEK THE LORD (2:1–3)

It is startling that Zephaniah never uses the verb *sûb*, "to turn, or repent," in his cry for a change in the lives of his listeners, since that was the hallmark of almost every other prophet's message. Nevertheless, he clearly desires that his audience humble themselves before God, for then *"it may be that you will be hidden in the day of the LORD's anger"* (2:3d). In saying "it may be that," Zephaniah was not casting doubt on the character or consistency of God; rather, he was pointing, even at this late moment, to the compassion of the Lord and His power to suspend or to restrain the judgment He had announced—if humans would but change. Often this "it may be that," or "perhaps," or "unless," is left unstated in the prophecy, but it is always implied. Did not the king and people of Nineveh infer from Jonah's prophecy that the Lord might be compassionate (Jonah 3:9)? What would we mortals ever do without this conditionality in all of God's threatening and warning?

Zephaniah's summons was: *"Gather yourselves together, yes, gather together, O undesirable nation"* (2:1). In Hebrew this summons contains several little barbs and derogatory notes. It refers to the Jews as a *gôi,* "nation," the word usually reserved for a Gentile nation, and it calls them "undesirable" or "shameful." By these negative words the prophet intended to refer to all of God's chosen people on whose heads he has called down judgment—the merchants, leaders, officers, money-brokers, rich, self-complacent, apathetic, and priests.

The reason why the nation should gather together in this special assembly is given in 2:2. There was still time *"before the decree is issued."* Surely that day of the decree will come speedily—like chaff is blown in the wind. Three times verse 2 stresses that the people should listen to what God is urging "before" the decree comes, "before" the Lord's anger comes, "before" the day of the Lord's wrath comes upon them.

As Amos did a century earlier (Amos 5:5, 14), Zephaniah advises the people to *"Seek the Lord"* (2:3). That is one of the four ways that the writer of 2 Chronicles, in the post-exilic period, would declare that God would send a revival: "If My people who are called by My name will humble themselves, and pray and *seek My face,* and turn from their wicked ways, then I will hear from heaven, and will forgive their sin and heal their land" (2 Chron. 7:14; italics ours).

To seek the Lord was to turn to Him with all of one's heart and being. It was to depend on Him rather than oneself and to let His eye guide in all the affairs of life. This text enjoins the people to seek three objects: the Lord himself, first of all; righteousness; and humility.

To seek anything or anyone other than the Lord was to fall into idolatry. The genus of idolatry was, simply, making something or someone else equal to, or greater than, God. He alone must be the object of our affections and worship.

To seek righteousness meant to seek God's standard in human behavior. It meant making God's Law, His will, and His covenant normative, for He alone was "in-the-right," or "righteousness." Righteousness was not obtained merely by obeying the Law, but by having faith in God that resulted in a lifestyle of obedience (Deut. 30:16, 20).

To seek humility meant the opposite of asserting one's self-will and pride. Blessed are the meek (not to be confused with the "weak"), asserted our Lord. Those who have gone into spiritual bankruptcy in order to gain the treasures of heaven are not foolish, but wise followers indeed. Their hearts and spirits were broken and contrite before God (Ps. 34:18; 51:17; Isa. 57:15; 66:2; 1 Pet. 5:6).

THE LORD'S PURPOSE IN PUNISHING THE NATIONS (2:4–15)

In these verses the prophet selects two nearby nations (Philistia [vv. 5–7] and Moab-Ammon [vv. 8–11]) and two distant nations (Ethiopia [v. 12] and Assyria [vv. 13–15]) to represent all the nations of the world. These nations were at the four points of the compass: Philistia to the west, Moab-Ammon to the east, Ethiopia to the south and Assyria to the north. Thus while mentioning in particular only these four nations, all the nations of the world were included in Zephaniah's indictment of the nations.

Further, four of the five cities of the famous Philistine Pentapolis were warned of impending destruction. If Pharaoh Psammetichus's twenty-nine year siege of Ashdod had begun, as Herodotus claims (*History* II. 157), then Ashdod was experiencing as much an immediate crisis as it would in the eschaton. Zephaniah saw both crises as united under the single concept of the day of the Lord.[9] Gaza Ashkelon, Ashdod, and Ekron would be *"forsaken"* then made *"desolate"* (v. 4). Gath, apparently, had already been left in ruins by the repeated attacks of the Assyrians.

Verse four begins with the word *"for,"* linking it with the call to "seek the LORD" in verse 3 and the worldwide judgment announced in chapter 1. Zephaniah did allow just a pinch of playfulness in his text, using the assonance and alliteration in "Gaza" (*ʾāzzâh*) being "forsaken" (*ʾāzûbâh*) (v. 4a) and "Ekron" (*ʾeqrôn*) being "uprooted" (*ʾāqēr*).

The Philistine inhabitants of the seacoast mentioned in verse 5a had originally migrated from Asia Minor (present day Turkey) and the island of Crete; hence they were called *"Cherethites"* (v. 5b; cf. 1 Sam. 30:14; 2 Sam. 15:18; Amos 9:7; Ezk. 25:16). To them Zephaniah proclaims: *"The word of the LORD is against you"* (v. 5c). God was not a spectator who sat on the sidelines of history anxiously observing the world, unable to do anything to stop people's actions or direct them. His laws and requirements were just as relevant to the Gentiles as they were to the Jews in the Old Testament. Unless the Gentiles too sought the Lord, they might expect to witness the same horrifying results that God had already disclosed in this prophecy. Interestingly, this is the only place in the Old Testament where *"Canaan"* is placed parallel to and used as a synonym for the *"Philistines"* (v. 5e). (*See also* Joshua 13:3f, where the territory of the Philistines was included with the Canaanites.)

Zephaniah's prediction is that these well-heeled cities of the coastal plain would be destroyed and left without any inhabitants. The seacoast pastures would become grazing grounds and sheepfolds for *"the remnant of the house of Judah"* (v. 7). This indeed is a startling prophecy to contemplate in our time, for in recent days the world's attention has been focused once again on the difficult topic of a national home for the Palestinian Arabs. Some, noting that the term "Palestinian" is related to the word "Philistine," have suggested that the Gaza Strip, our modern name for the area of the five cities of Philistia, be given as a national homeland for the Palestinian Arabs. But this text, the first in this prophecy of Zephaniah to mention the hopeful word of the "remnant," declares that *"the LORD their God will intervene for them and return their captives"* (v. 7d) to the very territory formerly claimed by the Philistines but now known as the Gaza Strip. This formula, literally "to restore [the] fortune[s]," has a substantial place in the theology of Jeremiah and Ezekiel.

While the day of the Lord will be a time of great judgment, it will also be a time of hope. There will emerge a "remnant" of Israel and Judah that will signal God's ability to deliver all who trust in Him as this remnant did. The prophets often mention this "remnant" (Amos 5:15; Mic. 2:12; 5:7–8; Jer. 23:3). The people of the remnant will be exempt from judgment in the day of the Lord. The Judahite refugees, in particular, will inhabit the Philistine coast in the day of the Lord!

Verses 8–11 turn to Judah's eastern neighbors, Moab and Ammon. These nations had historically had a tumultuous relationship with

Judah. Though related to Judah, through the descendants of Lot (Gen. 19:30–38), they had repeatedly hurled *"reproach"* and *"revilings"* (v. 8) at God's people. But to attack God's people was to attack God Himself; He was the "God of Israel."

Not only did the people of Moab and Ammon reproach God's people, but they *"made arrogant threats against their borders"* (v. 8d). In this they presumed to countermand the expressed plan and purpose of God. So this issue has stood all these years as the rock on which Judah's eastern neighbors would hurt themselves; further, this issue of the nations' borders will eventually force all the nations of the earth to come to terms with the fact that God has been in charge of history all along. This was only the most visible evidence of the general rebellion of all the nations against God himself!

Comparing Moab and Ammon to Sodom and Gomorrah (v. 9b) was surely a warning of the dire nature of the threats being raised against the two nations. Like Zephaniah, other prophets warned Moab and Ammon (Isa. 15–16; Jer. 48–49; Ezk. 25:1–11; Amos 1:13–15; 2:1–5).

These nations would become *"overrun with weeds and saltpits, and a perpetual desolation"* (v. 9d)—steril and barren. So weakened would they become that *"the residue of My people shall plunder them, and the remnant of My people shall possess them"* (v. 9f-g). Moab and Ammon's loss would be complete; the nations would be handed over to Israel instead.

From a theological perspective, Moab and Ammon's problem was not their sense of racial superiority, but their *"pride"* (v. 10a). Both Isaiah (16:6) and Jeremiah (48:26) cite "pride" as the one sin that led Moab and Ammon to insult and mock the people of God.

However, the time was coming when the Lord would *"reduce to nothing all the gods of the earth"* (v. 11b). Every alleged deity would be exposed for what it really was—impotent and, indeed, nonexistent! That would finally clear the way for all people to worship the Lord, *"each one from his place, indeed all the shores of the nations"* (v. 11 d-e). This startling text (for so it must have seemed to all who were accustomed to thinking that only in Jerusalem did true worship of God take place) is very similar to Malachi 1:11. Pilgrimages to Jerusalem would not always be necessary, for everyone could legitimately worship God in their own country. Undoubtedly, Zephaniah is referring to those days when the Messiah rules and reigns in the Millennium, but everything we have experienced along these lines in part in the New Testament era is a foretaste of what will come.

In verse 12 Zephaniah turns his attention to the south and foretells God's judgment on Ethiopia. Often the Hebrew word *Cush* denoted more than Ethiopia; it also embraced Nubia, and parts of Arabia bordering the Red Sea.

"You Ethiopians also," continues Zephaniah, *"shall be slain by My sword"* (v. 12), just as Philisita, Moab and Ammon will be. The instrument of God's judgment will be His "sword" (cf. Isa. 34:5; Ezk. 30:25). God often used other nations as the implements in His judgment, while maintaining that the "sword" was His. Judgments against Ethiopia were also given in Isaiah (18) and Ezekiel (30).

Finally, in verses 13–15 Zephaniah describes God's judgment on Assyria. Right about this time, the colossal empire of Assyria was beginning to crumble and another nation and empire (in this case, Babylon) was about to take its place. But God would *"stretch out His hand"* (cf. 1:4) and Assyrian's capital city of Nineveh, famous for its strong walls and magnificent buildings, would become a debris-ridden dump with birds (variously identified as cormorants, vultures, pelicans and desert owls—not the ordinary city-dwelling pigeons!) roosting on the debris.

The reason for God's judgment on Assyria was Nineveh's arrogance in saying, *"I am it, and there is none besides me"* (v. 15d). So successful had Assyria become that she believed in her own self-deification. Self-worship cannot be more arrogant than this. It showed itself in the Assyrian field commander's speech against King Hezekiah and Judah in Isaiah 36:4–10, 13–20.

The result of God's judgment on Assyria would be that everyone who passed by would *"hiss and shake [the] fist"* (v. 15 f)—the ultimate disgrace for an oriental. The people could handle everything but the hissing, for hissing was tantamount to an attack on their person.

THE LORD'S PURPOSE IN PUNISHING JUDAH (3:1–8)

After Zephaniah declares what God will do to the nations on a worldwide scale, he turns again (cf. 1:4–13) to Judah and Jerusalem. The city that should have been the model for all the world had instead become the home of the rebellious (who refused to submit to God's will), the polluted and defiled (who practiced sinful deeds, especially as they related to the use of blood and being pure in cultic matters of worship), and the oppressing (who disregarded the rights and needs of the poor, the orphans and the widows).

"Woe to her" (v. 1), cries the prophet in the standard lament form. Though Zephaniah does not say to what city he is referring, there is no doubt what city he intends; it is Jerusalem. Each of the three participles in verse 1 that expose the sins of the city are graphic: the *"rebellious,"* mutinous, and disobedient; the *"polluted,"* defiled, bloodstained, and unclean; the *"oppressing,"* repressive, bullying, and crushing! These three charges indicated the three directions in which Jerusalem's sin manifested itself: to God, to religious practices, and to fellow humans.

In verse 2 Zephaniah elaborates on these three charges by listing four specific indictments that God has against His people Israel (Note that in the Hebrew the negative particle is placed in the foreward and emphatic position in the first two indictments; in the last two, the name of God is pushed to the front.): (1) *"She has not obeyed His voice"* (v. 2). The voice of God through His prophets was simply disregarded. (2) *"She has not received correction."* The Law of God and His Word through His servants meant as little to the people of Israel as they did to the pagans around them. They went unheeded. No response to God's Law and Word was needed, the people seemed to think. (3)*"She has not trusted in the Lord."* The people of Israel acted as though more confidence and security were to be found in treaties and alliances with foreign nations than were to be gained from depending on the Lord. (4) *"She has not drawn near to her God."* When the people of Judah worshipped at all they had preferred to draw near to Baals, Ashtoreth, Chemosh, Milkom, the astrological bodies, and pagan priests.

In verses 3 and 4, God condemns four classes of Judah's leaders, representative of all her people, in turn:

1. *"Her princes"* or "officials." The people in power did not rule with justice and equity in mind, but, like *"roaring lions,"* were eager to pounce on any victim on whom they could exercise their greed and avarice.

2. *"Her judges"* or "rulers." Just as guilty were the civil magistrates, who were compared to *"evening wolves"* that prowled under the cover of darkness and devoured their victims so thoroughly that not even their bones were left the next morning! Surely this greed is inhuman!

3. *"Her prophets."* Always ready to give the people what they wanted, her teachers became "light," "frivolous," "unstable," and

"treacherous." Rather than faithfully representing the One that had sent them, they felt obliged to present what the people thought and thus their message descended to the lowest common denominator of the spiritual attainments of the people, which were not that magnificent!

4. *"Her priests."* This group of religious leaders profaned all that was holy or sacred (a better translation of *"sanctuary"*). By allowing the people to blur the distinction between what was sacred or holy and what was not, and by disregarding what had been specifically taught in the law, the priests acted as agents for the populace, not as ministers of God! They profaned what was holy—i.e., they "unhallowed" the holy. Further, like many contemporary pastors, Judah's priests did *"violence to the law"* (v. 4c) by replacing God's Holy Word with their own ideas, adapting the words of Scripture so as to fit the popular eddies and moods of the day! By so doing, they conveniently did not mention the "whole counsel of God" (Acts 20:27), for not all of it fitted their own interests or the interests of the people.

One would have thought that the presence of the Lord (v. 5) in their midst would have been enough to deter most, if not all, of the sins described in verses 1–4. The indicted leaders had been *"in her midst"* (v. 3), but so had the Lord been *"in her midst"* (v. 5). No one could implicate the Lord in any wrongdoing; *"He will do no unrighteousness"* (v. 5b). On the contrary, *"Every morning He brings His justice to light; He never fails"* (v. 5c). So why doesn't everyone see what is as plain as the morning sunlight on their face? God's moral standards are plainly visible to all; He never fails! Nor have His standards failed!

The wicked could not have been less interested. They knew no shame; as their excesses continued to grow, they became more impervious to the Law of God (v. 5e).

At this point, the Lord takes the people of Judah (and all who would eventually read this text) to school, and gives them (and us) a lesson in world history. *"I have cut off nations, their fortresses are devastated"* (v. 6a), the Lord reminds. History is full of examples of nations that are no longer on the scene, but had anyone thought to ask why? Wasn't their wreckage directly related to their moral collapse and disregard for the basic principles of righteousness taught in the Word of God—whether or not they were believing nations? Judah needed to look no further for such an example than the Northern kingdom that had gone into captivity in 721 B.C.

Nations and peoples are responsible to learn from history. It was hoped that Judah would heed the tragic realities of the past and reverse her headlong rush into disaster. Revealing again His mercy and compassion, God pleads, *"Surely you will fear Me, you will receive instruction"* (v. 7). But Judah did not. There was no trembling in the face of the presence and power of God, nor any evidence of a willingness to receive His instruction.

Despite all divine hope, Judah had resisted every loving attempt—in the form of divine punishments—to drive her back onto the right path. It was almost as if the people could not disengage themselves from a vice-grip of sin.

"Therefore wait for Me," says the LORD (v. 8a). This was not a promise. It was a warning that there was no chance of escaping God's threatened judgment. The facts against Judah were undeniable; God would simply rest His case and let history play out the realities that He had tried to warn His people against. That "day" would now come on Judah.

In verse 8 God gives the final summation of the case against the whole world: *"My determination is to gather the nations to my assembly of kingdoms, to pour on them My indignation, all my fierce anger; all the earth shall be devoured with the fire of My jealousy."* Thus, in language very similar to Joel 3 and Zechariah 14, God promises to bring all the nations of the earth together so that He might execute His judgment against all of them. They have all failed to keep His moral laws and to execute justice, much less to believe in Him. Where they will be gathered, this text does not say; but parallel texts indicate that they will gather in Jerusalem itself. They will gather on that final day in history when God personally enters the battle to judge all nations, including Judah.

THE LORD'S PURPOSE IN THE RESTORATION (3:9–20)

These verses mark the end of the prophet's long parade of indictments and announcements of judgment. Here he declares a worldwide conversion and a time when God will restore His people to their land.

The Conversion of the Nations (3:9–10)

Just when things looked darkest during the great judgment threatened in the preceding verses, *"then"* (v. 9) Yahweh would assume center stage and the long-awaited redemption promised by so many prophets would commence. *"I will restore to the peoples a pure language, that they all may call on the name of the LORD, to serve Him with one accord"* (v. 9). The Hebrew word translated "to restore" is a vigorous word meaning a turning around, a turning away, a transformation, a collapse, or a total change. It is not a slow, developing change, but a sudden and radical break with the past. The word was used of Saul when "God gave him another heart" (1 Sam. 10:9; cf. also Gen. 19:21, 25, 29; Deut. 29:33—all of the "collapse" of the cities of Sodom and Gomorrah). This radical change, amazingly enough, will affect the Gentile nations, consistent with the worldwide scope of the work of God described in 1:2–3. And when God promises to restore a "pure language," He is referring to more than a type or quality of speech; human language is merely the outward indicator of the inner ego and person. Thus the promise of a radical change of language was another statement of the uniqueness of God's re-creative work. (Answering Isaiah's confession that he was "a man of unclean lips [Isa. 6:5]" God would purify those lips and the inner disposition which they symbolized.)

Now mortals with new hearts would *"call on the name of the LORD"* and *"serve Him,"* literally, "with one shoulder," or as we say in our idiom, "shoulder to shoulder," or *"with one accord"* (v. 9c). When a team of oxen were yoked together, the task went best when they pulled the load as if they were one. In the day of the Lord, amazingly, the Gentile nations will worship and serve God alongside Israel with one accord.

From as far away—the ends of the earth it was thought in those days—as *"the rivers of Ethiopia My worshipers, the daughter of My dispersed ones, shall bring My offering"* (v. 10). This could mean either that all the world's peoples, not just the Jewish Diaspora, will come to worship Yahweh and to make offerings, or that all the exiled Israelites, even those dispersed so far away as to seem irretrievable, will return to worship and offer sacrifices to God. Given Zephaniah's universal outlook and the all-encompassing announcement in verse 9, the first interpretation must be the correct one. The concept of God's redemption extending to all the nations and peoples of the earth is not initiated by Zephaniah; it appears in Isaiah 2:2–4; Micah 4:1–4; Isaiah 11:9; 19:23–25; 49:5–6.

The "offering" mentioned here is the *minhâh*, a voluntary "gift" offering (cf. Lev. 2) made in addition to the regular offerings and expressing deep gratitude to God.

The Preservation of the Remnant (3:11–13)

Once again God refers to the day of the Lord, this time as *"in that day"* (v. 11a). So complete will be the cleansing of God that it will completely remove both the burden of "shame" and the feeling of disgrace for past transgressions. Moreover, all who are proud will be removed. Haughtiness will be abolished on God's *"holy mountain,"* Jerusalem (v. 11f).

The new people of God will carry three marks: (1) meekness, that attitude of life in which a person does not exalt himself above God or another person, but bows the head in submission to one's Lord; (2) humility, an attitude of genuine dependence on God as opposed to a self-satisfied indifference and bold assertion of one's rights above everyone else's; and (3) trust in the name of the Lord, a decision to seek refuge in the character, works, and truth of the Living God (v. 12).

This new people of God are once again called *"the remnant"* (v. 13a). They are those who have been cleansed by the Lord and who now remain in the land. They are pictured in this new day of the Millennium as being free of all unrighteousness, deception, or duplicity. In that day, there will be no perversity, treachery, crookedness, fraud, intrigue, cheating or deceit. Those who attempt to place this prediction somewhere within the present historic process will find that they have an impossible task, for it will exceed all constraints of language to make it fit our present world. This must be a day when our Lord has returned and our lips, hearts and lives have been drastically changed!

A picture of perfect tranquility and security is given at the end of verse 13; flocks quietly feed while their owners have not a worry in the world—*"no one shall make them afraid"* (v. 13e).

A Psalm of Joy (3:14–17)

She who once was the "rebellious," "polluted," and "oppressing city" (3:1) is given three titles of honor in this hymn or ode of joy to the Lord: *"daughter of Zion," "Israel,"* and *"daughter of Jerusalem"* (v. 14). In biblical poetry, cities and their inhabitants are often referred to as women, hence *"daughter of Zion"* and *"daughter of Jerusalem,"* both of which mean Israel.

The messianic era is set forth with great joy; it is a time to rejoice. To describe this era, Zephaniah uses four terms for joy: *"sing," "shout," "be glad,"* and *"rejoice"* (v. 14). Redeemed men and women were to enter into the exaltation of the triumphant Lord *"with all [their] heart"* (v. 14).

All fear and apprehension over being punished are gone, for the Lord *"has taken away your judgments"* (v. 15); *"He has cast out your enemy"* (v. 15). Zephaniah uses the "prophetic perfect tense" since he views the events he describes as being so certain that they may be spoken of as having already been accomplished (cf. Isa. 40:2). Since God has forgiven Jerusalem's iniquity and totally removed any resulting guilt, there will no longer be a need to use any of the nations as instruments of His judgment. The nations too will be cast out.

"The King of Israel, the LORD, is in your midst" (v. 15c). No longer will He be present only in His shekinah glory, or as the Angel of the Lord; indeed, He will personally reside in Jerusalem "in [their and our] midst." Therefore, *"you shall see disaster no more"* (v. 15d). The personal presence of the Lord shall render ineffective all the powers of evil and harm.

In that day of Messiah there will be no more reason to fear anything or anyone. And the discouraged, who wondered if there was reason to continue, can put their shoulder to the task. "Weak" or "slack hands" (v. 16c) indicated despair, disheartenment, and lack of involvement (Isa. 13:7; Jer. 6:24; Heb. 12:12).

In verse 17a, Zephaniah repeats the fact that *"The LORD your God [is] in your midst."* He is *"the Mighty One";* therefore, He is able to save and to deliver us.

There is no need, as a good number of commentators suggest, to place these verses in the post-exilic times solely because of their gentility and comforting effect. The tender note struck here is typical of God's final redemption promised all through the Old Testament. Our Lord is depicted as being happy in His work of delivering His people (v. 17). He will hush up His crying people with an overwhelming demonstration of His love. He will take great delight in all He has redeemed; He will break forth in singing over His people! Most of us had never thought there would be that much to sing about in the people of God—given all our warts and plain sinfulness. We cannot imagine that we could bring pleasure to the heart of God; but this text assures us that God definitely thinks differently. Some regard verse 17 as the most beautiful verse in the whole book of Zephaniah.

The Regathering of Israel (3:18–20)

Verse 18 is admittedly difficult to interpret. It seems to say that another cause for rejoicing may be seen in the fact that God will gather in that day all who previously could not enjoy the *"appointed assembly,"* or festivals in Jerusalem, and will reunite those who are far removed from the place of worship (cf. Ps. 24:4; 42:3; 44:2; 63:3).

At that very time, God will deal with all the nations who had oppressed Israel (cf. Isa. 60:14), and they will be destroyed (Isa. 59:17–21; 66:15–16). God will save *"the lame"* (cf. Mic. 4:7) and *"those who were driven out"* or "scattered" (v. 19). He will gather His flock from the Diaspora.

But there is more; the Lord *"will appoint them for praise and fame"* (v. 19e). Previously the people of Israel had received mostly shame, but now they will receive fame and honor. They will enjoy receiving praise. This thought is so important that Zephaniah states it twice.

Zephaniah repeatedly stresses that these things will occur *"At that time"* (vv. 19, 20). In that day, our Lord will assure that Israel is restored to her land. He will *"return your captives before your eyes"* (v. 20). Of course very few, if any, of the generation to whom Zephaniah spoke would be alive when the people returned almost one hundred years later. (In 536 B.C. the first group of people returned from Babylon under Zerubbabel). If the words "before your eyes" were meant to have any normative significance, then the fulfillment of this return could not have been accomplished until the Millennium. Furthermore, Judah could never have gained any kind of recognition or honor from any of the nations at that time, nor could she gain any since. Indeed, she has received more shame and contempt than anything else. It is clear, then, that this text talks about something we have never before seen. As someone said, "The Messiah will need to appear before the nations-at-large begin to give the credit to Israel." And so He shall!

CONCLUSION

Zephaniah's passionate appeal is to *"seek the Lord!"* His reasons are multiple, but one overwhelmingly important reason why mortals all over the planet should seek Him is that He has planned a final day of judgment, known as the "Day of the LORD," when He will finally make right all wickedness, unrighteousness, and injustice.

The nations will be judged; but, praise God, all who believe will be delivered. Israel will experience the direct intervention of God on her behalf against her enemies, and the Jews will be restored to their land.

At last God will dwell on earth in the midst of His people and the joy of all beings will be unspeakably great. Great is the day of our Lord, the Christ!

NOTES

1. For a discussion of the Scythian hypothesis, *see* Henri Cazelles, "Zephaniah, Jeremiah and the Scythians in Palestine," trans. Leo G. Perdue, in *A Prophet to the Nations: Essays in Jeremiah Studies*, eds. Leo G. Perdue and Brian W. Kovacs (Winona Lake, In.: Eisenbrauns, 1984), pp. 129–49.

2. Herodotus, *History* II. 157.

3. Herodotus, *History* II. 157.

4. These criticisms of the tripartite division are drawn from Marvin A. Sweeney, "A Form-Critical Reassessment of the Book of Zephaniah," *Catholic Biblical Quarterly* 53 (1991): 389–90.

5. Ibid, p. 403.

6. George Adam Smith, *The Book of the Twelve Prophets* (New York: Harper and Brothers, 1928), II: 47.

7. Maria Eszenyei Szeles, *Wrath and Mercy: A Commentary on the Books of Habakkuk and Zephaniah*, trans. George A. F. Knight (Grand Rapids: Eerdmans, 1987), p. 82.

8. Tr. William J. Irons, as cited by Charles L. Taylor, Jr., "The Book of Zephaniah," in *The Interpreter's Bible* (Nashville: Abingdon, 1956), VI: 1012.

9. The uniting of the *already*-fulfilled with the *not-yet*-fulfilled into one single concept of the "day of the Lord" is a common figure in the Bible and usually referred to by theologians as "inaugurated eschatology." To use another end-day event, 1 John 2:18 warns "Antichrist is coming," yet "even now many antichrists have come."

SECTION FIVE:

The Book of Haggai

Haggai 1:1–2:23

Introduction to Haggai

Some scholars criticize this compact message from Haggai as being a single-issue book concerned only with the rebuilding of Solomon's temple. This criticism can take severe forms, as it does in the volume by Oesterley and Robinson. Their judgment about Haggai was, "His whole mental outlook and utilitarian religious point of view (see 1:9–11) is sufficient to show that he can have no place among the prophets in the real sense of the word."[1] No less displeased was Paul Hanson, who accused Haggai and Zechariah of surrendering the prophetic word to a particular political program, thereby leading the prophetic office down "an ignominious path."[2]

But such criticisms fail to recognize the significance attached to the restoration of the temple and the function this book has as Scripture. The restored temple was a prelude to even greater acts of God. Neither these critical scholars nor we readers should despise the day of small things (Hag. 2:3, 7). For just as Haggai's contemporaries needlessly worried that the restored temple would fail to compare physically to the former Solomonic temple in all its glory, so we will commit a grave error if we fail to see a connection between this little beginning and the grand climax of history in the final day of our Lord Jesus Christ. The *"temple"* of 2:3 will be the same *"temple"* of 2:7 when God shakes the heaven and the earth in His climactic work in history. Here indeed was God's prelude to His even greater works in the eschaton.

Had not Martin Luther also warned against focusing on the temple per se to the neglect of hearing the Word of God? He cautioned:

> If we should consider the subject matter unsympathetically, the prophet will seem quite trivial on the surface, especially in our day. Everything about which he prophecies, especially about rebuilding the temple, has ceased. As a consequence, we must consider the subject matter correctly, so that we look not so much at it as at the Word of God.[3]

Reading the text of Haggai only to learn how the construction of the temple was resumed is too limited an outlook. The book contains an abiding word of God that still wishes to address us over the years, as the book itself states.

In spite of the fact that few people today know much about the book of Haggai, it has been used by God in several exceedingly significant ways over the centuries. For example, Savonarola, often called the morning star of the Reformation, preached a mighty series of sermons from the book of Haggai in November 1494 (just two years after Columbus sailed for America). Later John Knox turned to the prophet to lead Scotland in a memorable time of renewal and reformation. Few can argue with these results; they are part of the history of interpretation of Haggai.

THE AUTHOR

But how is it that a prophet whose ministry lasted for a mere five months in the year 520 B.C. should have so lasting an impact on so many? Haggai was quite different from his fellow prophets. His complaints against the nation of Judah did not focus on the usual flagrant sins of idolatry, unrighteousness, and injustice; instead, his concerns were over his people's apathy in their worship and service of God. He called his people to reexamine their priorities. His message concerned the interior of the person and the heart of the matters raised; external issues were merely symptoms of the deeper problem that must be addressed if any change was to come in those external issues.

Unfortunately, we know very little about Haggai. We do know that he was a contemporary of the prophet Zechariah and that both were used by God in 520 B.C. to prod the exiles that had returned to Jerusalem under Zerubbabel to pick up the neglected task of rebuilding the temple that had been destroyed by the Babylonians in 586 B.C. Immediately upon returning from a seventy-year exile, the people had undertaken this project with a mighty vigor. Sadly, disillusionment, discouragement, and controversy so quenched the hearty spirit of the restorationists that they dropped the project shortly after the foundation for the new footprint of the temple was laid. For the next sixteen years no one touched this project—nor did anyone seem to care! Then God sent Haggai and Zechariah to warn the people about their indifference, complacency, apathy, and faulty priorities.

The only other references to Haggai in the Bible are in Ezra 5:1 and 6:14. In the book of Haggai, Haggai is identified as "the prophet" (1:1, 3; 2:1, 10) and as "the LORD's messenger [or "angel"]" (1:13).

Haggai's name means "festival," suggesting that he may have been born on one of the Israelite feast days. In Latin, that name would be Festus and in Greek it would be Hilary. Haggai's father's name is not given in the book, nor is any other pertinent piece of biographical information.

BACKGROUND TO THE BOOK

This brief work of two chapters, totalling thirty-eight verses, was written in prose form, rather than the poetic form preferred by so many of the prophets. The writer refers to himself in the third person; or possibly, one of Haggai's disciples or other designated person (like the secretary Baruch that Jeremiah used) collected and arranged his messages.

The timing of Haggai's messages is of major importance in understanding what this book has to offer to the contemporary reader. Some sixty-six years earlier, in 586 B.C., Jerusalem was decimated by the Babylonian armies. Tragically for Judah, her temple, built in 967 B.C. by King Solomon, was totally destroyed, and God's covenant people did not have a place to worship for the first time since Moses had built the tabernacle, the forerunner of Solomon's temple. The temple lay in ruins. Most of Judah's population was forced to go into exile some 1100 miles away in ancient Babylon, now called Iraq. Very few escaped the awful effects of this invasion; only a very small cadre of people were left in the land. Devoid of leadership and the means or place to worship the Living God, their resolve melted. Little, if anything, was accomplished during those years, and there is no evidence that any vital faith remained. It was a period of stagnation for those who were left as well as for those who were deported into Babylon or who had fled into other foreign countries for safety.

In 539 B.C. the international picture changed abruptly as the newly-formed power of Media-Persia emerged. Under the masterful leadership of Cyrus, Babylon was captured on the very night the drinking and dining described by the prophet Daniel (Dan. 5) took place. The coup was sudden and complete; it happened virtually without a single shot of a bow or the thrust of a spear. King Belshazzar had retreated to his magnificent city of Babylon thinking that he had enough supplies—up to twenty years' worth—to outlast any siege. But Cyrus outsmarted him. He diverted the waters of the Euphrates River, which at that time flowed under the walls and river gates of the city of Babylon, and was able to march into town, sloshing through the now dangerously-receeded waters of the Euphrates. The Babylonians, meanwhile, were toasting Marduk and all their other gods in vessels specially brought out of storage, the vessels taken years ago from the temple of Yahweh in Jerusalem and singularly dedicated to the honor and glory of His name.

Perhaps as early as 538 B.C., Cyrus issued a decree (recorded in Ezra 1:2–4; 6:2–5) that made it possible for the exiles to return to their homeland. Under the governor Zerubbabel and the High Priest Joshua, almost 50,000 Jews (a rather disappointingly small percentage of the exiles living in Babylon) returned to Jerusalem and Judah.

Immediately upon the return of the "remnant" (Hag. 1:14), the people were united "as one person" (Ezra 3:1) in their resolve and direction. The first thing they did was build an altar of God in order to sacrifice burnt offerings in accordance with the Law of Moses (Ezra 3:2). Here on the foundations of the previous Solomonic altar they offered the morning and evening sacrifice and the New Moon sacrifices, and made regular burnt offerings and freewill offerings (Ezra 3:3–6).

But even more important, by the second month of the second year after their return (Ezra 3:8), the former exiles began work on rebuilding the temple. Quickly the foundations were completed for what would later be referred to as the "Second Temple." Then the trouble began: it started with the elders who had seen the beauty and splendor of Solomon's temple. They literally wept when they saw how scaled down this building was compared to what had been destroyed. Meanwhile, the younger generation rejoiced. So confusing was the commotion and dissonance between the weeping and the rejoicing that one could not tell which it was that the people were doing (Ezra 3:12–13). Then came the request from Judah's enemies in Samaria (the polyglot mixture of peoples whom the Assyrian King Esarhaddon had imported in order to keep the former inhabitants from uniting in a revolt against his kingdom). They offered to help the exiles build the temple, but Zerubbabel declined their offer on religious grounds: "You have no part with us in building a temple to our God" (Ezra 4:3 NIV). That led to more trouble, for now these enemies began to discourage and frustrate the exiles and make them afraid. Indeed, these disaffected persons were so incensed by the refusal of Zerubbabel to allow them to work on the temple that they wrote to the Medo-Persian potentate and were able to get an injunction against any further work on the house of God. Thus the work on the temple came to a grinding halt, and there matters rested until the second year of Darius the King, when God stirred up Haggai and Zechariah, two prophets who had been part of that first group of returning exiles. The book of Haggai, then, is a record of what God did through His prophet.

In order to summarize the key historic events and to give our readers a handy guide to some of the key dates, we offer the following chronology:

539 B.C.	The fall of Babylon
538	Cyrus's decree to allow the return of the exiles
537	49,897 Jews return home (Neh. 7; Ezra 2)
536	Work on the temple stopped (Ezra 3)
530	Cyrus dies
530–522	Cambyses II, Cyrus's son, reigns
522–486	Darius I (Civil War; Behistun stone erected)
520	Darius I confirms Cyrus's decree (Ezra 6)
520	Haggai's messages
516	Temple completed and dedicated (Ezra 6:15)

But now it is time for us to get into the message of the book of Haggai itself.

An Outline of Haggai

The book of Haggai is carefully laid out chronologically. It has five sections, each precisely dated to "the second year of King Darius," which is 520 B.C. on our Julian calendars. The sections (each containing one revelation, or message) and dates are:

I. 1:1–11   6th month, 1st day: August 29, 520 B.C.
II. 1:12–15   6th month, 24th day: September 21, 520
III. 2:1–9   7th month, 21st day: October 17, 520
IV. 2:10–19   9th month, 24th day: December 18, 520
V. 2:20–23   9th month, 24th day: December 18, 520.

But even more important than the dates of these messages is their content—what is communicated from the Spirit of God to the prophet, and thus to our generation. For our purposes, we will treat the five revelations to Haggai under four teaching blocks:

I. A Call to Renew the Work of God   1:1–15
    A. By Refusing to Offer Our Excuses   1:1–2
    B. By Setting Our Priorities   1:3–6
      1. God's Work Must Come Before Our Work
      2. God's Ways Must Come Before Our Ways
    C. By Getting Involved in Our Lord's Work   1:7–12
      1. The Purposes of Obedience
      2. The Costs of Disobedience
      3. The Beauty of Obedience
    D. By Our Receiving God's Enablement   1:13–15
    E. Conclusion
II. A Call to Reject a Negative Spirit   2:1–9
    A. For Our Present Needs: A Divine Formula   2:1–5
      1. Of Human Responsibility   2:4a
      2. Of Divine Presence   2:4b

   3. Of Divine Promise   2:5a
   4. Of the Divine Spirit   2:5b
   B. For Our Future Participation: A Divine Finale   2:6–9
   1. An Immovable Kingdom   2:6
   2. An Immovable King   2:7
   3. An Immovable Glory   2:8–9
   C. Conclusion
III. A Call to Personal Holiness   2:10–19
   A. Holiness is Not "Contagious"   2:10–12
   B. Evil is "Contagious"   2:13
   C. Holy Works Do Not Make Holy Persons   2:14
   D. A Holy God Gives All Good Gifts to Holy Persons
       2:15–19
   E. Conclusion
IV. A Call to Participate in God's Triumph   2:20–23
   A. Loosely Hang on to the Perishable Things of Life   2:20–21
   B. Firmly Grasp the Unshakable Kingdom of God   2:22–23
   C. Conclusion

CHAPTER ONE

A Call to Renew the Work of God

Haggai 1:1–15

1:1 In the second year of King Darius, in the sixth month, on the first day of the month, the word of the LORD came by Haggai the prophet to Zerubbabel the son of Shealtiel, governor of Judah, and to Joshua the son of Jehozadak, the high priest, saying,

2 "Thus speaks the LORD of hosts, saying: 'This people says, "The time has not come, the time that the LORD's house should be built."'"

3 Then the word of the LORD came by Haggai the prophet, saying,

4 "Is it time for you yourselves to dwell in your paneled houses, and this temple to lie in ruins?"

5 Now therefore, thus says the LORD of hosts: "Consider your ways!

6 "You have sown much,
     and bring in little;
   You eat, but do not have enough;
   You drink, but you are not filled with drink;
   You clothe yourselves, but no one is warm;
   And he who earns wages,
   Earns wages to put into a bag with holes."

7 Thus says the LORD of hosts: "Consider your ways!

8 "Go up to the mountains and bring wood and build the temple, that I may take pleasure in it and be glorified," says the LORD.

9 "You looked for much, but indeed it came to little; and when you brought it home, I blew it away. Why?" says the LORD of hosts. "Because of My house that is in ruins, while every one of you runs to his own house.

10 "Therefore the heavens above you withhold the dew, and the earth withholds its fruit.

11 "For I called for a drought on the land and the mountains, on the grain and the new wine and the oil, on whatever the ground brings forth, on men and livestock, and on all the labor of your hands."

12 Then Zerubbabel the son of Shealtiel, and Joshua the son of Jehozadak, the high priest, with all the remnant of the people, obeyed the voice of the LORD their God, and the words of Haggai the prophet, as the LORD their God had sent him; and the people feared the presence of the LORD.

13 Then Haggai, the LORD's messenger, spoke the LORD's message to the people, saying, "I am with you, says the LORD."

14 So the LORD stirred up the spirit of Zerubbabel the son of Shealtiel, governor of Judah, and the spirit of Joshua the son of Jehozadak, the high priest, and the spirit of all the remnant of the people; and they came and worked on the house of the LORD of hosts, their God,

15 on the twenty-fourth day of the sixth month, in the second year of King Darius.

Haggai 1:1–15

All too frequently this chapter is cited only in those times in the life of the believing community when a new building program has been announced. It is as if this chapter is reserved solely for the purpose of raising up exterior monuments to God.

But the immediate problem in Haggai of rebuilding the house of God serves only as a metaphor for the broader principle of doing the work of God in all its variety of forms. To conclude that the people of Judah, or the people today, have adequately responded after they have erected some kind of material structure is to miss the point badly.

Small wonder, then, that this chapter issues four *ways* in which we, like the remnant that returned from exile, can be involved in renewing the work of God.

A. By Refusing to Offer Our Excuses   1:1–2
B. By Setting Our Priorities   1:3–6
   1. God's Work Must Come Before Our Work
   2. God's Ways Must Come Before Our Ways
C. By Getting Involved in Our Lord's Work   1:7–12
   1. The Purposes of Obedience
   2. The Costs of Disobedience
   3. The Beauty of Obedience
D. By Our Receiving God's Enablement   1:13–15

BY REFUSING TO OFFER OUR EXCUSES (1:1–2)

The times had definitely changed! No longer were the prophets dating their revelations by the Davidic king in the line of the future Messiah; instead, we are *"In the second year of King Darius."* The times of the Gentiles had now dawned!

But the first line of the book of Haggai was momentous for more than its announcement of the Gentile influence in Judah; this was the first time God had spoken in the post-exilic era. It was the first time God's voice had been heard in the land since the days of Jeremiah. The prophets Daniel and Ezekiel had spoken during the seventy years of the exile, but they had spoken from the land of their captivity!

In this part of chapter 1 Haggai is writing *"in the sixth month, on the first day of the month."* On our Julian calendars that would be August 29, 520 B.C. Since it was the first day of the month, it was a holy day to the Lord and a holiday for Judah. This was the time of New Moon (Ps. 81:3; Isa. 1:13–14; Hos. 2:11; Amos 8:5; Num. 10:10; 28:11). It was a time to recall once again all that God had done for His people.

The sixth month, however, signalled somewhat ominously the end of the grape, fig, and pomegranate harvests and, with no refrigeration, the end of the summer fruits. Haggai may be alluding to Jeremiah's mournful word that the summer is over and we are not yet saved (Jer. 8:20). Or he may be alluding to Amos 8:1, where a basket of summer fruit signalled that the "end" had come for Israel. The dateline, at any rate, signalled more than a location in time. It carried its own overtones for those familiar with the culture and the failures of those times.

Once again, God patiently sent His Word by the hand of His prophet. This had been God's appointed means of notifying His people since the time of Moses—and even earlier. The Word was from God; it was not an editorial on current Jewish thought, nor the consensus of an elite group of the exiles.

That Word was addressed first to the nation's two leaders, Zerubbabel the governor and Joshua the High Priest. Zerubbabel was the grandson of Jehoiachin, a former king in Judah who had been taken captive in 598 B.C. (2 Kings 24:15) and carried off to Babylon. Zerubbabel means "Seed of Babylon" or "Shoot of Babylon." The title *"governor,"* pehâ, serves as a reminder of his Babylonian appointment since the word is borrowed from the Babylonian Akkadian language. Zerubbabel is probably the same person as the one called "Sheshbazzar" in Ezra 1:8 and 5:14, for the same work Zerubbabel is said to have done in Ezra 3:8 is attributed to Sheshbazzar in Ezra 5:16.

The miracle of Zerubbabel's being governor is itself another story of God's faithfulness to His promise to David. The story begins with the tragic declaration of God to Jehoiachin (also called King Coniah, or Jeconiah) in Jeremiah 22:30. There God declared Jehoiachin "childless," meaning that no son of his would ever sit on the Davidic throne. The signet ring, seal of the office of Davidic King, was stripped from him, and Jehoiachin and his five sons went into captivity. His five sons, also known to us from the tablets archaeologists have found at the famous Ishtar Gate in Babylon, were made eunuchs (as prophesied by Isaiah in Isaiah 39:7), and thus could raise no sons for the throne.

Consequently, Jehoiachin adopted the seven sons of Neri, a descendant of David from David's son Nathan. So it was that the line of David through Solomon terminated with Jehoiachin, but continued through Neri's son Shealtiel. But Shealtiel also died childless, so his brother Pediah had to perform the duty of Levirate Marriage (Deut. 25:5–10) out of which Zerubbabel was born. Hence, Zerubbabel was the legal son of Shealtiel, but the actual son of Pediah, a descendant of King David.

Joshua the High Priest was a descendant of the line of High Priests coming from Zadok.

The message that Haggai gives as he steps into his task of motivating God's people to reevaluate what they had been doing is this: *"This people says, 'The time has not come, the time that the* LORD's *house should be built'"* (v. 2). How odd that God should refer to His people using the distant form of *"This people."* Even during their time in

Egypt the people of Israel had been known as "My people." But clearly the gap had widened between what God expected and how His people were living; there was an obvious distance between God and His people. God's displeasure was evident.

The primary cause of the distance that had come between the people and their God was their excuse that the time had not come to rebuild the temple. This excuse was, in effect, a roundabout accusation (circumlocution) that it was God's fault things had not improved. The people seemed to be thinking "if God wanted His house to be built, He should have made us wealthier." Further, relations with the Medo-Persians had not yet been normalized. And the exiles needed time to recoup from the mighty losses they had sustained during all those years in Babylon and by a slow recovery of the economy at the time. In this way, the exiles ostensibly blamed their inaction on the "time"; but they were really pointing their fingers toward heaven and blaming God.

How quick we mortals are to find excuses and to blame God when we have not done His work, though we are at fault. Often our excuses are mere pretexts for our laziness and our selfish reinvestment of time on our own projects. The returned exiles had the time to do God's work if they wished to make the time. Matthew Henry remarked: "It is bad [enough] to neglect our duty, but it is worse to vouch Providence for the patronizing of our neglects."[4] For the person "who wills to do right, the time is always present; however, [we] mortals are ingenious when [we] wish to hide our delinquencies."[5]

And, just as the exiles' problem never was "time," so "time" has not been the problem for others since. We must recognize the rebuke of God in our general national mess. The only responsible thing to do is to refuse to attribute the symptoms of our nation's deep ills to God's mistreatment either of our nation or of us. The fault for not doing God's work is ours; it must not be attributed to God!

By Setting Our Priorities (1:3–6)

God's Work Must Come Before Our Work

God's response to the exiles' pitiful excuse-making was swift and direct: *"Is it time for you yourselves to dwell in your paneled houses, and this temple to lie in ruins?"* (v. 4). God's work in rebuilding His house ought to have had priority over the exiles' work on their houses, even as it must take priority over *our own* work. The religious condition of the people's hearts could be directly gauged by their attitude toward working on God's house. In that sense, the building of the temple was a barometer of the people's spiritual condition. And insofar as the house of God was being neglected, the people were committing an act of spiritual treason. How could they call their God Lord when they refused to do what He commanded? This was a patent violation of their claim that they served God as their King.

However, by rejecting God as their King and Lord the people were inviting God to reject their own labors (v. 6). How disingenuous was the exiles' excuse that the time was not right and that conditions and circumstances prevented them from doing what they really wanted to do.

If the times were so adverse, how did it happen that so many of the exiles were able to live in "paneled houses?" We are not exactly sure how we should translate the Hebrew word. Some translations render it "wainscoted" houses; others suggest "vault-roofed" (LXX), "panel-ceiled" (Vulgate), or "covered with cedar boards" (Chaldee). Regardless of how the word is rendered, the point is fairly clear. The people's position that they were too poor to rebuild the temple due to the bad economy, inflation, and the poor value of the shekel was untenable. Their lavish spending on themselves exposed their hypocrisy and lies.

"*Consider Your ways!*" (v. 5), the prophet urged. This must have been one of Haggai's favorite expressions, for in this short book of thirty-eight verses, he uses it in four verses (1:5, 7; 2:15, 18). Haggai was pointing to the people's desperate need to examine their hearts and to search out the direction of their lives (cf. Lam. 3:40). If God's work was not at the top of their list of priorities, how could they be sure they had not fallen into serious idolatry? Was not the genius of idolatry putting any idea, person, goal, or commitment on a par with or above the Living God?

God's Ways Must Come Before Our Ways

The Hebrew text uses a series of infinitive absolutes in the questions that are asked in verse 6 to emphasize their eternal and universal relevance. Put in modern parlance, Haggai's questions from the Lord ask: Are you sowing more and harvesting less? Are you eating and drinking more and enjoying it less? Are you wearing more and feeling less warmth? Are you earning more and able to buy less?

No one cheats God without cheating himself at the same time! The old Puritan commentator T. V. Moore said it best: "The events of life are hieroglyphics in which God records His feelings towards us, the key to which is found in the Bible."[6]

One point made in verse 6 is that there is a real correlation between the productivity of the land and the spiritual growth of the believing remnant. This correlation was first established after the fall in the Garden of Eden. Because of the sin of Adam and Eve, the land was cursed. When our Lord returns again, Romans 8:20–22 announces, the whole created order—including the dirt, or land—will experience release from bondage and enjoy the effects of the redemption of our Lord Jesus Christ. In the meantime, substantial healing can and will come every time God's people experience a major revival or reformation and turn back to Him. So let us believers not be unsure whether we are the keepers of our nation and part of the solution to some of the ecological disasters that visit us from time to time. We are!

Had not Amos (Amos 4:6–10) warned about such things in verse 6? Five times God sent one calamity after another in order to capture the attention of His people who were not hearing and responding to His Word. Unfortunately, none of the calamities that came upon them was successful in convincing the people that it was time to turn back to the Lord. Five times Amos records the mournful words, "Yet you did not return to me." Then the national judgment fell: "Prepare to meet your God." The capital of Samaria would be destroyed by the Assyrians, for there had been no sign of repentance. No less emphatic are Hosea 4:10 ("They shall eat but not have enough") and Micah 6:15 ("You shall sow, but not reap; you shall tread the olives, but not anoint yourselves with oil").

Some of us will protest: "Don't get so personal," while admitting, "I *am* less satisfied; I *do* work longer and harder, yet I seem to get further and further behind in my bills and cannot buy or do as much with my earnings." May I suggest that one possible reason we seem to be getting further behind is that God is trying to capture our attention. If in studying His Word we cannot hear our Lord calling us to turn back to Him, to set Him at the top of our priorities, then so great is His love for us that He will speak to us at the check-out counter in the grocery store. He will shout at us through our wretched state of misery and dissatisfaction with our jobs and our life's achievements.

All too often we have placed other goals, interests, and joys ahead of the place we should have reserved for the Living God: our children's educations, our children's little league games, our advancement in the company, our leisure time on the weekends. The priorities we set in our day-to-day lives testify to our concurrence with modern advertisements that we should "have it our way," or that "we are the one" around which everything ought to revolve. However, God calls us to make a radical break with all of that type of thinking and planning and to place His ways, His cause, His goals in first place, ahead of every other earthly desire. Doing anything less is simply a modern form of ancient idolatry. We may as well name our earthly distractions Baal, Anat, Asherah or any other of the gods or goddesses of Canaan, for our idols are no better than those of ancient Israel.

By Getting Involved in Our Lord's Work (1:7–12)

As he did in verse 5, in verse 7 Haggai calls us to ponder carefully the effects of what we are doing to ourselves and to our nation. So significant is Haggai's message in verses 7–12 that, in announcing its divine origin, Haggai refers to God as the *"Lord of hosts."* This title for our Lord occurs about 300 times in the Old Testament. Two hundred forty-seven of such occurrences are in the prophets, and in this slight volume of Haggai the title occurs fourteen times. Zechariah uses it fifty-three times and Malachi twenty-four times for a total of ninety-one times in these three post-exilic prophets alone. The title never appears in the Pentateuch, Joshua, or Judges; its first appearance is in 1 Samuel 1:3. Surely it has reference to the fact that the Lord is sovereign over the armies of Heaven and earth (1 Samuel 17:45; Ps. 24:7–10). He is absolutely sovereign without any rival!

The Purposes of Obedience

The response God wanted from His people was to go up to the mountains, cut down timber, and begin to build (v. 8). The fact that the people are commanded to cut down timber raises the question of what had happened to the cedar logs that they had cut down over sixteen years earlier in Lebanon (Ezra 3:7). Had they rotted on the abandoned building site? Or had they been stolen and improperly used to build their own "paneled houses?" Either answer was not a good testimony to the people's goodness or faithfulness.

This verse does not say that the people repented, but that may be fairly implied. For the people demonstrated by their actions that they had turned from their former apathetic ways and wanted to do God's work.

The purpose of obedience was not merely to see a building raised; it was first and last to bring pleasure to God and to glorify Him. As God says in verse 8, He wants the people to be obedient: *"that [He] may take pleasure in it and be glorified."* God makes it clear, then, that His pleasure does not come from buildings per se; it comes, rather, from the people's attitudes and the condition of their hearts while they are working on the buildings. The chief end of the work of every man and woman of God is not so much to build temples, or to carry out other external works of righteousness or good works, as it is to glorify God and to enjoy Him forever.

The Costs of Disobedience

Some will respond, "Give me the other side of the picture. What will I loose if I do not choose to go the route of pleasing God and glorifying His name?" Verse 9 answers that question. *"You looked for much, but indeed it came to little; and when you brought it home, I blew it away. Why?" says the* LORD *of hosts. "Because of My house that is in ruins, while every one of you runs to his own house."* Once again Scripture underscores the intimate connection between nature's health and the performance of men and women in grace. Moses warned Israel years earlier about the same judgments. Haggai 1:6 echoes Deuteronomy 28:38–40, Haggai 1:10 recalls Deuteronomy 28:23–24, and Haggai 1:11 captures the informing theology of Deuteronomy 28:22. Therefore, none of the judgments spoken of in Haggai were unexpected; they were in the book to teach people to avoid them.

The cost of disobedience is high. People generally experience shortages of raw materials, manufactured goods, food, and wages. Disobedience is never a profitable shortcut to success; on the contrary, it is ultimately a very costly way to go. Naturally, "one swallow does not make a summer," as the saying goes, but a series of these shortages experienced over a long period of time by a believing community that has been seriously reluctant to follow the voice of the Lord signals that God is giving His final call to any in that community who are still alert enough to hear it.

Because God's house was in "ruins," *ḥāreb* (v. 4), He had called for a "drought" (*ḥōreb*) on the land, mountains, grain, new wine, and oil (v. 11). Mount Horeb (Mount Sinai) was a dry and desolate land. If men and women wanted to abandon the work of God, ultimately God would help them appreciate the significance of what they had done by abandoning their lands, works, and endeavors. Doing the work of God was not an end in and of itself, but was an external barometer of a change going on in the souls of those who had refused—up to this point—to put their shoulder to the load.

The Beauty of Obedience

I wish there were more verses like verse 12 in the Bible. What an amazing text! Starting with the leadership and continuing down through the rank and file, the people all *"obeyed the voice of the LORD their God."* Suddenly, as a result of Haggai's preaching and the convicting power of the Holy Spirit, the people—who had been, in effect, practicing atheists—started to obey the Lord.

The people decided that the Lord had indeed sent Haggai and given him the message he had delivered. They *"feared the presence of the LORD."* Fear, in this context, is not to be confused with the state of being frightened; rather, it is that attitude that is borne out of a trust in the Living God. To fear the Lord is to depart from evil (Prov. 8:13; 9:10) and to rejoice in the Lord with trembling (Ps. 2:11).

BY OUR RECEIVING GOD'S ENABLEMENT (1:13–15)

This section is dated as a separate message, as discussed in the introduction. Yet this message and the message that precedes it are so closely tied that they belong together. On September 21, 520 B.C., some twenty-four days after laying down His challenge, the Lord gave His great word of assurance: *"I am with you, says the LORD"* (v. 13). Isn't it true that when we take one move towards the Lord He gives us the ability to complete the task? And He gives us the wonderful promise of His presence.

God promises to be "with" us over 100 times in the Old Testament. It's too bad that we have ruined the word "with" by our careless use of it in everyday speech. "Yes, I'm with you; I'm behind you," we say to our friends, but we never say how far behind we are. However, when God promises that He is with us, He means that He is right there alongside us with His strong presence. In fact, so real is His presence that when He is with us our service to our Lord is not a solo performance, but a team effort; the strong Son of God stands alongside us as we teach, sing, or serve in His name. That was the assurance the returned exiles had.

God also granted a new vitality to the community of exiles as He *"stirred up"* (v. 14) the people and their leadership. This involved restoring their vision and renewing their energy for the tasks that lay before them. A complete change of heart had taken place, and the leadership and people now wanted to do the work of God. Now the community shared a common vision and enthusiasm for the work, for God had met the people and had changed them from the inside out.

Conclusion

Once again, it was revival time for God's people. They had dabbled with disobedience too long and the results of drought, shortages, and suffering were all too plain, just as Deuteronomy 28:23–24 had predicted.

One of the key ways to fight inflation, crop failure, blight, and the shrinking dollar is to ask God to renew His work in each of our hearts. A righteous few can still be the keepers of their nation. But when we pretend we are too poor or too busy to seek first the kingdom of God and His righteousness (Matt. 6:33), our possessions and our investments of time begin to witness against us.

Let us stop giving God the scraps of our time and energy. Let us start obeying God and doing His will. For if we will honor our Lord, He will stir us up by His Holy Spirit and enable us to do His will by working in us that which is well pleasing in His sight.

As Zechariah 4:6 reminds us, "Not by might nor by power, but by my Spirit, says the LORD of hosts."

Ours is a most critical moment in history. Will we experience revival or revolution? In the midst of all the angry and strident voices of our day, will the believing body not hear His call to be different? Let us ask God to renew our hearts as we turn to Him in full repentance. Therein lies the hope for history and for our nations until we see our Lord face to face.

CHAPTER TWO

A Call to Reject a Negative Spirit

Haggai 2:1–9

2:1 In the seventh month, on the twenty-first day of the month, the word of the LORD came by Haggai the prophet, saying:

2 "Speak now to Zerubbabel the son of Shealtiel, governor of Judah, and to Joshua the son of Jehozadak, the high priest, and to the remnant of the people, saying:

3 'Who is left among you who saw this temple in its former glory? And how do you see it now? In comparison with it, is this not in your eyes as nothing?

4 'Yet now be strong, Zerubbabel,' says the LORD; 'and be strong, Joshua, son of Jehozadak, the high priest; and be strong, all you people of the land,' says the LORD, 'and work; for I am with you,' says the LORD of hosts.

5 'According to the word that I covenanted with you when you came out of Egypt, so My Spirit remains among you; do not fear!'

6 "For thus says the LORD of hosts: 'Once more (it is a little while) I will shake heaven and earth, the sea and dry land;

7 'and I will shake all nations, and they shall come to the Desire of All Nations, and I will fill this temple with glory,' says the LORD of hosts.

8 'The silver is Mine, and the gold is Mine,' says the LORD of hosts.

9 'The glory of this latter temple shall be greater than the former,' says the LORD of hosts. 'And in this place I will give peace,' says the LORD of hosts."

Haggai 2:1–9

Whereas Haggai's first message addressed the people's unwarranted contentment with things as they were, his second message addresses the people's unwarranted discontent: the new danger that emerged as the work on the temple progressed. This message is a call to reject despondency, despair, and pessimism.

Those who had seen the first temple, that magnificent structure standing in all its glory, were liable to rate the present effort as a poor imitation. With such an inferior replacement of Solomon's temple, despair could quickly snuff out any spirit of enthusiasm or joy that the building could have symbolized to those who had never seen the first temple. Given this possibility, actually experienced sixteen years earlier (Ezra 3), Haggai's second message was needed.

God offers in Haggai's second message two *cures* for the myopia and debilitating comparisons between the past and the present. The first cure will aid us in the present, and the second will help us face the future.

> A. For Our Present Needs: A Divine Formula   2:1–5
>   1. Of Human Responsibility   2:4a
>   2. Of Divine Presence   2:4b
>   3. Of Divine Promise   2:5a
>   4. Of the Divine Spirit   2:5b
> B. For Our Participation: A Divine Finalé   2:6–9
>   1. An Immovable Kingdom   2:6
>   2. An Immovable King   2:7
>   3. An Immovable Glory   2:8–9

FOR OUR PRESENT NEEDS: A DIVINE FORMULA (2:1–5)

Human hands could never construct a building, no matter how magnificent, deserving of God or in any way equal to His glory. Even Solomon had to acknowledge in his prayer that, if the highest heaven could not contain the Living God, neither could any house built by any mortal—even his temple, in all its cedar, cyprus, and gold carvings and appointments—since a house built by a mortal cannot begin to rival the splendor of the heavens (1 Kings 8:27). Isaiah made the same point in Isaiah 66:1: if heaven is God's throne and the earth is His footstool, where is the house that would be adequate to match His person or to serve as His resting place? There is none; therefore, one should be hesitant in complaining about whether this present structure was as beautiful as a previous one or comparable to any other such structure.

Invidious comparisons are not always all that helpful. However, since the people had started this little game some sixteen years earlier (*see* Ezra 3), it was now best to face the problem and recognize it for what it was (v. 3). The Bible never covers up matters—especially where sin might be involved. Instead, it invites us to face up to the matter and declare what is troubling our souls.

The question in verse 3, then, has a rhetorical note to it: *"In comparison with it, is this not in your eyes as nothing?"* (v. 3). Here was an invitation to confess that what was being built was thought to be small and worthless by many in the returned community. But how could any work done for God and connected with His great triumph in that final day ever be judged to be small or worthless?

The twenty-first day of the seventh month, the date of this second message, was the last day of the Feast of Tabernacles. This was a public holiday, and the crowds from the countryside would be interested in what progress had been made during the preceding month, when work began on the temple. But in the first twenty-one days of the month the builders had already taken time out for the week-long festivities of the Feast of Tabernacles and for the celebration of *Yom Kippur* (the Day of Atonement). There could not have been any measurable progress in such a short period of time considering the few days the builders had worked (especially since the building materials had to be gathered and prepared); not seeing any real progress, pessimism once again set in.

Of Human Responsibility (2:4a)

The thrice-repeated exhortation to *"be strong"* (v. 4) is especially applicable to a downhearted people. In other national emergencies, God had given the same exhortation to Joshua (Deut. 31:7; Josh. 1:6, 7, 9, 18). David had shared the same encouragement with his son Solomon when he began to build the first temple: "Consider now, for the LORD has chosen you to build a house for the sanctuary; be strong, and do it. . . . Be strong and of good courage, and do it; do not fear nor be dismayed, for the LORD God—my God—will be with you. He will not leave you nor forsake you, until you have finished all the work for the service of the house of the LORD" (1 Chron. 28:10, 20).

The people were to be strong and to get on with the work because God was at work. Surely their Lord would equip them with enough energy to do what needed to be done, for in their weakness, as we have learned, God's power would be at its peak (2 Cor. 12:9; cf. Heb. 13:21).

The prophet Zechariah would give the same counsel in Zechariah 8:9: "Thus says the LORD of hosts: 'Let your hands be strong, you who have been hearing in these days these words by the mouth of the prophets.'" Men and women are responsible to act once God has spoken.

Of Divine Presence (2:4b)

Behind God's call for us to "be strong" is His promise *"for I am with you."* As we have said (see our discussion of 1:13–15), over 100 times in the Old Testament the preposition "with" sounds one of the deepest sources of encouragement a person can be given. It is part of His name and reflects His very character: Immanuel, "God with us." Beginning as early as Genesis 21:20, 22, the theology of the presence of God builds throughout the Old Testament.

It is impossible to dissociate from our Lord's assurance any strength that we might muster up. Without our Lord's presence and help, we do not have any strength or vitality. We dare not disconnect ourselves from our source of strength if we seek to carry on the work of God.

Of Divine Promise (2:5a)

What God promises to do here is *"According to the word that I covenanted with you when you came out of Egypt."* The Lord does not do anything on the spur of the moment. It was part of His eternal plan that He was carrying out even in the face of what many would have called a real setback. God had given His word to the patriarchs and Moses that He would be and do something unique for Israel so that, through Israel, all the families of the earth could receive His blessing. He would give an heir from the seed of the woman—Abraham, Isaac, and Jacob; an inheritance of the land to the nation of Israel; and the heritage of the gospel that said "And in you all the families of the earth shall be blessed" (Gen. 12:3; Gal. 3:8).

This promise doctrine can be put in that famous tripartite formula that appears almost fifty times in the Old and New Testaments: "I will be your God, You shall be my people, and I will dwell in the midst of you." That was the promise that was repeated when God brought His people out of Egypt in Exodus 29:45.

Of the Divine Spirit (2:5b)

"My Spirit remains among you; do not fear!" Just as Ephesians 6:12 warns us against thinking that ordinary human sagacity and ability are equal to the job before us (for we wrestle not against flesh and blood), here Haggai makes the point that the Holy Spirit is continually abiding (the Hebrew verb is a present participle) in the midst of all of us.

All too frequently, the ministry of the Holy Spirit in ancient times is not given the full recognition from modern readers it deserves. Our Lord was obviously startled that Nicodemus, though a teacher of the Jews, did not know how to be born again or what the ministry of the Holy Spirit was (John 3:10).

Further, David prayed in Psalm 51:11 that the Holy Spirit would not leave him. Likewise, Zechariah confessed in 4:6b, "Not by might nor by power, but by My Spirit, says the LORD of hosts." Indeed, the presence of the Holy Spirit was one more antidote for the community's despair.

With the comforting and enabling assurances of God's presence, His ancient promise, and His Holy Spirit, was there any room for weakness, fear, or frustration? This was not just sentimental talk realizable only in the future; the present could be an earnest and downpayment for the power and results of the Holy Spirit's work in the future.

FOR OUR FUTURE PARTICIPATION: A DIVINE FINALÉ (2:6–9)

The future belonged totally to God; He would reorder all things and establish His kingdom on earth. No shake-up that this world had ever seen would compare to that shake up of the heavens and the earth. For just as God had once shaken the earth—ever so slightly—at the Exodus from Egypt (Ps. 114) and at Sinai (Exod. 19:18; Judg. 5:4–5; Ps. 68:6; Hab. 3:6), so He would once again shake up things—this time in an extraordinary way.

An Immovable Kingdom (2:6)

Very soon, now, warns the prophet, God is going to really rock this old planet—more violently than anything experienced at Sinai, on Mount Saint Helens or anywhere else. Our Lord will do this to remove everything changeable; the transitory will be replaced with the eternal.

The shaking of the earth at the presence of the Lord during the Exodus (Ps. 114:1, 3, 7: "When Israel went out of Egypt, . . . the sea saw it and fled. . . . Tremble, O earth, at the presence of the LORD, at the presence of the God of Jacob. . . .") and the shaking of Sinai (Exod. 19:18: "Now Mount Sinai was completely in smoke, because the LORD descended upon it in fire . . . and the whole mountain quaked greatly.") were merely precursors of the appearance of God that would come in the final day. In the last day there would be a shake-up that would engulf the whole world, signalling that the final appearance of Christ would take place momentarily. Then Christ would come and reign on earth in all His glory forever and ever.

The New Testament apostles similarly warned about the imminence of the Lord's coming. Paul cautioned in 1 Corinthians 7:29, 31 that "the time is short," "for the form of this world is passing away." Similarly, Peter urged us to be vigilant, for "the day of the Lord will come as a thief in the night, in which the heavens will pass away with a great noise, and the elements will melt with fervent heat. . . . Therefore, since all these things will be dissolved, what manner of persons ought you to be in holy conduct and godliness, looking for and hastening the coming of the day of God. . ." (2 Peter 3:10–11).

The writer to the Hebrews even made this section of Haggai the basis of one of his messages. He said in Hebrews 12:26–28, "Now he has promised 'Yet once more I shake not only the earth, but also heaven.' Now this, 'Yet once more,' indicates the removal of those things that are being shaken, as of things that are made, that the things which cannot be shaken may remain. Therefore, since we are receiving a kingdom which cannot be shaken, let us have grace, by which we may serve God acceptably with reverence and godly fear."

That ought to convince us to hold on to that which cannot be shaken. All that can be shaken, the transitory, we ought to hold on to loosely. Why would we risk eternity, the health of our souls and everything enduring in order to enjoy the ephemeral pleasures of sin for a brief season?

On September 13, 1988, I was in Kingston, Jamaica, teaching Old Testament theology when hurricane Gilbert blew into town at 11:00 A.M. For three hours gale winds clocking up to 200 miles per hour at the center of the storm tore that island apart. After a reprieve of some sixty-five minutes as the eye of the storm went over, the winds returned from the opposite direction. The storm illustrated graphically the necessity of fixing ones hopes, goals, and affections on that which is abiding, for few things survived the desolation of those gale-force winds. I saw coconut trees and telephone poles snap as if they were matchsticks. Entire second stories of buildings rose skyward and disappeared. Tin roofs were ripped off and turned into instruments of death as they whipped down the street with a force that severed in half human bodies and automobiles tires alike! In the midst of such destruction, one comes to the realization that very little is abiding or permanent in this world of material goods. Most is transitory.

But we have a kingdom from our God that *is* abiding. With thankful hearts let us enter into His presence with thanksgiving and into His courts with praise. Let us serve Him with reverence and a godly fear, as the writer of Hebrews urges us to do, "[f]or our God is a consuming fire" (Heb. 12:29).

An Immovable King (2:7)

"[A]nd I will shake all nations, and they shall come to the Desire of All Nations." Almost all recent translations challenge the fact that this passage is messianic. The question arises because of the use of the plural form of the Hebrew verb "come." Since most recent translators link the verb with the singular noun "desire," they render the noun as a singular collective, "desired things." Thus the 1901 American Standard Version of the Bible changed "desire" into "precious things," while the New American Standard Bible reads "They will come with the *wealth* of all nations." The New English Bible reads "The *treasure* of all nations shall come hither," and the New International Version reads "And the *desired* of all nations will come." [Italics mine.]

But the consonants that make up the noun could as well be read as a plural form, without changing the received Hebrew text, if one supplies different vowels. The third century B.C. Greek translation, the Septuagint, also rendered the noun as a plural.

Both the singular and the plural forms of the word "desire" are used in the Old Testament in reference to an individual. Using the singular form, Saul is called "the desire of Israel" in 1 Samuel 9:20, and Daniel 11:37 refers to the Antichrist who does not have "the desire of women." Daniel is described three times as "greatly beloved" (Dan. 9:23; 10:11, 19)—all in the plural form using the same consonants found in Haggai 2:7.

Could it be, then, that Haggai deliberately uses a form of "desire" that has both singular and plural connotations in order to bring out the idea that God is at the head of all precious things—that He is more precious than all the wealth of the world? There is, after all, much biblical evidence suggesting that the "wealth" of the nations will come flowing to the people of God in that day: "The wealth of the Gentiles shall come to you" (Isa. 60:5, using a different word for "wealth," *ḥayîl*); Zechariah's reference to the "wealth of all the surrounding nations" (Zech. 14:14; cf. Rev. 21:26).

Therefore, we conclude that in verse 7 "desire" refers to the Messiah who will come. He is the preeminent "desired One." Yet, just as He is the epitomy and center of all that is valuable, so in His train will flow all the wealth and treasures of the nations. Christ is that "Messenger of the Covenant" who shall come (Mal. 3:1), and it is He who is the focus of all the longing of the believing community. Whether verse 7 refers to prized persons or possessions, the expression "the Desire of All Nations" points to that which is "precious" and of utmost value in the eyes of its beholders. It is similar to the idiom "vessels of desire," which occurs in the singular in 2 Chronicles 32:27 ("desirable items"), 2 Chronicles 36:10 ("costly articles"), and Daniel 11:8 ("precious articles"), but appears in the plural form in 2 Chronicles 20:25 ("valuables") and Daniel 11:43 ("precious things"). It would seem, then, that the word "desire" used in verse 7 of Haggai comprises both singular and plural connotations and that most translators and modern commentators are much too timid in failing to extend their understanding of the word to include the singular connotation and to see a clear Messianic reference here.[7]

An Immovable Glory (2:8–9)

"I will fill this temple with glory" (v. 7) Along with an unshakable kingdom and King, God promises in these verses to fill the rebuilt

temple with glory in that day when He shakes up the heavens and the earth.

Glory could, in this case, refer to material splendor, for verse 8 reminds us that "'*The silver is Mine, and the gold is Mine,' says the* LORD *of hosts*" (v. 8). Surely this follows from the fact that the earth belongs to the Lord and all that is in it (Ps. 24:1). He is in a very good position, then, to lavish upon His house an abundance of material splendor and glory.

Equally well, however, glory could refer to the personal presence of the Lord. His presence alone would be more than enough to compensate for all the perceived inadequacies of the second temple as compared to the Solomonic temple. Verse 9 supports the translation of "glory" as the Lord's personal presence. Could it not be that in their use of "glory," as in their use of "desire," Haggai and our Lord have deliberately brought together the material and personal connotations of the word in order to underscore how unique and transcending were the benefits God alone was able to bring those who previously were too focused on the present to the exclusion of the future? We think so.

CONCLUSION

God has planned, and has already inaugurated, a kingdom that will never be destroyed (Dan. 2:44). He is the only One that the nations and the people of the earth should really be desiring. If only men and women knew that what they hungered for and sought in a thousand other distractions was really the Living God!

So the word for discouraged people who feel they may be off in the hinterlands of God's service is this: God's work done in God's way will never lack in splendor, eternal significance, or the personal presence of our Lord. For that Sunday School class, that rural pastorate, that little-known unheralded ministry and all other works for good are directly linked to the final manifestation of the Kingdom of God in the last day. In this way, too, "this temple" referred to in verse 3 is directly connected to "this latter temple" referred to in verse 9!

The kingdom, the glory, and the person of our Lord will remain when everything else has given way. They are unshakeable. Let us, therefore, forsake all negative attitudes about the work of God; His name, His cause, and His kingdom will most certainly triumph over everything!

CHAPTER THREE

A Call to Personal Holiness

Haggai 2:10–19

10 On the twenty-fourth day of the ninth month, in the second year of Darius, the word of the LORD came by Haggai the prophet, saying,

11 "Thus says the LORD of hosts: 'Now, ask the priests concerning the law, saying,

12 "If one carries holy meat in the fold of his garment, and with the edge he touches bread or stew, wine or oil, or any food, will it become holy?"'" Then the priests answered and said, "No."

13 And Haggai said, "If one who is unclean because of a dead body touches any of these, will it be unclean?" So the priests answered and said, "It shall be unclean."

14 Then Haggai answered and said, "'So is this people, and so is this nation before Me,' says the LORD, 'and so is every work of their hands; and what they offer there is unclean.

15 'And now, carefully consider from this day forward: from before stone was laid upon stone in the temple of the LORD—

16 'since those days, when one came to a heap of twenty ephahs, there were but ten; when one came to the wine vat to draw out fifty baths from the press, there were but twenty.

17 'I struck you with blight and mildew and hail in all the labors of your hands; yet you did not turn to Me,' says the LORD.

18 'Consider now from this day forward, from the twenty-fourth day of the ninth month, from the day

> that the foundation of the LORD's temple was laid—
> consider it:
>
>   19 'Is the seed still in the barn? As yet the vine, the fig
> tree, the pomegranate, and the olive tree have not yielded
> fruit. But from this day forward I will bless you.'"
>
> *Haggai 2:10–19*

Haggai addressed the people's unwarranted contentment in his first message and their unwarranted discontent in his second message. In this third message he rebukes the people's misplaced values. It is all too common to rest on one's laurels after completing a major task. Thus it became important to warn that one must build with pure motives. Building the temple cannot be the sum and substance of all there is to life.

In this message, Haggai conducts what almost looks like a television quiz show with a panel of experts. Haggai, acting as the host, has a series of questions for his panel of priests, who are to supply the answers. The relevant passages that form the basis of his questions are Leviticus 6:27; 22:4–6 and Numbers 19:11. The principles learned from Haggai's interchange with the priests form the basis for our discussion of this text.

Illustrations

    A.   Holiness Is Not "Contagious"   2:10–12
    B.   Evil Is "Contagious"   2:13

Applications

    C.   Holy Works Do Not Make Holy Persons   2:14
    D.   A Holy God Gives All Good Gifts to Holy Persons   2:15–19

HOLINESS IS NOT "CONTAGIOUS" (2:10–12)

It may have been that the community now reasoned: if God is going to shake the nations, then what is the sense of our continuing to build this temple? Or was the problem a different one? Did the returned exiles reason instead that since the temple construction had started all would be well and they could relax in their efforts to serve our Lord? The second supposition appears closer to the truth.

This message came on *"the twenty-fourth day of the ninth month,"* which would be December 18, 520 B.C., exactly three months after the people had responded to Haggai's initial challenge. Once again, God took the initiative by disclosing His will to His people. Like Haggai's first message, this one has an introductory formula followed by a challenge to the people, culminating in the phrase in verse 15, *"And now, carefully consider from this day forward"* (see 1:5, 7).

"Now, ask the priests concerning the law" (v. 11). Since the priests were the legal experts, the Lord wished to direct a question to them; Haggai's use of questions and answers piqued and sustained the people's interest. Haggai asks the priests, *"If one carries holy meat in the fold of his garment, and with the edge he touches bread or stew, wine or oil, or any food, will it become holy?"* (v. 12).

To put the question as succinctly as possible: Is it possible to communicate holiness to the third degree? The priests' answer will have relevance for all God's people in every age.

The people must have been arguing that since the restoration of the temple and its ritual had begun, there was no more occasion for any blight on their labor or on their efforts to make a living. Haggai is instructed by God to raise the question he poses with the priests in order to rid the community of any possible misconceptions concerning this issue.

The priests, of course, answer correctly when they reply in the negative. They knew that the Law of Leviticus 6:27 taught that direct contact with holy meat made one holy, but nowhere did the text teach that indirect communication of holiness to the third degree was just as effective as communicating holiness by direct contact.

Accordingly, holy acts have no power to make persons holy; only a holy God can make us holy. Thus, the temple is the holy sanctuary of God; but that does not automatically sanctify the land of Judah and all its inhabitants, just as it is not true that because our grandparents knew God and served Him things will go all right for us as the benefits from their holy lives. Building the temple could not serve as a good luck charm or an amulet to ward off evil. It is amazing how poorly we understand spiritual things sometimes.

If the amulet mentality was the ditch on one side of the road, the ditch on the other side of the road was the misconception that worshipping in a temple would automatically cleanse unholy persons. This trust in ritualism to remedy and atone for unsanctified hearts was anathema in the Old and New Testaments. Over and over again the prophets warned that external religiosity was not an adequate substitute for true repentance of the heart. The prophets warned that obedience was preferred to mere sacrifice (1 Sam. 15:22) and that knowledge of God was to be given priority over sacrifice (Hos. 6:6; Amos 5:21; Mic. 6:6–8; Isa. 1:11–17; 58:3; Jer. 7:21–22). God warned that He would not hear us if we regarded iniquity in our hearts (Ps. 66:18). The one who turns his ear from hearing the Law would find that even his prayer was an abomination to God (Prov. 28:9). Thus religious works that do not flow from faith and love for our Lord will have little or no effect in maturing a person in his faith. Repentance to God does not cancel the consequences of our sins, but it can, by the grace of God, remove the guilt of those sins. Accordingly, a repentant murderer may truly be forgiven, even though the state may demand that he still pay for the consequences of his act.

EVIL IS "CONTAGIOUS" (2:13)

Our panel of priests, having answered the first question correctly, is now given a second question: *"If one who is unclean because of a dead body touches any of these, will it be unclean?"* This time the priests answer, *"It shall be unclean"* (v. 13).

Evil and defilement are much more easily transmitted—and can be transmitted more extensively—than holiness. Drop a little filth in a container and soon the entire contents are contaminated. Sin is much more contagious and corrosive than most realize.

It is surprising to see how poorly many reason in this area. They feel that environmental determinism (the view that things will change for the better if the surroundings change for the better) will sufficiently secure the holiness they hope for themselves and their children. But that is about as reasonable as saying that one healthy specimen in their midst will heal a hospital ward full of people with infectious diseases, or, that what a bushel of rotten apples needs is one healthy, succulent Yakima Valley apple. Surely everyone can see the flaws in such reasoning. So why do we continue to insist that holiness is contagious and transferable while, ironically, maintaining that evil is not all that dangerous, especially if there are good examples around for our children? Though I have spent my life in Christian education, I cannot endorse the view that our children's mere contact or association with holiness—by attending Christian schools throughout their education or by receiving training from their parents—will preserve them. This text warns against such thinking; one holy environment is not a panacea.

God's people had tainted their sacrifices and work by their disbelief and by reducing their worship to mere functionalism; they had hoped that one act of getting the temple started was enough and that they could now rest on their laurals. But religion is not "caught." To grow spiritually one needs more than a good environment, good influences, and good associates or playmates.

According to the Mosaic Law, contact with a dead body was the thing that most defiled a person, making him ceremonially unclean (Lev. 21:10–21; Num. 11:6; 19:11–21). Death had such a strong polluting effect because it is the result of sin.

HOLY WORKS DO NOT MAKE HOLY PERSONS (2:14)

As He did in 1:2, in verse 14 God refers to the people not as "my people" but as *"this people,"* thus implying a continuing rift between God and man. Reinforcing this rift, in this verse God also refers to the people as *"this nation."*

The people had hoped that their holy work of rebuilding the temple would automatically make their land, its products, and all the work of their hands holy. But their logic was flawed. The holiness of the temple could be transmitted to the land but did not thereby pass on to the products of the land.

Only cleansed men and women can serve God with clean hands and clean hearts. Without these, the people's gifts to God—no matter how costly or how frequently given—are unclean. Some had offered to God sacrifices in the midst of great scarcity (Ezra 3:3), but they still lacked the spiritual prerequisite of clean hands and clean hearts, and their gifts were thus of no value to God or man.

Righteousness cannot come from what a person does for God; it comes from what God does in the heart of a person. Unfortunately, too many in Haggai's day were like we are today; they wrongly thought their work on the temple could bring the sanctification that can only come from the Lord.

A HOLY GOD GIVES ALL GOOD GIFTS TO HOLY PERSONS (2:15–19)

Here, as we have said, Haggai again asks for some very careful reflection: *"And now, carefully consider from this day forward."* The

Hebrew word translated here as "forward" has been rendered in at least four different ways: (1) It has been rendered "backwards," although in only one translation. This is likely not an accurate translation since it gives the phrase a meaning not found elsewhere and imposes on the phrase the opposite of the meaning it has in verse 18; (2) The word is deleted altogether in some translations, though for no apparent reason; (3) It has also been rendered "foreward," a meaning definitely favored because of its parallel usage in 1 Samuel 16:13; 30:25; and Haggai 2:18; and (4) Finally, the word has been rendered "forward," with the additional words "what will come to pass" in the RSV, though the added words are not in the Hebrew and are actually unnecessary. [8] The third meaning is preferred, for the reason stated.

In directing his people to consider "from this day forward," Haggai is inviting his people to compare what God is going to do in the future with the conditions that existed before one stone was laid upon another in the building of the temple. There, nothing seemed to work and all labor was a waste. Instead of the expected "twenty ephahs, there were but ten," a fifty-percent reduction in the expected grain harvest. The grape harvest was even worse. "When one came to the wine vat to draw out fifty baths from the press, there were but twenty" (v. 16). The wine press was a hollowed out stone trough, usually with lattice work overhead that functioned like trolley straps to keep those tramping on the grapes in their bare feet from slipping and breaking their necks. A deep notch was cut into the end of the trough so that when the vat was filled with skins at the bottom and juice at the top, the juice would spill over and be caught in jars for storage and later use. But alas, the grape harvest yielded only forty percent of what was expected, a loss of sixty percent!

That was all worth thinking about as Haggai urged once again in verse 18, "Consider now from this day forward." Things were really going to change since the revival and repentance of chapter 1 had taken place. The curses of verse 17 were the standard ones warned about in Deuteronomy 28:22—"blight and mildew and hail." The "blight," or "blasting wind," is that scorching east wind called Khamsin in Arabic, a hot wind that blows in off the desert and scorches everything (cf. Gen. 41:6, wherein Pharoah dreams of grain blighted by the east wind). The "mildew" is probably a fungus that kept the grain from ripening properly. These two terms occur not only in Deuteronomy

28:22, but also in 1 Kings 8:27 and 2 Chronicles 6:28. The third term, "hail," is another adverse weather condition that usually comes with the north winds (cf. Prov. 25:23). Heavy hail can damage crops and even injure people and cattle (Exod. 9:25–35; Josh 10:11). Accordingly, this passage might be paraphrased: "I sent hot dry winds to wither your grain and damp winds to make it rot." [9]

The tragedy had been this: *"yet you did not turn to Me"* (v. 17). This verse is word-for-word what Amos had concluded in his day (Amos 4:9; cf. Jer. 3:6–10). The single word "turn," or "return," summarizes the heart of every prophet's message (Zech. 1:4). It is the Old Testament word for "repent," and it issues God's most persistent invitation in that testament.

Some have spotted what seems to be a contradiction between Haggai 2:18, which speaks of the twenty-fourth day of the ninth month (December 18, 520 B.C.) as the time when the foundation of the new temple was laid, and Ezra 3:8–10, which places the laying of the foundation in the second month of the second year of the return of the exiles from Babylon (c. 537 B.C.). But Ezra 3:8–10 does not conflict with Haggai 2:18 because the date given in Ezra is the date the exiles began their first, aborted, work on the temple—work that was halted for sixteen years. While a different date for the start of the first work on the temple is given in Haggai 1:15, that is the date when the people began to clear the site and gather the materials for building. Therefore, Ezra 3:8–10 and Haggai 1:15 likewise do not conflict. Ezra 4:24 tends to support the fact that on December 18, 520 B.C., the rebuilding of the temple got under way in earnest after the completion of the preliminary preparations.

God expects a negative answer to His question in verse 19: *"Is the seed still in the barn?"* Since early rains are expected in October and November, that is when the ground is ploughed and planted with the grain seed for the winter months. Haggai's revelation came towards the end of December; therefore, the seed for next year's crop had better be in the ground if the people expect to harvest it next year. From verse 19 the people were to infer: you know what bad harvests you have been having up to this point. But watch what I the Lord am going to do now that you have begun to build the temple. I have seen the change in your hearts that this work signals.

In verse 19 God also asks the rhetorical question: *"As yet the vine, the fig tree, the pomegranate, and the olive tree have not yielded fruit. But from this day forward I will bless you."* The trees must have looked better than they had looked at that time of the year in any previous year. Here was another sign that God would now turn toward His people with blessing. Progress in the spiritual realm was the first indication that success was coming in the agricultural realm as well.

Conclusion

It is clear that physical pollution and spiritual defilement are more effectively transmitted than purity and holiness. Purity and holiness are not gifts that can be communicated simply by contact or association—especially to the second and third person or situation and beyond.

Neither can an external work or participation in a ritual substitute for the commitment of the heart that is the first step necessary to validating the authenticity of any act of worship.

Even though it would be dangerous apart from revelation to attempt to predict the quality or quantity of a harvest that may not have fully germinated, yet a bounteous harvest can be anticipated when a nation's righteous remnant begins to please God from their hearts, for positive results are felt even in nature and in people's labors. In that sense, the believing remnant, who truly fear God, are their nation's keepers. They know that one benevolent or religious act of mercy, like starting to build the temple, is not all that there is to serving God. Holiness is not something that can be transferred merely on contact with religious acts, and thus excuse us from involving ourselves for the rest of our lives. Rather, we must wholeheartedly dedicate the entirety of our lives—every facet of our lives—to our Lord.

CHAPTER FOUR

A Call to Participate in God's Triumph

Haggai 2:20–23

20 And again the word of the LORD came to Haggai on the twenty-fourth day of the month, saying,

21 "Speak to Zerubbabel, governor of Judah, saying:

'I will shake heaven and earth.

22 I will overthrow the throne of kingdoms;
I will destroy the strength
    of the Gentile kingdoms.
I will overthrow the chariots
And those who ride in them;
The horses and their riders shall come down,
Every one by the sword of his brother.

23 'In that day,' says the LORD of hosts, 'I will take you, Zerubbabel My servant, the son of Shealtiel,' says the LORD, 'and will make you as a signet ring; for I have chosen you,' says the LORD of hosts."

Haggai 2:20–23

In verses 20–23 Haggai adds to God's promise to bless the produce of the land (2:18–19) God's promise of the work He will do in the consummation of history. This message features Zerubbabel, Judah's governor, a descendant of David, but offers encouragement to any believer faced with tough decisions similar to those which Zerubbabel's culture presented him. Its two words of advice are:

A. Loosely Hang on to the Perishable Things of Life   2:20–21
B. Firmly Grasp the Unshakable Kingdom of God   2:22–23

LOOSELY HANG ON TO THE PERISHABLE THINGS OF LIFE (2:20–21)

For the second time on December 18, 520 B.C., God spoke to His servant. Using the language of 2:6–9, Zerubbabel was warned that *"[God] will shake heaven and earth"* (2:21). This shake-up did not refer to any impending revolt that would disrupt the Persian empire; disruptive revolts had occurred in 521 B.C., and order had already been restored by the time this message came to God's people. No, this shake-up was to be an eschatological one to occur in connection with the coming of our Lord. (*See* our comments on Haggai 2:6–9).

Facing the certain fact that this world and all of its things were going to pass away, how important it now was for all believers to monitor themselves carefully in the way they regarded (and clung to) the stuff of the world. What was the sense of selling one's soul for that which was going to perish anyway? That was the first principle Haggai wanted his people, and us, to learn.

FIRMLY GRASP THE UNSHAKEABLE KINGDOM OF GOD (2:22–23)

God's future victory over all human governments is now declared in the most graphic terms possible. Haggai cannot actually describe the future. No one can describe the future, since no one has been there and no one, except God, has any knowledge of it. Haggai therefore does the only thing any writer can do to give his readers some idea of the future; he recalls the past.[9] Thus, under the inspiration of God, Haggai uses the "overthrow" of Sodom and Gomorrah (Deut. 29:23; Isa. 13:19) to describe the future collapse of kingdoms. The experience of Pharaoh and his armies as they "went down" into the sea (Exod. 15:1, 5), both horse and rider, and were vanquished, serves as the best analogy of what God will do in the future in His final conquest of competing nations. Likewise, Gideon serves as the best illustration of how completely disarmed the enemy will be in that day when they try to oppose God, for they will pull the sword on each other (Judg. 7:22).

The nations that try to oppose God in that final day will only succeed in destroying themselves, for they will find themselves entering self-destructive wars, in which God will annihilate them as He did the five cities of the plain, Pharaoh's army that chased the people of Israel, and the Midianites.

The final promise of Haggai's prophecy is this: "'*In that day,' says the LORD of hosts, 'I will take you, Zerubbabel My servant, the son of Shealtiel,' says the LORD, 'and I will make you as a signet ring; for I have chosen you,' says the LORD of hosts*" (v. 23). Here is a passage replete with Messianic allusions and predictions. "My servant" is a well known title for the Messiah; in fact, of all the terms used for the coming Christ (including "Messiah," "servant," or "Servant of the LORD,") it is the most frequently used. Not only does this title appear twenty times in the singular form in Isaiah 41–53 (e.g., Isa. 41:8; 42:1; 44:1) and eleven more times in the plural in Isaiah 54–66, but it is the very title used for the new David who is to come—Christ himself—in Ezekekiel 34:23 and 37:24.[11] The preeminent Servant is Jesus Christ who is to come, though the word "servant" also denotes corporate solidarity and can refer to all of Israel. The One to come represents the whole group. But the hope and identity of the group rests on its identification with the Messiah himself.

A second Messianic allusion is the "signet ring." This God-ordained emblem of the office and authority of the Davidic kingship—the family through whom the Messiah would come—had been taken from one of David's descendants through the Solomonic line, Jehoiachin (also named Coniah) (Jeremiah 22:24). God later gave the ring to another Davidite through the line of David's other son, Nathan (*see* our discussion on Haggai 1:1), and gives it now to the Davidic descendant Zerubbabel.

In a sense, too, our Lord is the "signet seal" of the Father and His authority. He is that signet as man, not as God. Thus it was that Christ came to earth and took on flesh—manhood—in the race and family of David.

God again alludes to Zerubbabel's anointed roots when He says that He has "chosen" him (cf. Isaiah 42:1, where the coming Servant of the Lord is called God's chosen or Elect One). He was singled out by God for this task long before the world began. These were the very words spoken to the One who came as the long-expected Messiah, that were heard from heaven on the day that John baptized Jesus (Matt. 3:16–17).

The last allusion to the coming Messiah is found in the words "*I will take you.*" No doubt, these words denote God's special selection of Zerubbabel (cf. Exod. 6:7; Josh. 24:3; 2 Sam. 7:8). Historically they contained overtones of God's special designation for a special task.

The unshakeable kingdom of our Lord centers on the Lord Christ who would come to do the will of the Father. He will restore the fallen hut of David (Amos 9:11–12) and receive the king's seal, or signet, and, thereby, the assurance that His elevation and status are in accord with His person and character.

CONCLUSION

When all the nations of the earth have been shaken and reduced to what they are in reality, then the Lord himself will emerge as God's unshakeable Messiah. The fact that Zerubbabel emerged at this time in the life of the struggling nation was just another sign that God had not forgotten His promises to Abraham and David.

Therefore, believers ought to be holy just as the Lord their God is holy (1 Pet. 1:15–16). Our sinful passions which grew out of our former ignorance ought to be squelched. We had better sieze with all spiritual understanding the abiding rule and reign of God, for in the end everything will be shaken except the coming King and His kingdom.

Our enemy is subtle and he is ever at work. If he cannot draw us away from God's service by one means, he will try another. But thanks be to God that He that is in us is greater than he that is in the world. Believers will recognize the clandestine efforts of the enemy to turn us aside from the call of God in our misdirected focus on the external form or the institution in and for itself; but our focus must be fixed on Christ and our heart relationship to Him must never be traded for cheap ritualism or external works valued only for themselves.

NOTES

1. W. O. E. Oesterley and Theodore H. Robinson, *An Introduction to the Books of the Old Testament* (London: SPCK, 1946), p. 409.

2. Paul D. Hanson, *The Dawn of Apocalyptic* (Philadelphia: Fortress, 1975), p. 247.

3. Martin Luther. *Luther's Works: Lectures on the Minor Prophets*, XVIII, ed. by Hilton C. Oswald (St. Louis: Concordia, 1975) p. 367, as cited by Elizabeth

Achtemeier in *Nahum–Malachi, Interpretation: A Biblical Commentary for Teaching and Preaching* (Atlanta: Knox, 1986), p. 93.

4. Matthew Henry, *Commentary on the Whole Bible: Isaiah to Malachi* (New York, Fleming H. Revell Co., 1800 [1712]), IV: 1390.

5. John Calvin, *Commentaries on the Twelve Minor Prophets IV* (Grand Rapids: Eerdmans, 1950), *in loco.*

6. T. V. Moore, *Haggai, Zechariah and Malachi* (New York: Robert Carter and Brothers, 1856), p. 66.

7. The most helpful discussion, and the one I used to shape my discussion here, is found in Herbert Wolf, "'The Desire of all Nations' in Haggai 2:7: Messianic or Not?," *Journal of the Evangelical Theological Society* 19 (1976): 97–102. Also largely contained in Herbert Wolf, *Haggai and Malachi: Rededication and Renewal* (Chicago: Moody, 1976), pp. 35–38.

8. David J. Clark, "Problems in Haggai 2:15–19," *Bible Translator* 34 (1983): 432–33.

9 Clark, ibid., p. 434.

10. *See* Walter C. Kaiser, Jr., *Back Toward the Future: Hints for Interpreting Biblical Prophecy* (Grand Rapids: Baker, 1989). The title of the book sets the theme for this type of interpretation.

11. *See* the magnificent chapter XII by Willis Judson Beecher, *The Prophets and the Promise* (Grand Rapids: Baker, 1963; reprint of New York: Thomas Crowell, 1905), pp. 263–88.

The Book of Zechariah

Zechariah 1:1–14:21

Introduction to Zechariah

Zechariah is not only the longest of the books of the twelve Minor Prophets, it is one of the most frequently quoted. There are seventy-one quotations from or allusions to Zechariah in the New Testament. One third of these appear in the Gospels and thirty-one are found in the book of Revelation (including twenty from chapters 1–8 and eight from chapters 9–14). Of all the Old Testament books, Zechariah is second only to Ezekiel in its influence on the book of Revelation.

THE AUTHOR

Zechariah means "Yahweh remembers." It is a name filled with hope, reminding the many people who felt God had abandoned them during the seventy long years of exile in Babylon that God will exercise His "grace," or "covenantal love" (*ḥesed*); He will not forget His own.

The name Zechariah was quite popular, for there are some thirty different individuals in the Old Testament who bear this name. The Zechariah who was the author of our book was *"the son of Berechiah, the son of Iddo the prophet"* (1:1). In Ezra 5:1 and 6:14, he is referred to as the "son of Iddo," with no reference to Berechiah. It is not necessary, however, to posit scribal confusion between two different Zechariahs (cf. Isa. 8:2), for there is ample evidence in the Old Testament that the word "son" was used as an equivalent of "grandson" (cf. Gen. 31:28). Thus, we can conclude that Zechariah was Berechiah's son and Iddo's grandson.

Interestingly enough, Nehemiah speaks of an Iddo who is one of the heads of the priestly families that returned to Judah from Babylon (Neh. 12:4, 16). If this is the same Iddo, and it appears it is, then Zechariah was from the tribe of Levi and therefore served as a priest as well as a prophet. Other prophets in the Old Testament similarly had a dual role of priest and prophet: e.g., Jeremiah (Jer. 1:1) and Ezekiel (Ezk. 1:3). Zechariah must have succeeded his grandfather Iddo as head of his priestly family (Neh. 12:16). We must infer, then, that Zechariah's father Berechiah died at an early age, making it necessary for Zechariah to step in and fill his place in the cycle of priests. The text does suggest that Zechariah was, indeed, a young man when he received his visions in chapters 1–8, for Zechariah 2:4 notes that the angel said *"Run, speak to this young man."* That would have been *"On the twenty-fourth day of the eleventh month, which is the month Shebat, in the second year of Darius"*(1:7). On our Julian calendar, that would have been October 15, 519 B.C.

Zechariah began his ministry *"In the eighth month of the second year of Darius,"* which would have been November, 520 B.C. Thus he entered his prophetic ministry two months after his contemporary, Haggai. Haggai commenced his labors on August 29, 520 B.C. (Hag. 1:1), and his first revelation was followed by additional words from our Lord on September 21, 520 B.C. (Hag 1:15), October 17, 520 B.C. (Hag. 2:1), and twice on December 18, 520 B.C. (Hag. 2:10, 20). Zechariah received his first message after Haggai received the message given in Haggai 2:1–9 and before Haggai received his last messages (Hag. 2:10–19, 20–23).

While the first eight chapters of Zechariah's prophecy were written in 520 B.C., chapters 9–14 may have been, and probably were, composed much later, in Zechariah's old age. Some conservatives suggest this may have been as late as 480 to 470 B.C.[1] If Zechariah was around thirty years old when he wrote the first eight chapters, he must have been around seventy years old when he wrote the last six chapters. If so, the composition of chapters 9–14 would have taken place in the days when the Persian empire was waning, perhaps after the revolt of Egypt in 486 B.C. and the death of Darius in 485 B.C. The changes in the author's age and in the political circumstances of the empire arguably account for the differences in style, outlook, and themes found in chapters 1–8 and chapters 9–14.

The Unity of the Book

Most critical scholars do not regard all fourteen chapters of the book of Zechariah to be from one and the same hand. They attribute chapters 9–14 to an anonymous author from a much later period and assert that these chapters were made part of Zechariah in order to make sure they were included in the canon, riding in on Zechariah's coattails, as it were.

Apparently this division of Zechariah into at least two separate works began rather innocently when a Cambridge scholar, Joseph Mede (1586–1638), suggested that the quotation from Zechariah 11:13 that Matthew (Matt. 27:9–10) attributed to Jeremiah was actually written by Jeremiah because Jeremiah was the author of chapters 9–14.[2] Others took Mede's idea and argued that Zechariah 9–14 was written much later than 1–8, in the Hellenistic, or even Maccabean, period.

The arguments for a so-called "Deutero-Zechariah"—that the last six chapters have a different content, style, and vocabulary—are not as convincing as some seem to think. The most damaging argument against a Deutero-Zechariah is that since there is no agreement on who the shepherds of chapter 11 were, it is not possible to place chapter 11 within a definite later period. The difference in content between the first chapters and the last is not conclusive; naturally, the chapters would address different issues if they were written during two different time periods (as we have stated), approximately forty years apart. Zechariah chapters 1–8 contain words that would encourage those returning from exile to turn from their sin and receive God's forgiveness. In chapters 9–14 Zechariah focuses on God's great work in the last day and on how the people should live knowing they will one day face the Lord.

Finally, the difference in vocabulary is not persuasive. It is true that the phrase "Thus says the LORD" (1:3) occurs frequently in chapters 1–8, but only once in the second section of 9–14, viz. chapters 12–14. However, the different chapters do contain similar vocabulary: the phrase "says the LORD" appears fourteen times in chapters 1–8 and six times in chapters 9–14. Further, "LORD of hosts" occurs three times in each of 1–8 and 9–14.

Neither is the difference in style evidence of a Deutero-Zechariah. One could hardly expect that after forty years a writer's style would show no change or development, particularly if it adjusts to a change of subject matter.

The truth of the matter is that all talk about a lack of unity in the book is really hypothetical, for no Hebrew manuscript showing such a break between chapters 8 and 9 has ever been discovered. In fact, the Greek manuscript found in the Dead Sea Scrolls containing the end of Zechariah 8 and the beginning of Zechariah 9 shows no gap or space between the two chapters.

Moreover, while some have concentrated on the differences, the similarities between chapters 1–8 and 9–14 are even more striking. All the chapters exhibit a fondness for the vocative and metaphors followed by meanings. Further, tell-tale characteristic phrases and certain idiosyncrasies of the writer appear in all the chapters of 1–14. [3]

It is true that Zechariah's name appears in the book only three times, all in the first eight chapters (1:1; 1:7; 7:1). It is also true that all of the first eight chapters are in prose (except the poetic sections of 2:6–13 and 8:1–8) while chapters 9–11 are poetic (except the prose section of 11:4–16) and chapters 12–14 are once again in prose (except 13:7–9). But none of this evidence amounts to a full proof for either side. Furthermore, when the book is taken as a unit, it is easier to see that a master plan does seem to be in mind and that there are linking themes, concerns, and shared perspectives that strengthen the overall impact of the message of the book.

HISTORICAL BACKGROUND TO THE BOOK

The setting of this book is the same as the setting of the book of Haggai (see the Introduction to that book). Like Haggai, Zechariah's most immediate concern was the rebuilding of Solomon's temple.

Also like Haggai, Zechariah develops the messianic theme, although he does so much more extensively. Messiah's coming would be God's answer to all the political challenges that had arisen to dash the hopes of the fallen kingdom and the throne of David.

Zechariah, of course, continued to minister long after Haggai's brief five-month ministry from August 29 to December 18, 520 B.C. Zechariah's ministry may have stretched as long as fifty years, from 520 B.C. to 470 B.C.

THE STRUCTURE OF THE BOOK

Zechariah contains three main blocks of material following a memorable introduction that is one of the "most intensely spiritual calls to repentance to be found in the Old Testament"[4] (1:1–6): (1) the visions (1:7–6:15), (2) messages answering questions about fasting, and

(3) eschatological writings divided into two oracles (9–11 and 12–14).

Recently, what critical scholars regarded as the chaotic order of events in chapters 9–14 was given a new explanation by Paul Lamarche. He argues that chapters 9–14 were built on a chiastic pattern; i.e., just as the Greek letter *chi* is in the form of an "x," so the pattern of thought moves so that the *a: b* line or section is matched by a *b: a* line or section.

As the following illustration shows, the introductory announcement of judgment and salvation on the neighboring peoples (9:1–8) was balanced by the concluding message of judgment and salvation on all nations (14:16–21)—all labelled a: items in the chiasm. In between these two bookends, as it were, are the two sections (chapters 9–11 and 12–14) wherein three themes can be distinguished: b: the king, or shepherd, as the Lord's representative (9:9–10; 11:4–17; 12:10–13:1; 13:7–9), (and in this case, expanded to) c: Israel's war and victory (9:11–10:1; 10:3b–11:3; 12:1–9; 14:1–15), and d: judgment on idols (10:2, 3a; and 13:2–6).

The Plan of Zechariah 9–14
(according to Paul Lamarche)[5]

a: Judgment and salvation of neighboring peoples 9:1–8				a: Judgment and salvation of all nations 14:16–21
b: Arrival and description of the king 9:9–10	b1 Shepherds rejected by the people 11:4–17	c2: War and victory of Israel 12:1–9	c3: War and victory of Israel 14:1–15	
c: War and victory of Israel 9:11–10:1	c1: War and victory of Israel 10:3b–11:3	b2: LORD's representative pierced 12:10–13:1	b3: Shepherd struck; people tested, return 13:7–9	
d: Presence of idols; judgment 10:2,3a		d1: Suppression of idols 13:2–6		

The great advantage of this explanation of the structure of 9–14 is that it does not call for a rearrangement of the text. Some consternation may be expressed over the fact that four passages are marked "b," but Zechariah is doing no more than what he has observed in the prophets that preceded him; the king is set side by side with the "shepherd" (*see* Jer. 23:1–8 and Ezk. 34:23–4).

The grand chiasm of chapters 9–14 is not the only one used by

Zechariah. The eight night visions in 1–6 form an *a,b,b,c,c,b,b,a* pattern with the theological climax coming in the fourth and fifth vision *(c,c)*. Further, as Joyce Baldwin points out, the call in the introductory message (1:1–6) is repeated in the sermons at the end of the first section (7:4–14 and 8:9–17). Finally, the climax of section one concerns the nations (8:20–23) flocking to Jerusalem to be with the Lord of hosts, and section two similarly ends with the nations finally with the Lord in Jerusalem (14:16–29).[6]

An Outline of Zechariah

CHAPTER ONE

Calling God's People to Repentance

Zechariah 1:1–6

1:1 In the eighth month of the second year of
Darius, the word of the LORD came to Zechariah the
son of Berechiah, the son of Iddo the prophet, saying,
2 "The LORD has been very angry with your
fathers.
3 "Therefore say to them, 'Thus says the LORD of
hosts: "Return to Me," says the LORD of hosts, "and I
will return to you," says the LORD of hosts.
4 "Do not be like your fathers, to whom the
former prophets preached, saying, 'Thus says the
LORD of hosts: "Turn now from your evil ways and
your evil deeds."'' But they did not hear nor heed
Me," says the LORD.
5 "Your fathers, where are they?
And the prophets, do they live forever?
6 Yet surely My words and My statutes,
Which I commanded My servants the prophets,
Did they not overtake your fathers?"
"So they returned and said:
'Just as the LORD of hosts determined
to do to us,
According to our ways
and according to our deeds,
So He has dealt with us.' " ' "

Zechariah 1:1–6

This text, which G. L. Robinson has called "one of the strongest
and most intensely spiritual calls to repentance to be found in the Old

Testament,"[7] issues four summons to repentance for all peoples in all ages. It was delivered three months before the eight night visions that follow in 1:7 to 6:8. It has now been eighteen years since Cyrus issued his famous decree (538 B.C.) allowing the Jews to return to their land.

The 50,000 Jews who returned, under the governorship of Zerubbabel and the High Priesthood of Joshua, immediately began to build the new temple, although they soon became discouraged and stopped. Then, in 520 B.C., God sent two prophets, Haggai and Zechariah. Haggai's task was to rouse the people to continue the task they had started sixteen years earlier. Zechariah's task was to convince the people to accompany that work with a complete spiritual change, the fruit of which could be seen, at least in part, in the rebuilding of the temple.

The four summons Zechariah issues are:

A. We Must Repent if We Wish to Experience All of God's Blessings   1:3
B. We Must Be Responsive to the Lessons of History if We Do Not Wish to Be Destroyed   1:4
C. We Must Realize How Brief the Time and Opportunities are if We Wish to Do Anything Positive   1:5
D. We Must Count on the Unchangeableness of Our God's Word if We Wish to Do Anything That Lasts   1:6

WE MUST REPENT IF WE WISH TO EXPERIENCE ALL OF GOD'S BLESSINGS (1:3)

Zechariah identifies himself as one who brought *"the word of the LORD"* to the people on that November day of 520 B.C. during the reign of the Medo-Persian king Darius. No longer were the biblical prophecies dated by the Judean kings in the line of David, for these were now the times of the Gentiles. (On the prophet's pedigree and background, see the introduction.)

Zechariah begins with the most emphatic statement one could make: *"The LORD has been very angry with your fathers"* (v. 2). The verb "has been angry" is emphasized by a noun made up of the same consonants as the verb. It is high time Israel recognized this fact.

Some will immediately protest that the God of the New Testament is a God of love and ask why the Old Testament chooses to focus on His wrath.

God is, of course, a God of love; this we must stress. But we must not lose sight of the fact that His infinitely holy character demands that He be angry with sin. In fact, it is a mark of a sick society when we are willing to listen only to pronouncements of God's love and not to messages that also declare God's wrath with sin. The Lord is "slow to anger" (Nah. 1:3), but persons must not view His patience as a weakness or hesitance to deal with sin; God will deal with sin (2 Pet. 3:9). Both testaments affirm God's wrath as well as His Love (Exod. 34:6–7; Deut. 7:7–11; John 3:16, 36).

The text of verse 2 gives a triple emphasis to God's anger toward sin. The people knew, moreover, that God had been extremely displeased with them, for the experience of seventy years in captivity had not been lost altogether on the nation, except on the most obtuse and hardened sinners.

The simple, but profound, solution to Israel's current state of sin was to *"return"* (v. 3) to the Lord. No other single word epitomized the prophets more accurately than this single word to "turn," or "return." In all of Scripture that is the one prerequisite to receiving any of God's blessings.

The summons to "return" is God's call to us to reverse our directions; when we are following our own goals and aims God asks us to do a 180 degree turn and make Him the goal and aim of our lives. I learned this lesson the hard way. In June of 1952, I had just finished my freshman year at Wheaton College. My parents had driven from the Philadelphia area to Chicago to drive me back home for a summer job.

Those were the days prior to the completion of the Interstate system. We left campus after I had participated in an evening concert with the College Chapel Choir. In order to gain time, we drove through the night on the old Lincoln Highway, Route 30. Some time past midnight I took my turn driving in western Ohio, and suddenly I encountered a detour that was poorly marked. I carefully followed the signs for Route 30, but I could not tell whether it was Route 30 east, which is what I wanted, or Route 30 west.

About five o'clock in the morning I was surprised to notice another town named Bryan, Ohio, in what I thought was eastern Ohio. I thought that was strange, for we had passed a Bryan, Ohio, the night before as we entered Ohio. Then the terrible reality set in: we had reversed our direction at that detour, half way through the state and had now gone back to where we had been hours before. Once more we had to turn around and head east. That is what Zechariah's word "return" means. It is a "U-turn" theology, which calls us to head in the direction that will take us back to the Savior.

The message summoning us to "return" to the Lord has ever been the earmark of all of God's true messengers. Isaiah cried, "Seek the LORD while He may be found, call upon Him while He is near. Let the wicked forsake his way, and the unrighteous man his thoughts; let him return to the LORD, and He will have mercy on him; and to our God, for He will abundantly pardon" (55:6–7). Likewise Joel urged, "Turn to me with all your heart. . . . rend your heart, and not your garments; return to the LORD your God, for He is gracious and merciful, slow to anger, and of great kindness. . ." (2:12–13). Even as the voice of the Old Testament fades, we hear Malachi cry once more, "Return to Me and I will return to you" (Mal. 3:7). John the Baptist cried out, "Repent, for the kingdom of God is at hand" (Matt. 3:2), and Jesus proclaimed the identical message (Matt. 4:17). Jesus was not the last to issue the summons to repent; the apostles declared that mortals must "repent" (Acts 2:38; 3:19; 5:31; 17:30; 20:21; 26:20; and 2 Cor. 7:10). It is imperative that this message of repentance be preached in all the world.

Is this preaching needed any less today than in Zechariah's day or in the day of the New Testament apostles? No! People today are not more heavenly inclined. Is this preaching needed by Christians as well? Yes! It is always time to repent of our sins if we wish to experience the power of the gospel and the joy of walking with our Lord.

We return to the Lord, for we live only by God's grace. He asks only that we be willing to turn our backs on our sins and turn to face Him, the only source of every blessing. It is so important that we do so that Zechariah three times (in the Hebrew text) notes that it is the Lord who says we should return to Him. Thus he drums into our consciousness an idea we would usually resist.

The idea of repentance, or "turning," is not abstract; it is very personal, for God summons us to *"Return to Me."* Repentance from sin is the prerequisite for any fellowship with the living Lord (1 John 1:9).

The title *"LORD of hosts"* designates our Lord as ruler over the whole universe, including the armies of Israel (Judg. 5:14; 1 Sam. 17:45) and the armies of heaven (1 Kings 22:19; Luke 2:13; Rev. 19:14). It was the favorite of the post-exilic prophets; of the 261 times it appears in the Old Testament they used it 91 times (Haggai-14, Zechariah-53 and Malachi-24). The title celebrates God's sovereignty and omnipotence: He is Lord.

WE MUST BE RESPONSIVE TO THE LESSONS OF HISTORY IF WE DO NOT WISH TO BE DESTROYED (1:4)

Four times *"the fathers"* figure in the brief text of verses 1–6 (vv. 2, 4, 5, 6). The previous generations are cited for their negligence, inattentiveness, and disobedience.

The fathers had sinned in two ways: in their *"evil ways"* and in their *"evil deeds."* "Evil ways" denotes a direction, mind-set, path or tendency always to go towards the evil option. "Evil deeds" denotes the actual practice or activity of evil. Some will only lean towards evil, while others will actually do evil. Both forms of evil are condemned here.

One could hardly blame the *"former prophets"* for the fathers' continued sin; the former prophets had presented the truth—and had done so tactfully. Had they not pled with those previous generations, *"Turn [please]"*? The Hebrew word for "please" is more than just a grace note added to the text. It marked the earnestness of Zechariah's appeal to his audience.

What do any of us learn from history? Is history "bunk," as Henry Ford suggested? Or is history "His-story"? Surely, it is risky business to waste the lessons of previous generations.

God waits patiently for each succeeding generation to weigh the calamities and blessings of the past. If any generation will heed the words to "turn" to God, or heed the growing storm clouds that forewarn of the certain coming judgment of God, He will forgive.

WE MUST REALIZE HOW BRIEF THE TIME AND OPPORTUNITIES ARE IF WE WISH TO DO ANYTHING POSITIVE (1:5)

The prophets and the fathers are not viewed from the same perspective here in verse 5. The point of the prophet is this: the time is extremely short for both the prophets and the fathers. It may have seemed as if the prophets would be around forever, for so it appeared in what many regarded as a constant haranguing from them. But look how fleeting life is! Neither the prophets nor the fathers lived forever! Most of them are gone; and so will all mortals eventually be.

If there is so little time in which to do anything for the glory of God, how important it is that we should do so now while we still have life and breath.

WE MUST COUNT ON THE UNCHANGEABLENESS OF OUR LORD'S WORD IF WE WISH TO DO ANYTHING THAT LASTS (1:6)

If the prophets seemed to be fragile and transitory, God's Word did not partake of either liability. Verse 6 begins with a strong adversative that could also be translated as "Nevertheless." And it is that permanence, immutability or unchangeableness of the Word of God and His purpose that distinguishes them from His servants the prophets.

If only we would learn to distinguish between the weakness and fragility of the best of God's servants and the abiding veracity and eternal effectiveness of the message that these prophets bring! Recent months have brought to light many startling revelations about the failures of some of the more famous televangelists and pastors of our day. But our trust must not be in televangelists or pastors; it is to be in the Lord who sent them and in the truthfulness of the word that they speak, for that word belongs to God.

"Did [my words] not overtake your fathers?" (v. 6c). What a graphic word picture! God's words functioned just like a highway patrol officer who spots a speeder, turns on the flashing lights of his patrol car, and pulls the speeder over. So God's Word will "curb" us. The Word of God will drive right up alongside us and nail us with precision for the infractions we commit.

Interestingly enough, the word *"overtake"* is a direct quote from Moses' speech in Deuteronomy 28:15, 45. There God had warned that His Word would "overtake" us if we tried to run away from Him. God's Word endures forever (1 Pet. 1:25; Isa. 40:6–8). God spoke and the world was created (Ps. 33:6, 9). God spoke in revelation and that word was like a "hammer" (Jer. 23:29) that breaks the rocks in pieces. It would do what it promised or threatened to do.

The plan and purpose of God would be carried out for Judah and the nations. He did *"just as [He] [had] determined to do to us"* (v. 6d). The Lord has done exactly what He had planned to do. No one can say to Him, "What have you done?" (cf. Dan. 4:35d).

The *"words"* and *"statutes"* of God were summaries of His own requirements embodied in His covenants. They were the announcements of what He would do in the face of the alternative responses that Israel could make. God did as He pleased and no one stopped Him or frustrated His will.

CONCLUSION

God's word is forever sure. What He has said He would do in judgment of a generation or people, He has done—unless that generation turned back to the Lord.

Both national and personal repentance are extremely important if we are to participate in the blessings of God. How can we as individuals, or as a nation, expect to continue to reap the benefits of our godly parents if we ourselves do not walk with the Lord and repent of our sins?

While there were external symbols of a turning back to God in the Old Testament, such as using sackcloth (Jonah 3:6, 8; Neh. 9:1; Dan. 9:3; Joel 1:8; Isa. 58:5) and sitting in ashes (Isa. 58:5; Dan. 9:3; Esther 4:3), Joel advises us that it is more important to rend our hearts than it is to rend our garments in grief over our sins (Joel 2:13). Let those who have never turned to the Lord before, and those who already have but who have gotten away from Him and have fallen into sin, repent and turn 180 degrees to face the One who is the author and finisher of our faith.

CHAPTER TWO

Waiting in the Calm Before the International Storm

Zechariah 1:7–17

7 On the twenty-fourth day of the eleventh month, which is the month Shebat, in the second year of Darius, the word of the LORD came to Zechariah the son of Berechiah, the son of Iddo the prophet:

8 I saw by night, and behold, a man riding on a red horse, and it stood among the myrtle trees in the hollow; and behind him were horses: red, sorrel, and white.

9 Then I said, "My lord, what are these?" So the angel who talked with me said to me, "I will show you what they are."

10 And the man who stood among the myrtle trees answered and said, "These are the ones whom the LORD has sent to walk to and fro throughout the earth."

11 So they answered the Angel of the LORD, who stood among the myrtle trees, and said, "We have walked to and fro throughout the earth, and behold, all the earth is resting quietly."

12 Then the Angel of the LORD answered and said, "O LORD of hosts, how long will You not have mercy on Jerusalem and on the cities of Judah, against which You were angry these seventy years?"

13 And the LORD answered the angel who talked to me, with good and comforting words.

14 So the angel who spoke with me said to me, "Proclaim, saying, 'Thus says the LORD of hosts:

> "I am zealous for Jerusalem
> And for Zion with great zeal.
> 15 I am exceedingly angry with the
>   nations at ease;
> For I was a little angry,
> And they helped—but with evil intent."
> 16 'Therefore thus says the LORD:
> "I am returning to Jerusalem with mercy;
> My house shall be built in it,"
> says the LORD of hosts,
> "And a surveyor's line shall be stretched out
>   over Jerusalem."'
> 17 "Again proclaim, saying, 'Thus says the LORD
> of hosts:
> "My cities shall again spread out
>   through prosperity;
> The LORD will again comfort Zion,
> And will again choose Jerusalem." ' "
>
> *Zechariah 1:7–17*

On February 15, 519 B.C., some three and one-half months after his initial message in 1:1–6, and two months after Haggai's final message (Hag. 2:20–23), Zechariah was given eight night visions. It appears that all eight visions were given in one night, but we cannot be sure.

The eight visions can best be understood in the chiastic pattern of *a, b, b, c, c, b, b, a,* with the theological climax coming in the fourth and fifth visions.[8] The first and the eighth vision bear a strong resemblance to one another, while the second and third, fourth and fifth, and sixth and seventh are in pairs. The resulting pattern would appear something like this:

   a Waiting in the Calm Before the International Storm 1:7–17

     b Watching the Nations Punish One Another 1:18–21

     b Expecting the Glory of God on Earth 2:1–13

       c Symbolizing the Removal of Sin All in One Day 3:1–10

       c Receiving God's Spirit for Doing His Work 4:1–14

     b Purging Evil From Israel 5:1–4

     b Removing Wickedness From Israel 5:5–11

   a Executing Judgment on the Gentile Nations 6:1–15

There is one other noteworthy pattern found in these visions. Typically each begins with what Zechariah *"saw,"* followed by the question *"what are these [or, "What does this mean"]?"* and concludes with an explanation by the interpreting angel, *"Then the angel of the* LORD *answered and said. . . ."*

In the first vision of Zechariah, he observes a man riding on a red horse among some myrtle trees in a ravine, or deep valley. Accompanying the red horse rider are other riders on red, sorrel, and white horses. These horsemen return after patrolling the earth with the disappointing news that *"all the earth is resting quietly"* (v. 11).

The focal point of this vision is 1:14, a message about the *"zeal"* of the Lord. The Hebrew word for "zeal," *qin³â*, is connected with the Arabic root *qana³a*, meaning "to become very red," as in the red face of a person with burning passion. (The Greeks took their word for this idea from the root "to boil.")

Zeal takes the form of hatred, envy or competition with others when a person is zealous only to advance his own interests; but when zeal is directed towards others it makes one capable of the most noble deeds. When God is spoken of as being "zealous," or "jealous" (Exod. 20:5; 34:14; Deut. 5:9), what is being described is the intensity of His love towards His own, not any kind of hatred, envy, or competition with others. The Lord is described as being a jealous God and a devouring fire (Deut. 4:24; 6:15; 29:18,19; 32:16, 21). Indeed, the fire of God's jealousy will be experienced in all kinds of events, even in the defeat of Israel's enemies.

Grounded in His zeal, and the intensity of His love, this first vision exhibits three mercies God gives as He moves on the international scene towards the climax of history.

A.   In Granting the Vision of His Plan for the Future   1:7–8
B.   In Granting the Interpretation of the Vision   1:9–12
C.   In Granting Three Declarations and Four Comforting
      Words for the Future   1:13–17.

IN GRANTING THE VISION OF HIS PLAN FOR THE FUTURE (1:7–8)

In this vision Zechariah sees two groups of angelic beings. The man riding the red horse is probably the same as the "Angel of the LORD." The "angel who talked with me" is an interpreter that accompanied the prophet (1:8; 2:3; 4:1,5; 5:5; 6:4).

At the center of this vision, and at the center of all of history, is the rider on the red horse, none other than *"the angel of the* LORD*"* (v. 11).

Some scholars identify the angel of the Lord in the Old Testament as the second person of the Trinity. (In Exodus 23:20–21, God's "name" was "in" this one called the Angel of the Lord. He is the One sent from the Father.) The other riders, said in verse 8 to be riding behind him on *"red, sorrel, and white"* horses, are only angels. The fact that Zechariah uses a present participle here means that the riders were in the act of riding at the time of the vision.

Christ is said to be *"among the myrtle trees"* (v. 8). The "myrtle," or *hadassah* shrub (the Jewish form of the name Esther), was an indigenous shrub that grew all over Israel and was a popular name for Israel. Thus, in this vision the myrtle tree symbolizes Israel.

The rider on the red horse is also located *"in the hallow"* (v. 8), a glen, ravine, or valley. This may well indicate that the nation of Israel was at the time in a period of deep humiliation. This low time in the nation's history is directly related to the fact that we have now passed into the "times of the Gentiles" (Luke 21:24). That period would last from the time of Nebuchadnezzar's first captivity in 605 B.C. until just before the second coming of Christ.

The variegated coloring of the horses may well indicate that the mission of God would be mixed. "Red" usually points to the judgment of war, and "white" usually points to mercy and peace. "Sorrel" (also translated "speckled," "dappled," "tawny," or a reddish-brown color) suggests a combination and mixture of God's works.

IN GRANTING THE INTERPRETATION OF THE VISION (1:9–12)

The prophet asks the same question we would have asked: *"What are these?"* (v. 9). The interpreting angel sent from the Lord, who is to be distinguished from the "Angel of the LORD," is called *"the angel who talked with me"* (v. 9).

The interpreting angel answers: *"These are the ones whom the LORD has sent to walk to and fro throughout the earth"* (v. 10). Their job was to reconnoiter and patrol the events, movements, and happenings on the earth. They went "to and fro," a phrase very similar to that used to describe Satan's activities in Job 1:7 (cf. also for patrolling, Genesis 3:8, God walking in the Garden; Exodus 21:19, the daily work-a-day movements of men; and 2 Samuel 11:2, David's restless pacing on his palace roof one night as he spotted Bathsheba bathing the village below).

The patrol's report was disappointing and disquieting, for the riders declare, *"all the earth is resting quietly"* (v. 11). This was disappointing because it meant that the great shake-up of the heaven and earth that God had promised in Haggai 2:21–2 had not come about as immediately as some had hoped.

The cry that goes up—from the Angel of the LORD, surprisingly enough—is: *"How long will You not have mercy on Jerusalem and on the cities of Judah, against which You were angry these seventy years?"* (v. 12). Obviously, the return of the exiles from Babylon was not in and of itself regarded as the fulfillment of the prophecy of Jeremiah 25:11 and 29:10. There had to be more to come.

And the wait continues to the present moment, even though the State of Israel was reestablished in May, 1948. Yes, even though Jerusalem has been in Israeli hands since the Six-day War in 1967, the fact remains that modern Jews are still scattered all over the world. So the question still demands an answer: "How long will it be before God's promise is finally realized?"

IN GRANTING THREE DECLARATIONS AND FOUR COMFORTING WORDS FOR THE FUTURE (1:13–17)

This text sets forth three declarations and four comforting words. The first of the three declarations is: *"[God is] zealous for Jerusalem"* (v. 14). The covenant God made with the people of Israel will never be revoked; it will be fulfilled, for the Lord made it unconditionally. One day Israel will be brought back to her land, not because she deserves it, but because God will be faithful to His Word.

The second declaration is: *"[God is] exceedingly angry with the nations"* (v. 15). These Gentile nations are altogether too complacent and self-reliant. Whereas God was but *"a little angry"* with His people, when God used nations such as Assyria or Babylon to discipline Israel (Isa. 10; Hab. 1–2) these nations *"helped—but with evil intent"* (v. 15); they used the occasions to try to destroy Israel and remove her from the family of nations. They disciplined Israel beyond what God had intended.

The third declaration, necessarily implicit in a text about God's zeal or jealousy, is that God will judge these nations. God will judge them before His earthly kingdom comes (Joel 3:1ff; Zech. 6:1–8).

These declarations are followed by four *"good and comforting words"*

(v. 13). The first is that Messiah will come again to Jerusalem (v. 16a). The book of Ezekiel describes how the "glory of the LORD" departed from Jerusalem, left the Holy of Holies to go to the porch of the temple, moved out to the eastern gate of the city, and finally, went up the Mount of Olives, where the glory of the Lord went up to heaven and where it will return when our Lord returns the second time (Ezk. 10:18–19; 11:23). By the term "glory," of course, the writer means the presence of God. In the meantime, Zechariah declared that His return would signal His restoration of the people to *"mercy"* (v. 16a).

The second wonderful word of hope and comfort for God's people is *"My house shall be built in [Jerusalem]"* (v. 16b). The project of rebuilding the so-called "second temple" in the days of Haggai and Zechariah was only a partial fulfillment of the command to build a temple when our Lord returns to rule and reign in the Millennium. God's glorious promise of a temple—the details and dimensions of which had never before been seen (Ezk. 40–48)—was to be realized far in the future. Zechariah will have more to say about this structure in Zechariah 2 (*see also* Isa. 2:2–3).

The third comforting word promises that Jerusalem's boundaries would expand (v. 16c). This city, ravaged as it was by the Babylonians in 587 B.C., the Romans in A.D. 70, and many other conflicts since—and still ravaged in our present day—would experience unusual urban renewal and expansion. The surveyor's line would *"be stretched out"* to measure an enlarged Jerusalem.

The fourth comforting word is that Jerusalem would once again be the city God had chosen (v. 17). Somewhat like our "Governor's Award" for a model city in a state, the Lord will select Jerusalem once again as His chosen place. The reason God will do this is because "the gifts and the calling of God are irrevocable" (Rom. 11:29). Having set His affection once on this city, our Lord will not forget what He has promised, even though He must judge the people of Jerusalem in the interim. The cities of the Promised Land will *"spread out,"* or "overflow" just as the springs of water overflowed into the streets in Proverbs 5:16.

CONCLUSION

Since the life of the Church is found in the olive tree on to which we, the Gentile "wild branches," have been grafted, we cannot be disinterested in what happens to the Jewish nation. We should derive comfort from what comforts Israel.

In the meantime, the Gentile nations are not the sovereign powers they think they are; nor will they remain the owners of all power, wealth, and authority. God alone is sovereign and He will overcome all the nations and all their threats against Jerusalem.

The patience of God wears thin with these nations. While He patiently waits for the planned moment to begin His judgment, neither Israel nor the Church should slip into thinking He will not vindicate His name. He will come and restore all things.

The gospel we preach is the "good news" of salvation, which includes the "gospel of the kingdom" (Acts 20:24–25). Consequently, Gentile believers are brought into the same kingdom as believing Jews, and all recline at the table of Abraham, Isaac, and Jacob (Matt. 8:11–12). In no sense was this kingdom postponed, nor did Jesus teach such when Israel failed to believe in Him. Had that kingdom been postponed, God's predetermined plan to have Christ go to the cross to die for our sins would have been placed in jeopardy.

The Church is a part of Messiah's kingdom (Luke 13:28–29). We still await the full establishment of Messiah's kingdom when our Lord returns in the future the second time. In the meantime, we already have eternal life because we have tasted of the powers of the age to come and His kingdom has begun already within us.

CHAPTER THREE

Watching the Nations Punish One Another

Zechariah 1:18–21

18 Then I raised my eyes and looked, and there were four horns.

19 And I said to the angel who talked with me, "What are these?" So he answered me, "These are the horns that have scattered Judah, Israel, and Jerusalem."

20 Then the LORD showed me four craftsmen.

21 And I said, "What are these coming to do?" So he said, "These are the horns that scattered Judah, so that no one could lift up his head; but the craftsmen are coming to terrify them, to cast out the horns of the nations that lifted up their horn against the land of Judah to scatter it."

Zechariah 1:18–21

The second night vision of Zechariah focuses on the "four horns" and the "four craftsmen." In the previous vision the Lord expressed His anger over what other nations had been doing to His people Israel, but there was no sign that His vindication had begun. Now, God would reveal how He would begin to deal with the other nations.

Two forces are revealed in this second vision:

A. The Scatterers 1:18–19
B. The Avengers 1:20–21

THE SCATTERERS (1:18–19)

"Horns," the pride and symbol of strength of the animals that sport them, are used here figuratively to represent the nations that plagued Israel. As such, the "horn" is a symbol of strength and virility (Ps. 75:4,5; 102: 10; Amos 6:15).

Because of God's strength, "horn" is a title for God (Ps. 18:2; 2 Sam. 22:3). To "lift up one's horn" was a sign of victory (2 Sam. 2:1), but "to lower one's horn" was a symbol of defeat (Job 16:15). Here, the horn is simply used as a metaphor for the strength of each nation, just as the horn was the pride of the bull.

In his second vision, Zechariah sees *"four horns"* (v. 18b). The most natural question for him to ask was *"What are these?"* (v. 19).

The answer given by the interpreting angel is: *"These are the horns that have scattered Judah, Israel, and Jerusalem"* (v. 19b). Many, including Jerome and most patristic commentators, have interpreted the four horns to be the Babylonians, Medo-Persians, Greeks and Romans. Rabbi Kimchi has also interpreted them in this way: "These are the four monarchies—and they are the Babylonian monarchy, the Persian monarchy, and the Grecian monarchy, and so the Targum of Jonathan has it instead of the four horns)—the four monarchies."[9] (Kimchi does not identify the fourth empire because it had not yet shown itself to either Daniel or Zechariah.) These four great empires generally mark "the times of the Gentiles" (Luke 21:24). They move from 605 B.C. until the second coming of Christ.

Today the four horns are more commonly identified as the four directions from which opposition comes—a totality of opposition. Either view is acceptable, for ultimately each nation only stands for a successive empire that will finally be manifested in the complete opposition to Israel in the end day.

The order in which Judah, Israel, and Jerusalem are mentioned is somewhat unexpected, since Israel fell first in 722 B.C. The Greek LXX omits the reference to Israel, but it appears in all Hebrew manuscripts and in the partial Greek text of this passage found at Qumran. The prophet merely wanted to indicate it was the whole of the Jewish people scattered in exile, not just Judah.

The repetition of the words "to scatter" (vv. 19, 21) and "to lift up" (to lift up one's eyes obediently [v. 18], to fail "to lift up" one's head as an indication of defeat [v. 21a], and "to lift up" one's horn defiantly [v. 21b]), is a stylistic device used to emphasize the key ideas of the vision.

THE AVENGERS (1:20–21)

The *"four craftsmen"* (v. 20) could come from any trade, whether carpenters (wood-workers, 2 Sam. 5:11), metalurgists (workers in metal, 1 Sam. 13:19), or masons (workers in stone, Exod. 28:11).

The prophet did not ask about their identity, as he did the four horns; he asked about their function: *"What are these coming to do?"* (v. 21a). The verb is an active participle in Hebrew, indicating that what they were doing was now in process: the craftsmen were in the process of destroying the four horns. *"The craftsmen are coming to terrify [the four horns]"* (v. 21c). This vision thus teaches that for every enemy raised up against God's people, God graciously raises up a counteracting power to destroy it. So thorough was God's counteracting move against the four horns that "that one did not lift up his head" (v. 21c; literal translation). God will *"cast out"* (v. 21c), or, literally, "throw down" in defeat, all who lifted their horn to scatter Israel. Note that in Hebrew "lifting up" horns against the land of Judah is an active participle, indicating that the persecution of the Jews had been continuous, not sporadic.

God's craftsmen seem to move slowly, but they are constantly at work and move relentlessly onward in their work of destroying each other's predecessor. Thus, each horn was vanquished by the succeeding horn, which then acted as the most recent craftsman ordained by God to remove the former power. "In spite of dungeon, fire, and sword," God's truth was still abiding and on course.

CONCLUSION

The second vision demonstrates that God is sovereign over the nations (cf. Dan. 4:17, 35). It also displays His power, authority, and superintendence over all the evils done in the world, particularly as they affect His people Israel.

The vision makes two points for all who hear God's word: first, God will keep His covenant with Israel; second, we are not to be anxious to vindicate ourselves. The apostle Paul reminded us: "Beloved, do not avenge yourselves, but rather give place to wrath; for it is written, 'Vengeance is Mine, I will repay,' says the Lord" (Rom. 12:19).

CHAPTER FOUR

Expecting the Glory of God on Earth

Zechariah 2:1–13

2:1 Then I raised my eyes and looked, and behold, a man with a measuring line in his hand.

2 So I said, "Where are you going?" And he said to me, "To measure Jerusalem, to see what is its width and what is its length."

3 And there was the angel who talked with me, going out; and another angel was coming out to meet him,

4 who said to him, "Run, speak to this young man, saying: 'Jerusalem shall be inhabited as towns without walls, because of the multitude of men and livestock in it.

5 'For I,' says the LORD, 'will be a wall of fire all around her, and I will be the glory in her midst.'"

6 "Up, up! Flee from the land of the north," says the LORD; "for I have spread you abroad like the four winds of heaven," says the LORD.

7 "Up, Zion! Escape, you who dwell with the daughter of Babylon."

8 For thus says the LORD of hosts: "He sent Me after glory, to the nations which plunder you; for he who touches you touches the apple of His eye.

9 "For surely I will shake My hand against them, and they shall become spoil for their servants. Then you will know that the LORD of hosts has sent Me.

10 "Sing and rejoice, O daughter of Zion! For behold, I am coming and I will dwell in your midst," says the LORD.

11 "Many nations shall be joined to the LORD in that day, and they shall become My people. And I

will dwell in your midst. Then you will know that the
LORD of hosts has sent Me to you.

12 "And the LORD will take possession of Judah as
His inheritance in the Holy Land, and will again
choose Jerusalem.

13 "Be silent, all flesh, before the LORD, for He is
aroused from His holy habitation!"

Zechariah 2:1–13

In his third vision, the prophet sees a man measuring Jerusalem, a
scene that evokes the reference in the first vision, "And a surveyor's
line shall be stretched out over Jerusalem" (1:16). The message of the
third vision is that the city would have a vast population and would
be protected by the Lord himself as He resided within the city.

Two great affirmations are found in the third vision:

A. Our Lord's Return Will be Glorious   2:1–9
B. Our Lord's Future Blessings Will be Glorious   2:10–13

OUR LORD'S RETURN WILL BE GLORIOUS (2:1–9)

The controlling thought of this text is found in verse 5, "'For I,' says
the LORD, 'will be a wall of fire all around her, and I will be the glory in her
midst.'" The "I" is emphatic, and, contrary to normal Hebrew practice, the verb "to be" is expressed as incomplete or future action. And
to make sure no one misses the point, our Lord adds, as it were, His
signature, "says the LORD."

This "wall of fire" reminds us of the pillar of cloud and the pillar of
fire that accompanied Israel through the wilderness and separated
the Egyptians from the Israelites at the Red Sea (Exod. 14:19–24).

The "glory" in her midst recalls the tragic reversal of that presence
when the threefold steps of departure of that glory of God abandoned
the people of God in Ezekiel's day (Ezk. 9:3; 10:19; 11:23). Not until
our Lord returns a second time would His "glory" come back (Ezk.
43:1–7). The "glory" of God points primarily to His presence among
men and secondarily to the luminous effects His presence produces.
Note that the Angel of the LORD, usually regarded as an appearance
of Christ in a pre-incarnate form, had been associated with the cloud
of glory earlier in the Old Testament (Exod. 13:21–22).

The "man" (v. 1) with a measuring line in his hand cannot be the interpreting angel, but must be the one the text has previously

identified as "The Angel of the LORD" (e.g., 1:12). This is no one else but Christ, the Rider of the red horse in 1:8. That this messianic person is a "man" will be affirmed even more radically in Zechariah 6:12: "Behold, the Man whose name is the BRANCH!" Likewise, in Ezekiel 40:2–3, a "man" surveyed the millennial temple, again a clear reference to Christ.

One message of the measuring line and expansion of the city is that believers should not draw in the kingdom too narrowly. Our Lord has sheep that are not of the fold of Israel that He must win (John 10:16). The expansion of the city does not refer only to a spiritual enlargement of the Kingdom of God, however; God's kingdom will house an actual enlarged city of Jerusalem wherein the Lord himself will reside just as truly as He did during the thirty years of His earthly pilgrimage.

The big news is that, due to a huge increase in population, Jerusalem will be a city without walls (v. 4). The word translated "city" is literally "plains." In Ezekiel 38:11, the same word is used to refer to a land where people dwell in peace without walls, bolts, or gates. Isaiah had taught the same truth: "For your waste and desolate places, and the land of your destruction, will even now be too small for the inhabitants; and those who swallowed you up will be far away. The children you will have, after you have lost the others, will say again in your ears, 'The place is too small for me; give me a place where I may dwell'" (Isa. 49:19–20). It cannot be without significance that Israel has received enormous numbers of immigrants in the past year or two—witness the Ethiopian airlift in the Spring of 1991 and the massive influx of people from the former Soviet Union in 1990 and 1991. Surely this is an important sign for all who take Scripture seriously.

Zechariah writes the remainder of chapter 2 in poetry: verses 6–13 are divided into two equal stanzas (vv. 6–9 and 10–13). Each stanza begins with a command followed by the exhortation *"for."* Beginning in verse 6 we also see a different speaker and a different audience. Zechariah now speaks, instead of the angel, and he addresses, first, the exiles in Babylon and, then, the people of the Zion whose return will act as a symbol of God's work in the final day of our Lord.

We are startled by the command in verse 6; it literally begins with "Ho! Ho!" or "Hey there! Listen!" Zechariah commands his audience: *"Flee from the land of the north"* [v. 6]. . . ."*Up, Zion! Escape, you who dwell with the daughter of Babylon"* (v. 7).

This is the same command Jeremiah had given in Jeremiah 51:6 ("Flee from the midst of Babylon") and in Jeremiah 50:8 ("Move from the midst of Babylon"). Now, if Jeremiah's command had been intended to warn the residents of the exile to flee Babylon before it fell in 539 B.C., why did the prophet and statesman Daniel remain in Babylon the very night Babylon collapsed if, as we know, Daniel knew the prophecy of Jeremiah and regarded it already as Scripture? (Dan. 9:2; cf. Jer. 25:12; 29:10). When Belshazzar called Daniel into the banquet hall in Daniel 5 to interpret the writing on the wall, Daniel should have quickly excused himself and made a beeline out of town if the words "Flee from the midst of Babylon" pertained to that day. But apparently they did not; they referred to an eschatological event in which Babylon, perhaps modern–day Iraq, would be involved in the final events of history before the coming of the Lord.

Verses 6 and 7 appear to be dependent on Isaiah 13–14 and Jeremiah 50–51. Thus, when God would finally deliver Israel, He would render His final judgment on Babylon. That would take place as Israel was being gathered from all over the world and restored to her land (Jer. 50:4–5, 20). It would be a day when the nations of the earth had drunk the cup of wine from Babylon and had gone mad (Jer. 51:6–7). (Could it be that the wine in this case may have been black, i.e., oil?) Zechariah commands his audience to flee from Babylon in that future day with assurance that God would protect His city Jerusalem and display His glory (v. 7b).

Mystery of mysteries, Yahweh is Lord, yet He was also *"sent"* (v. 8). This teaching is the same as that of Isaiah 61:1–2 (emphasis ours): "The Spirit of the LORD is upon Me, because the LORD has anointed Me to preach good tidings to the poor; He has *sent Me* to heal the brokenhearted, to proclaim liberty to the captives, and the opening of the prison to those who are bound." That truth is repeated in John 10:30 and 36: "I and My Father are one, . . . the Father . . . sent [Me]." The Father and Son are one, yet the Father has *sent* the Son. That is the mystery of the Trinity.

The nation or person that *"touches [Israel] touches the apple of His eye"* (v. 8). That is what Deuteronomy 32:10 had taught as well: "He kept him [Israel] as the apple of His eye" (cf. Ps. 17:8; Prov. 7:2, 9). Interestingly, although in Hebrew the usual word for "apple" of the eye is *ʾîšôn*, meaning "pupil (on the eye)," Zechariah uses the word *bābâ*, a word that occurs only once in the Hebrew Bible. In this context, where the Judeans have just been told to flee Babylon, *bābâ* appears to be a cognate of "Babylon," Hebrew *bābili*, which in the Akkadian logographic writing would be KÄ.DINGIR.RA.KI, where KÄ means "gate" and DINGER signals the presence of a deity. It could well be, then, that Zechariah's "gate of the eye" is an ironic pun on the pride of Babylon, which called herself the gateway to god![10] How dangerous it is for the nations to try to oppose God by picking on the people of Israel—whom God had used as the means of bringing His oracles and messianic line to the world!

OUR LORD'S FUTURE BLESSINGS WILL BE GLORIOUS (2:10–13)

Since God is going to enlarge Jerusalem, the people of the city are addressed as the *"daughter of Zion"* (a term used to refer to the people of Jerusalem in 2:4,5; 8:3 and to the population around Jerusalem in 3:14). The people are urged to *"sing and rejoice"* (v. 10a). The fact that the Lord will finally be made king in Zion is more than enough cause for breaking loose in jubilant celebration of doxology.

Four beautiful promises are built upon the vision of 2:1–6. Each one tells of what God is going to do when He returns to earth to rule and reign during the Millennium.

The first promise is: *"Behold, I am coming and I will dwell in your midst"* (v. 10b). The second coming of our Lord is that blessed hope that the believer cherishes. It is also the climax of the oft-repeated tripartite formula: "I will be your God, you shall be my people and I will dwell in the midst of you." The verb "to dwell" *(shakan)* is connected with the *Shekinah* (hence, the verb *shakan*) glory of God and with the word for the tabernacle *(Mishkan;* Exod. 25:8).

How sad it is that so many modern interpreters have turned their backs on the premillennial interpretation of texts such as these. It is especially sad, since this premillennial coming of Christ was practically the only view taken by the Church for the first four centuries of the Christian era. In modern Christianity, some scholars maintain that this view is held only by cultic groups or groups with an off-beat brand of theology. But premillennialism's roots and significance go far beyond any of these token criticisms. God will conclude history just as He promised Abraham, Isaac, and Jacob. He will bring Israel back to her land, and then He will personally reside in the land and will be her King and Sovereign.

The second promise is: *"Many nations shall be joined to the* Lord *in that day, and they shall become My people"* (v. 11). The term "My people" was generally reserved for Israel, but now it refers to *goyim*, or "Gentiles," who would be joined, by faith, to Israel to form the new, one people of God. Isaiah 19:25 used the same term to describe converted Egypt; the Egyptians, too, would one day become "My people." This work of joining believing Jew and Gentile into one people would fulfil the second part of the tri-partite formula mentioned in our commentary on verse 10.

The conclusion to verse 11 is almost identical to the conclusion to verse 9: *"You will know that the* Lord *of hosts has sent Me to you."* This work of God would be the proof that God was who He said He was.

The third promise is: *"The* Lord *will take possession of Judah as His inheritance in the Holy Land, and will again choose Jerusalem"* (v. 12). This is the only time in the Bible where the Promised Land is referred to as the *"Holy Land."* (This name will, however, appear later in the Apocrypha [Wisdom 12:3; 2 Maccabees 1:7]). God certainly is not finished with the city He chose years ago in 1000 B.C. for the throne of David. It will be God's chosen center of worship and place of adjudication during the messianic rule and reign of Christ on earth during the Millennium.

The fourth promise is that there would be worldwide judgment at the second coming of Christ. *"All flesh"* will be hushed by His awesome presence (v. 13). God will once more "arouse" (cf. Isaiah 51:9, where the same word is translated "Awake, awake") himself from *"His holy habitation."* Such stirring would surely indicate that He was about to commence His work of judgment as He had prophesied in His word. He will leave his heavenly temple (Hab. 2:20; Ps. 68:6; Jer. 25:30; Deut. 26:15) and come to earth.

No wonder the earth is instructed to *"Be silent!"* There would be little more left to do than to catch one's breath and to wait to see what God would do (Hab. 2:20; Zeph. 1:7). Great would be the day of the Lord.

Conclusion

Here is the hope, not only of Israel, but of the Church and the nations. As Isaiah cried, "Say to the cities of Judah [and, we add, the world], 'Behold your God!'" (Isa. 40:9d).

What a day that will be:

1. The Lord will return.
2. The Gentiles will come to know the Lord.
3. Jerusalem will be rebuilt and become the new world center.
4. World judgment from God will show right cannot forever be denied. The Lord will be King and truth will be the normal way of life, not the exception.
5. Babylon will be judged and Israel will be restored.

Great will be that day, the day of the Lord!

CHAPTER FIVE

Symbolizing the Removal of Sin all in One Day

Zechariah 3:1–10

3:1 Then he showed me Joshua the high priest standing before the Angel of the LORD, and Satan standing at his right hand to oppose him.

2 And the LORD said to Satan, "The LORD rebuke you, Satan! The LORD who has chosen Jerusalem rebuke you! Is this not a brand plucked from the fire?"

3 Now Joshua was clothed with filthy garments, and was standing before the Angel.

4 Then He answered and spoke to those who stood before Him, saying, "Take away the filthy garments from him." And to him He said, "See, I have removed your iniquity from you, and I will clothe you with rich robes."

5 And I said, "Let them put a clean turban on his head." So they put a clean turban on his head, and they put the clothes on him. And the Angel of the LORD stood by.

6 Then the Angel of the LORD admonished Joshua, saying,

7 "Thus says the LORD of hosts:
'If you will walk in My ways,
And if you will keep My command,
Then you shall also judge My house,
And likewise have charge of My courts;
I will give you places to walk
Among these who stand here.

> 8 'Hear, O Joshua, the high priest,
>   You and your companions who sit before you,
>   For they are a wondrous sign;
>   For behold, I am bringing forth My Servant
>   the BRANCH.
> 9 For behold, the stone
>   That I have laid before Joshua:
>   Upon the stone are seven eyes.
>   Behold, I will engrave its inscription,'
>   Says the LORD of hosts,
>   'And I will remove the iniquity of that land
>   in one day.
> 10 In that day,' says the LORD of hosts,
>   'Everyone will invite his neighbor
>   Under his vine and under his fig tree.'"
>
> *Zechariah 3:1–10*

The "good and comfortable words" (1:13) of the first three visions promise not only the overthrow of the Gentile powers (1:18–21), the restoration of the Jewish Diaspora (1:12; 2:4), and the future habitation of Jerusalem (2:4), but also the restoration of spiritual relations between God and His people (2:5, 10, 11). It is the last promise that this vision focuses on.

One of the most famous ink spots in the world is the one on the wall of Wartburg Castle, Germany, where, it is said, Martin Luther had it out with the Devil over the evil one's constant dredging up of Luther's past sins. In a letter to Melanchthon dated May 24, 1521, Luther wrote:

> I do see myself insensible and hardened, a slave to sloth, rarely, alas! praying—unable even to utter a groan for the Church, while my untamed flesh, burns with devouring flame. [11]

The story is that Luther dreamt that Satan appeared to him reading a long scroll with all his many sins from his birth on. As the reading of the list proceeded, Luther's terrors grew until finally he jumped up and cried, "It is all true, Satan, and many more sins I have committed in my life which are known to God only; but write at the bottom of your list, 'the blood of Jesus Christ, God's Son, cleanses us from all sin.'" Then grasping the inkwell on his table, he threw it at the Devil, who immediately fled. The memorial of this incident is now the famous spot on the Wartburg Castle.

This fourth vision deals with that same problem of sin. The focal point of the vision is 3:8–9, where Joshua, the High Priest, and his companions are declared to be *"a wondrous sign."* God promises that He would *"remove the iniquity of that land in one day."* Four acts of God would complete this promise:

> A. Christ Intervenes For Us As Our High Priest   3:1–2
> B. Christ Cleanses Us As Our High Priest   3:3–4
> C. Christ Challenges Us As Our High Priest   3:5–7
> D. Christ Delivers Us As Our High Priest   3:8–10

CHRIST INTERVENES FOR US AS OUR HIGH PRIEST (3:1–2)

The problem that this vision wrestles with is: How can a morally defiled and sinful people be made fit to appear in the presence of God, much less to be priests and ministers for the Holy One who inhabits heaven (Exod. 19:6)? There is only one way; it is God who is faithful and who mercifully forgives sin. And blacksliding Israel has received God's promise of a restoration.

In Zechariah's vision, the High Priest Joshua (who had returned from the Babylonian exile with Zerubbabel, the governor, and 49,697 other exiles) stands before "the Angel of the LORD" (3:1), whom we have already identified (in our commentary on 1:7–8) as a preincarnate appearance of the second person of the Trinity. Thus it was that Joshua stood before Jesus (v. 1). Joshua was to minister to the Lord, for so the Lord had set apart the tribe of Levi to serve Him, especially the family of Aaron, from whose family Joshua also descended. The High Priest was a mediator for the people.

Unfortunately, Satan is right there as well. He came *"to oppose him [Joshua]"* (v. 1d). As the sworn enemy of Israel and the Church, Satan acts as an adversary and an accuser of the brethren (Job 1:6–10; 2:1–7; Rev. 12:10).

But it is the Lord who pleads Israel's cause and ours: "He is near who justifies Me; who will contend with Me? Let us stand together. Who is my adversary? Let him come near Me. Surely the Lord GOD will help Me; who is he who will condemn Me?" (Isa. 50:8–9a). Paul asked similar questions in Romans 8:33–34: "Who shall bring a charge against God's elect? It is God who justifies. Who is he who condemns? It is Christ who died, and furthermore is also risen, who is even at the right hand of God, who also makes intercession for us."

Thus, the Lord himself will rebuke the Devil (cf. Jude 9, where the archangel Michael says to the Devil, "The Lord rebuke you."). Interestingly, Jude used two other phrases from the prophet Zechariah (thereby showing the close affinity between the two and the way the inspired New Testament writers viewed Zechariah's meaning): "a brand plucked from the fire" (Zech. 3:2) is echoed in Jude 23: "pulling them out of the fire"; and "filthy garments" (Zech. 3:3) is echoed in Jude 23c: "hating even the garment defiled by the flesh."

Our Lord has not cast off His people or forgotten His promise just because Israel's garments have become "filthy," i.e., sinful. Paul makes the same point in Romans 11:1: "I say then, has God cast away His people [Israel]? Certainly not!"

God's answer to Satan's accusations is that Israel has already endured quite a bit; she is *a brand plucked from the fire* (v. 2c). (Amos 4:11 had used the same figure of speech: "'And you [Israel] were like a firebrand plucked from the burning; yet you have not returned to Me,' says the LORD.") But, despite the series of misfortunes, trials, and judgments that have passed over the Jewish nation, in the mercy of God, He has prevented Israel from being destroyed.

Joshua the High Priest, then, is the representative of his people, but the accusations that are brought by Satan are brought against all the people. But God's mercy exceeds all accusations through all of Israel's afflictions—even the "iron furnace" of Egypt (Deut. 4:20). The Lord has chosen Zion and He will not recant or back down from His promise.

CHRIST CLEANSES US AS OUR HIGH PRIEST (3:3–4)

In this vision, Joshua the High Priest stands *"clothed with filthy garments"* (v. 3) before the Angel of the Lord. That is a picture of us all: "But we are all like an unclean thing, and all our righteousnesses are like filthy rags" (Isa. 64:6a). Even more graphic, the High Priest himself is filthy from being dung-spattered!

God's command is: *"Take away the filthy garments from him"* (v. 4), for the Angel said he would cloth him instead with *"rich robes"* (v. 4d). What a graphic picture of the free, gracious forgiveness of and removal of sin from all who confess their sin to our Lord! Joshua could no more cleanse himself than we can! Someone had to take the filthy clothes from him! These "rich robes" are the garments of salvation. They are the perfect righteousness of our Lord in which all who believe are attired. Joshua was reinstated and reconsecrated by this act of replacing his garments, and, since he was a "sign," so were all who believed thereby assured of complete cleansing from God. In fact, the sin of the land would be removed in *"one day"* (v. 9d). In exchange for the polluted clothes of sin, the Lord would wash away the filth of the daughter of Zion (cf. Isa. 4:3–4; Ezk. 36:16–32).

CHRIST CHALLENGES US AS OUR HIGH PRIEST (3:5–7)

Our Lord did not stop with clothing Joshua in richly appointed robes; He also *"put a clean turban on his head"* (v. 5). This turban, or mitre, was worn with a plate on the forehead that reminded the wearer of his special task before God: "You shall also make a plate of pure gold and engrave on it, like the engraving of a signet: HOLINESS TO THE LORD. . . . So it shall be on Aaron's forehead, that Aaron may bear the iniquity of the . . . children of Israel . . . that they may be accepted before the LORD" (Exod. 28:36, 38).

God's original, and ultimate, plan is that all His people should be "to Me a kingdom of priests" (Exod. 19:6). Again, in Isaiah 61:6, the whole nation is to be called one day to be "the Priests of the Lord." This doctrine of the priesthood of all believers is reinstituted in the New Testament (1 Pet. 2:5; Rev. 1:6).

Joshua is robed in festal attire, like those who attend the marriage feast of the Lamb, the great supper of God. There, too, believers will be arrayed in "fine linen, clean and bright," and in "wedding garments" (Matt. 22:1–14; Rev. 19:6–18). These robes of righteousness were acquired by faith. They were given not to Joshua alone, but to all who believe.

At this point, our Lord, as the Angel of the Lord, solemnly admonishes Joshua with the identical words that were often found in Deuteronomy, the words dying David gave to Solomon, and the words that were given to Joshua in the conquest: *"If you will walk in My ways, and if you will keep My command, then you shall also judge My house. . ."* (v. 7). God's "house" in this context means His people. The same metaphor was used in Numbers 12:7: "My servant Moses [who] is faithful in all My house." That same word is used again in Hebrews 3:2; verse 6 of the same chapter affirms, "Christ as a Son over His own house, *whose house we are* if we hold fast [italics ours]." Thus, the first reward that Joshua's obedience would yield him is being judge over the "house," or people, of God.

The second reward for Joshua's obedience and faithfulness is that he would *"have charge of [God's] courts"* (v. 7c). Joshua is promised the privilege of exercising authority over the temple—now in ruins for over seventy years—and its courts.

Joshua's third reward is that *"I will give you places to walk among these who stand here"* (v. 7d). This promise is more difficult to understand, but it appears to mean free access among the angelic beings, thereby suggesting direct access to God. But that surely is a clumsy way to express that thought, if that is indeed what is meant. The Jewish Targums make this comment on the promise: "In the resurrection of the dead, I will revive you and give you feet walking among the seraphim." The meaning, then, promised those who kept God's charge and lived according to His Word, that they would have the honor of being transplanted to higher service in heaven, after their work on earth was done, to walk among the angels.

Our pardon and justification are free gifts from our Lord, but the honor and privilege of future reward, which Joshua is promised here three times, are directly conditioned on obedience and faithfulness here and now.

CHRIST DELIVERS US AS OUR HIGH PRIEST (3:8–10)

Just as Isaiah and his sons were "signs" (Isa. 8:18), so Joshua and his companions were *"a wondrous sign"* (v. 8c). Even though Joshua and his companions were imperfect signs of the person and work of Joshua's greater namesake, Jesus, Zechariah's vision was divinely given in order to teach us something about our Lord Jesus. (The Greek name Jesus, incidentally, was the same as the Hebrew name Joshua.)

Whereas the adversary accused Joshua (v. 1), the Lord now reinstates and recommissions him, granting to him the right of direct access to God the Father, even as our Lord grants direct access to God to all believers (Heb. 4:4–16).

Two marvelous titles of our Lord appear in the last part of verse 8: *"My Servant"* and *"the BRANCH."* The first, "My Servant," is the most frequently used title for the coming Messiah; it is even more frequently used than "Messiah." A large number of the twenty appearances of the title "Servant" in Isaiah 41–53 refer to Christ.

But it is the use of the title "BRANCH" that is significant. This title appears in the Old Testament in four wonderful promises about the coming Messiah. These prophetic promises give four presentations of the Branch that correspond to the four presentations of Christ in the four gospels. They are:

(1) The Branch as *Royal King*. "I will raise to David a Branch of righteousness" (Jer. 23:5); "Behold your King" (corresponds to the presentation of the Messiah in Matthew).

(2) The Branch as *Servant*. "My Servant the BRANCH" (Zech. 3:8); "Behold My Servant" (corresponds to the presentation of the Messiah in Mark).

(3) The Branch as *Fully Man*. "The Man whose name is the BRANCH" (Zech. 6:12); "Behold the Man" (corresponds to the presentation of the Messiah in Luke).

(4) The Branch as *Fully God*. "The Branch of the LORD" (Isa. 4:2); "Behold the Son of God" (corresponds to the presentation of the Messiah in John).

In addition to the messianic title Branch, this passage uses the messianic title "stone." This abrupt change in metaphor has troubled some interpreters so much that they have rearranged the text (cf. the NEB). But there is absolutely no textual or manuscript evidence for doing so.

The *"stone"* (v. 9) was set before Joshua. The stone had seven eyes and this inscription: *"And I will remove the iniquity of that land in one day"* (v. 9d). The stone must be the same one that Isaiah talked about: "Behold I lay in Zion a stone for a foundation, a tried stone, a precious cornerstone, a sure foundation; whoever believes will not act hastily" (Isa. 28:16). Again, Psalm 118:22 declares, "The stone which the builders rejected has become the chief cornerstone." This stone is also reminiscent of the "stone" in Daniel 2:44–45.

The number seven, in the reference to the seven eyes, may be used here because seven is the number of completeness, or it may be a deliberate reference to the sevenfold fulness of the one Spirit of Yahweh given to Messiah (Isa. 11:2): the spirit of the LORD, the spirit of wisdom, the spirit of understanding, the spirit of counsel, the spirit of might, the spirit of knowledge, and the spirit of the fear of the LORD.

In this passage about the stone, God promises, as we have said, that He would remove the iniquity of the land in one day (v. 9). Such a cleansing of the land is typical of the spiritual cleansing that Messiah will accomplish on Calvary. This action is the key to the whole fourth vision. The "one day" promised here is "that day" of Zechariah 9–14, i.e., the "day" of Israel's national repentance when her people will look on Him whom they have pierced (Zech. 12:10).

The fourth vision concludes in verse 10 with a picture of tranquility and rest, since sin has been pardoned and removed. This domestic scene of everyone sitting under his own vine and fig tree is the epitome of contentment and happiness (cf. 1 Kings 4:25; 2 Kings 18:31; Mic. 4:4).

CONCLUSION

In our new Joshua, Jesus Christ, God has intervened on behalf of our sins. Christ's atoning death has cleansed us from all our sins. Therefore, our forgiven sins are gone, and they are removed as far as the east is from the west.

In one day, God will so move on Israel that she too will confess her sins and be forgiven by God in a single day. All those who are part of God's "house" will want to rejoice in what God will do for Israel, for they will benefit by the same work of grace.

CHAPTER SIX

Receiving God's Spirit for Doing His Work

Zechariah 4:1–14

4:1 Now the angel who talked with me came back and wakened me, as a man who is wakened out of his sleep.

2 And he said to me, "What do you see?" So I said, "I am looking, and there is a lampstand of solid gold with a bowl on top of it, and on the stand seven lamps with seven pipes to the seven lamps.

3 "Two olive trees are by it, one at the right of the bowl and the other at its left."

4 So I answered and spoke to the angel who talked with me, saying, "What are these, my lord?"

5 Then the angel who talked with me answered and said to me, "Do you not know what these are?" And I said, "No, my lord."

6 So he answered and said to me:

"This is the word of the LORD to Zerubbabel:
'Not by might nor by power, but by My Spirit,'
Says the LORD of hosts.

7 'Who are you, O great mountain?
Before Zerubbabel you shall become a plain!
And he shall bring forth the capstone
With shouts of "Grace, grace to it!"'"

8 Moreover the word of the LORD came to me, saying:

9 "The hands of Zerubbabel
Have laid the foundation of this temple;
His hands shall also finish it.
Then you will know

327

> That the LORD of hosts has sent Me to you.
>
> 10 For who has despised the day of small things?
> For these seven rejoice to see
> The plumb line in the hand of Zerubbabel.
> They are the eyes of the LORD,
> Which scan to and fro throughout the
>   whole earth."
>
> 11 Then I answered and said to him, "What are
> these two olive trees, one at the right of the lampstand
> and the other at its left?"
>
> 12 And I further answered and said to him,
> "What are these two olive branches that drip into the
> receptacles of the two gold pipes from which the
> golden oil drains?"
>
> 13 Then he answered me and said, "Do you not
> know what these are?" And I said, "No, my lord."
>
> 14 So he said, "These are the two anointed ones,
> who stand beside the Lord of the whole earth."
>
> *Zechariah 4:1–14*

The fifth vision, which along with the fourth forms the apex of the chiastic arrangement of the eight visions, focuses on the completion of the temple. The central message of this vision is that the temple would not be completed by human ingenuity or drive, but by the Spirit of God (4:6). Of special concern is the "lampstand" that, in most cases, stood in the "Holy Place" (for a description of the lampstand in the tabernacle, *see* Exod. 25:31; and in the temple, *see* 1 Kings 7:49). The lampstand occupies the central place in this vision and in the eight visions taken as a whole.

Three principles are taught in this vision:

    A. God's Work Will Be Accomplished by God's Spirit   4:1-6
    B. God's Work Must Not Be Despised for Its Small Beginnings   4:7-10
    C. God's Work Values People More than Institutions   4:11-14[12]

GOD'S WORK WILL BE ACCOMPLISHED BY GOD'S SPIRIT (4:1-6)

The interpreting angel had to arouse Zechariah, for it appears he had fallen into a listless stupor. When the angel asks Zechariah what he saw, he replies: *"a lampstand of solid gold with a bowl on top of it, and on the stand seven lamps with seven pipes to the seven lamps"* (v. 2).

This lampstand could not be the seven-branched menorah known to us from the famous Titus' Roman arch representation found in later Jewish art. Rather, it was probably a cylindrical pedestal, made out of gold, with a bowl on top. The bowl, or, in some translations, the flared feature on top of the column, had seven lamps, each with seven pinches, or spouts, to hold seven wicks. Similar lamps, or saucer-shaped lamps, dating from 900 B.C., with seven pinches around their lip have been found at Dan and Dothan.[13]

In addition to this seven-fluted lampstand, Zechariah sees *"two olive trees . . . one at the right of the bowl and the other at its left"* (v. 3). Additional information on these two olive trees appears in verse 12, where the prophet asks: *"What are these two olive branches that drip into the receptacles of the two gold pipes from which the golden oil drains?"* The word "branches" may also be rendered as "clusters" of fruit on the olive trees. The word "pipes" is only a guess, since this is the only place where it appears in the Old Testament. Nevertheless, the idea of "pipes" or "funnels" works well in this context. Presumably, "the golden oil" is the oil from the crushed olives that is channelled to the lamps in order to keep them burning.

The prophet is again stymied, so he inquires, *"What are these, my lord?"* (v. 4). The interpreting angel responds by asking, *"Do you not know what these are?"* (v. 5). Zechariah simply retorts, *"No, my lord."* This is not the only time that the prophet asks the interpreting angel to explain this vision; three times he has to repeat the question (vv. 4, 11, 12). The prophet needed divine enablement and revelation if he was going to be able to interpret this vision.

Surprisingly enough, the angel does answer his question directly and immediately; he gives Zechariah a word for governor Zerubbabel. It is this: *"'Not by might nor by power, but by My Spirit,' says the LORD of hosts"* (v. 6). While the previous vision (which, as we have said, we regard along with this vision as central to the eight night visions) focused on Joshua the High Priest, this one focuses on Zerubbabel the governor.

Verse 6 is the focal point of this vision. Any work this group of returnees from exile were going to do would only be accomplished by the power of the Spirit of God. Relying solely on human resources, human sagacity and human strength, their efforts would be worthless.

The community had tried to rebuild the temple by their own strength immediately upon their return from Babylon over sixteen years earlier, but that turned out to be a fiasco (Ezra 3:8–13).

Human effort without the supply of the "oil" of the Holy Spirit would burn itself out. What the golden olive oil was to the seven fluted oil lamps the Spirit of God is to all aspects of any work done in His name; God's work done in God's way will never lack God's provision and power. Those who resist this principle will learn the hard way that they will be powerless to do God's work.

G. Campbell Morgan reminds us how important divine enablement is:

> Not by resources, nor by resoluteness. These may be high, pure, mighty; but in so far as they are human they cannot accomplish the work of God in the world. By might and by power, by resources and resoluteness, we may be able to legislate for [ourselves]. . . . we can do much on the human level; but by these things we cannot shine as lights in the world. . . . We are very far from believing that. If I were asked to-day to give what I think to be the reason for the comparative failure of the Church of God in missionary enterprise, I would say that we are terribly in danger of imagining that by our own splendid resources and resoluteness we can accomplish the work.[14]

GOD'S WORK MUST NOT BE DESPISED FOR ITS SMALL BEGINNINGS (4:7–10)

The application of the principle stated in verse 6 is immediately taken up in verse 7. *"Who are you, O great mountain? Before Zerubbabel you shall become a plain!"* The "great mountain" must be a metaphorical allusion to some set of obstacles or difficulties that those rebuilding the temple were facing (Ezra 4:1–4; 5:3–5). But the mountain of obstacles would quickly be flattened out in front of God's man Zerubbabel, for the work of rebuilding the temple was now proceeding according to the divine principle announced in verse 6.

Zerubbabel would *"bring forth the capstone with shouts of 'Grace, grace to it!'"* (v. 7c,d). This must refer to completing the temple, not to laying its foundation, for the foundation had already been laid (Ezra 3:1–10). The "capstone" represents the "topping out" of the project. And the shouts that would accompany this culminating act would be shouts praising God's favor to the people in helping them complete the task, as well as shouts praising the temple's "beauty" and "grace."

Verse 9 reaffirms the fact that verse 8 refers to completing the temple: *"The hands of Zerubbabel have laid the foundation of this temple; his hands shall also finish it. Then you will know that the LORD of hosts has sent Me to you."* The job was finished during Zerubbabel's days; it did not drag on for centuries as did the construction of some of the great cathedrals of Europe. The fact that the temple was completed in Zerubbabel's time as Zechariah predicted is further evidence that the Lord truly spoke through Zechariah. The clause *"Then you will know that the LORD of hosts has sent Me"* repeats the identical promise made in 2:9 and 11.

Yet some may have been tempted to *"despise the day of small things"* (v. 10a; cf. Hag. 2:3). That would have been tragic, for such a view is a short-sighted evaluation of the significance of completing the temple. It is an unacceptable view because it fails to connect the *"small thing*[s]*"* like rebuilding the temple with either the ongoing triumph of the work of God or God's great wrap-up of history in the final day (*see* our commentary on Haggai 2). Often those who mock small beginnings have a lot of common sense, but, unfortunately, common sense can just as easily restrict or even block out one's vision in matters of faith.

The remainder of verse 10 is much more difficult to interpret. *"For these seven rejoice to see the plumb line in the hand of Zerubbabel. They are the eyes of the LORD, which scan to and fro throughout the whole earth."* The "seven" are best understood to be the "seven lamps" (since the subject is the lampstand with its wicks), rather than the "seven eyes" of the fourth vision (Zech. 3:9), notwithstanding that this vision and the fourth vision are best interpreted together.

Even more difficult is the "plumbline," for it literally means "stone of tin." The word used here is not the usual word for "plumbline" used in the Old Testament. Judging from the verbal root of the same word for "tin," the word used here can be translated "the stone of separation," signifying the distinctive nature of the community of God. The *Jerusalem Bible* renders the word "the chosen stone," a short step from "the stone of separation." Thus, just as the topstone was set apart in verse 9 for capping off the temple, so here a special stone is set apart for just such a unique place in the capstone of the temple. All could rejoice, therefore, in the laying of this final, special, separate capstone.

The "seven eyes of the LORD" may also be translated as the seven "springs" (since the Hebrew word for "eye" is the same as "spring" or "fountain") of the Lord. But once again, as we did in 3:9, we opt simply for the concept of completeness in the number seven. God's eyes scan the earth, going to and fro in an act of completeness—an act that points to His omniscience. He, the Lord, will see when that final, special, capstone is laid, for He sees all. Therein lies another reason why we must not belittle or demean the day of small beginnings, for one small work or one small worker plus God is always a majority.

GOD'S WORK VALUES PEOPLE MORE THAN INSTITUTIONS (4:11–14)

The questioning returns to the identity and meaning of the two olive trees. Zechariah does not become so preoccupied with buildings and things that he cannot keep his value system straight. The vision forces him to notice that the two olive trees on either side of the central lampstand are more than just props.

He is told straightaway in verse 14 that *"These are the two anointed ones, who stand beside the Lord of the whole earth."* "Anointed ones" are, literally, "sons of oil"; they are set apart as God's representatives in the office of political and priestly leadership. They *"stand beside the Lord of the whole earth"* (v. 14b) to do His bidding in the service of their Lord.

People are still more important in this vision, and in the program of God, than the temple—home of the lampstand—or any of the rest of the furniture in the building itself. What fueled the lampstand were the two olive trees, Zerubbabel and Joshua. The temple needed the lampstand, and the lampstand needed the fuel of the olive oil. Thus priority must be given in God's work to the humans God uses to fire the instruments in the institutions of God. As Peter C. Craigie remarks:

> The Church, as an institution, is never enough; no anonymous organization will by itself transform the world. People are always needed, for through them the life and light of God may flow. And as both Joshua and Zerubbabel had a part to play, . . . so too the Church depends for its vitality upon both the clergy and the laity.[15]

CONCLUSION

God will accomplish His purposes through His chosen instruments, mortals who are willing to fuel the fires that give light and life to the house and mission of our Lord. Our Lord will accomplish His purposes in spite of mountainous obstacles that tasks such as the rebuilding of the temple pose. Moreover, while God values men and women more than He values institutions, men and women must not think that their work for God in building the institutions is accomplished by their own might and power. Rather, it is done only by His Holy Spirit.

That is why men and women must not negatively judge any work of God based on how it appears to them at present, for any demeaning or belittling of small beginnings is premature and ill-founded. All so-called "small things" are directly linked to God's ongoing triumph and, especially, to His climactic victory in the final day.

CHAPTER SEVEN

Purging the Wicked from Israel

Zechariah 5:1–4

5:1 Then I turned and raised my eyes, and saw there a flying scroll.

2 And he said to me, "What do you see?" So I answered, "I see a flying scroll. Its length is twenty cubits and its width ten cubits."

3 Then he said to me, "This is the curse that goes out over the face of the whole earth: 'Every thief shall be expelled,' according to what is on this side of the scroll; and, 'Every perjurer shall be expelled,' according to what is on that side of it."

4 "I will send out the curse,"
    says the LORD of hosts;
"It shall enter the house of the thief
And the house of the one who swears falsely
    by My name.
It shall remain in the midst of his house
And consume it, with its timber and stones."

Zechariah 5:1–4

Visions six and seven are twin messages in the chiastic arrangement detailed in our introduction. The sixth vision reveals that the wicked will be purged from Israel, while the seventh demonstrates that wickedness itself will as well be removed from Israel; Zechariah 5:1–4 warns that individual sinners will be judged, while Zechariah 5:5–11 promises that the very principle of evil will be removed from Israel.

Each of Zechariah's last three visions is conversely related to one of the first three. Vision three describes a brand new Jerusalem wherein the Lord dwells, and its corresponding vision, vision six, announces the removal of the wicked from Jerusalem. In vision two Zechariah sees the removal of the horns that had been raised up against Israel by God's craftsmen, while in vision seven evil itself is removed from Israel to the land of Babylon. (We will discuss the relationship of the first and eighth vision in our discussion of the eighth vision.)

The central teaching point of this vision is that the pervasiveness of sin and crime is enough to cancel out the blessing that one would think might come from rebuilding the temple of God. In this respect, this vision is quite similar to the point made by the prophet Haggai when he asks the priests if holiness is as "catchy" or contagious as evil is. It is not, of course. Similarly, one work of obedience does not offset the need for holiness in all aspects of living. In this vision, theft and perjury (i.e. using the name of the Lord in vain or for no valid or legitimate purpose) are crimes and offenses against God and neighbor that had to be faced, regardless of the fact that the nation was actively involved in building a house for God.

This vision exposes two judgments against the wicked:

A. The Evil of the Wicked Unfurled   5:1–2
B. The Evil of the Wicked Condemned   5:3–4

THE EVIL OF THE WICKED UNFURLED (5:1–2)

On the prophet's visionary landscape he views *"a flying scroll"* (v. 1). This scroll was of unusual proportions, measuring in *"its length . . . twenty cubits and its width ten cubits"* (v. 2). Since a "cubit" is about eighteen inches, this scroll was about 30 feet x 15 feet. Scrolls, which antedated our modern books, were usually long strips of papyrus or parchment, but this scroll was unusually wide.

This text assigns no significance to these dimensions; many interpreters have noted nevertheless that they are the same as the Holy Place in the tabernacle (Exod. 26:15–28) and the porch of Solomon's temple (1 Kings 6:3); they have inferred that the scroll is given the similar dimensions since judgment must begin at the house of God and with the people of God. It is true that Scripture holds us responsible to make inferences in texts that are not explicit, as the commentator George Bush observes:

> If inferences are not binding in the interpretation of divine law,
> then we would ask for the *express* command which was violated
> by Nadab and Abihu in offering strange fire [Lev 10:1–3], and
> which cost them their lives. Any prohibition in set terms on that
> subject will be sought for in vain. So again, did not our Saviour
> tell the Sadducees that they *ought to have inferred* that the doctrine
> of the resurrection was true, from what God said to Moses at the
> bush?[16]

These interpreters may well be drawing the correct inference from
this text; Zechariah may have taken the trouble to describe the odd
shape of the scroll when its dimensions would only have had significance for those who remembered that the messages it brought were
aimed at the people of the house of God—and that the house shared
the same dimensions. Judgment *did* begin at the house of God!

The fact that the scroll was "flying" likens its messages to some of
the advertisements one can see at a seashore, fair or football stadium,
where a small aircraft flies overhead trailing a long sign. In the case
of the scroll, however, the message was being guided by God. It is
almost as if the scroll were on automatic pilot.[17]

THE EVIL OF THE WICKED CONDEMNED (5:3–4)

This flying scroll had writing on both sides, just like the one in
Ezekiel 2:10. Its messages were words of judgment: *"This is the curse
that goes out over the face of the whole earth"* (v. 3).

Two classes of evildoers were enjoined on the scroll: thieves and
perjurers. These two classes of sinners violated injunctions on both
tables of the Law of God. Exodus 20:7 warns "You shall not take the
name of the LORD your God in vain." Exodus 20:15 warns against
sinning against our neighbor: "You shall not steal." Perhaps these
two sins represent the whole Law of God on both tables, and the message means that the same people who were now engaged in building
the temple of God were violating the whole law of God and needed
to turn back to God.

In the "curse" of God (vv. 3,4) rested the warning that had so often
been given in Deuteronomy 28–30. Obedience to the commands
given by Moses to the people would have resulted in "blessing," but
disobedience of any kind would result in "cursing." The word
"curse" (ʾalah) is closely identified with "covenant." In the covenant

there was a bonding together of the Lord and His people, but when there are infractions and violations of that covenantal relationship, the punishments are spelled out in God's "curses."

Crime did not pay in Zechariah's time, nor will it ever pay—regardless of whether law enforcement agencies and the legal profession handle criminals adequately. Criminals will come under the judgment of God. Apparently, in the community of returned exiles, theft and perjury were two very common abuses of God's Law. How could the people committing theft and perjury expect God's blessing on their lives, even if they were rebuilding the temple?

Both the thief and the perjurer could expect to *"be expelled"* (v. 3c). They would be "purged away," or removed from the community. So certain was this fact that God advertised it on His flying announcement!

The "curse" would *"enter the house of the thief,"* and in the house of the perjurer the curse would *"remain in [his] midst"* (v. 4). Surely this indicates the severity of the judgment that God would bring against those who violated His covenant. Moreover, the curse would *"consume [the houses], with its timber and stones"* (v. 4d). Such a consuming judgment from God reminds us of the fire that fell from heaven when the prophet Elijah prayed for God to answer his prayer by fire (1 Kings 18:38). The fire ate up the sacrificed animal, the twelve stones of which the altar was made, and the water-filled trench surrounding the altar. The wicked may not expect to escape the judgment of God.

CONCLUSION

There was great thanksgiving to God for the completion of the temple and the way the people had responded to the call to work.

But the people could not use this as an excuse for tolerating residual wickedness in their midst. God would pursue the unrepentant thief and the one swearing falsely in His name into his very house with His consuming judgments. Further, the pervasiveness of the crimes within the community of returned exiles might cancel out any blessing on that community that might have come from the rebuilding of the temple.

CHAPTER EIGHT

Removing Wickedness from Israel

Zechariah 5:5–11

5 Then the angel who talked with me came out and said to me, "Lift your eyes now, and see what this is that goes forth."

6 So I asked, "What is it?" And he said, "It is a basket that is going forth." He also said, "This is their resemblance throughout the earth:

7 "Here is a lead disc lifted up, and this is a woman sitting inside the basket";

8 then he said, "This is Wickedness!" And he thrust her down into the basket, and threw the lead cover over its mouth.

9 Then I raised my eyes and looked, and there were two women, coming with the wind in their wings; for they had wings like the wings of a stork, and they lifted up the basket between earth and heaven.

10 So I said to the angel who talked with me, "Where are they carrying the basket?"

11 And he said to me, "To build a house for it in the land of Shinar; when it is ready, the basket will be set there on its base."

Zechariah 5:5–11

The seventh vision depicts the removal of wickedness from the land of Judah to Babylon. Sin, symbolized as a woman, since wickedness is a feminine word, is thrust into an ephah, sealed with a lead disc, and carried by two women to the ancient land of Shinar (modern-day Babylon/Iraq).

As in vision six, God will move against evil in two dramatic acts. These two acts are:

A. Wickedness Will Be Placed Under Wraps 5:5–8
B. Wickedness Will Be Housed in Babylon 5:9–11

WICKEDNESS WILL BE PLACED UNDER WRAPS (5:5–8)

This time the prophet is shown *"a basket that is going forth"* (v. 6). The weight and measurements of this "basket," or "ephah," like most from that time, are difficult to describe. The ephah held somewhere between 3/8 to 2/3 of a U.S. bushel.[18] By any estimate, it was too small for any woman to fit into. But that fact is not all that significant for apocalyptic literature where it is not necessary for the images, especially those that occur in dreams or visions, to conform in all aspects to reality.

When Zechariah, true to his previous form, asks "What is it?", he is told that *"This is Wickedness!"* (v. 8). Wickedness stood for everything that was the opposite of righteousness—whether in the ethical, civil or religious realm. This was wickedness personified. (The possible connection between Babylon being the ancient center of mercantile commercialism and its current ascendency to the center of the economic forces through the oil cartel should not be missed.)

To make the image of the personified wickedness even more vivid, wickedness is depicted as *"a woman sitting inside [a] basket"* (v. 7). The picture is reminiscent of a kind of genie in a jar. This woman's influence would be capped by the *"lead disc"* (v. 7). Surely that would be God's concluding act of placing wickedness under wraps.

Wickedness had grown to such proportions that it looked as if iniquity came by the bushel-fulls. But no longer would it prevail; in God's concluding acts of history He would remove the wicked (vision six) and, as this vision shows, wickedness itself.

WICKEDNESS WILL BE HOUSED IN BABYLON (5:9–11)

In the second half of this vision, the prophet suddenly sees *"two women, coming with the wind in their wings; for they had wings like the wings of a stork"* (v. 9bc). The Hebrew word for "stork" is ḥasîdâ, meaning "faithful one," and is similar to the Hebrew word for "grace," ḥesed. The faithful one—the stork—may symbolize God's gracious removal of sin and iniquity from His people, just as God had removed the sin of the dung-spattered High Priest Joshua by His "grace" (Zech. 3:4).

The woman in the ephah will be removed to *"Shinar,"* the ancient name for that part of Babylon that contained such cities as Babel (Babylon), Erech, Accad, and Calneh (Gen. 10:10; 11:2; Dan. 1:2). This was the area that from earliest times was opposed to the will of God (Gen. 11:1–9). In this land, which had also served most recently as the place of Judah's captivity, God would *"build a house for [wickedness]"* (v. 11).

God would give wickedness a home far removed from His people. A home like the ancient ziggurats, exhibited first, perhaps, in the tower of Babel. *"When it is ready, the basket will be set there on its base"* (v. 11c). Once located on its "base," or "pedestal," wickedness would be worshipped like the idol it was for those who had so consistently resisted God's will.

Given the part that Babylon plays in the eschatological drama of the closing days of this present age, the removal of wickedness to Babylon might have been in preparation for the final conflict between good and evil. Isaiah 13–14, and, especially, Jeremiah 50–51, place a revived Babylonian empire at the center of the final contest between God and "all the nations of the earth" that have been gathered into the Near East for history's finale. But God will triumph, for He has full control over evil. That can be seen in His ability to pack up evil and literally ship it to the center of wickedness where He is able to deal with it conclusively at the end of the age.

Conclusion

The only successful way to deal with evil conclusively is to remove it completely. This God will do as He concludes the times of the Gentiles and moves in grace and love to restore His people Israel.

CHAPTER NINE

Executing Judgment on the Gentile Nations

Zechariah 6:1–15

6:1 Then I turned and raised my eyes and looked, and behold, four chariots were coming from between two mountains, and the mountains were mountains of bronze.

2 With the first chariot were red horses, with the second chariot black horses,

3 with the third chariot white horses, and with the fourth chariot dappled horses—strong steeds.

4 Then I answered and said to the angel who talked with me, "What are these, my lord?"

5 And the angel answered and said to me, "These are four spirits of heaven, who go out from their station before the Lord of all the earth.

6 "The one with the black horses is going to the north country, the white are going after them, and the dappled are going toward the south country."

7 Then the strong steeds went out, eager to go, that they might walk to and fro throughout the earth. And He said, "Go, walk to and fro throughout the earth." So they walked to and fro throughout the earth.

8 And He called to me, and spoke to me, saying, "See, those who go toward the north country have given rest to My Spirit in the north country."

9 Then the word of the LORD came to me, saying:

10 "Receive the gift from the captives—from Heldai, Tobijah, and Jedaiah, who have come from

Babylon—and go the same day and enter the house of
Josiah the son of Zephaniah.

11 "Take the silver and gold, make an elaborate
crown, and set it on the head of Joshua the son of
Jehozadak, the high priest.

12 "Then speak to him, saying, 'Thus says the
LORD of hosts, saying:

> Behold, the Man whose name is the BRANCH!
> From His place He shall branch out,
> And He shall build the temple of the LORD;

13 Yes, He shall build the temple of the LORD.
> He shall bear the glory,
> And shall sit and rule on His throne;
> So He shall be a priest on His throne,
> And the counsel of peace shall be between
>   them both.'"

14 "Now the elaborate crown shall be for a
memorial in the temple of the LORD for Helem,
Tobijah, Jedaiah, and Hen the son of Zephaniah.

15 "Even those who are far away shall come and
build the temple of the LORD. Then you shall know
that the LORD of hosts has sent Me to you. And this
shall come to pass if you diligently obey the voice of
the LORD your God."

Zechariah 6:1–15

The eighth vision corresponds to the first; both visions concern
Israel's relation to the Gentile nations.

The first vision concludes with the disappointing news of the equestrian
patrol that all the Gentile nations were at rest. In the eighth vision, war
chariots are attached to the horses so they can now dispense judgment.

The crowning of Joshua, High Priest, and a second oracle concerning the Branch (6:9–14) form a fitting conclusion to all eight visions
and therefore belong to them. The conclusion also contains another
reference to building a temple, one which will be built by men from
the ends of the earth (v. 15).

God will execute His judgment over the nations of the world in
two ways:

A. By Appeasing God's Wrath Against the Gentile Nations   6:1–8
B. By Installing God's Priest-King as Ruler Over All Nations
     (6:9–15).

By Appeasing God's Wrath Against the Gentile Nations (6:1–8)

The mission of the horses and chariots supplies the central theme to all eight visions, for they acted as a pair of book-ends at the front and back of the visions. Together, the eight visions say more than that the temple must be rebuilt and the leadership revived; they argue that God's kingdom in the whole world would be renewed and governments that had opposed His kingdom would be totally vanquished.

In the eighth vision *"Four chariots"* (v. 1) are immediately presented to us, not just the four horses seen in the first vision. These are obviously war chariots, so the intention to dispense judgment is clear from the start of the vision.

Instead of coming out from "a hallow," or "valley" (1:8) as in the first vision, the four chariots come out from *"two mountains, . . . mountains of bronze"* (v. 1). The interpreting angel never identifies these two mountains, nor does the prophet inquire as to what they stand for. But where the evidence is thin, the suggestions are legion. A favorite identification is Mount Zion and the Mount of Olives. But why would Zechariah say these limestone mountains are made of "bronze?" Another suggestion is that the mountains refer to Babylon, which claimed to be the gateway to the gods. In truth no one can be certain what these mountains stand for; nor is it clear that we must decide. The mountains may simply be part of the apocalyptic drapery that functions only to let us know that the vision has a supernatural, not natural, setting.

The colors of the horses figure prominently in the eighth vision, as they did in the first. *"With the first chariot were red horses, with the second chariot black horses, with the third chariot white horses, and with the fourth chariot dappled horses—strong steeds"* (vv. 2–3). These horses bear a strong resemblance to the four horsemen of Revelation 6:1–8. Generally it is said that red indicates martyrdom, white stands for victory, black stands for famine, and dappled (or "pale"), a mixture of some white on a darker background, points overall to death. In spite of what some allege, more seems to be implied by the vividness of such detail than the four corners of the globe. This will be clear from our discussion, which follows.

When the prophet asks his usual question, *"What are these, my lord?"* (v. 4b), the angel replies, *"These are four spirits of heaven, who go out from their station before the Lord of all the earth"* (v. 5). The verb "to go out" is one of the most frequently used words in the last three visions. It occurs twelve times. The whole world is being prepared for God's concluding acts in the historic process as He restores Israel to her land and assumes the reign of the world.

"The one with the black horses is going to the north country" (v. 6a). If the vision has both a now (fulfilled) and a not-yet (fulfilled) aspect about it, as many prophecies do, then this text points both to ancient Babylon (a country north and east of Jerusalem, approached from a road leading north out of Jerusalem) and to an eschatological country (or countries) where God would prepare for His concluding acts by sending first a time of deep famine—either in modern Iraq (ancient Babylon) or, perhaps, Syria—then a victory over one or more of these countries—with *"the white [horses which] are going after [the black ones]"* (v. 6b)—in the latter days, i.e., the time connected with the second coming of our Lord.

"The dappled are going toward the south country" (v. 6c), continues the angel. If this pale, or dappled, horse has the same symbolic value as it does in Revelation 6, then death would spread to the south of Judah, perhaps to Egypt, or even to the African continent. One immediately wonders whether the tremendous foothold the disease AIDS has on that continent is a harbinger of things to come!

The angel does not comment on the red team of horses. Some scholars have concluded that the word "after," or "behind" (hence "west" of) the white team, means the "west." However, no manuscripts contain this word, and there are no other textual reasons for making this conclusion; for the same reasons translations like *The Jerusalem Bible* and the *New English Bible* that read "The red horses went towards the east country" are not supported by the text. The red team seems to be held in reserve.

God's *"strong steeds"* were *"eager to go, that they might walk to and fro throughout the earth"* (v. 7). Unlike the steeds in the first vision which report that "all the earth is resting quietly" (1:11), in this vision the "strong steeds" did their work in their war chariots and "appeased [God's] wrath," or, literally, "they have caused my spirit to rest" (*"have given rest to My Spirit"*; v. 8). God could now rest because His messengers of wrath had executed what He sent them to do. Cyrus's overthrow of Babylon in 539 B.C. was the first of the promised victories. But victory over Babylon is also a key focus of an even greater victory over the Gentile nations; only when the Babylon of the final day has fallen will God's Spirit find its complete rest and will the full vindication of the persecuted people of Israel be accomplished.

BY INSTALLING GOD'S PRIEST-KING AS RULER OVER ALL NATIONS (6:9–15)

The climactic concluding act of the eight night visions is the symbolic crowning of Joshua. Rather than portraying this for Zechariah in a vision, the prophet is now placed in the midst of his people, where he receives a delegation of three men from Babylon who come bearing a special gift of *"silver and gold"* (v. 11).

The three recent arrivals from Babylon had entered *"the house of Josiah the son of Zephaniah"* (v. 10c). The prophet is told to go to Josiah's house in order to receive this *"gift from the captives"* (v. 10).

From the gift of silver and gold from those still among the exiled community in Babylon (who had not participated in Zerubbabel's return in 537 B.C., Ezra's return in 458 B.C. or Nehemiah's return in 445 B.C.), Zechariah was to fashion *"an elaborate crown, and set it on the head of Joshua the son of Jehozadak, the high priest"* (v. 11). The most surprising news here is that the high priest is given a dual role of priest and king! The word "crown" in Hebrew is actually the plural "crowns" and may well point to the double-ringed priestly and royal tiara, thus pointing to the Messiah who was to come as both priest and king.

The coronation ceremony of the high priest (and not of the Davidic governor, Zerubbabel) introduces five messianic promises that are of great significance for all of biblical revelation.

1. *"Behold, the Man whose name is the BRANCH"* (v. 12b) promises that a Davidic king would rule in the coming new age (*see* our comments on the title "Branch" in Zech. 3:8; cf. Jer. 23:3–5; 33:14–26; Isa. 4:2).

2. *"From His place He shall branch out"* (v. 12c). Messiah, though He came out of dry and parched ground (Isa. 53:2), would be elevated and prosper in accordance with His very own nature—He would, as the BRANCH, branch out! (cf. 2 Sam. 23:1; Ps. 89:19).

3. *"And He shall build the temple of the LORD"* (v. 12d). While Zerubbabel the governor, under the prompting of the prophets Haggai and Zechariah, built the so-called second temple in 515 B.C., Messiah himself would build a new temple in that coming new age (Isa. 2:2–4; Ezk. 40–42; Mic. 4:1–5; Hag. 2:7–9). Not only would Messiah be in

charge of the building of this new temple, but *"He shall bear the glory"* (v. 13b). Bearing "glory," or "honor," signifies all the majesty and splendor that a royal position affords (cf. Ps. 96:6). There would be nothing "wimpish," or indecisive about the Messiah's exercise of royal authority.

4. *"And [He] shall sit and rule on His throne"* (v. 13c). God had long ago promised that the scion of David would sit on the throne of his family and that that throne would endure forever, unlike all other mortal empires (2 Sam. 7:12–16). Though some Davidic kings would not personally participate in the present spiritual benefits of this line, they would be compelled to pass on the lineal benefits of God's gracious gift to David until the Messiah himself came (cf. Luke 1:32–33). All power and all authority in heaven and earth belong to the Messiah, who would one day sit on David's throne.

5. *"So He shall be a priest on His throne, and the counsel of peace shall be between them both"* (v. 13d, e). This is the greatest Old Testament passage on the fact that the coming Messiah will be both a Davidic king and a Priest (cf. Heb. 7). So amazing is this prediction that it has troubled many a commentator. Was it likely that a "priest" would "sit upon His throne?" The Greek Septuagint translation attempts to soften this prediction by substituting "at His right hand" for "on His throne." But as we know from the royal Psalms (e.g., Ps. 110:4), the Anointed One would exercise an everlasting priesthood in addition to His royal and prophetic offices. Thus, Zechariah daringly combines the priestly and kingly offices into one person, "the Branch." Only the Lord himself could bring "peace" to this earth by dealing with the iniquity of the earth in one day (3:8–9). Jesus, our Savior, will once again deal with sin decisively and remove the sin of Judah, all in one day. Further, in this one person of the coming Branch, all tensions between the offices of religious and political leadership would be resolved.

The crown of verse 11 would be stored *"for a memorial in the temple of the LORD"* (v. 14), both as a reminder of the gift from the captives in Babylon and as a testimony to the coming union of the priest and king in the one office of Messiah. There that crown would stay "Until He comes whose right it is" (Ezk. 21:27; cf. Gen. 49:10—"Until Shiloh comes").

In this passage, which has already had more than its share of surprises, we are further startled by the words in verse 15: *"Even those who are far away shall come and build the temple of the* LORD. *Then you shall know that the* LORD *of hosts has sent Me to you. And this shall come to pass if you diligently obey the voice of the* LORD *your God.*" This verse does not refer, of course, to Zerubbabel's temple, but to the millennial temple that Isaiah (2:1–4), Micah (4:1–4), and Ezekiel (40–48) spoke of. Like the Jews from Babylon who brought gifts of silver and gold to make the double crown, "those from afar" (by New Testament times a subtle circumlocution for Gentiles; e.g., Acts 2:39; Eph. 2:13) would pitch in with their gifts and labor to construct the millennial temple. These "princely gifts coming from the far-off Babylon were but a harbinger and precursor of the wealth of the nations that would pour into Jerusalem when Messiah the Branch was received as King of kings and Lord of lords."[19]

The eight visions, and the first main block of the book of Zechariah, conclude with a warning, from Deuteronomy 28:1, that God's blessings were promised to those who walked in obedience.

CONCLUSION

The eight visions surely indicate that God was going to do more than help the newly-returned exiles now in Jerusalem to complete the building of the temple. This work would be connected to, but exceeded by, what the Messiah was going to do in the final day.

Not only would a new temple be built, but Messiah, as the unifier of the priestly and kingly offices, would remove the guilt of iniquity in one day, restore the nation of Israel back to her land, subdue all the nations that had for so long harassed Israel, and sit on His throne over the whole world as undisputed king of all the nations.

CHAPTER TEN

What It Means to Be the People of God, Then and Now

Zechariah 7:1–8:23

7:1 Now in the fourth year of King Darius it came to pass that the word of the LORD came to Zechariah, on the fourth day of the ninth month, which is Chislev,

2 when the people sent Sherezer, with Regem–Melech and his men, to the house of God, to pray before the LORD,

3 and to ask the priests who were in the house of the LORD of hosts, and the prophets, saying, "Should I weep in the fifth month and fast as I have done for so many years?"

4 Then the word of the LORD of hosts came to me, saying,

5 "Say to all the people of the land, and to the priests: 'When you fasted and mourned in the fifth and seventh months during those seventy years, did you really fast for Me—for Me?

6 'When you eat and when you drink, do you not eat and drink for yourselves?

7 'Should you not have obeyed the words which the LORD proclaimed through the former prophets when Jerusalem and the cities around it were inhabited and prosperous, and the South and the Lowland were inhabited?'"

8 Then the word of the LORD came to Zechariah, saying,

348

9 "Thus says the LORD of hosts:
   'Execute true justice,
   Show mercy and compassion
   Everyone to his brother.

10 Do not oppress the widow or the fatherless,
   The alien or the poor.
   Let none of you plan evil in his heart
   Against his brother.'

11 "But they refused to heed, shrugged their shoulders, and stopped their ears so that they could not hear.

12 "Yes, they made their hearts like flint, refusing to hear the law and the words which the LORD of hosts had sent by His Spirit through the former prophets. Thus great wrath came from the LORD of hosts.

13 "Therefore it happened, that just as He proclaimed and they would not hear, so they called out and I would not listen," says the LORD of hosts.

14 "But I scattered them with a whirlwind among all the nations which they had not known. Thus the land became desolate after them, so that no one passed through or returned; for they made the pleasant land desolate."

8:1 Again the word of the LORD of hosts came, saying,

2 "Thus says the LORD of hosts:
   'I am zealous for Zion with great zeal;
   With great fervor I am zealous for her.'

3 "Thus says the LORD:
   'I will return to Zion,
   And dwell in the midst of Jerusalem.
   Jerusalem shall be called the City of Truth,
   The Mountain of the LORD of hosts,
   The Holy Mountain.'

4 "Thus says the LORD of hosts:
   'Old men and old women shall again sit
   In the streets of Jerusalem,
   Each one with his staff in his hand
   Because of great age.

5 The streets of the city
   Shall be full of boys and girls
   Playing in its streets.'

6 "Thus says the LORD of hosts:
  'If it is marvelous in the eyes of the remnant of
      this people in these days,
  Will it also be marvelous in My eyes?'
  Says the LORD of hosts.
7 "Thus says the LORD of hosts:
  'Behold, I will save My people from the land of
      the east
  And from the land of the west;
8 I will bring them back,
  And they shall dwell in the midst of Jerusalem.
  They shall be My people
  And I will be their God,
  In truth and righteousness.'
9 "Thus says the LORD of hosts:
  'Let your hands be strong,
  You who have been hearing in these days
  These words by the mouth of the prophets,
  Who were in the day
  That the foundation was laid
  For the house of the LORD of hosts,
  That the temple might be built.
10 For before these days
  There were no wages for man
      nor any hire for beast;
  There was no peace from the enemy for
      whoever went out or came in;
  For I set all men, everyone, against his neighbor.
11 'But now I will not treat the remnant of this
      people as in the former days,' says the
  LORD of hosts.
12 'For the seed shall be prosperous,
  The vine shall give its fruit,
  The ground shall give her increase,
  And the heavens shall give their dew.
  I will cause the remnant of this people
  To possess all these things.
13 And it shall come to pass
  That just as you were a curse among
      the nations,
  O house of Judah and house of Israel,
  So I will save you, and you shall be a blessing.

350

> Do not fear,
> Let your hands be strong.'
> 14 "For thus says the LORD of hosts:
> 'Just as I determined to punish you
> When your fathers provoked Me to wrath,'
> Says the LORD of hosts,
> 'And I would not relent,
> 15 So again in these days
> I am determined to do good
> To Jerusalem and to the house of Judah.
> Do not fear.
> 16 These are the things you shall do:
> Speak each man the truth to his neighbor;
> Give judgment in your gates for truth, justice,
> and peace;
> 17 Let none of you think evil in your heart against
> your neighbor;
> And do not love a false oath.
> For all these are things that I hate,'
> Says the LORD."
> 18 Then the word of the LORD of hosts
> came to me, saying,
> 19 "Thus says the LORD of hosts:
> 'The fast of the fourth month,
> The fast of the fifth,
> The fast of the seventh,
> And the fast of the tenth,
> Shall be joy and gladness and cheerful feasts
> For the house of Judah.
> Therefore love truth and peace.'
> 20 "Thus says the LORD of hosts:
> 'Peoples shall yet come,
> Inhabitants of many cities;
> 21 The inhabitants of one city shall go to another,
> saying,
> "Let us continue to go
> and pray before the LORD,
> And seek the LORD of hosts.
> I myself will go also."
> 22 Yes, many peoples and strong nations
> Shall come to seek the LORD of hosts in Jerusalem,
> And to pray before the LORD.'

23 "Thus says the LORD of hosts: 'In those days ten
men from every language of the nations shall grasp
the sleeve of a Jewish man, saying, "Let us go with
you, for we have heard that God is with you."'"

Zechariah 7:1–8:23

The second main block of Zechariah's prophecy is contained in
chapters 7 and 8. These two chapters contain some of the most succinct statements of what all the prophets had been trying to say.[20] The
messages contained within these chapters were prompted by questions posed by a delegation sent to Jerusalem, presumably from the
town of Bethel (twelve miles north of Jerusalem). The NKJV does not
identify the town as "Bethel" (except in the margin), but says only
that the delegation was coming *"to the house of God"* (v. 2). Others
identify the site with a compound, proper name, "Bethel-Sharezer,"
for which there is a Babylonian equivalent from the relevant time period.[21] Unlike the town of Bethel, Bethel-Sharezer was a considerable
distance from Jerusalem, and this distance could have been the reason
for the three-and-a-half-month delay between the fast commemorating the destruction of the temple, which occurred in the fifth month
and seventh day (2 Kings 25:8), and the arrival of the delegation in
the ninth month on the fifth day (7:1). However, there could have
been other reasons for the delegation's delay, and our preference is to
view the delegation as a Jewish delegation from the city of Bethel.

The messages in these chapters were also occasioned by the fact
that the people needed guidance on whether they were to continue to
observe the fasts connected with the tragic events surrounding the
fall of Jerusalem. Verse 3 of chapter 7 raises the question about continuing the fast commemorating the destruction of the house of God
in the fifth month, seventh day (c. August 7th), and 8:19 asks whether
the people should continue to observe three other fast days, viz., (1) the
Breaching of the walls, in the 4th month, 9th day (Jer. 39:2), (2) the Murder of Governor Gedaliah, in the 7th month (2 Kings 25:25; Jer. 41:1–2),
and (3) the Beginning of the Siege of Jerusalem, in the 10th month,
10th day (2 Kings 25:1–2; Jer. 39:1).

Interestingly enough, God had only commanded that the people
observe one fast day—*Yom Kippur*, the "Day of Atonement" (Lev.
16:29; 23:27,29, 32). The people had increased their burden by adding
four more days. This is so true to life. We religionists often fail to get
it straight; we either go overboard on one side or on the other!

352

Chapters seven and eight are best divided on the basis of the recurring quotation formulae. These will show that chapters seven and eight have four major paragraphs: 7:4–7; 7:8–14; 8:1–17; and 8:18–23. The formula in each of the four paragraphs that functions as a marker is *"Then the word of the LORD [of hosts] came."* Naturally, 7:1–3 serves as an introduction. The delegation from Bethel poses the question: *"Should I weep in the fifth month and fast as I have done for so many years?"* (7:3). Since the temple was almost complete, it was very natural to ask about the proper method of worship there. It is worth noting that once the reality has come, the commemoration of a past event is somewhat passé in the thinking of the people. That should help us answer the similar question whether there will be sacrifices as memorials in the millennial temple when the Lamb of God is present!

A second set of recurrent quotation formulae that divide these paragraphs into sub-paragraphs is *"Thus says the LORD [of hosts]"* (7:9; 8:2, 3, 4, 6, 7, 9, 14, 19, 20, 23).[22]

One last observation is worth noting before we begin our exposition of the chapters. Chapter seven records the negative side of the issue and concludes with Israel being scattered among the nations, while chapter eight focuses on the positive side, concluding with the nations grasping for the robe of the Jews so that they might go up to Jerusalem with them.

Chapters seven and eight, like the texts beginning at 1:1 and 1:8, have as their date line *"the fourth day of the ninth month, which is Chislev"* (7:1), December 7, 518 B.C., on our Julian calendars. The chapters give us snatches from Zechariah's sermons as he urges God's people not to substitute empty formalism for the reality of the living presence of the Lord of glory. Zechariah gives us the answers to four questions which, in turn, reveal four characteristics of what it means to be the people of God, both in Zechariah's day and in our own. The four questions, which form our teaching and preaching outline, are:

    A. Are We Serving Ourselves or God?   7:4–7
    B. Are We Listening To Ourselves or God?   7:8–14
    C. Are We Believing a Lie or the Truth?   8:1–17
    D. Are We Ready for the Future?   8:18–23

ARE WE SERVING OURSELVES OR GOD? (7:4–7)

"In the fourth year of King Darius" (7:1; 518 B.C.), things were looking much better for the returned exiles. Every impediment to building

the temple had been removed by Darius's royal decree (Ezra 6). Homes were being built (Hag. 1:4). Life seemed to be returning to normal.

Still something seemed to be wrong. A delegation of two prominent men, with some attendants, was sent from the former calf-worshipping center of the former Northern Israel, i.e., from Bethel. The lessons of the destruction of Samaria in 722 B.C. had not been lost on these sensitive souls. The dispute that raged from 931 to 722 B.C. as to whether the Jews should worship in Jerusalem had been resolved. Jerusalem was the legitimate place to worship. The delegation came, in fact, *"to pray before the LORD"* (v. 7:2c) *"and to ask the priests who were in the house of the LORD of hosts"* (v. 7:3) about whether they should continue to fast now that the temple had almost been completed. The word for "to pray" was literally "to stroke [or smooth] the face of the LORD," i.e., "to entreat" Him urgently.

The fifth month, Hebrew *Ab* (August), will live forever in infamy in the hearts and minds of Israel. It was on August 9th, 587 B.C., that Jerusalem was finally taken and destroyed by Nebuchadnezzar. According to the Talmud, it was also the day when God decreed that the people in the wilderness should not enter the land because of their unbelief. Further, it was the day on which not only the first, or Solomonic, temple was destroyed, but the second temple was destroyed by the Romans. Moreover, it was the day on which the city of Bethar was taken under Bar Kokbah (A.D. 135), only to fall in turn into Gentile hands who put everyone to death including Bar Kohbah, the messianic pretender in the second Christian century. Finally, on that day, August 9th, wicked Turnus Rufus ploughed up the hill of the sanctuary and thus fulfilled Micah's prophecy, "Zion shall be ploughed as a field."

Implicit in the delegation's question about fasting is another question: Will God honor His promises to raise up the nation of Israel once again, as the earlier prophets had predicted, or what should we expect? The answer given is practically identical to the call for repentance in the introduction to the book (Zech. 1:1–6).

The Word of the Lord came to the prophet with this response to the people: *"When you fasted and mourned in the fifth and seventh months during those seventy years, did you really fast for Me—for Me? When you eat and when you drink, do you not eat and drink for yourselves?"* (vv. 5b–6). Clearly, ritual in and of itself can be, and in this case was, little

354

more than empty formalism that satisfied only the people's selfish interests.

It is a false notion that abstaining from food and mourning over God's past acts of judgment are necessarily meritorious. It is possible to use fasting and mourning as a way of calling attention to ourselves, instead of to God. True fasting and mourning are outward signs of genuine inward grief and a decision to repent of sin. Self-imposed religious acts, not prescribed in Scripture, are merely self-glorifying. They are expressions of our preoccupations with ourselves and our own importance. God's antidote for such egocentrism is this: "Therefore, whether you eat or drink, or whatever you do, do all to the glory of God" (1 Cor. 10:31).

"Should you not have obeyed the words which the LORD *proclaimed through the former prophets when Jerusalem and the cities around it were inhabited and prosperous, and the South and the Lowland were inhabited?"* (v. 7). Isaiah, one of the former prophets, had dealt with the topic of fasting. The people of the eighth century B.C. complained: "'Why have we fasted,' they say, 'and You have not seen? Why have we afflicted our souls and You take no notice?'" (Isa. 58:3). But if they wished to have a fast, Isaiah advised, here was one for them: feed the hungry, clothe the naked, help your relatives, loose those fraudulent contracts you forced others into, let the oppressed go free; there's a "fast" if you want one. But that was not the sort of thing they were hoping God would say.

Isaiah's point, and the point of this text, is that if we want to serve God rather than ourselves, there is a proper set of priorities to observe: obedience takes precedence over sacrifices; walking humbly with God is more important than scores of rituals (1 Sam. 15:22–23; Mic. 6:6–8).

Therefore, let us not waste a lot of time and motion. Let us return to the true and tested paths first set out by the former prophets. There just is no substitute for heart righteousness; all religious acts must flow out of a genuine response of faith and obedience to God, or they are merely self-serving, self-glorifying and, consequently, self-condemning.

ARE WE LISTENING TO OURSELVES OR GOD? (7:8–14)

Have we heard the message of the former prophets yet? Zechariah conveys the substance of Isaiah 58:6–12 in verses 9–10. He urges:

"Execute true justice, show mercy and compassion everyone to his brother. Do not oppress the widow or the fatherless, the alien or the poor. Let none of you plan evil in his heart against his brother" (v. 9–10).

Even though our prior duty to God is presumed, our duty to our neighbor is set forth as a test of the genuineness of our commitment to God. This is not a so-called "social gospel," for the gospel is addressed first and foremost to individuals, but the gospel surely has social implications or it would not be the powerful Word of God that Scripture portrays it to be.

Neglect of the duties listed in verses 9–10 leads to a society that has gone dead towards God. In such an insensitive society there is no fair and just administration of justice, no demonstration of mercy and compassion for weak and hurting individuals, no looking out for widows, orphans, aliens or the poor, and no end of conjuring up ways of doing evil. Instead, there is simply a "dog-eat-dog" mentality in the business world, the domestic scene, and the ecclesiastical realm. In effect, society says "down with the fetus," "down with the victim of crimes," "down with the oppressed." What a tragic state of affairs.

No one is listening: *"But they refused to heed, shrugged their shoulders, and stopped their ears so that they could not hear"* (v. 11). Surely this says it all. They refused to listen! They pulled away the shoulder, a body-language sign of rejection (cf. Neh. 9:29) and, literally, they "made their ears heavy" (cf. Isa. 6:10: "Make the heart of this people dull, and their ears heavy."). *"Yes, they made their hearts like flint, refusing to hear the law and the words which the LORD of hosts had sent by His Spirit through the former prophets"* (v. 12ab). In Jeremiah 17:1, this hard stone is rendered a "diamond." What a waste of the prophet's and God's revelation!

One result of such adamant spirits and stopped-up ears was that when *"[the people] called out"* in prayer, the Lord said He *"would not listen"* (v. 13bc) to their requests! This should not have come as a surprise, for Isaiah had taught the same truth in Isaiah 58:9—only when the people obeyed would God say "Here I am" when they called out to Him in prayer. Perhaps this is the reason why in our own day so few of some people's prayers are answered!

Another result was that Israel was *"scattered . . . among all the nations"* (v. 14). Leviticus 26:14–43 and Deuteronomy 28:15–68 had warned about precisely such a result, but Israel had maintained her adamant behavior with a deaf ear to the commands of God "till there was no remedy" (2 Chron. 36:16). Sadly, on the last page of the Bible (in the Hebrew order of the canon) is this note: "But they mocked the messengers of God, despised His words, and scoffed at His prophets, until the wrath of the LORD arose against His people, till there was no remedy" (2 Chron. 36:16). How important it is to listen to God and the words He has sent through His apostles and prophets.

ARE WE BELIEVING A LIE OR THE TRUTH? (8:1–17)

The bad memories of past acts of disobedience gradually faded and were replaced by an expectation of hope for the future. Though Zechariah speaks of judgment where he needs to, he does not play that string to the exclusion of all others. In this text God reveals to Zechariah what He will do beyond the painful realities of the present. The ten occurrences of the formula *"Thus says the LORD [of hosts]"* (8:2, 3, 4, 6, 7, 9, 14, 19, 20, 23) divide the text into subthemes—perhaps a *potpourri* of themes from a number of Zechariah's messages given over the years. In our discussion of the text we have expressed each of the subthemes as a question.

1. *Do we believe that God's zeal for His promise to Israel and His hot anger against the nations that oppress her are still controlling facts of life?* (8:1–2). God declares to Zechariah: "I am zealous for Zion with great zeal; with great fervor I am zealous for her" (v. 2). The Hebrew word *qinʿâh* can be rendered "zealousness" or "jealousness." "Zeal" is an aspect of God's internal intensity and the passion that He brings to everything that He does and says. Of course, our Lord was not jealous in the sense that we use that word today—our Lord was not a green-eyed monster—for of what and whom would our Lord need to be jealous? Everything anyone has comes from Him and, ultimately, is His—in that sense, in this text it is better to translate *qinʿâh* as "zealousness"; the Lord was zealous for His name, reputation, and mission.

God had announced His zeal for Jerusalem in 1:14; He was zealous because He had given His covenantal promise that He would be faithful to what He had promised to do. Unfortunately, however, when the Lord was but "a little angry" (1:15) with Israel and used her enemies to punish her, her enemies exceeded their divine orders and showed no mercy on Israel. God judged those nations; so what will He do to modern nations that engage in the same type of excess?

2. *Do we believe that God will return to dwell in Jerusalem?* (8:3). God's anger against the nations that oppress Israel will by no means be the end of the matter. *"I will return to Zion, and dwell in the midst of Jerusalem"* (v. 3ab). As we have discussed in 1:16 and 2:10, God had promised that He would come down to live personally in Jerusalem, fulfilling the third part in the tri-partite formula, "I will be your God, you shall be my people, and I will dwell in the midst of you." In that coming day when Messiah would rule and reign from "the midst of Jerusalem," *"Jerusalem shall be called the City of Truth, the Mountain of the LORD of hosts, the Holy Mountain"* (v. 3cde). Because He is the God of Truth, the city where He would reign—Jerusalem—would finally be known as the "City of Truth." This title is appropriate as well because "The remnant of Israel shall do no unrighteousness and speak no lies" (Zeph. 3:13). The mountain of Jerusalem is "holy" because of the Lord's holy presence there and because "HOLINESS" will be on the hearts and foreheads of all who reside there in that future day (Zech. 14:20–21).

3. *Do we believe Jerusalem will be repopulated?* (8:4–5). Two groups of people, frequently overlooked—*"Old men and old women"* and *"boys and girls"* (v. 4a, 5c)—will be able to live in Jerusalem once again without fear of being mugged or abused, or of being victimized by a criminal or pervert. The fact that the men and women are described as old indicates that the text is speaking of another day and age, when there will be peace, security, and the sound of children enjoying their play in the streets. Elizabeth Achtemeier quips, "God's kingdom will not have come on this earth until its streets are fit for its children. But by the same token, it will not have come until its children are fit for its streets."[23]

4. *Do we believe it is too difficult for God to bring back a full remnant?* (8:6). The Hebrew word *pālā* rendered *"it is marvelous"* in verse 6 is a magnificent word with a rich history of associations and a deep theological heritage. It is one of the titles Isaiah used for the Son who was to be born in the Davidic line. His name was to be *"Wonderful."* It means the One who does "difficult things," or "miraculous" or "hard" tasks.

The same Hebrew word was used in Genesis 18:14, where God quizzed Abraham on why it was that Sarah, who was ninety years of age and in menopause, laughed when she and her 100-year-old husband were told they were going to bear a son? "Is anything *too hard* for the Lord?" The word was used, too, in Jeremiah. Jeremiah was told to buy some land just as the Babylonians were about to close in on and capture the land. Jeremiah affirmed, "there is nothing *too hard* for the LORD" (32:17). Later the Lord asked Jeremiah: "Is anything *too hard* for Me?" (32:26).

"Will it also be marvelous in My eyes [or too hard for Me]" (v. 6b)? No, it will not be too marvelous or too hard for the Lord! He will bring back His people to the land of Palestine, though most Christians think it will be something too difficult even for God to do.

5. *Do we believe the restored remnant will come from all over the world?* (8:7–8). Verses 7 and 8 contain perhaps the most succinct yet comprehensive statement in all of Scripture on the fact that God is intending to restore Israel to her land. *"Behold, I will save My people,"* Zechariah announces. They will come from *"the land of the east"* and *"from the land of the west,"* and God *"will bring them back, and they shall dwell in the midst of Jerusalem."* East and west function here as a figure of speech known as a merism (cf. Ps. 50:1; 113:3; Mal. 1:11); the remnant shall come from all over the earth.

Then the tri-partite formula discussed, earlier will be realized: *"They shall be My people and I will be their God."* To be God's own people and to be betrothed to Him forever was the great dream of the prophets and of the covenant itself (e.g., Hos. 2:19–20; Jer. 32:38–41).

Some commentators dispute the notion that the restored remnant will come from all over the world, noting that the world's present population of over fourteen million Jews would not all fit into Jerusalem. But, we note in response, there are modern cities with populations approaching or, in the case of Mexico City, exceeding that number. Further, the correct interpretation of verse 8 may be that Jerusalem will be the place where the people's worship will be centered, not where they will actually reside. Finally, the reference in verse 8 to Jerusalem may be a figure of speech called a synecdoche, wherein a part is used for the whole; i.e., the city of Jerusalem may stand for the whole land.

In that marvelous day of return, "truth" and "righteousness" would characterize the relationship between God and His people. In the past, only God was truthful and righteous, but now His people would be as well. Surely, that is a different day!

6. *Do we believe God will give the increase?* (8:9–13). Verses 9–13 contain a practical application of the promises about the future set forth in 8:1–8 that would give comfort to all.

God's encouraging words *"Let your hands be strong"* (v. 9) are similar to those Haggai gave in Haggai 2:4: "Now be strong," or "Be of good courage." These words are an idiom more frequently used in exhortations for those going into battle (Judg. 7:11; 2 Sam. 2:7; 16:21). The basis for this encouragement was the words God had given *"by the mouth of the prophets"* (v. 9d; cf. 1:4; 7:7, 12). Zechariah refers in particular to the prophets who spoke *"in the day that the foundation was laid for the house of the LORD of hosts"* (v. 9ef). Since Ezra 3 mentions no other prophets that were ministering during such time, this reference may well be to the message of Haggai (1:6–11; 2:15–19).

Like Haggai (1:6), God contrasts conditions at a time *"before these days"* (v. 10a)— i.e., before the days when the people heard the words of the prophets—with conditions *"now"* (v. 11a). In the earlier days, when the Samaritans were bitter foes of the returned exiles (Ezra 4:1– 5), there was no stability, security, or prosperity for man or beast. But in spite of Sanballat, Tobiah, and Geshem, and their conspiracies, God would *"now . . . treat the remnant of this people as in the former days"* (v. 11ab). Repentance alone had provided the grounds for God to reverse the adverse conditions this fledgling community of returned exiles had experienced for so long.

Again like Haggai (2:19), Zechariah proclaims that prosperity of the soil would follow genuine repentance and turning to God (v. 8:12). There is a connection, begun in the Garden of Eden, between the sin of mankind and the decreased productivity of the land. In the Garden of Eden, creation was subjected to bondage and waits for its release when our Lord returns the second time (Rom. 8:20–22). Nevertheless, in times of repentance and turning to the Lord, God can bring substantial healing even to the created order. That is what He promises in verse 12 to do for the spiritually revived remnant.

Using a *"just as"/"so"* construction (cf. Zech. 1:6; 7:13), verse 13 offers another comparison of the past and the future. While in the recent past the nations of Israel and Judah had been *"a curse among the nations,"* God would *"save [them], and [make them] a blessing."* Significantly, God's promise is addressed to both Israel and Judah, not to the returned Judahites alone (v. 13b); like Ezekiel 37:15–22, which pictured the reunion of the divided kingdom, so Zechariah depicts one revived nation.

7. *Do we believe God wants us to speak the truth, to render sound judgment, and not to plot evil against our neighbor?* (8:14–17). In what

appears to be another outline of a sermon, in this text Zechariah first tells what God proposes to do (vv. 14–15), then tells what God expects His people to do (vv. 16–17).

Using another *"just as"/"so"* construction (v. 14a, 15a), the Lord contrasts His past use of punishment (e.g., the exile that God had *"determined"* [v. 14] ever since Moses' day should the people disobey. Deut. 28:38–41; Jer. 4:28; 51:12) with His plan and determination *"to do good to Jerusalem"* (v. 15). Jeremiah had taught the same truth: "Just as I have brought all this great calamity on this people, so I will bring on them all the good that I have promised them"(Jer. 32:42). And since God is not a man that He should back down on His promises (Num. 23:19; 1 Sam. 15:29), the people could expect the "good" promised in verses 12–13.

In the meantime, God expected four deeds from the redeemed people: (1) *"Speak each man the truth to his neighbor"* (v. 16a). Since God is truth (Exod. 34:6), He expects no less than truth from His people in their daily dealings with each other (Ps. 15:2; Eph. 4:25); (2) Render sound judgments in the dispensing of justice everywhere (v. 16c). Corruption in the courts corrupts God's purpose in the world; (3) Keep your hearts pure by not indulging in vindictiveness or hatred against your neighbor (v. 17a). Once the inner dispositions give way, every conceivable act of violence and sin against our neighbor is possible. As Jesus taught, "For out of the heart proceed evil thoughts, murders, adulteries, fornications, thefts, false witness, blasphemies" (Matt. 15:19); and (4) *"Do not love a false oath"* (v. 17b). Falsified testimony against our neighbor is unacceptable to God because, once again, God is the God of truth. Referring to all four sins, the Lord says: *"For all these are things that I hate"* (v. 17c). These sins are listed in Proverbs 6:16–19 among the seven abominations that the Lord hates.

ARE WE READY FOR THE FUTURE? (8:18–23)

This final section of chapter 8 depicts the joys God's people will experience in the future. Israel and Judah will be joined by many nations as Jerusalem becomes "the place to be" in that day.

In the future God would turn the fasts that the people had devised on the fourth, fifth, seventh, and tenth months—mournful times of self-denial—into times of *"joy and gladness and cheerful feasts"* (v. 19ef; *see* our comments on 7:1–3). Therefore, the Lord desires that His people espouse and value *"truth and peace"* above all else (v. 19g). The fruit of benefitting from God's promises should be righteousness, truth, love, and peace. His promises about the future should provide the incentive to live a holy life in the present.

Also in the future there would come a great turning to the Lord, as was predicted in Isaiah 2:1–4 and Micah 4:1–5. The number of people who would turn to the Lord is significantly large (*"many peoples,"* v. 22a), and people would view the matter of turning to the Lord as urgent enough to demand immediate attention (*"let us continue to go,"* or better translated, "let us go *at once,"* v. 21b).

The people from every nationality will travel to Jerusalem to *"seek the LORD of hosts"* (v. 21c). That Jerusalem will be the center of worship in that future day can be seen as well in Isaiah 66:20, Micah 4:1–2, and Ezekiel 40–44.

So intense will be the desire of all the people of the earth to join the revived Jewish nation in the worship of the Living God *"[i]n those days"* (as contrasted with *"these days,"* 8:23, cf. 8:9, 15) that *"ten men from every language of the nations shall grasp the sleeve of a Jewish man, saying, 'Let us go with you, for we have heard that God is with you'"* (v. 23). The number "ten" is used here as an indefinite number signifying a large multitude. The Gentiles will clutch on to the robes of any Jew whom they can find and beg him to let them go along with him as they go up to worship God. The Gentiles will be this persistent and intense because they will have finally heard that the ancient promise that God made to His people is true. Indeed, God is with His people (Gen. 21:22; 26:3, 24; Exod. 3:12; Josh. 1:5; Isa. 45:14).

CONCLUSION

What God wants from His people is authenticity. Too often we serve only ourselves, rather than the Lord. Too frequently we listen only to what we wish to hear, with little or no care for what God is saying.

It is sometimes much easier to fulfill the outward demands of formal and ritualistic worship than it is to prepare for these acts by coming with a pure heart and an inner disposition that responds to God's grace. Where there is all form, function, and routine, invariably there is no joy, no heart-felt involvement, and no true worship of the Living God.

God hates substitutes for the real thing as much as (and even more than) our generation hates substitutes for natural foods. Therefore, it is wrong to think that mere attendance at God's house can substitute for a personal holiness as the proper preparation for meeting God. It is likewise wrong to substitute ceremonial observances for obedience to God as a basis for those acts of religious ritual that will follow. It is wrong to substitute mere possession of God's Word, or even knowledge of that Word, for a genuine response to what that word teaches.

God wants us to love truth and peace. If we do, we shall enjoy the marvelous works that He predicts will follow in those days and events surrounding His second coming.

Two Burdens Concerning Israel and the Nations

FIRST BURDEN:

Zechariah 9–11

The last six chapters of the book of Zechariah deal mainly with the future of Israel. In many ways, the tone takes a change, even though the chapters are not unrelated to the previous eight, as we explained in the introduction.

This third main block of the book of Zechariah is divided into two equal divisions, chapters 9–11 and chapters 12–14. Each is introduced with *"The burden of the word of the LORD"* (9:1; 12:1). In general, the first "burden" is counter-balanced with predictions of our Lord's first coming, while the second "burden" is offset by the promise of Messiah's second coming. Further, the first burden describes the rejection of the messianic "shepherd" (11:4–17), while the second teaches that Messiah shall finally be recognized by Israel as a spiritual renewal takes place among the people (12:10–13:1).

CHAPTER ELEVEN

Dispossessing the Gentile Powers of the Promised Land

Zechariah 9:1–8

9:1 The burden of the word of the LORD
Against the land of Hadrach,
And Damascus its resting place
(For the eyes of men
And all the tribes of Israel
Are on the LORD);

2 Also against Hamath, which borders on it,
And against Tyre and Sidon, though they are
very wise.

3 For Tyre built herself a tower,
Heaped up silver like the dust,
And gold like the mire of the streets.

4 Behold, the LORD will cast her out;
He will destroy her power in the sea,
And she will be devoured by fire.

5 Ashkelon shall see it and fear;
Gaza also shall be very sorrowful;
And Ekron, for He dried up her expectation.
The king shall perish from Gaza,
And Ashkelon shall not be inhabited.

6 "A mixed race shall settle in Ashdod,
And I will cut off the pride of the Philistines.

7 I will take away the blood from his mouth,
And the abominations from between his teeth.
But he who remains,
even he shall be for our God,
And shall be like a leader in Judah,
And Ekron like a Jebusite.

> 8 I will camp around My house
> Because of the army,
> Because of him who passes by
>   and him who returns.
> No more shall an oppressor pass
>   through them,
> For now I have seen with My eyes.
>
> *Zechariah 9:1–8*

The literary structure of this text argues for its unity. P. Lamarche has shown that there is a chiastic pattern in 9:1–8 within the larger chiastic pattern to chapters 9–14 (*see* our discussion in the introduction, *The Structure of the Book*). Verses 1–4 speak of cities in the northern part of the Promised Land; verses 5–8 speak of cities in the southern part of the Promised Land. But even more extraordinary, verses 1–2 and 7b–8 describe God's salvation while verses 3–7a speak of His judgment, giving the resulting form of *a, b, b, a*. The repeated use of the phrase the "eye of the LORD" in verses 1 and 8 is further confirmation of the unity of this text.[24]

This text prophesies the most extensive outreach of the borders of Israel, to include the Philistine seaboard, the northern cities of Tyre and Sidon and a corridor through Damascus. It seems to be consistent with a number of other texts, such as Numbers 13:21–24; 34:1–12; Deuteronomy 1:7; Joshua 1:3–4; 1 Kings 8:65; 2 Kings 14:25, 28; and Ezekiel 47:16. The phrase "From Dan to Beersheba" (Judg. 20:1; 1 Sam. 3:20; 2 Sam. 17:11) was the conventional way to refer to the territory that Israel actually held during most of her history—a territory far less extensive than what is prophesied in Zechariah 9:1–8; God had always marked out more for Israel than she ever possessed.

Chapter 9 describes Yahweh as a Divine Warrior, and most contemporary scholars who focus on this title do so in order to avoid comparing the prophecies of this chapter with the actual subsequent history of Israel, since few, if any, of the events described have actually taken place already in history.[25] But this chapter could be describing events that are still to come in our future, and thus we would not need to—and could not—find historical analogues at this time. Further, nothing in this chapter suggests that a kind of cosmic war is being waged to provide an opportunity to raise a hymn to God as the warrior who vindicates the interests of the faithful.

In this teaching block, God will win back two areas as part of His originally promised land:

366

A. Winning Back the Northern Territory   9:1–4
B. Winning Back the Southern Territory   9:5–8

Winning Back the Northern Territory (9:1–4)

The division comprising chapters 9–11, like chapters 12–14 (and Malachi 1:1), has as its heading, *"The Burden of the word of the Lord."* The Hebrew term *māsās'* is best translated as "burden," rather than "oracle," or "proclamation," since it comes from the verbal root meaning "to lift up," or "to bear," hence, something that is heavy or a "burden." The term *māsās'* occurs more than sixty times in the Old Testament and usually refers to a burden "imposed by a master, a despot or a deity on their subjects, beasts, men or things."[26] In prophecy, however, a "burden" is a declaration of judgment involving a catastrophic event that is to come.

The first place against which God has issued this burden is *"the land of Hadrach"* (v. 1). Nowhere else in the Old Testament is this site mentioned, but the site is known from the Assyrian cuneiform inscriptions as "Hatarikka," a city and country against which Assyria waged war in the eighth century.[27] Apparently, it was located to the north of Hamath on the Orontes River, southwest of Aleppo. *"Damascus"* (v. 1c), the second place mentioned in this burden, was the capital of Aram, modern Syria. The Arameans, on more than a few occasions, were pitched in battle against Israel.

The remainder of verse 1 explains why God gave this message of a catastrophe against the land of Hadrach and Damascus: *"For the eyes of men and all the tribes of Israel are on the Lord."* It is now time for God to act as He said He would and to fulfill His pledge of long ago.

"Hamath," *"Tyre,"* and *"Sidon"* are likewise subjects of this prophetic judgment. Hamath, on the Orontes River, is one of the northern-most limits of the Promised Land (e.g., Num. 13:21; Josh. 13:5; Judg. 3:3), while Tyre and Sidon belong to the Phoenician coast of the Mediterranean Sea. Even *"though [Tyre and Sidon] are very wise"* (v. 2) in their business dealings as great maritime powers, they will not escape the ominous consequences of this judgment.

Tyre built up enormously impressive defenses (v. 3a), including a breakwater that was 2460 feet long and 27 feet thick to defend her island city, yet *"the Lord will cast her out"* (v. 4a). God will *"destroy her power in the sea"* (v. 4b), or, more accurately, "hurl her wealth into the sea." The Assyrians besieged Tyre for five years and finally took it in 722 B.C. Later, the Babylonian King Nebuchadnezzar laid siege on Tyre for thirteen years (572 B.C.), only to have the mainland city move out one-half mile in the Mediterranean Sea to the island city without too much satisfaction for his efforts (Ezk. 29:18). But when Alexander the Great met with the same resistance that had frustrated the Babylonians, more than two centuries after the Babylonians, he scrapped up the timbers, stones, and dust of the mainland and "hurled them into the sea," as he built a causeway one-half mile out into the Mediterranean Sea to capture the island city (Ezk. 26:12). The seemingly invincible city fell in 332 B.C. Will history repeat itself in the end day, or is this the event that Zechariah predicted?

WINNING BACK THE SOUTHERN TERRITORY (9:5–8)

The news of the fall of Tyre brought fear into the hearts of the Philistine cities. Only four of the five cities in the Philistine pentapolis are mentioned here: Ashkelon, Gaza, Ekron, and Ashdod. Apparently Gath, the fifth city, had already lapsed into decline (2 Chron. 26:6). It is interesting to compare the eighth century judgment pronounced on these same cities by the prophet Amos with Zechariah's burden. In Amos's judgment the king of Ashkelon would be killed and Ashdod's citizens would be decimated, while in Zechariah's burden Gaza's king would be killed, Ashkelon's citizens would be decimated (v. 5), and Ashdod would experience a mixed population from the time of the exile onwards. In fact, as evidence of the great assimilation into Ashdod of this mixed population, the Persians borrowed the name Ashdod for a division of the fifth satrapy (v. 6a).

In the middle of verse 6, the pronoun referring to the Lord changes from third person to first person singular. The Lord is the speaker as He describes what He will do to and for the Philistines. God will deal first with the Philistines' *"pride"* (v. 6b). For years the Philistine military machine had been the bane of David and Saul's existence. That would cease. Then the Lord would *"take away the blood from [Philistine's] mouth, and the abominations from between his teeth"* (v. 7ab). "Blood" and "abominations" are references to practices with idolatrous connections which God had forbidden (Lev. 17:14; Isa. 65:4; 66:3, 17). If the Philistines were going to be assimilated into the Jewish people, they needed to abstain from eating meat that was not well-bled and abandon all practices that carried any connotation of magic or idolatry.

By now it is evident that this part of Zechariah's message has a broader purpose than to reveal God's geographic or military objectives. Through these objectives, people whom most would not have regarded as candidates for incorporating into the body of the believing community were included in the family of God! Philistines would have God as their God, just as the Jebusites of old Jerusalem were incorporated into the people of Israel when David captured Jerusalem (v. 7e).

The victorious march of Yahweh will end up at His house, the temple in Jerusalem (v. 8a). There the Lord will camp, not only to protect His house, but to symbolize that He will now protect the whole land, of which His house is the center. God's all-seeing eye will not let anything escape His notice (v. 8bd). In fact, 9:8 contains two clauses that link the first eight chapters with the last six (and thereby argues against the favorite modern position that there is no unity to the book): the clause *"No more shall an oppressor pass through them"* is found in 9:8c and 7:14, and the expression *"For now I have seen with My eyes"* is found in 9:8c and 4:10b. God has been an eyewitness to Israel's distress, but He will now be personally present to make sure no one ever again oppresses her.

CONCLUSION

Many view the word *"Philistine"* as so removed from anything sacred that it is often used in modern speech as a synonym for an uncultured barbarian. But this text challenges all our misrepresentations and includes the Philistines as part of the people of God in that day when the Lord personally will camp at His house in Jerusalem!

Surely the Lord's victory over the nations in the northern and southern parts of the Promised Land is as certain as can be. Moreover, many of those who had been alien to both the Lord and His people will now be incorporated into His body as an integrated part of the people of faith.

These truths will prepare us for the coming universal worship of Messiah as the ruling and reigning King in Jerusalem (14:16–19). Men and women shall literally come from all tribes, languages, and nationalities (including the Philistines) to worship the Living God in that day when He personally resides as Sovereign over all the earth.

CHAPTER TWELVE

Processing in with the Messianic King in Jerusalem

Zechariah 9:9–10

9 "Rejoice greatly, O daughter of Zion!
Shout, O daughter of Jerusalem!
Behold, your King is coming to you;
He is just and having salvation,
Lowly and riding on a donkey,
A colt, the foal of a donkey.
10 I will cut off the chariot from Ephraim
And the horse from Jerusalem;
The battle bow shall be cut off.
He shall speak peace to the nations;
His dominion shall be 'from sea to sea,
And from the River to the ends of the earth.'

Zechariah 9:9–10

At the heart of chapter 9 stands one of the most famous predictions about the coming messianic king. Whether it should be treated separately, as we do here, or linked with 9:1–8 or with 9:11–17, is a difficult question. On the one hand, it does continue in the poetic form of verses 1–8, and it does describe both the Messiah and the way He will govern the kingdom of God announced in both verses 1–8 and verses 11–17. On the other hand, it is distinctive in nature and functions as a pivotal point for both 1–8 and 11–17, and these factors persuade us that it is best to treat verses 9–10 as a distinctive oracle that enlarges on the messianic teaching of 3:8 and 6:9–15.

Zechariah 9:9–10 contains four announcements that are worth shouting about:

A. The Arrival of Our King   9:9a-c
B. The Character of Our King   9:9d-f
C. The Disarmament of Our World   9:10a-c
D. The Kingdom of Our Lord   9:10d-f

THE ARRIVAL OF OUR KING (9:9A-C)

In 9:9ab the prophet urges the people of Jerusalem, here personified as *"daughter of Zion"* and *"daughter of Jerusalem,"* to *"Rejoice greatly"* and *"Shout"* (v. 9ab). These spontaneous outbursts of exuberant joy are expressions of enormous jubilation and celebration over the fact that the earth will finally receive her King. Isaac Watts paraphrased Psalm 98, which celebrates the same event, with the words: "Joy to the world, the Lord has come. Let earth receive her King." Few events in the history of our planet are more worthy of shouting over. The prophet Zephaniah had already issued the same call for jubilation when he urged in Zephaniah 3:14–15: "Sing, O daughter of Zion! Shout, O Israel! . . . The King of Israel, the LORD, is in your midst." And Zechariah had earlier quoted the Lord's similar call for rejoicing: "'Sing and rejoice, O daughter of Zion! For behold, I am coming and I will dwell in your midst,' says the LORD" (Zech. 2:10). In that coming day, the Lord will dwell in Jerusalem.

THE CHARACTER OF OUR KING (9:9D–F)

Our coming King is described here as being *"just,"* i.e., "in-the-right." Since His nature and character set the norms for what "righteousness" is, He can uphold what is right in His exercise of the office of ruler.

The Messiah is also described as *"having salvation."* To be "endowed with salvation" can mean either to experience deliverance and victory or to be a Savior of others. In Zephaniah 3:17 the verb *"to save"* is found in the active form: "The LORD your God in your midst, The Mighty One, will save," or "who gives victory." But in the Hebrew text of our passage, the verb "to save" is in the passive form, meaning the Messiah has experienced the Father's deliverance and victory.

Finally, the Messiah is described as lowly. The Hebrew word ʿ*ān·* may be translated as one who has experienced "humility," "affliction" or the trial of being "stricken." The Messiah had just such an experience or trial when He was brought low through the affliction He bore on our behalf on the cross (Isa. 53:7).

The Messiah will come to us *"riding on a donkey, a colt, the foal of a donkey"* (9ef). In the ancient Near East the donkey was not thought of as a lowly beast of burden, as we might think today. Rather, the donkey was the preferred mount of princes (Judg. 5:10; 10:4; 12:14), kings (2 Sam. 16:1–2), and leaders who mingled with the people in a peaceful manner (Gen. 49:11; 2 Sam. 19:26; 1 Kings 1:33). Horses, especially when linked to chariots, were instruments of war (Deut. 17:16; Ps. 33:16–17; Isa. 33:1). The fact that the Messiah is not said to come on a horse signifies that He would not come, this time, as a conqueror. These verses also seem to allude to Jacob's blessing on the line of Judah in Genesis 49:11, where "the One whose right it is" (cf. Ezk. 21:27) is described as "binding his donkey to the vine, and his donkey's colt to the choice vine." Thus, the Davidic Ruler promised in Genesis 49:11 would come mounted on a donkey. Note, too, that He would come riding on the colt of the ass, a purebred, born of an ass and not of a mule.[28]

Both Matthew (21:2–7) and John (12:12–15) refer to these verses in their depiction of Jesus's triumphal entry into Jerusalem on the Sunday before the events of Good Friday and Easter Sunday. Matthew notes that both the donkey and the colt were brought, while John says specifically that Jesus rode on the "young" animal.

THE DISARMAMENT OF OUR WORLD (9:10A-C)

When the Messiah comes—these verses apparently refer to the Messiah's second coming—three weapons of war will be abolished: *"the chariot," "the horse,"* and the *"battle bow."* These and, I would assume, their modern equivalents, will be banished from Messiah's realm.

Specifying *"Ephraim"* and *"Jerusalem"* as cities from which the implements of war will be banished is one more reminder that God's plan involves both the restoration and reunification (8:13; Ezk. 37:15–28) of the northern and southern kingdoms that have been split apart since 931 B.C. But the work of God would not stop there; peace would come to the whole world.

The Kingdom of Our Lord (9:10d-f)

Messiah *"shall speak peace to the nations."* With a Ruler who is just and victorious, it will not be necessary to settle disputes among nations and territories by warfare. As citizens of God's future kingdom, we will delight in Messiah's righteous decrees and Law, not in using arms. By such peaceful means, the dominion of our Lord will extend out over the whole earth.

The scope of Messiah's realm is traced in language reminiscent of Psalm 72:8. We refer again to Isaac Watts' paraphrase of that Psalm: "Jesus shall reign wher'er the sun, does its successive journeys run. His kingdom spread from shore to shore. Til moons shall wax and wane no more." In Zechariah's words, *"His dominion shall be 'from sea to sea, and from the River [probably the Ephrates, not the Nile] to the ends of the earth'"*(v. 10). Finally our whole earth will realize what everyone has always longed for—a just and lasting peace.

Conclusion

Like His celebrated entrance into Jerusalem on Palm Sunday, Jesus will come once again as King of kings and Lord of lords in order to rule and reign forever and forever.

What a triumphant return that will be! If ever there was a reason to shout, this is it. The Messiah King is Lord of the whole earth!

CHAPTER THIRTEEN

Releasing the Captives: The Jewels in the Crown

Zechariah 9:11–10:1

11 "As for you also,
Because of the blood of your covenant,
I will set your prisoners free from the
waterless pit.
12 Return to the stronghold,
You prisoners of hope.
Even today I declare
That I will restore double to you.
13 For I have bent Judah, My bow,
Fitted the bow with Ephraim,
And raised up your sons, O Zion,
Against your sons, O Greece,
And made you like the sword of a
mighty man."
14 Then the LORD will be seen over them,
And His arrow will go forth like lightning.
The Lord GOD will blow the trumpet,
And go with whirlwinds from the south.
15 The LORD of hosts will defend them;
They shall devour and subdue with sling
stones.
They shall drink and roar as if with wine;
They shall be filled with blood like basins,
Like the corners of the altar.
16 The LORD their God will save them in that day,
As the flock of His people.
For they shall be like the jewels of a crown,

> Lifted like a banner over His land—
> 17 For how great is their goodness
> And how great their beauty!
> Grain shall make the young men thrive,
> And new wine the young women.
> 10:1 Ask the LORD for rain
> In the time of the latter rain.
> The LORD will make flashing clouds;
> He will give them showers of rain,
> Grass in the field for everyone.
>
> *Zechariah 9:11–10:1*

Now that the King has been announced, the captives of Northern and Southern Israel can be released. Their release, and what follows, are depicted in words charged with emotion and color and in rich metaphors, especially battle metaphors.

God's kingdom will be populated by released captives. Involved in that release will be three unforgettable factors. They are:

A. The Blood of the Covenant   9:11–13
B. The Theophany of the Divine Warrior   9:14–15a
C. The Eschatological Banquet of the Released   9:15b–10:1

THE BLOOD OF THE COVENANT (9:11–13)

The phrase *"As for you also"* that begins verses 11–13 link these verses to verses 9–10; the particle "also" alerts us to the fact that in verses 11–13 the Lord will develop His description of the future day begun in verses 9–10. Thus the chapter has a real unity of both form and content.

Everything that will happen in that future day—the arrival of the King and the rule and reign of Messiah as absolute Lord over the whole earth, with His personal headquarters in Jerusalem—will have been made possible by *"the blood of your covenant"* (v. 11a). The phrase "the blood of your covenant" is mentioned only one other time in the Old Testament (Exod. 24:8), even though the Old Testament does mention the idea of a blood sacrifice on occasions when the covenant was being ratified (Gen. 15:9–11, the covenant with Abraham; Exod. 24:8, the covenant with Moses; and Exod. 29:38–46, ratification of the covenant through daily offerings in the temple).

What makes these words seem so familiar to us is the fact that Jesus used them at the institution of the last supper in Mark 14:24:

"This is My blood of the new covenant, which is shed for many." They are also frequently heard in the benediction that comes from Hebrews 13:20: "May the God of peace . . . through the blood of the everlasting covenant . . . make you complete."

"Blood," in all these sacrifices, does not refer to a transfusion that would impart life; instead, it signifies that the life that was in the blood (Lev. 17:11) was spilt on the ground in death, as a substitute for the one presenting the sacrificial offering, so that the benefits of the covenant might be continued. Thus, in the sacrificial ceremony, when the people and the altar were sprinkled with blood, they were united together with the Lord.

Because of the substituted life that had been yielded up on our behalf (at first, and only temporarily, in the form of an animal's life, but later in the form of the perfect God-Man's life, i.e., the Messiah's life), *"I will set your prisoners free from the waterless pit"* (v. 11c). Some have balked at this reference to the "waterless pit" (omitted in the NEB and bracketed in the JB), but one need only remember that there were no jails in that day. Cisterns that normally served as holes in the earth to collect rain-water during the rainy season often had to double as retention centers or jails. Joseph was cast into "a pit. . . . [with] no water in it" (Gen. 37:24) as was Jeremiah (Jer. 38:6–13). But when our Lord returns, He will empty these pits, or jails.

Zechariah dubs those released from jail *"prisoners of hope"* (v. 12b). The liberated could now return to Zion, here called *"the stronghold"* (v. 12a).

In verse 12d God says He would *"restore double"* to the former prisoners. This means, first, that as God's "firstborn" they would receive a double share of the inheritance (Deut. 21:17). It probably also implies that theirs would be a full measure—full and running over.

God would involve Judah and Ephraim in His act of liberating the captives. (Once again He showed no favoritism to the southern nation of Judah, but featured both parts of the divided kingdom in the restoration.) God would use both of them as His *"bow."* Some difficulty has been expressed over the translation *"For I have bent Judah, My bow, fitted the bow with Ephraim"* (13a). However, a recently found Akkadian equivalent to the Hebrew *hapax legomenon* ("A word appearing only once") can now clarify the unusual idiom "to fill" with the subject of the "bow." It means "to fill [i.e., to fit an arrow on the string of or, technically, to nock] the bow." Thus, according to Shalom M. Paul,[29] 13a should be rendered "For I have bent Judah, my bow; I have nocked Ephraim." Whether this verse points to the actual use of the two parts of the divided kingdom in God's final stand against evil, or merely describes how the Lord can handle both of these nations just as efficiently as a battle-tested soldier handles his weapons, we cannot say for certain, although the verses that follow give some support to the latter view.

In verse 13c-e God declares that He has *"raised up your sons, O Zion, against your sons, O Greece, and made you like the sword of a mighty man."* Proponents of the Deutero-Zechariah theory (*see* our discussion of this theory in the Introduction, in the section *Unity of the Book*) use this verse to support their theory because, they say, the metre is over-loaded and the lines must be a later intrusion, since Greece only became a threat to Judah in Maccabean times (166–135 B.C.)[30]. But the name *Javan* (an older name for Greece) was around long before then. It appears in the Table of the Nations in Genesis 10:2, 4 and, in the eighth century B.C., Isaiah 66:19. While in some contexts Javan, or Greece, may stand for any distant or unknown peoples, it may also stand for any confederation of western powers, as best known during the days of Alexander the Great, as the nation coming from the Greek Pelopennesis.

THE THEOPHANY OF THE DIVINE WARRIOR (9:14–15A)

The Old Testament contains many theophanies, or appearances of God. So awesome were these dramatic appearances that they were frequently accompanied by thunder, lightning, smoke and earthquakes (cf. Exod. 19:16–19; Judg. 5:4–5; 2 Sam. 22:8–18; Ps. 29; 68:7–8; Hab. 3:3–15).

In this theophany, *"His arrow will go forth like lightning. The LORD GOD will blow the trumpet, and go with whirlwinds from the south"* (v. 14b–d). The thunder is the Lord's trumpet, which sounds not only the call to battle, but also the beginning of the festivals. The southern windstorms our Lord uses as His tanks, for on them He comes into town to conquer and to reign.

It is the Lord who shall defend His people (v. 15a).

THE ESCHATOLOGICAL BANQUET OF THE RELEASED (9:15B–10:1)

The language used to describe the banquet of the released prisoners— *"they shall devour and subdue with sling stones. They shall drink and roar as if with wine"* (v. 15b–c)—has appeared odd to many. This language does not connote eating the flesh or (as mis-translated by the RSV) drinking the blood of enemies. Eating and drinking are simply metaphors for celebrating Yahweh's victory over the nations. The sling stones shall "be tread down" as worthless reminders from previous battles; they will be of no more use than the gravel under our feet.

The food at this victory celebration will be so abundant that the released prisoners *"shall be filled with [drink] like [a sacrificial] basin, like the corners of the altar"* (v. 15d). This verse does not contain any word that could be translated "blood," as suggested in the NKJV rendering "They shall be filled with blood like basins, like the corners of the altar." It simply makes the point that the provisions for the victory celebration would be so extensive that the released prisoners would remind a person of the way an altar looks when the meat on it overflows even into its corners.

"In that day," continues Zechariah in verse 16a, Yahweh *"will save"* His people, and His *"flock"* will be safe, for *"they shall be like the jewels of a crown."* Using "jewels" to stand for God's flock simply continues the metaphor begun in Exodus, where God announces to Moses that His believing remnant are His "treasured possession" (Exod. 19:5; this term means moveable valuables or treasures, as opposed to real estate [cf. Mal. 3:17]). These "jewels" are God's pride and joy, for they will be unfurled over the land just like a banner or flag (v. 16d).

In the prosperity of the future days, there will be an abundance of grain and wine. How wonderful it will be to live and thrive in a land in which the Lord is in charge and from which evil has been vanquished forever (Amos 9:13; Joel 3:18).

The prosperity that is expected in those days will depend on rain; therefore 10:1 urges us to *"Ask the LORD for rain in the time of the latter rain."* And the promise is that the Lord will send *"showers of rain"* in the latter part of the springtime and *"grass in the field for everyone."* Everything will function as it ought to in that day. What a different day it will be!

CONCLUSION

So long to the nightmare of earth's darkest moments. In that day when the King comes back into town, we shall be liberated.

The blood of God's covenant has made possible the release of the captives. Consequently, we will watch as the wicked and evil are forever vanquished. Then it will be time to celebrate as we have never celebrated before.

CHAPTER FOURTEEN

Punishing the Shepherds and Regathering the People in the Land

Zechariah 10:2–12

2 For the idols speak delusion;
   The diviners envision lies,
   And tell false dreams;
   They comfort in vain.
   Therefore the people wend their way
      like sheep;
   They are in trouble because there is
      no shepherd.
3 "My anger is kindled against the shepherds,
   And I will punish the goatherds.
   For the LORD of hosts will visit His flock,
   The house of Judah,
   And will make them as His royal horse
      in the battle.
4 From him comes the cornerstone,
   From him the tent peg,
   From him the battle bow,
   From him every ruler together.
5 They shall be like mighty men,
   Who tread down their enemies
   In the mire of the streets in the battle.
   They shall fight because the LORD is with them,
   And the riders on horses shall be put to shame.
6 "I will strengthen the house of Judah,
   And I will save the house of Joseph.
   I will bring them back,
   Because I have mercy on them.

> They shall be as though I had not cast
>   them aside;
> For I am the LORD their God,
> And I will hear them.
> 7 Those of Ephraim shall be like a mighty man,
>   And their heart shall rejoice as if with wine.
>   Yes, their children shall see it and be glad;
>   Their heart shall rejoice in the LORD.
> 8 I will whistle for them and gather them,
>   For I will redeem them;
>   And they shall increase as they once increased.
> 9 "I will sow them among the peoples,
>   And they shall remember Me in far countries;
>   They shall live, together with their children,
>   And they shall return.
> 10 I will also bring them back from the
>   land of Egypt,
>   And gather them from Assyria.
>   I will bring them into the land of
>   Gilead and Lebanon,
>   Until no more room is found for them.
> 11 He shall pass through the sea with affliction,
>   And strike the waves of the sea:
>   All the depths of the River shall dry up.
>   Then the pride of Assyria shall be brought down,
>   And the scepter of Egypt shall depart.
> 12 "So I will strengthen them in the LORD,
>   And they shall walk up and down
>   in His name,"
> Says the LORD.

Zechariah 10:2–12

A new metaphor is introduced in chapters 10–11, the metaphor of the shepherd as leader. The metaphor is used to contrast good and bad leaders. The contrast can be traced to the key verse in chapter 10: *"I will bring them back, because I [will] have mercy on them"* (v. 6b). The good leader, or true shepherd, has compassion for the people; the bad leader, or false shepherd, could not care less.

This text exhibits two strong contrasts:

    A. The Contrast Between Corrupted Shepherds and Compassionate Shepherds   10:2–5

B. The Contrast Between the Nation's Former State and Its
Future Regathering in the Land   10:6–12

THE CONTRAST BETWEEN CORRUPTED SHEPHERDS
AND COMPASSIONATE SHEPHERDS (10:2–5)

The word "shepherd" in the ancient Near East was used to designate any number of leadership positions: teachers, prophets, priests, judges, rulers, kings, and governors. In Zechariah's time, tragically, the leaders had turned their positions of privilege into occasions for abuse. And the people, being sheep, were powerless to do anything for themselves. They needed to be rescued. Like sheep, humans require guidance but often lack the sense to choose a leader. Instead, they choose another sheep, which often needs guidance itself. Consequently, everyone wanders off on their own and everything suffers.

One of the mistakes the leaders made was to look in the wrong direction for guidance. They commonly looked to the idols for guidance, but *"the idols [teraphim] speak delusion"* (v. 2a). The teraphim used as household idols used to divine the future (Gen. 31:19; Judg. 17:5; 18:5; 1 Sam. 15:23). No less disturbing, the leaders taught their people to put their trust in diviners, even though *"The diviners envision lies, and tell false dreams; they comfort in vain"* (v. 2b-d). The problem with the diviners was not that they used dreams, for surely God often used dreams to communicate with His prophets; the problem was that they used false dreams spun out of the leaders' own imaginations! Prophets who used false dreams were castigated by the prophet Jeremiah in no uncertain terms (Jer. 23:32; 27:9–10). Some diviners would even inspect the entrails of birds and animals to determine what direction or course of action should be taken (Josh. 13:22; 1 Sam. 6:2). All of it was a sham and an outright denial of the revealed will of God.

The results of this misguided leadership were devastating. *"Therefore the people wend their way like sheep"* (v. 2e). "Wandering" sheep is the only way one could describe the people. Moreover, *"They are in trouble because there is no shepherd"* (v. 2f). With only unreliable and false sources of leadership, the people were, in effect, leaderless. They had no real shepherd who cared for them or knew what to do.

Such subterfuges by these unreliable tricksters excite the anger of God. *"My anger is kindled against the shepherds, and I will punish the goatherds. For the* LORD *of hosts will visit His flock"* (v. 3ab). Our Lord will not abandon His flock; neither will He let these "he-goats" or "goatherds"—a most uncomplimentary term (cf. Ezk. 34:17)—get away with what they have inflicted on His flock. Judah's faithless leaders will be brought into judgment. Whether they had preyed upon the weak, pushed the poor around, or bullied the masses, they would not go unpunished. What a warning to all leaders in the household of God and in the state!

But that was not the end of things. Contrasted with these alien leaders were a group of faithful and compassionate leaders whom God was raising up from the *"house of Judah"* (v. 3d). God would take His bullied sheep and turn them into *"His royal horse in the battle"* (v. 3e). God would strengthen His people by turning them into warhorses that would rebell and overthrow their oppressive leaders.

A new, stable, leadership would now be given directly *"From him"* (v. 4a), i.e., from the Lord himself. This new brand of leaders would find its model in the One who Himself was *"the cornerstone," "the tent peg,"* and *"the battle bow"* (v. 4). The word "cornerstone" is used in Psalm 118:22 to refer to the stone—Messiah—that men rejected, but that became the chief cornerstone. Surely it symbolizes steadfastness and reliability. In other passages in the Old Testament it is used figuatively to refer to a "ruler" (cf. Isa. 19:13).

A "tent peg" depicts either the hook in the center of a tent where frequently-used items are kept or the peg in the ground that secures a tent and keeps it taut and secure. The reference in verse 4 is probably to the hook since the same imagery was used in Isaiah 22:23 to refer to Eliakim, the son of Hilkiah, who had a leadership position. God declared that He would "fasten him as a peg in a secure place." There, too, the imagery referred at once both to Eliakim and to the coming Messiah, who would be a leader in the house of Judah, and to whom "the key of the house of David" would be given.

A "battle bow" is the symbol of strength for military conquest (2 Kings 13:17). The new brand of leaders would be ready to take up the cause of the Lord, just as the Messiah who sits on the white horse in Revelation 6:2 had a "bow" as He "went out conquering and to conquer."

Here, then, are three graphic pictures of the model leader, our Lord Jesus Christ.[31] *"From him every ruler together"* (v. 4d) would go forth, for in the future Messiah would be the source of compassionate leaders.

Linked to this concept, by way of the figure of synecdoche, may also be the idea that God would empower all His people to over- throw all false leaders and oppressors. This figure of speech (wherein the part is put for the whole) may explain verse 5, in which Zechariah describes the people as *"mighty men, who tread down their enemies. . . . They shall fight because the LORD is with them, and the riders on horses shall be put to shame."* So expert will this revived people be that even the exalted cavalry will be handily defeated and embarrassed.

THE CONTRAST BETWEEN THE NATION'S FORMER STATE AND ITS FUTURE REGATHERING IN THE LAND (10:6–12)

When God *"will strengthen the house of Judah, and . . . save the house of Joseph"* (v. 6ab), it will be known that something new and dif- ferent is happening in accordance with His ancient promises. The "house of Judah" represents, of course, the southern kingdom, and the "house of Joseph" stands for the northern ten tribes which broke away in 931 B.C. after Solomon's death.

Both houses God would *"bring . . . back"* (v. 6c) into the land, because He would have mercy on them. This is an amazing predic- tion for the simple reason that it was made some time after December 7, 518 B.C. (Zech. 7:1), if Zechariah's prophecies are in chronological order, almost twenty years after the return from exile had begun. The promise was still being repeated. Moreover, it is a promise that the Jewish people would return not just from the Babylonian exile (as many twentiety-century scholars have taught), but from all over the world, (cf. 10:9–10). Furthermore, God would rectify not just the Judean captivity in Babylon, but also the Assyrian captivity that began in 722 B.C. with the fall of Samaria, the capital of the ten Joseph tribes. The ten lost tribes would never be lost as long as God maintained the ancient promise He had given to Abraham, Isaac, Jacob and David concerning the everlasting inher- itance of the land.

The Lord God would *"hear them"* (v. 6f); they would be delivered in that day of the Lord. The northern tribes, here also referred to as *"Ephraim"* since the largest Joseph tribe was the clan of Ephraim, would be transformed into mighty warriors (v. 7a), just as Judah would be (v. 5). There would be plenty of reason for rejoicing and celebrating over this new work of God.

As the shepherd signals for his sheep (cf. Judg. 5:16), so the Lord would *"whistle for [his people] and gather them"* (v. 8). Once again He would *"redeem them"* (v. 8b). This redemption involved both a redemption from sin and a deliverance from the Diaspora whereby God's people had been scattered all over the world. Then *"they shall increase as they once increased"* (v. 8d). There was a striking contrast between the way God had blessed the work of their hands from the time of Abraham—with abundant fruit of the land and cattle and an increase in their families—and the people's experiences since the exile, when God had withheld such blessings. But the *"increase"* God will give when He restores His people will be another indication that those former days had passed.

Though the Lord is the One who will make all this possible, the people must first fulfill the prerequisite that they *"remember Me in far countries"* (v. 9b). That is what the Lord had taught them to do in Leviticus 26:40–42: "But if they confess their iniquity . . . in which they were unfaithful to Me, . . . then I will remember My covenant with Jacob. . . ." Not only would the people *"return,"* but they would *"live, together with their children"* (v. 9cd). Here was real life, the kind of living that is by faith (Hab. 2:4). This, then, is what it means to *"sow them among the peoples"* (v. 9a). To counter judgment of scattering His people, Hosea had offered God's promise that He would again "sow" them: "I will sow her for Myself in the earth, and I will have mercy on her" (Hos. 2:23). The Hebrew word for "to sow" also means "to scatter," since the seed in the hand of the sower is scattered as he walks across the field.

In verse 10 God names the nations from which He will bring back His people to Israel: *"Egypt"* and *"Assyria."* "Egypt" had long been a byword for bondage (Isa. 11:11; Hos. 11:1, 11; Mic. 7:15). "Assyria" no doubt refers here to all the lands to the north and east of Israel where the captives had been taken, including Assyria (northern Mesopotamia), Babylon (southern Mesopotamia), and Persia.

"I will bring them into the land of Gilead and Lebanon, until no more room is found for them" (v. 10cd). Gilead and Lebanon are part of the greatly-expanded boundaries of Israel described in the promise-covenant. "Gilead" was primarily the area that is referred to today as the "Golan Heights," the extension of the promised Holy Land that reaches in a northeasterly direction to the Euphrates River through the Damascus corridor. Lebanon, of course, is north of present-day

Israel and encompasses the coastal cities of Tyre, Sidon, Beirut, and Byblos. The number of returned exiles will be so great that, even with its expanded boundaries, all of Israel's space will be exhausted. That is the problem present-day Israel is confronting, as witnessed by its difficulty in absorbing the recent immigrants airlifted from Ethiopia and the massive number of Russian Jewish immigrants.

The Lord himself will *"pass through the sea [of] affliction, and strike the waves of the sea: all the depths of the River [Nile] shall dry up"* (v. 11). The Lord will go ahead of His people to remove all barriers to their return from exile, just as He had opened up the Red Sea (Exod. 14:21–32) and the Jordan River (Josh. 3:14–17) when He led Israel out of captivity the first time. The Hebrew word translated here as "River" is literally the "Nile," but, figuratively, it refers to the "Euphrates River," which God will dry up in the new, latter-day, exodus (Isa. 11:15).

Those nations that had opposed God will suffer a loss of prestige, pride, and status. In the last part of verse 11 "Egypt" and "Assyria" are again used figuratively to refer to the opponents of God.

Lest one think that all of this talk of "remembering" the Lord and turning back to Him is solely the work of individuals and the result of *chutzpah* (Yiddish for "nerve," "audacity," and the like), verse 12 affirms that such a return of the Jews back to Israel just before our Lord returns the second time will be accomplished by the power of God. *"'So I will strengthen them in the LORD, and they shall walk up and down in His name,' says the LORD."* God will supply the strength they need; they can not supply it themselves.

The figure of "walking up and down in the name of the LORD" appeared earlier in Micah 4:5 to refer to those who are in Messiah's kingdom. This confirms that Zechariah is also speaking of that time when the benefits of the new covenant will be fully realized.

CONCLUSION

The contrasts in this passage are striking. There is no comparison between the ruthless shepherds Israel has had in the past and the ones God will give her in the future. In particuarly sharp contrast is the Good Shepherd himself, who is our "Cornerstone," our "Tent-peg," and our "Battle bow."

Even after the return from the Babylonian exile had begun, God was pledging that He would restore His people from all over the world to the land of Israel. This is one of the most important of the two to three dozen major texts in the Old Testament prophesying the return of the Diaspora simply because the date of the prophecy places it after the return from the Babylonian exile. The return of the Diaspora will happen, this text reminds us, through the strength that will come from the Lord God himself.

CHAPTER FIFTEEN

Detailing the Destiny of the Good Shepherd

Zechariah 11:1–17

11:1 Open your doors, O Lebanon,
   That fire may devour your cedars.
 2 Wail, O cypress, for the cedar has fallen,
   Because the mighty trees are ruined.
   Wail, O oaks of Bashan,
   For the thick forest has come down.
 3 There is the sound of wailing shepherds!
   For their glory is in ruins.
   There is the sound of roaring lions!
   For the pride of the Jordan is in ruins.
 4 Thus says the LORD my God, "Feed the flock for slaughter,
 5 "whose owners slaughter them and feel no guilt; those who sell them say, 'Blessed be the LORD, for I am rich'; and their shepherds do not pity them.
 6 "For I will no longer pity the inhabitants of the land," says the LORD. "But indeed I will give everyone into his neighbor's hand and into the hand of his king. They shall attack the land, and I will not deliver them from their hand."
 7 So I fed the flock for slaughter, in particular the poor of the flock. I took for myself two staffs: the one I called Beauty, and the other I called Bonds; and I fed the flock.
 8 I dismissed the three shepherds in one month. My soul loathed them, and their soul also abhorred me.

9 Then I said, "I will not feed you. Let what is dying die, and what is perishing perish. Let those that are left eat each other's flesh."

10 And I took my staff, Beauty, and cut it in two, that I might break the covenant which I had made with all the peoples.

11 So it was broken on that day. Thus the poor of the flock, who were watching me, knew that it was the word of the LORD.

12 Then I said to them, "If it is agreeable to you, give me my wages; and if not, refrain." So they weighed out for my wages thirty pieces of silver.

13 And the LORD said to me, "Throw it to the potter"—that princely price they set on me. So I took the thirty pieces of silver and threw them into the house of the LORD for the potter.

14 Then I cut in two my other staff, Bonds, that I might break the brotherhood between Judah and Israel.

15 And the LORD said to me, "Next, take for yourself the implements of a foolish shepherd.

16 "For indeed I will raise up a shepherd in the land who will not care for those who are cut off, nor seek the young, nor heal those that are broken, nor feed those that still stand. But he will eat the flesh of the fat and tear their hooves in pieces.

17 Woe to the worthless shepherd,
   Who leaves the flock!
   A sword shall be against his arm
   And against his right eye;
   His arm shall completely wither,
   And his right eye shall be totally blinded.

Zechariah 11:1–17

Three metaphors for human rulers dominate the beginning of chapter 11: trees, lions, and shepherds. Our conclusion that these are metaphors for human rulers is based both on the fact that they are used as metaphors for human rulers throughout Scripture and on the fact that this chapter of Zechariah concerns the role of human leaders in the violence and warfare against the nations that will precede the coming of God's kingdom to earth.

The fact that Zechariah does not place this chapter in a precise historical context has made the identification of its participants extremely difficult; in fact, the "three shepherds" of verse 8 have never been convincingly identified. Over forty possibilities have been suggested, covering a range of persons from the earliest days of Israel's history to Roman times.

Despite this admitted obscurity, we can discern the main themes of this chapter. Students of prophetic interpretation must remember that our Lord warned that history (i.e., the fulfillment of the predictions in the real world) would be the final interpreter of prophecy—"Now I tell you before it comes, that when it does come to pass, you may believe that I am He" (John 13:19).

This chapter distinguishes between three types of shepherds—national shepherds, good shepherds, and worthless shepherds—and the respective outcome of their roles:

A. The Collapse of National Shepherds   11:1–3
B. The Rejection of the Good Shepherd   11:4–14
C. The Appointment of a Worthless Shepherd   11:15–17

THE COLLAPSE OF NATIONAL SHEPHERDS (11:1–3)

The short poem of verses 1–3 centers primarily on the collapse of Lebanon and Bashan, the areas to the north and east of Israel. Lebanon, renowned for its majestic cedars, and Bashan, equally famous for its mighty oaks, will both experience the humiliation of being levelled, just as all national and human pride must eventually give way before the sweeping hand of God's judgment on the nations and their kings.

How the mighty cedars and oaks have fallen, sighs the prophet! The cedar, cypress, and oak trees are metaphors for kings and their kingdoms. Trees are metaphors for rulers in many passages throughout the Old Testament. For example: David's royal house would come out of the stump of Jesse (Isa. 11:1); Pharaoh is depicted as a cypress or a cedar tree in Eden (Ezk. 31:1–9); and Nebuchadnezzar was likened to a tree (Dan. 4; *see also* Ezk. 17:22–24).

It does not appear that the cedar is a metaphor for the royal house of Judah in this passage, as it is in Ezekiel 17:3–4, 12–14. Rather, it more likely symbolizes pride, as it does in Isaiah 2:13, particularly the pride of Lebanon and its ruler. But the cedar could be chopped down just as quickly as the Assyrian king was reduced in Isaiah 10:33–34.

The nations represented by the cedars and oaks were the alien powers that revolted against God and His kingdom. Lesser trees—lesser kings and their nations—might well grieve over the destruction of the mighty, for their felling would come in due season as well. Others would be lost by fire. Their destruction was certain.

Perhaps verse 3 is an allusion to Jeremiah 25:34–37, wherein Jeremiah refers to those kings who grieved over the loss of their glory, because the Lord plundered their pasture. *"The sound of roaring lions"* (v. 3c) refers metaphorically to the kings who have been stirred up out of their lairs and are roaming around threateningly in search of prey.

In the last verse of this poem we learn that another area has been laid waste: *"the pride of the Jordan"* (v. 3d). This may also be translated "the jungle of the Jordan River," i.e., the clustered growth of trees and bushes that grow along the banks of the Jordan River and provide shelter for wild beasts.

If verses 1–3 were meant to describe events that would take place in the regular course of history, they must be referring to a time still in the future, since there are no known historical events like the events they describe. Verses 1–3 may, however, be a poetic description of the collapse of all surrounding nations before God's triumph in the final day. We must await history's unravelling of this mystery.

THE REJECTION OF THE GOOD SHEPHERD (11:4–14)

This is a most difficult section to interpret. A shepherd is requested to look after a flock that has been slated for slaughter. It would appear that the prophet is to act out a parable that has prophetic truth. He dresses in the garb of a shepherd and acts out a ministry to the people, assuming both a religious and a civic function as he discharges his commission.

The prose narrative begins with this instruction to the prophet: *"Feed the flock for slaughter"* (v. 4a). A better translation that makes the meaning clearer is: "Become shepherd of the flock doomed to slaughter." This the prophet did, according to verse 7a: "So I became the shepherd of the flock doomed for slaughter."

The flock entrusted to the shepherd-prophet is Israel. The nation had been abused by other owners who slaughtered the people, like sheep, without any feeling of guilt (v. 5a). So ruthless were these heartless leaders that they said, *"Blessed be the LORD, for I am rich"* (v. 5b). They had no more concern for the flock than did the hireling in John 10:13. In fact, the foreign rulers, who must be the *"owners"* and the shepherds who felt no guilt (v. 5), trafficked in human slave trade, a practice the prophets sternly decried (e.g., Amos 1:6). Meanwhile, *"their [own] shepherds"* (v. 5d; a reference to the Jewish leaders) did *"not pity them"* (v. 5d). The Jewish leaders' abandonment of God's flock was surely as reprehensible as the profiteering motives of the foreign shepherds.

What would happen to God's people Israel? Verse 6 reveals what they could expect in the future: *"'For I will no longer pity the inhabitants of the land,' says the LORD."* The whole land would be handed over to Israel's neighbors and foreign kings. Now the wicked shepherds and wicked citizens would find themselves powerless to defend themselves. The foreign kings would *"attack the land, [but God would] not deliver them from their hand"* (v. 6c). The end had come for rebellious Israel!

What was Zechariah to do? He became Israel's shepherd, in spite of the certain doom that awaited her (v. 7a). The correct translation of the clause rendered here *"in particular the poor of the flock"* (v. 7b) has been hotly debated, even though it is the reading of the Hebrew text and the Targums. But a number of commentators argue—on the well-known principle "choose the more difficult reading"—that the Greek Septuagint has the more difficult reading and should therefore be adopted. The Septuagint reads "for the Canaanites," where Canaanite means "merchant," as it often does in Scripture (e.g., Ezk. 16:29; 17:4). Most translators adopt the Greek text, for it makes sense in the context of this discussion of a class of merchants trading in human lives.

Zechariah shepherded his flock with two staffs, one named *"Beauty"* (i.e, "Grace," or "Favor") and the other named *"Bonds"* (i.e., "Union"; v. 7d). The staffs indicate that Zechariah was to serve as shepherd of his people; they symbolize further what the prophet wanted to achieve through his ministry. Through his ministry, he wanted his people to enjoy God's "favor," and he wanted to realize national "unity" of the northern and southern kingdoms.

Verse 8 is the most problematic verse in the chapter. As the good shepherd was carrying out his duties, he had to dismiss *"three shepherds in one month"* (v. 8a). If this verse refers to three shepherds who appeared in pre-exilic times, it means that the Lord removed Jehoiakim, Jehoiachin, and Zedekiah all within a very short period (cf. Hos. 5:7; "one month" means a brief span of time). But that interpretation is far from solid. It is best not to attempt to identify the three shepherds at this time, since no convincing arguments can be sustained, based on history to the present time.

Zechariah's patience was beginning to run out with the flock he was attempting to pasture, and *"their soul[s] also abhorred [him]"* (v. 8c). How could a shepherd perform his duties under those conditions?

At this point the prophet appeared to give up; he declared that he would no longer feed his people. *"Let what is dying die, and what is perishing perish"* (v. 9b), he sighed. The flock could now just as well become cannibals: *"Let those that are left eat each other's flesh"* (v. 9c). That is literally what the people did during the famines that resulted from the siege on Jerusalem in 587 B.C. and 70 A.D. (Deut. 28:54–57; Lam. 4:10; Josephus, *Wars*, VI, 201–13). Moreover, figuratively they acted like cannibals in the way they verbally and emotionally went after one another. People can't attack God's messenger without developing the bad habit of attacking each other.

Unfortunately, few recognized that Zechariah, as a model of the good shepherd, was acting on their behalf. Not only did they fail to appreciate Zechariah's dismissal of the detestable shepherds, but, showing their true character, they turned on Zechariah, the good shepherd! That is when the prophet broke the staff of "Beauty," or "Favor" (v. 10a). The period of God's graciousness had ended!

Verse 10b reads, *"I might break the covenant which I had made with all the peoples."* Could this mean that the inviolable covenant made with the patriarchs (Gen. 12:1–3) and David (2 Sam. 7:12–16) had now come to an end? In 8:11–15 and 10:6–12 Zechariah had promised that God would never break that covenant. The phrase "with all the peoples" is key to understanding verse 10b. It refers to all the Gentile nations (cf. Joel 2:6). One need only remember that God's people had been protected from decimation by a covenant that had restrained the Gentile nations (Job 5:23; Ezk. 34:25; Hos. 2:18); that was the covenant that had been broken. God would now remove Judah from the shadow of His protecting hand, so that the nations could be the rod of punishment in His hands (cf. Isa. 10:15–16).

The reaction of *"the poor of the flock, who were watching [Zechariah]"* (v. 11b) was one of sudden realization that this was coming from the hand of God (v. 11c), *"that it was the word of the LORD."* The implications of Zechariah breaking the staff of "Beauty" could not be missed.

Then Zechariah, still acting out the parable of the good shepherd, requested that he be paid his wages for shepherding the people (v. 12). Now that his contract had been terminated (11:9), he reluctantly asked to be released with his final paycheck: *"if it is agreeable to you, give me my wages"* (v. 12a).

The authorities determined that *"thirty pieces of silver"* (v. 12c) was all the shepherd was worth! That is the sum owed an owner of a slain slave under the Mosaic law (Exod. 21:32). That was also, of course, the same sum Judas received for betraying Jesus (Matt. 26:15; 27:9). (There are two plausible explanations for the fact that Matthew ascribed the quote to Jeremiah rather than Zechariah. First, Matthew may have referred to Jeremiah because his book may have appeared at the head of the whole collection of the prophets. Second, Matthew combined Zechariah 11:12–13 with Jeremiah 18:1–4 and 32:6–9, thus he may have meant to refer to both prophets by using the name of the first-mentioned prophet whose book stood at the head of the collection or was the name of the more prominent prophet.) The thirty pieces of silver had to be *"weighed out"* (v. 12c), since in Zechariah's time coins were not yet stamped.

The Lord's instructions to Zechariah, after he had received such a *"princely price!"* (v. 13c; note the irony), were that Zechariah *"'Throw it to the potter'"* (v. 13a). Since the Hebrew words for "potter" (*yôṣēr*) and "treasury" (*'ôṣār*) sound alike, and since both ideas were found in Matthew 27:6–9 (the money in the treasury was used to buy a potter's field), many have adopted the Syriac emendation for verse 13 and have read "throw it into the treasury." But that is not necessary, since to "throw it to the potter" was simply a proverbial expression with a note of contempt—"throw it away."

It is clear, though, that the money was to be cast into *"the house of the LORD"* (v. 13d). One must remember that the potters were connected with the temple, for they made the sacrificial vessels (Lev. 6:28); there may even have been a guild of potters serving on a regular basis in the temple (Jer. 18:6; 19:1).

After he cast away his thirty shekels, Zechariah broke the other staff, *"Bonds,"* or "Unity" (v. 14). The people had rejected their good shepherd; the national unity they had hoped for would not be realized at this time, for as Ezekiel had prophesied, the people would be reunited under the rule of the One Good Shepherd who would glue the stick of Joseph to the stick of Judah in the final day (Ezk. 37:16–28).

THE APPOINTMENT OF A WORTHLESS SHEPHERD (11:15–17)

Amazingly, the Lord asks Zechariah to continue the parable by impersonating a worthless shepherd (v. 15). Presumably *"the implements of a foolish shepherd"* (v. 15b) were the same as those of a good shepherd; the difference would only be in the different attitudes and usages that each shepherd attached to these instruments and to the position the shepherds held in the community.

Verse 16 supplies the explanation. God would raise up leaders who would not only neglect their flock, but would destroy them (remember that what God permits may be charged directly to Him, since he is Lord of all the universe anyway). So brutally would these leaders treat the sheep that their treatment would be likened to *"eat[ing] the flesh of the fat and tear[ing] their hooves in pieces"* (v. 16e). What savage treatment!

A poem concludes this parable involving a symbolic action that the Prophet was told to enact for the benefit of his audience. The worthless and foolish shepherds have much to fear, for all who have abandoned their flock will be judged. The sword would take their arms and their right eyes out of action (v. 17c). The arm that should have protected the sheep would *"completely wither"* (v. 17e), and the eye that should have looked in pity on those whom they were to shepherd would be *"totally blinded"* (v. 17f). While certain aspects of this decree of judgment can be seen in the judgment that befell King Herod (who was stricken by a type of instant withering disease in 64–3 B.C.) and Alcimus (a High Priest in 163–59 B.C. who betrayed the Maccabees, 1 Macc. 7:1–25), the character and work may well point to the antichrist of Daniel 7:25–7; 11:36–9; 2 Thessalonians 2:1–12; and Revelation 13:1–10.

CONCLUSION

There is a world of difference between the Good Shepherd and all the worthless and foolish shepherds this world has seen so far. The differences are extremely and painfully visible.

What a tragedy that although the Good Shepherd called to His flock, and continued to extend His grace, unity, and security from other nations, Israel did not respond.

The resulting fracture of graciousness and unity will not be restored until the nation returns to our Lord with belief and trust.

The prediction that the Good Shepherd would be sold for the trifling price of a slave underscores how costly our salvation really is in comparison to how most non-believers value it. Judas is more than a fall-character; he is another forerunner of all the worthless shepherds yet to come, who are themselves harbingers of the last in this long line of leaders who will come to challenge Messiah—the Antichrist.

SECOND BURDEN

Zechariah 12–14

In the first of the two burdens that make up the last six chapters of the book of Zechariah, Zechariah prophesies that the Gentile powers will be destroyed as the kingdom of God comes into its full manifestation (chapters 9–11). Only after these world powers are overthrown can Messiah's kingdom be finally and fully established.

In the second burden (chapters 12–14) Zechariah describes how Israel will be sifted and purged in the final conflict of earth's history as she is forced to face the nations of the earth alone. This burden cannot be applied to any calamities we have seen so far in the history of the earth—including the calamities that befell Nebuchadnezzar of the Babylonian empire or Antiochus Epiphanes of the Greco-Macedonian empire—simply because in no known calamities of the past did Messiah appear on the Mount of Olives with His saints, as He does in the second burden.

One of the key phrases of chapters 12–14, occuring seventeen times, is *"In that day."* It refers to the time of the second coming of Messiah, our Lord Jesus Christ. The other two terms that have the highest frequency of repetition are *"Jerusalem"* (occuring twenty-two times) and *"nations"* (occuring thirteen times).

CHAPTER SIXTEEN

Cleansing Judah and Jerusalem of Foreign Invaders

Zechariah 12:1–9

12:1 The burden of the word of the LORD against Israel. Thus says the LORD, who stretches out the heavens, lays the foundation of the earth, and forms the spirit of man within him:

2 "Behold, I will make Jerusalem a cup of drunkenness to all the surrounding peoples, when they lay siege against Judah and Jerusalem.

3 "And it shall happen in that day that I will make Jerusalem a very heavy stone for all peoples; all who would heave it away will surely be cut in pieces, though all nations of the earth are gathered against it.

4 "In that day," says the LORD, "I will strike every horse with confusion, and its rider with madness; I will open My eyes on the house of Judah, and will strike every horse of the peoples with blindness.

5 "And the governors of Judah shall say in their heart, 'The inhabitants of Jerusalem are my strength in the LORD of hosts, their God.'

6 "In that day I will make the governors of Judah like a firepan in the woodpile, and like a fiery torch in the sheaves; they shall devour all the surrounding peoples on the right hand and on the left, but Jerusalem shall be inhabited again in her own place—Jerusalem.

7 "The LORD will save the tents of Judah first, so that the glory of the house of David and the glory of the inhabitants of Jerusalem shall not become greater than that of Judah.

8 "In that day the Lord will defend the inhabitants of Jerusalem; the one who is feeble among them
in that day shall be like David, and the house of
David shall be like God, like the Angel of the Lord
before them.
    9 "It shall be in that day that I will seek to
destroy all the nations that come against Jerusalem.
                                        Zechariah 12:1–9

The main theme of these verses is that Israel will be delivered from
a future siege by the nations by a sudden intervention of God. The
world powers will come up against Jerusalem in that final day, bent
on eradicating Israel from the face of the earth, but God will con-
found those powers, and the inhabitants of the Holy City will
triumph decisively.

The venerable Dean Alford was quoted as saying that in that day
Israel will learn the truth of the saying: "Our only true triumphs are
God's triumphs *over us*, and that *His defeats of us* are our only true vic-
tories."[32]

Verses 1–9 exhibit four major works of God:

A. His Authenticating Word   12:1
B. His Intoxicated Enemies   12:2
C. His Immovable City   12:3
D. His Astonishing Deliverance   12:4–9

His Authenticating Word (12:1)

We have already commented on the phrase *"burden of the word of
the Lord"* (see our discussion of 9:1). The second burden, or the message of judgment, is *"against Israel"* (12:1).

There must be no doubt about the certitude of what is about to
be announced, for it comes from the mouth of the Lord—the same
Lord who demonstrated His creative power in creation and who
formed everything that now exists. (Zechariah's use of the three
participial verbs *"stretches out"* [the heavens], *"lays the foundation"*
[of the earth], and *"forms"* [the spirit of man within him] are very
reminiscent of Isaiah's style, e.g., Isa. 42:5.) The God who worked in
creation in the past is the same Lord who continues to work in rev-

elation, providence, and deliverance in the present and future. He who formed us and shaped us right down to our spiritual being is the One who will continue to shape and guide us by His word and His Spirit up to the end of the age. He is sovereign over the cosmos, over the earth, and over man himself.

HIS INTOXICATED ENEMIES (12:2)

God is also sovereign over Israel and her enemies. The Hebrew text emphatically begins "Behold I, I am going to make Jerusalem a cup of reeling to all the surrounding peoples."

Verses 2 and 3 contain two metaphors for Jerusalem: an intoxicating cup and a heavy stone that will hurt all who try to lift it.

The *"cup of drunkenness"* (v. 2a) is often used in Scripture as a symbol of the divine judgment God brings on mortals. God's judgment reduces them to a state of helplessness and misery similar to that of a drunken, staggering, intoxicated man. For example, Psalm 75:8 advises, "For in the hand of the LORD there is a cup, and the wine is red; it is fully mixed, and He pours it out; Surely its dregs shall all the wicked of the earth drain and drink down." Even though the Hebrew word for *"cup"* in Psalm 75:8 is not *saph*, but *kôs*, the concept is the same. Further, Isaiah warned: "Thus says the Lord, The LORD and your God, who pleads the cause of His people: 'See, I have taken out of your hand the cup of trembling, the dregs of the cup of My fury; you shall no longer drink it. But I will put it into the hand of those who afflict you, who have said to you, 'Lie down, that we may walk over you.' And you have laid down your body like the ground and as the street, for those who walk over'" (Isa. 51:22–23). Zechariah actually uses the Hebrew word for "bowl," not "cup"; the larger vessel is needed to allow all the nations to get drunk.

The tables will now be turned: No longer will Israel suffer at the hand of her enemies. But first the battle of the ages must take place; Judah and Jerusalem must be paired off to face the whole world! The nations will come against Judah and Jerusalem to lay siege against them (v. 2b). Literally, the last part of verse 2 says: "And also on Judah shall be [or 'fall', this 'cup of drunkenness'] in [or 'during'] the siege [which is] against Jerusalem."

HIS IMMOVABLE CITY (12:3)

"All nations of the earth" (v. 3c) will be *"gathered against"* Jerusalem as history swings into its final phase. The magnitude of this final battle cannot be overemphasized. In the words of Revelation 16:14, the "spirits of demons . . . go out to the kings of the earth and of the whole world, to gather them to the battle of that great day of God Almighty." The prophet Joel similarly said: "In those days and at that time, when I bring back the captives of Judah and Jerusalem, I will also gather all nations and bring them down to the Valley of Jehoshaphat; and I will enter into judgment with them there on account of My people, My heritage Israel, whom they have scattered among the nations . . ." (Joel 3:1–2).

But the city will not budge. Jerusalem will prove to be such a heavy stone that all nations that attempt to lift it will hurt themselves or, more literally, herniate themselves.

Some believe Psalm 118:5–6 and 10–12 apply to the type of situation Judah will face in that day:

> I called on the LORD in distress [same word as "siege" in 12:2];
> The LORD answered me and set me in a broad place.
>
> The LORD is on my side;
> I will not fear.
> What can man do to me?
>
> All nations surrounded me,
> But in the name of the LORD I will destroy them.
>
> They surrounded me,
> Yes, they surrounded me;
> But in the name of the LORD I will destroy them.
>
> They surrounded me like bees;
> They were quenched like a fire of thorns;
> For in the name of the LORD I will destroy them.

HIS ASTONISHING DELIVERANCE (12:4–9)

According to verse 4a the decisive battle will occur *"In that day."* This is the time of God's judgment on the wicked and His deliverance of the righteous.

In that battle God will intervene to cause afflictions: *"confusion,"* *"madness,"* and *"blindness"* (v. 4). These afflictions had been promised as long ago as Moses's time in Deuteronomy 28:28: "the LORD will strike you with madness and blindness and confusion of heart" if you walk contrary to His way and will. Now, in the eschatological battle of the ages, every horse and rider will be afflicted either with confusion, blindness or madness. It is unlikely that "horses" will be used in that final battle as the main means of carrying the battle forward; the writer describes the implements of future war using battle imagery he knew in his own day, just as the writers of the Old Testament described worship in the future day when our Lord will be present using familiar terms for worship in their day.

God *"will open [His] eyes on the house of Judah,"* and then the battle will turn against the nations. This is the fourth time Zechariah mentions Yahweh's eyes (3:9; 4:10; 9:8). (As we have discussed in our section entitled Unity of the Book, the repeated references to Yahweh's eyes argue for the unity of the book and for Zechariah being the author of the whole book.)

It is this look of pity and compassion on His people that will not only change the battle, but will melt the hearts of the people in repentance and contrition for their past sin (12:10). Then the cup of reeling and drunkenness (12:2) will be taken from the hands of Judah and placed into the hands of the nations. The resulting astonishment, panic, bewilderment, madness, and blindness will be obvious to all.

With the sudden realization that Yahweh is their God, Judah will turn on her enemy like a fire igniting dry tinder or ripe sheaves (v. 6). Judah will be *"like a firepan in the woodpile"* (v. 6a). *"They shall devour all the surrounding peoples on the right hand and on the left, but Jerusalem shall be inhabited again in her own place—Jerusalem"* (v. 6cd).

The inhabitants of Judah dwelling in the countryside will be delivered first so that the house of David and the inhabitants of Jerusalem will not exalt themselves above Judah. This will discourage rivalry and division.

The invasion of the land of Israel described here is discussed in more detail in 13:8–9 and 14:1–6. Two-thirds of the people of the land will die, and one-half of Jerusalem will be carried away into captivity before the Lord steps into the battle. But His intervention will be so decisive that there will be no question about the outcome of the battle. The Lord will reverse the fortunes of the battle!

The once broken and feeble Jewish remnant will finally recognize their Savior. It will almost be as if they had been given superhuman strength (v. 8). Even the feeblest of them will act valiantly and valorously.

Then it will happen that God will destroy those nations that came up against Jerusalem. The word to *"seek"* to destroy does not imply that the mission might not be successful, but means the Lord will make that object the focus and first priority of all His actions at that time.

CONCLUSION

"The battle is the LORD's." If this was true in David's day (1 Sam. 17:47), it will be especially true when the Lord moves for one last time against all the nations of the earth that wish to commit genicide against His people and sacrilege against His name.

Count on this event, for it is as authentic as the word that built the universe and that preserves both it and man in the meantime.

The Lord remains when all else has been removed. And the place of His ancient dwelling—Jerusalem—remains as well. What a Savior!

CHAPTER SEVENTEEN

Mourning for the Pierced One

Zechariah 12:10–13:1

10 "And I will pour on the house of David and on
the inhabitants of Jerusalem the Spirit of grace and
supplication; then they will look on Me whom they
have pierced; they will mourn for Him as one mourns
for his only son, and grieve for Him as one grieves for
a firstborn.

11 "In that day there shall be a great mourning in
Jerusalem, like the mourning at Hadad Rimmon in
the plain of Megiddo.

12 "And the land shall mourn, every family by
itself: the family of the house of David by itself, and
their wives by themselves; the family of the house of
Nathan by itself, and their wives by themselves;

13 "the family of the house of Levi by itself, and
their wives by themselves; the family of Shimei by
itself, and their wives by themselves;

14 "all the families that remain, every family by
itself, and their wives by themselves.

13:1 "In that day a fountain shall be opened for the
house of David and for the inhabitants of Jerusalem,
for sin and for uncleanness.

Zechariah 12:10–13:1

Essential to the nation's physical deliverance is the people's spiritual renewal and repentance. The jubilation of the promised victory
in the early verses of chapter 12 gives way in these verses to mourning over the sins of the nation.

The Lord will give a whole new spirit (12:10) and a new cleansing
(13:1) to those who are genuinely moved over the sight of the One

who was pierced on their behalf and the One who bore their own sin.

Zechariah 12:1–9 had just described a day like no other day in the annals of time, when the Lord directly intervened with His personal presence to grant a most decisive victory. The only thing similar to it was the triumph over Pharaoh at the Red Sea. God's triumph over the hearts of the Judahites would be even greater and more significant.

This text records two mercies that God will dispense in that day:

A.   A New Spirit of Grace and Supplication   12:10–4
B.   A New Cleansing for Sin and Uncleanness   13:1

A NEW SPIRIT OF GRACE AND SUPPLICATION (12:10–14)

Very few promises in Scripture are more compassionate than the one found in verse 10, and very few are more hotly debated.

God has promised to *"pour on the house of David and on the inhabitants of Jerusalem the Spirit of grace and supplication"* (v. 10a). The source of these gifts is clearly none other than the Lord. And the dominant gift is the "grace" or "compassion" of our Lord. This is a grace that forgives sin; in fact, it is a grace that forgives even the piercing of the Son of God. *"Then they will look on Me whom they have pierced; they will mourn for Him . . . and grieve for Him"* (v. 10b).

We do not mean by saying this to add fuel to the awful fire that has stigmatized our Jewish neighbors as "Christ killers"—a stigma that is as untrue as it is unfair. The fact is that all of us are involved in the murder of the Messiah, for it was for the sins of the whole world that He died. Furthermore, it is unfair to charge Jewish people of subsequent generations with an act committed by a group of first-Christian century Jews. And even the first-century Jews did not act alone, for the New Testament clearly says that both the Jews and Romans at Golgotha put Jesus to death. So caution and care must be exercised in discussing the Jews' role in piercing the Son of God.

But why is there so much controversy over this text? One of the greatest problems centers around a translation problem. The *New Jewish Publication Society* translation of the *Tanakh* (Old Testament) in 1988 rendered it: "But I will fill the House of David and the inhabitants of Jerusalem with a spirit of pity and compassion; and they shall lament to Me about those who are slain, wailing over them as over a favorite son and showing bitter grief as over a first-born." The 1896

Jewish translation in an Appendix to the Revised Version read, "And they [i.e., the house of David and the inhabitants of Jerusalem] shall look up to Me because of Him whom they [i.e., the nations which came up against Jerusalem] have pierced." A more ancient Jewish interpretation understands this prophecy to refer to Messiah ben ("son of") Joseph, a separate individual from Messiah ben ("son of") David. But the creation of these two Messiahs, one who would suffer (ben Joseph) and the other who would be glorified (ben David) finds no support from the *Tenakh* itself.

Probably no text in the Old Testament speaks more directly to the question of whether there are going to be two comings of the one Messiah than does verse 10. But, even aside from the question of whether this text points to one or two Messiahs, the hardest fact for most Jewish interpreters and readers to face is that "Me" and "Him" both refer to the same person. Most Jewish interpreters would prefer to have the Gentile nations look to God, whom these nations have attacked indirectly by inflicting suffering on His people Israel.

But each of these novel translations is problematic. Each ignores the fact that the subject of both the verb "to look" and the verb "to pierce" is the same in Hebrew. Therefore, those who pierced the One who will pour out a spirit of grace and supplication in that day, belong to the same national group that will "look" and "mourn" over the pierced One like one mourns over the loss of a firstborn.

In the debate over verse 10, interpreters argue that it is impossible to pierce God, since He is spirit and not flesh and blood (Isa. 31:3; John 4:24). But that is the point; it was Christ's flesh that was pierced, and the One who was pierced is at the same time One in essence and being with the God who speaks in this text. Note also that whenever the first person pronoun appears elsewhere in this chapter (vv. 2, 3, 4, 6, 9, 10) it refers to the Messiah. Zechariah had just referred in chapter 11 to the Good Shepherd who had been rejected by Israel, and whose rejection was followed by a terrible punishment. Only the Messiah fits all the details here. His piercing must have come in an earlier advent, for certainly when He comes again it will be with the victory promised in this section.[33]

Israel is described as God's *"firstborn"* (v. 10e) in Exodus 4:22 and Jeremiah 31:9. Used first to describe the whole nation, the term is then used to describe the representative of the whole group, the coming Messiah (Rom. 8:29; Col. 1:15, 18; Heb. 1:6; Rev. 1:5; cf. Heb. 12:23).

The mourning here is so intense that the only mourning that even begins to compare with it is the *"mourning at Hadad Rimmon in the plain of Megiddo"* (v. 11b). Presumably Hadad-Rimmon is the name of a place. But the reference to the plain of Megiddo surely indicates an intention to compare this mourning to that which followed the tragic death of King Josiah (2 Kings 23:29; 2 Chron. 35:25). Few kings had compiled a better record for godliness and righteousness than Josiah, but he perished at the Megiddo pass on his thirty-ninth birthday trying to stop Pharaoh Necho. His death stunned the nation and sent it into deep grief. The nation's mourning over King Josiah's death was a small foretaste of the nation's mourning of Messiah when it suddenly realizes that it has pierced the One who died for their sins, and for the sins of the whole world (Isa. 53:5).

Verses 12–14 identify those who would mourn Him. He will be universally mourned, by *"the land," "every family," "the house of David," "the house of Nathan," "the house of Levi," "the family of Shimei,"* the *"wives by themselves,"* and *"all the families that remain."* Thus, He will be mourned by the royal family, the priestly ministers and their household, and perhaps the prophetic line represented by Nathan the prophet (2 Sam. 7:2). His mourners may even include the Shimei who cursed David (2 Sam. 16:5), although Zechariah may be referring in verse 13 to the Shimei who was one of Levi's sons (Num. 3:18; Shimei the son of Gershom and grandson of Levi). If "family of Shimei" refers to the Shemei who was one of Levi's sons and if "house of Nathan" refers to David's son Nathan (who replaced Solomon in the genealogy of our Lord) rather than Nathan the prophet, Zechariah would have identified two families in the royal line and two families in the priestly line as representatives of the whole nation of Israel. In this way Zechariah describes national as well as individual grief and sorrow that will occur in that day.

In that day, as each person fully realizes in his heart the awfulness of the death and long rejection of the Messiah, the mourning will be so intense that each person will mourn apart from the rest with almost inconsolable grief.

A NEW CLEANSING FOR SIN AND UNCLEANNESS (13:1)

The Lord declares, *"In that day a fountain shall be opened for the house of David and for the inhabitants of Jerusalem, for sin and for uncleanness"*

(13:1). This fountain for cleansing sin is an extension of the cleansing of the High Priest Joshua in 3:3–5. There, only the High Priest was cleansed as representative of all the people, but, as 13:1 indicates, in that day all of Israel will be cleansed. As in verses 12:11–12, the reference in 13:1 to "the house of David" and "the inhabitants of Jerusalem" refers to the entire nation of Israel.

So generous will be the flow of the cleansing waters that it will be compared to the initial flow of an unplugged fountain. This is the cleansing that Ezekiel had promised in Ezekiel 36:25–28, and that our Lord must have assumed that Nicodemus knew about as a teacher of the Jews (John 3).

This cleansing would remove all *"sin"*—i.e., everything contrary to the will and Law of God—and all *"uncleanness"*—i.e., all impurities, including ritualistic and sexual impurities.

Here would come a repentant Israel, the very thing the apostle Paul had prayed for and desired above everything else in Romans 9–11. The times of the Gentiles would have ended, and a repentant Israel would be grafted back on to the very tree from which the branches of the olive tree had been temporarily lopped off (Rom. 11:26–27). The people of Israel would now be washed with the washing of the Word and renewed by the inner work of the Holy Spirit (Titus 3:5).

CONCLUSION

There is a fountain filled with the cleansing water of the Word of God and the forgiving mercy of our Lord Jesus Christ. And one day Israel will realize how mistaken she has been in not plunging into that fountain.

Israel will look on the pierced Son of God and mourn like she has never mourned before. And through Israel's mourning she will experience spiritual renewal and restoration. What a Savior!

CHAPTER EIGHTEEN

Cleansing the Land of False Prophets

Zechariah 13:2–6

2 "It shall be in that day," says the LORD of hosts, "that I will cut off the names of the idols from the land, and they shall no longer be remembered. I will also cause the prophets and the unclean spirit to depart from the land.

3 "It shall come to pass that if anyone still prophesies, then his father and mother who begot him will say to him, 'You shall not live, because you have spoken lies in the name of the LORD.' And his father and mother who begot him shall thrust him through when he prophesies.

4 "And it shall be in that day that every prophet will be ashamed of his vision when he prophesies; they will not wear a robe of coarse hair to deceive.

5 "But he will say, 'I am no prophet, I am a farmer; for a man taught me to keep cattle from my youth.'

6 "And someone will say to him, 'What are these wounds in your hands?' Then he will answer, 'Those with which I was wounded in the house of my friends.'

Zechariah 13:2–6

Much of this second burden is a mirror image of the first burden. For example, in this brief pericope of 13:2–6 Zechariah scolds the false prophets (cf. 10:2–3a, wherein Zechariah rebuked the sham leaders). There never seemed to be a shortage of counterfeit prophets; someone was always available to say what people wanted to hear.

Thus it was necessary throughout their careers for the true prophets of God to chastise the fraudulent prophets. Jeremiah devoted most of his twenty-third chapter to this theme, Ezekiel devoted the first half of his thirteenth chapter, and Micah devoted his third chapter.

According to this pericope, God will take two actions against false prophets:

A.   The Removal of the False Prophets   13:2
B.   The Exposure of the False Prophets   13:3–6

THE REMOVAL OF THE FALSE PROPHETS (13:2)

God will act against the false prophets *"in that day."* As God concludes history He will deal so decisively with all idols that their names will no longer be remembered. In the ancient Near East, to *"cut off the names of the idols"* was the equivalent of destroying the idols and everything that suggested they had ever existed. A person's name encompassed the person, his reputation, and his character.

Additionally, God would *"cause the prophets and the unclean spirit to depart from the land."* This is the only time in the Bible, except in the New Testament Gospels, where the phrase "unclean spirit" occurs.

All power and authority over men's hearts and minds that these alleged deities, prophets, and spirits had would now be removed from the land altogether.

THE EXPOSURE OF THE FALSE PROPHETS (13:3–6)

Should any false prophecy break out in that future day, public opinion will be so strong against it that even the false prophet's own parents will not tolerate it (v. 3). To speak *"lies in the name of the LORD"* will be a most reprehensible distortion of revelation and of God's character. Instinctively, the false prophet's parents *"shall thrust him through when he prophesies"* (v. 3d). This is the same penalty Deuteronomy 13:5 and 18:20 prescribed for such a serious offense. The only unusual aspect of the penalty described here is that the parents carry it out, not the judges or the community under the judges' instruction. The verb "to pierce" is the same verb that appeared in 12:10 and that describes Phinehas' act in Numbers 25:7–8.

Actually, there will be great hesitancy on the part of a false prophet to announce *"his vision."* This is a significant change from the false prophets' former brazenness. Now evil—not goodness or the sons of light—will be on the defensive.

Even the *"course hair"* garment, the symbol of the prophetic profession, will be shunned by the false prophets (2 Kings 1:8) in that day out of fear of being immediately challenged and dealt with by the populace (v. 4c). Gone are the days when deceiving the public was a favorite sport of false prophets!

So loathe will these false prophets be to claim the office that they will go to great lengths to deny that they are prophets, claiming instead that they have been farmers and herdsmen since their youth (v. 5).

When challenged to explain what the *"wounds in [their] hands"* (v. 6) are, the false prophets will try their best to make sure no one thinks the obvious—that they are Canaanite ecstatic prophets who indulged in masochistic beatings in order to attract the favor and oracular response of Baal and the other gods of Canaan (cf. 1 Kings 18:28). The false prophets will protest that the wounds are *"'Those with which I was wounded in the house of my friends.'"* This explanation sounds most unreal and unlikely. Some "friends" these "farmers" have!

CONCLUSION

It is an awesome responsibility to deliver the Word of God. Toying with it, distorting it, or twisting it to fit some subjective idea or loyalty other than to the Lord is extremely serious, since it involves the lives of other people for all eternity! Churchmen should be jarred out of their lethargy and their relational types of teaching. God's word is true, and He will never allow any human substitutes to adulterate His Word.

CHAPTER NINETEEN

Slaughtering the Shepherd and Scattering the Sheep

Zechariah 13:7–9

7 "Awake, O sword, against My Shepherd,
  Against the Man who is My Companion,"
  Says the LORD of hosts.
  "Strike the Shepherd,
  And the sheep will be scattered;
  Then I will turn My hand against the little ones.
8 And it shall come to pass in all the land,"
  Says the LORD,
  "That two thirds in it shall be cut off and die,
  But one third shall be left in it:
9 I will bring the one third through the fire,
  Will refine them as silver is refined,
  And test them as gold is tested.
  They will call on My name,
  And I will answer them.
  I will say, 'This is My people';
  And each one will say, 'The LORD is my God.'"

Zechariah 13:7–9

In these verses we return to the shepherd motif that we found in chapter 11, with its attendant teaching about leadership in chapters 12 and 13. Tragically, here the shepherd is slain and the sheep are scattered.

Two major events are described:

A. The Shepherd is Slain   13:7
B. The Sheep are Decimated   13:8-9

THE SHEPHERD IS SLAIN (13:7)

In a most vivid personification, the *"sword"* is addressed as an instrument of death and instructed to move against the shepherd.

Yahweh calls the shepherd *"My Shepherd,"* indicating that this Shepherd is no ordinary leader. Indeed, Yahweh also calls him *"the Man who is My Companion."* Surely that is more than high praise. This Shepherd is One who is side by side with, or the equal of, the Lord! The term "associate" (or "Companion," v. 7) is used to refer to those who are close neighbors or close companions (cf. Lev. 6:2; 18:20; 19:15). The equality that such a relationship brings to mind is the equality with God claimed by Jesus in John 10:30 and 14:9. The Shepherd's close association with the Lord strengthens the case for identifying him as the Shepherd of 11:4–14 and the One who was pierced in 12:10.

The sword is told, *"Strike the Shepherd"* (v. 7c). This accords with what Isaiah taught: "Yet it pleased the LORD to bruise Him" (Isa. 53:10). Thus Jesus was delivered up in accordance with the definite plan of God, although it is the men who did the deed who are culpable for what they did (Acts 2:23).

As a result of Messiah's death, the sheep were scattered. This act of dying was too much to accept for any contemporary Jewish view of the Messiah. The cross would continue to be an offense as long as the Gentile period lasted. Even *"the little ones"* (v. 7d) suffered as the tradition of resisting the significance of Jesus' hideous death was passed on from parents to children.

THE SHEEP ARE DECIMATED (13:8–9)

One of earth's most devastating disasters will take place in the end times. *"Two thirds in [the land of Israel] shall be cut off and die"* (v. 8a). Israel's present population is somewhere around five million. What it will swell to by the time this text is fulfilled we do not know, but God has promised to lead in a restoration of the Jewish people to the land of Israel. When that takes place there may be some eight to twelve million people in Israel. Think of it: "two-thirds" of whatever the population is in that day will be killed!

The remaining *"one third"* will be brought through this affliction (v. 9a). They will be like brands plucked from the fire (Ezk. 5:4; Mal. 3:3).

All impurities will have been refined away by this experience and by the cry of repentance already traced in this chapter. Finally, the remaining one-third shall *"call on [the LORD's] name"* (v. 9d). And the Lord has promised to answer them when they call. *"Each one will say, 'The LORD is my God'"* (v. 9f). Only then will the first part of the tripartite formula of the ancient promise-plan of God be reinstituted: "I will be your God, You shall be My people, and I will dwell in the midst of you" (e.g., *see* Hos. 2:23; Ezk. 36:23, 27, 28). In that day, as Paul exclaimed, "All Israel will be saved" (Rom. 11:26–7).

CONCLUSION

The Shepherd in 13:7–9 must be our Lord Jesus Christ. Who else has such a close relationship with the Father?

So what will it take for Israel—and all the world—to recognize who this Shepherd really is? We can be assured that at least Israel will finally come to her senses, but oh, by what a national bloodbath from the nations! Would that more Jews and Gentiles would come to the Messiah even now before these terrible days must be endured.

CHAPTER TWENTY

Waiting for the Second Coming of Messiah

Zechariah 14:1–15

14:1 Behold, the day of the LORD is coming,
And your spoil will be divided in your midst.
2 For I will gather all the nations to battle against
Jerusalem;
The city shall be taken,
The houses rifled,
And the women ravished.
Half of the city shall go into captivity,
But the remnant of the people shall not
be cut off from the city.
3 Then the LORD will go forth
And fight against those nations,
As He fights in the day of battle.
4 And in that day His feet will stand on the
Mount of Olives,
Which faces Jerusalem on the east.
And the Mount of Olives shall be split in two,
From east to west,
Making a very large valley;
Half of the mountain shall move
toward the north
And half of it toward the south.
5 Then you shall flee through My
mountain valley,
For the mountain valley shall reach to Azal.
Yes, you shall flee
As you fled from the earthquake

In the days of Uzziah king of Judah.
Thus the LORD my God will come,
And all the saints with You.
6 It shall come to pass in that day
That there will be no light;
The lights will diminish.
7 It shall be one day
Which is known to the LORD—
Neither day nor night.
But at evening time it shall happen
That it will be light.
8 And in that day it shall be
That living waters shall flow from Jerusalem,
Half of them toward the eastern sea
And half of them toward the western sea;
In both summer and winter it shall occur.
9 And the LORD shall be King over all the earth.
In that day it shall be—
"The LORD is one,"
And His name one.
10 All the land shall be turned into a plain from Geba
to Rimmon south of Jerusalem. Jerusalem shall be raised
up and inhabited in her place from Benjamin's Gate to the
place of the First Gate and the Corner Gate, and from the
Tower of Hananeel to the king's winepresses.
11 The people shall dwell in it;
And no longer shall there be utter destruction,
But Jerusalem shall be safely inhabited.
12 And this shall be the plague with which the
LORD will strike all the people who fought against
Jerusalem:
Their flesh shall dissolve
while they stand on their feet,
Their eyes shall dissolve
in their sockets,
And their tongues shall dissolve
in their mouths.
13 It shall come to pass in that day
That a great panic from the LORD
will be among them.
Everyone will seize the hand of his neighbor,
And raise his hand against his neighbor's hand;

14 Judah also will fight at Jerusalem.
  And the wealth of all the surrounding nations
  Shall be gathered together:
  Gold, silver, and apparel in great abundance.
15 Such also shall be the plague
  On the horse and the mule,
  On the camel and the donkey,
  And on all the cattle that will be in
    those camps.
  So shall this plague be.

Zechariah 14:1–15

In no other chapter of the Bible is the interpretation of the name "Israel" more important than in Zechariah 14. To say that "Israel" means the "Church," as many have done, would lead to a most confusing picture in this chapter and in the end of chapter 13. For example, 13:8–9 affirms that two-thirds of the land (Israel) will die, but few would be willing to say that two-thirds of the Church will be slaughtered in the final day. Clearly "Israel" refers to that geo-political unit known today as the nation of Israel.

The probable course of events leading up to the greatest crisis Israel will ever face in this world include: First, the people of Israel will be restored to the land of Canaan in large numbers. The exact timing of their restoration cannot be determined, but it would appear to occur prior to our Lord's second coming. Second, after a brief period of prosperity, one of Israel's darkest nights will set in. The nations of the world will gather against her in the siege predicted in Zechariah 12 and 14. Third, Israel will enter into a covenant with one who is otherwise known as the Antichrist. Unfortunately, Israel will readily accept any other person who comes in his own name, all the while rejecting the one who comes in the name of the Lord. Fourth, Antichrist will break his covenant with Israel after a period of three and a half years. Whether this covenant will have been public or not is impossible to say, but when it is broken it will lead to actions against the people of Israel that verge on genocide. Fifth, the nations of the earth will join Antichrist in their march in triumph over Israel, saying, "Come, let us cut off the existence of this nation so that the name of Israel may no longer be remembered." Sixth, the Lord shall intervene on that day. It shall be a day like none before or after it (Josh. 10:14). The Lord, as a "Mighty Man of War," will go forth to fight for

Israel—and He will be victorious. All these events will constitute the greatest crisis Israel has ever endured.

Three mighty events recorded in Zechariah 14:1–15 will distinguish the second coming of our Lord from all other events this earth has ever seen. At the heart of this pericope stands verse 9: *"And the LORD shall be King over all the earth. In that day it shall be—'The LORD is one, and His name one.'"* The three events that lead up to that magnificent moment are:

A. Our Nations Will Fight Jerusalem for the Last Time   14:1–3
B. Our Messiah Will Appear a Second Time   14:4–7
C. Our Messiah's Kingdom Will Be Established Over All   14:8–15

OUR NATIONS WILL FIGHT JERUSALEM FOR THE LAST TIME 14:1–3

In many ways, chapter 14 is simply an enlargement of 13:9—one day there will come a renewed relationship between God and all the nations of the earth.

This chapter begins with the final siege on Jerusalem. This siege was described earlier in 12:1–9. Now it will be described from a different angle, with a different point of view, and with a different purpose. In Zechariah 12, the siege was described in its final stages, although God's promised intervention had not yet taken place. In Zechariah 14 the siege is first described in its earlier stages; then Zechariah quickly moves to the climactic moments when God suddenly intervenes. Zechariah 12 notes God's coming in terms of grace and salvation, while Zechariah 14 depicts His coming with power and victory over all the nations and over all evil.

This siege on Jerusalem is to take place on a *"day"* that is known to the Lord (v. 1a). This is the time immediately before His second coming. It is a "day" when *"[Israel's] spoil will be divided in [their] midst"* (v. 1b). The nations will already be actively distributing the plunder, booty, and spoil they have taken from Jerusalem. This is the time known in Jeremiah 30:5–7 as the time of "Jacob's trouble."

God promised repeatedly in Scripture that He would *"gather all the nations to battle against Jerusalem"* (v. 2a). That is what the programmatic statement of Joel 3:1–5 had detailed—"For behold, in those days and at that time, when I bring back the captives of Judah and Jerusalem, I will also gather all nations, and bring them down to the

Valley of Jehoshaphat; I will enter into judgment with them there on account of My people, My heritage Israel. . . ." Thus it is clear that the *time* will be on that famous "Day of the LORD," also known variously as "in those days," "at that time," or the "latter days." The participants in the siege will be "all nations." The place will be "the Valley of Jehoshaphat" or, as Revelation 16:13–16 calls it, "Armageddon." There are four reasons God will enter into judgment with the nations, according to Joel 3:1–5: first, the nations scattered Israel (Joel 3:2c); second, the nations partitioned the land of Israel (Joel 3:2d); third, the nations made slaves out of the Jews (Joel 3:3); and fourth, the Babylonians carried off the sacred vessels (Joel 3:5).

For these reasons, God will assemble the nations in the Near East. Moreover, if God uses wicked hands as His secondary means to accomplish His will, His agents will be morally responsible for what they do.

The horrors of this siege are monstrous. *"The city shall be taken, the house rifled, and the women ravished. Half of the city shall go into captivity"* (v. 2). While two thirds of the land is perishing, one half of the city of Jerusalem will be taken captive. The remaining third of the country's population will be brought through these events, though refined and thoroughly chastened.

"Then the LORD will go forth and fight against those nations" (v. 3a). Just when Antichrist and his all-nation forces seem to have gained the upper hand, the Lord himself will enter the battle and the balance of powers will shift. The ominous terminology of war is now used to refer to the Lord: He will *"go forth."* This He only does when He enters as the "Man of War" (Exod. 15:3). The battle will belong to the Lord (1 Sam. 17:47) *"in the day of battle"* (v. 3c). Just as the Lord fought for Gideon, so the Lord will fight on that day (Judg. 7:21–22; cf. Josh. 10:14; v. 3c).

OUR MESSIAH WILL APPEAR A SECOND TIME (14:4–7)

The Lord will personally, physically, and actually reappear on this earth, just as He said He would, on the very spot where He left it at the end of His thirty-year pilgrimage. The early believers were told, "Men of Galilee, why do you stand gazing up into heaven? This same Jesus, who was taken up from you into heaven, will so come in like manner as you saw Him go into heaven" (Acts 1:11). Zechariah's "day of the LORD" is that promised day of return. Here on the

Mount of Olives, where Jesus had left Jerusalem, He would return again. This accords with what the Old Testament predicts. The "Glory of God," representing the very presence of God, had removed itself from the earth by stages, moving first from the Holy of Holies to the porch of the Temple, then to the eastern gate, and eventually to the mountain east of the temple (the Mount of Olives), only to be taken up into heaven to stay until His return and His name becomes "The LORD is there, Yahweh *Shammah*" (Ezk. 10:4, 18–19; 11:22–24; 43:1–5; 48:35b).

Ultimately, our Lord will come "with healing in His wings" (Mal. 4:2), but some major catastrophic events must precede this healing. When our Lord touches down on the Mount of Olives, the mountain will *"be split in two, from east to west, making a very large valley; half of the mountain shall move toward the north and half of it toward the south"* (v. 4cde). The major fault line in the Jordan valley runs north and south. There is a hair-line fault line that runs east and west through the Mount of Olives. That is where a new valley will be formed in that day. The seventh bowl of judgment in the book of Revelation (16:18–19) comes in the form of an earthquake splitting Jerusalem into three parts. Out of this seismic activity, a great plain will be formed from Geba to Rimmon. The believing remnant, it would appear, will escape by the newly-formed valley created by the division of the Mount of Olives.

Who should appear but the Lord himself! *"Thus the LORD my God will come"* (v. 5e). The great hope of Israel and of the Church will finally be realized: the epiphany of the Lord! Accompanying Him will be *"all the saints"* (v. 5f). The term "saints," or "holy ones," is used in the Old Testament to refer to angels (Deut. 33:3; Ps. 89:5–7; Job 15:15) or holy individuals (Lev. 11:44–45; Ps. 16:3; 34:9; 2 Chron. 35:3; Dan. 8:24). Using the same terms, the New Testament says that Christ will be accompanied both by His angels and His holy people: "and they will see the Son of Man coming on the clouds of heaven with power and great glory. And He will send His angels with a great sound of a trumpet, and they will gather together His elect from the four winds, from one end of heaven to the other" (Matt. 24:30b–31); also, when He comes, in that Day, He will be glorified in His saints and will be admired among all those who believe (2 Thess. 1:10). Again, it is promised "at the coming of our Lord Jesus Christ with all His saints" (1 Thess. 3:13b) and, in Jude 14, "Behold, the Lord comes with ten thousands of His saints." We conclude that our Lord will return with His angels and all who have believed in Him through all the ages.

And what a day that will be! The celestial luminaries will cease to function in the pattern they have known all these aeons. *"In that day . . . there will be no light"* (v. 6). Isaiah had prophesied, "For the stars of heaven and their constellations will not give their light; the sun will be darkened in its going forth, and the moon will not cause its light to shine" (Isa. 13:10; cf. Isa. 24:23; Joel 3:14–16; Matt. 24:29–30; Mark 13:24–25; Rev. 6:13; 8:12). Instead of the usual light of the sun and moon, a thick murkiness will cover the earth. This will be a day like none the earth has ever known.

But there will no longer be a need for the light from the celestial bodies, for the resplendent light of the glory of God's presence will be reflected over all the earth. A whole new order of creation will have dawned. And that glory will far exceed the glory of the previous creation.

Our Messiah's Kingdom Will Be Established Over All (14:8–15)

In paradise restored (Rev. 22:1), there will issue forth from the entrance of the sanctuary a life-giving stream of water (v. 8a). Half of it will flow to the Dead Sea *("the eastern sea")* and half of it will flow to the Mediterranean Sea *("the western sea"*; v. 8bc). It will never stop flowing, whether it be summer or winter (v. 8d). It will flow out to the entire region of the desert area of the Jordan (Ezk. 47:1–12). Joel had also predicted a day when all the brooks of Judah would flow full of water and a fountain would come from the house of the Lord (Joel 3:18).

More importantly, *"The LORD shall be King over all the earth"* (v. 9). Then "The kingdoms of this world [will] have become the kingdoms of our Lord and of His Christ, and He shall reign forever and ever!" (Rev. 11:15b). Christ will be regarded by all as "King of kings and Lord of lords" (Rev. 19:16): *"'The LORD is one,' and His name one"* (v. 9b). He will be acknowledged as the only Lord, with no rivals—our incomparably great Lord.

The peace of Jerusalem will never again be disturbed (v. 11). Even the landscape will be changed as a result of the seismic activity. The land from Geba, six miles northeast of Jerusalem, to Rimmon, thirty-three miles southwest of Jerusalem, will be uplifted into a great plain. Even the city of Jerusalem will be transformed; it too will be uplifted by the same earthquake. In order to accommodate her new status as the religious and governmental capital of the world in the millennial era, Jerusalem would be uplifted and inhabited from Benjamin's Gate on the north wall (the "Gate of Ephraim" in 2 Kings 14:3) to the "First Gate" on the northeast corner, from the "Corner Gate" on the northwest corner to "the Tower of Hananel," perhaps in the southeast corner, and to the "king's winepresses" in the king's gardens south of the city near the Valley of Hinnon.

No longer would there be a "curse," or "utter destruction," on the people or the city. The Hebrew word used here for "curse" is *herem*, which means placing something under an involuntary dedication for destruction, the opposite of the kind of voluntary dedication described in Romans 12:1–2.

Three formidable enemies will be unleashed against Israel's enemies: a deadly plague (v. 12), a panic among the enemies' troops (v. 13), and a superhuman valor to fight on the part of the remnant of Judah (v. 14). The plague will be so sudden and so deadly that the flesh of Israel's enemies will rot while they are standing on their feet. It almost sounds like some kind of nuclear blast will leave the flesh, eyes, and tongues of Israel's enemies festering with wounds and rotting on the battlefield. In addition to this plague, the Lord will cause the enemy to hear a roar similar to what Gideon's adversaries heard on the day of Gideon's victory. Upon hearing this roar, the enemy will turn on one another in their confusion, just as they did in the day of Gideon. Finally, Judah will fight *"at Jerusalem"* (v. 14). So valiant will the fighting of the Jews be that into their hands will fall *"gold, silver, and apparel in great abundance"* (v. 14d). The hoard of goods and wealth will be enormous.

The entire enemy retinue will be put under the *"plague"* (v. 15). The victory will be most decisive.

Conclusion

In that day, Christ will be King over all the earth, with none left to challenge His person, work, law, or rule. Righteousness and justice, truth and grace, mercy and beauty, will be the order of the day.

Gone will be all filth, evil, injustice, and unrighteousness and the rule of tyrants, dictators, and despots of wickedness.

Even so, come Lord Jesus. *Maranatha.*

CHAPTER TWENTY-ONE

Worshipping the Lord as King Over All

Zechariah 14:16–21

16 And it shall come to pass that everyone who is left of all the nations which came against Jerusalem shall go up from year to year to worship the King, the LORD of hosts, and to keep the Feast of Tabernacles.

17 And it shall be that whichever of the families of the earth do not come up to Jerusalem to worship the King, the LORD of hosts, on them there will be no rain.

18 If the family of Egypt will not come up and enter in, they shall have no rain; they shall receive the plague with which the LORD strikes the nations who do not come up to keep the Feast of Tabernacles.

19 This shall be the punishment of Egypt and the punishment of all the nations that do not come up to keep the Feast of Tabernacles.

20 In that day "HOLINESS TO THE LORD" shall be engraved on the bells of the horses. The pots in the LORD's house shall be like the bowls before the altar.

21 Yes, every pot in Jerusalem and Judah shall be holiness to the LORD of hosts. Everyone who sacrifices shall come and take them and cook in them. In that day there shall no longer be a Canaanite in the house of the LORD of hosts.

Zechariah 14:16–21

This text describes the worship of *"The King, the LORD of hosts"* (v. 16c). It parallels 8:20–23 in the first burden, which describe the nations going up to Jerusalem to worship the Lord.

Now that the nations are defeated and all evil vanquished, the thought dominating all hearts and minds is the worship of the Living God.

Three features will form the focus of worship in that day. They will be:

A. Jerusalem Will Serve as the Religious Center of the World   14:16
B. All Nations Must Come Annually to Jerusalem   14:17–19
C. Holiness to the Lord Will Dominate All Worship   14:20–21

JERUSALEM WILL SERVE AS THE RELIGIOUS CENTER OF THE WORLD (14:16)

Those survivors of the battle that was just described will go to Jerusalem each year to worship the Lord. It hardly seems that there would be any one left after the brutality of that battle, but there would be.

Now Messiah will be able to take His place on the throne of David. It will be the joy of the nations to worship only Him.

The nations will observe *"the Feast of Tabernacles"* along with Israel. This feast had been described in Leviticus 23:39, 42–43, and Deuteronomy 16:13–16. It commemorated Israel's years in the wilderness and her fall harvests. Some think that this fall harvest and Feast of Tabernacles anticipated the gathering of the nations into God's kingdom. Traditionally, this feast had been open equally to the stranger and to the people of Israel. It is mentioned in the post-exilic period as having continuing significance (Ezra 3:4; Neh. 8:14–18).

Just as the Passover Feast pictured the death of Messiah as our Redeemer; the Feast of Unleavened Bread depicted the walk of believers in fellowship with the Savior; the Feast of Firstfruits foreshadowed the resurrection of Christ; and the Feast of Pentecost predicted the coming of the Holy Spirit; so the Feast of Tabernacles would remain unfulfilled until the time of kingdom rest came in the world and Israel had been gathered in to her land. On the eighth day of the Feast of Tabernacles, the people of Israel returned to their homes—an event that looked forward to the eternal state and the rest God had promised so frequently in Scripture (Heb. 3–4).

The central feature, however, continued to be the fact that the King, the Messiah, was worshipped by every nation and by all of Israel.

ALL NATIONS MUST COME ANNUALLY TO JERUSALEM (14:17–19)

It will be a necessity for all nations to appear before the Lord each year (v. 17). Should any nation decide that they will not come, *"on them there will be no rain"* (v. 17c). In the past, God had reminded nations that they were apostate by shutting off the rain (Lev. 26:19–20; Deut. 28:24; 1 Kings 17:1; Hag. 1:11).

Egypt is singled out as an example of one that might not wish to come up to worship the Lord one of those years (v. 18). Perhaps she might feel she was exempt from God's threats of a drought, since she had depended for so many centuries on the Nile River. But the Nile will not save her. The waters that flow down the Nile from equatorial Africa might also be stopped, causing Egypt to experience drought.

It is interesting, nonetheless, to note that Egypt, the enemy of Israel for so many centuries, will be among the many nations that will worship the Lord in the final day. This is in accord with the prophecy of Isaiah (Isa. 19).

Worship is regarded in this context as a very necessary act, even when the King, our Lord, is himself present. It is tragic to think how loose we have become in our whole concept of worship. Many have begun to feel that it is not all that important. But in verse 19, a *"punishment"* is attached to a negligent disregard of worship.

HOLINESS TO THE LORD WILL DOMINATE ALL WORSHIP (14:20–21)

Just as the turban of the High Priest was inscribed on the gold headband *"HOLINESS TO THE LORD"* (v. 20a), so holiness now will be engraved on everything, including the bells of the horses (v. 20). The pots in the Lord's house will be as dedicated and as sacred as the bowls used at the altar in the temple (v. 20c). The old distinction between secular and sacred will no longer be necessary. In God's kingdom every lowly pot will be holy to the Lord (v. 21).

Moreover, in the kingdom age there will no longer be the need for merchants to sell their wares in the temple (*"Canaanite"* in v. 21 probably means "merchant"). All that was unclean and godless will have been removed in all of God's kingdom during the millennial rule and reign. The money-takers will no longer mar the temple courts of the house of God. The need for separating the secular and common from the sacred will have passed for all worship will center totally and exclusively on the Lord Almighty, the King of kings and Lord of lords.

CONCLUSION

Thus Zechariah brings his prophecy to a most elevated conclusion. The prophet whose name means "Yahweh remembers" proves that God had not forgotten His people. He would conclude history as He had promised in His covenant. While many others may have forgotten Israel, her Lord had not; the Lord could not forget Israel any more than a nursing mother could abandon her child (Isa. 49:14–15). He had remembered, and now He was Israel's sole King, Lord, God, and Sovereign. He was—and remains—Lord of all!

NOTES

1. E.g., Gleason L. Archer, Jr., *A Survey of Old Testament Introduction* (Chicago: Moody, 1964), pp. 414–15.
2. As cited by J. Carl Laney, *Zechariah* (Chicago: Moody, 1984), p. 8. It is possible that Jeremiah's name got connected with this citation because in one list of the prophets, Jeremiah heads the whole group and thus Zechariah would come under that general designation.
3. For lists of these similarities, *see* C. H. H Wright, *Zechariah and His Prophecies* (London: Hodder and Stroughton, 1879), pp. xxxv-xlii, and E.B. Pusey, *The Minor Prophets: Zechariah* (1907), pp. 4–37.
4. George L. Robinson, "Zechariah," in *International Standard Bible Encyclopedia*, ed. James Orr (Grand Rapids: Eerdmans, 1952), V: 3137.
5. Paul Lamarche, *Zacharie IX-XIV, Structure Littéraire et Messianisme* (Paris: Gabalda, 1961), pp. 112–13. The chart for Lamarche's material is found in Joyce Baldwin, *Haggai, Zechariah, and Malachi: An Introduction and Commentary* (Downers Grove, Il.: Inter-Varsity Press, 1972), pp. 78–79.
6. Baldwin, *Haggai, Zechariah, and Malachi*, p. 80.
7. Robinson, "Zechariah," V: 3137.
8. Baldwin, *Haggai, Zechariah, and Malachi*, pp. 80, 93.
9. As cited by David Baron, *Commentary on Zechariah: His Visions and Prophecies* (Grand Rapids: Kregel Publications, 1988), pp. 46–47.
10. For this suggestion and the general line of argument, I am indebted to T.J. Finley, "'The Apple of His Eye,' (BāBAT ʾÊNÔ) in Zechariah II 12," *Vetus Testamentum* 38 (1988): 337–38.
11. M. Michelet, *The Life of Luther*, Based on Luther's Letters and *Table Talk*, 2nd ed., tr. W. Hazlitt, pp. 101–102.

12. These principles are a reworking of a similar list proposed by Peter C. Craigie, *Twelve Prophets* (Philadelphia: Westminster, 1985), II: 178–79.

13. *See* Robert North, "Zechariah's Seven-Spout Lampstand," *Biblica* 51 (1970): 183–206. For a picture of a lamp on a pedestal with seven pinches for the seven wicks, see North's plate facing page 192.

14. G. Campbell Morgan, *The Divine Worker*, pp. 53–54, as cited by Elizabeth Achtemeier, *Nahum–Malachi*, Interpretation: A Bible Commentary for Teaching and Preaching (Atlanta: Knox, 1986), p. 125.

15. Craigie, *Twelve Prophets*, II:180.

16. George Bush, *Notes, Critical and Practical, on the Book of Leviticus* (New York: Newman and Ivison, 1852), p. 183. Emphasis in the original.

17. For these concepts of an airplane and automatic pilot, *see* Craigie, *Twelve Prophets*, II: 181.

18. Baldwin, *Haggai, Zechariah, and Malachi*, p. 128, n. 1, says that the capacity of this container was between 4 gallons 6 3/4 pints and 5 1/2 gallons. These are only estimates based on incomplete remains of two such measures, however, and the margin of variation is between 4.6 and 10.25 gallons.

19. Walter C. Kaiser, Jr., *Toward an Old Testament Theology* (Grand Rapids: Zondervan, 1978), p. 254.

20. Ralph L. Smith states that 7:7–10 contains "one of the finest summaries of the teachings of the former prophets," *Micah–Malachi* (Waco, Texas: Word, 1984), p. 225.

21. J. Phillip Hyatt, "A Neo-Babylonian Parallel to BETHEL-ŠAR-EZER, Zech 7,2," *Journal of Biblical Literature* 56 (1937): 387–94, as cited by J. Carl Laney, *Zechariah* (Chicago: Moody, 1984), p. 79, n.1.

22. David J. Clark, "Discourse Structure in Zechariah 7:1–8:23," *Bible Translator* 36 (1985): 328–35.

23. Achtemeier, *Nahum–Malachi*, p. 137. Even though Professor Achtemeier probably meant this in a different way than we are taking it here, it may be a case where an author writes better than she knows.

24. Lamarche, *Zacharie IX-XIV*, p. 42, as cited by Baldwin, *Haggai, Zechariah, and Malachi*, p. 158.

25. *See* Paul D. Hanson, "Zechariah 9 and the Recapitulation of an Ancient Ritual Pattern," *Journal of Biblical Literature* 92 (1973): 37–59, as cited by Laney, *Zechariah*, p. 94, n. 2.

26. P. A. H. de Boer, *An Inquiry Into the Meaning of the Term Massa'* (Leiden: Brill, 1948), p. 214. *See also* Walter C. Kaiser, Jr., "*Massaʾ*," in *Theological Wordbook of the Old Testament*, ed. R. Laird Harris, Gleason L. Archer, Jr., and Bruce K. Waltke, 2 vols. (Chicago: Moody, 1980), II: 602.

27. James B. Pritchard, *Ancient Near Eastern Texts: Relating to the Old Testament* (Princeton: Princeton Press 1955), pp. 282–83. ed. hereafter, *ANET*.

28. Baldwin, *Haggai, Zechariah, and Malachi*, p. 166, notes that *ANET*, p.

482, n. 6, attests the phrase "ass's colt" at Mari, where it means a "purebred."

29. Shalom M. Paul, "A Technical Expression From Archery in Zechariah IX 13a," *Vetus Testamentum* 39 (1989): 495–96.

30. The NEB omits the words of verse 13c-e and the JB brackets them.

31. David Baron, *Rays of Messiah's Glory: Christ in the Old Testament* (Grand Rapids: Zondervan, n.d.), pp. 151–78.

32. Dean Alford, as cited by David Baron, *Commentary on Zechariah: His Visions and Prophecies* (Grand Rapids: Kregel, 1988 [reprint of 1918 edition]), p. 437.

33. For more details on this text, *see* Walter C. Kaiser, Jr., *Toward Rediscovering the Old Testament* (Grand Rapids: Zondervan, 1987), pp. 109–111. The use of the first person pronoun to refer to the Messiah is noted in Merrill J. Unger, *Zechariah* (Grand Rapids: Zondervan, 1963), p. 217.

SECTION SEVEN:

The Book of Malachi

Malachi 1:1–4:6

Introduction to Malachi

The book of Malachi is often pushed to the back eddies of scholarly thought and contemporary preaching because of the low opinion held by all too many commentators of its style and subject matter. Part of this prejudice is due, as Beth Glazier-McDonald[1] notes, to the fact that scholars have a prejudice against "the relative significance of the reestablished temple cult and the realigned priestly hierarchy." But as Glazier-McDonald most adequately answers, "What scholars have failed to realize is that the central issue both for Malachi and for the 'classical' prophets, was the honor of Yahweh."[2] Added to this theme of Yahweh's honor in Malachi are the correlary themes of the greatness of the name of God (1:5, 11, 14; 2:2) and the unchanging love of God (1:2; 3:6).

THE AUTHOR

The prophet Malachi was the last of the Old Testament prophets. His name means "my messenger," or "my angel," but this may be an apocopated form of Malachiah, "messenger of Yahweh" (*see* 2:7) or "Yahweh is my messenger" (just as Abi, "my Father," in 2 Kings 18:2 appears as Abijah, "Yahweh is my Father," in 2 Chron. 29:1).

The Greek translation, the Septuagint, and most modern commentators do not view Malachi as the personal name of the writer of this book. Instead, they view it as an official name, or appellation—"by the hand of *his* angel," a title suggested by Malachi 3:1—and argue that the book is anonymous. To support their view, these commentators point to, among other things: (1) the absence of Malachi's father's name, (2) the absence of Malachi's place of birth, and (3) the fact that Zechariah 9:1 and 12:1; and Malachi 1:1 (the last three "burdens" in the Minor Prophets) share the same heading, marking them, presumably, as anonymous additions to the collection of what is commonly

431

called "The Twelve." But none of these points is persuasive. While Malachi's father's name is not given, neither is Obadiah's. Nor is any place of birth given for several of the prophets, including Habakkuk. Further, the three "burdens" cannot be considered apart from the other Minor Prophets because Zechariah 9:1–14:21 is an integral part of the book of Zechariah, as discussed above. Moreover, to take the view that Malachi is an official name one must change the pronoun "my" ("my messenger") to "his" ("his angel"), a change for which there is no Hebrew evidence. Therefore, it is best to treat Malachi as a personal name.

Further evidence argues against Malachi's being an official name rather than the personal name of the prophet. In the Jewish tradition, the person of Malachi was remembered along with Haggai and Zechariah as one of the men of the great synagogue. The Targum of Jonathan, Jerome, and Rabbi Rashi (1040–1105) all understood Malachi as a title for Ezra the Scribe, a view that Calvin preferred.[3] Pseudo Epiphanius and other church fathers[4] took the view that Malachi was a personal name and linked Malachi with the town of Sopha, or Sophira, in Zubulun, calling him a Levite. How trustworthy this information is cannot be evaluated from this distance in time. The most that can be said at the present is that no valid arguments can be made against the view that Malachi is a personal name and that his work is not anonymous.

THE DATE OF MALACHI

Almost all commentators agree that the book of Malachi was written sometime in the post-exilic age after Haggai and Zechariah began to prophesy (520 B.C.), since Malachi 1:6–14 and 3:10 assume that the temple worship has been restored. Furthermore, since Ben-Sira (Ecclesiasticus) 48:10 (a work dated c. 180 B.C.) quotes Malachi 4:6, Malachi could not have been written in the Maccabean era (168–143 B.C.). Indeed, the fact that Ecclesiasticus 48:10 makes reference to Malachi demonstrates that the book of the twelve Minor Prophets, including the prophecy of Malachi, was already recognized as being canonical by approximately 180 B.C.

The only historical reference in Malachi is to the destruction of Edom (1:3–5). Edom was first destroyed by Nebuchadnezzar in his 587 B.C. campaigns on Jerusalem and the surrounding nations. But it is more likely that the reference in Malachi is to the destruction carried out by the Nabatean Arabs, who totally drove out the Edomites between 550 and 400 B.C., thus replacing the Edomite Kingdom with their own Idumean state.[5] (Unfortunately, we do not have a more precise date for this second destruction of Edom.)

There is little doubt that the book of Malachi is to be dated close to the book of Nehemiah, for both share too many concerns not to have come out of the same general time period. These shared concerns include:

1. Marriage of heathen wives
   (Mal. 2:11–15 and Neh. 13:23–27)
2. Neglect in paying tithes
   (Mal. 3:8–10 and Neh. 13:10–14)
3. Disregard of the Sabbath
   (Mal. 2:8–9; 4:4 and Neh. 13:15–22)
4. Corruption of the priesthood
   (Mal. 1:6–2:9 and Neh. 13:7–9)
5. Existence of social wrongs
   (Mal. 3:5 and Neh. 5:1–13)

Further, since Malachi predicates several of his arguments on the existence and knowledge of the Law of Moses (e.g., 4:4), his book must be dated after Ezra arrived in Judah (458 B.C.), for it was Ezra who restored the knowledge and authority of the Law of God (Ezra 7:14, 25, 26). Moreover, since prior to Ezra's arrival the costs of worshipping God were paid out of the royal revenues of Persia (Ezra 7:15–17, 20–24), the abuses found in Malachi 1:6–9 could only have sprung up after Ezra's arrival (6:9–10).

With these guidelines in mind, the date for Malachi could fall within any of several periods very nicely: (1) the period of Nehemiah's absence from Jerusalem, (2) the period of Nehemiah's second visit to and governorship of Jerusalem, or (3) the period after Nehemiah's second term of office. We prefer to consider Malachi a forerunner to Nehemiah, one who paved the way for the extensive reforms initiated by Nehemiah after he returned to Jerusalem the second time, sometime after 433 B.C. Dating the book of Malachi within this period is also suggested by the extensive parallels between the book and Nehemiah 13.

Malachi's use of the term "governor" in Malachi 1:8 may help to date the book within the interval between Ezra's arrival in 458 B.C.

and Nehemiah's arrival in 445 B.C. Nehemiah 5:14 makes clear that there were "governors" prior to Nehemiah, and this is confirmed by the Elephantine Papyri. No doubt, the Persians took over the term "governor" (*pehah*), which was used under the Babylonian domination (Jer. 51:28, 57; Ezk. 23:6), even though the Persian's normal title was *tiršâtâh* (Neh 10; 2; however, *see* Esther 3:12 and Neh. 5:14). Further, many believe that had Malachi intended to refer to Nehemiah here he would have identified him by name just as Haggai identified Zerubbabel by name. Accordingly, the weight of these arguments is to place the book somewhere between 458 and 445 B.C.

THE DIVISIONS OF MALACHI

There is wide agreement that Malachi's prophecy falls into six clearly marked sections that follow the form of a running dialogue.[6] The six sections are:

1. 1:1–5   Introduction. God proves His love for Israel by contrasting it to His treatment of Edom.
2. 1:6–2:9   God rebukes the priesthood for their perversion of the ordinances and Law of God.
3. 2:10–16   God rebukes the people for perverting God's ordinance of marriage by marrying unbelieving partners and by divorcing their wives.
4. 2:17–3:6   God announces His messenger who will prepare the way for His Messiah as His answer to the people's search for God's justice.
5. 3:7–12   God rebukes the people for withholding the tithes and offerings owed to God.
6. 3:13–4:6   God predicts the destinies of the wicked and of the righteous.

THE STYLE OF MALACHI

Malachi is a gem of clarity, simplicity, and directness. In forty-seven of its fifty-five verses, the Lord addresses Israel using the first-person address.

It is generally conceded that Malachi uses a prose format. Malachi's skillful use of questions is reminiscent of Habakkuk's technique some 200 years earlier. The repetition of words and figures of speech—"says the LORD" appears twenty times in fifty-five verses, for example—further contributes to the strong style in this book. The most distinctive trait of Malachi's prose is his use of the disputational method to introduce each of the six sections; in fact, his entire message is punctuated with questions from both his audience and his Lord (1:2, 6, 7, 8, 9, 13; 2:10, 14, 15, 17; 3:2, 7, 8, 13).

Some commentators have made disparaging remarks about the literary skills of Malachi, particularly as compared to Isaiah or Amos. But their opinions are just that, and the standard by which they have judged Malachi is seldom disclosed or defended.

Typically, after introducing a declaration from God, Malachi records the audience's rebuttal or protestations with the words, "yet you say" (1:2, 6, 7, 13; 2:14, 17; 3:7, 8, 13). Even though the other prophets engaged in exchanges with their audiences (e.g., Isa. 40:27, 28; Jer. 2:23–25, 29–34, 35–36; 8:8–9; Ezk. 12:21–28; Hag. 1:2), Malachi is the master of this technique.[7] With consummate skill he fields each of the audience's protestations. How pathetic are these protestations! They reflect an artificial piety and gross misunderstanding of the program and message of God. Nevertheless, Malachi will not be sidetracked from his master theme: God loves His people, however hypocritical and insincere they remain.

Finally, one is struck in this book by another supporting theme— the majesty of God. He is, indeed, Master, Lord, and King. Add to this theme of God's majesty the greatness of the name of God (1:5, 11, 14; 2:2), the success of His coming Messiah, and the day of the Lord standing sure despite the people's lack of respect, and the profundity of the theology found in this book increases. A believing remnant nevertheless remains; they still "fear the LORD" (another theme of the book repeated in 1:6, 11, 14; 2:5; 3:5, 16; 4:2, 5). However, the two pivotal statements in the book are: "I have loved you" (1:2) and "For I am the LORD, I do not change" (3:6). Malachi, then, is the book about the unchanging love of God.

An Outline of Malachi

I. A Call to Respond to God's Love   1:1–5
  A. Our God's Election-Love   1:1–3a
  B. Our God's Justice-Love   1:3b–4
  C. Our God's Universal-Love   1:5
  D. Conclusion

II. A Call to Be Authentic   1:6–14
  A. In Our Profession   1:6–7
  B. In Our Gifts   1:8–9
  C. In Our Service   1:10–12
  D. In Our Time   1:13–14
  E. Conclusion

III. A Call to Love God Totally   2:1–9
  A. Love for God's Glory   2:1–3
  B. Love for God's Word   2:4–9
  C. Conclusion

IV. A Call to Be Faithful   2:10–16
  A. We Must Be Loyal to the God of the Covenant   2:10
  B. We Must Be Loyal to the People of God   2:11–12
  C. We Must Be Loyal to the Partner of Our Marriage   2:13–16
  D. Conclusion

V. A Call to Trust an Unchanging God   2:17–3:12
  A. Our God is Just   2:17–3:6
  B. Our God is Faithful   3:7–12
  C. Conclusion

VI. A Call to Take Inventory   3:13–4:6
  A. Is It Vain to Serve the Lord?   3:13–18
  B. Is There No Difference Between the Righteous and the Wicked?   4:1–3
  C. Are There No Guides for the Righteous?   4:4–6
  D. Conclusion

436

CHAPTER ONE

A Call to Respond to God's Love

Malachi 1:1–5

1:1 The burden of the word of the LORD to Israel by
     Malachi.
   2 "I have loved you," says the LORD.
     "Yet you say, 'In what way have You loved us?'
     Was not Esau Jacob's brother?"
     Says the LORD.
     "Yet Jacob I have loved;
   3 But Esau I have hated,
     And laid waste his mountains and his heritage
     For the jackals of the wilderness."
   4 Even though Edom has said,
     "We have been impoverished,
     But we will return and build
         the desolate places,"
     Thus says the LORD of hosts:
     "They may build, but I will throw down;
     They shall be called the Territory of Wickedness,
     And the people against whom the LORD will
         have indignation forever.
   5 Your eyes shall see,
     And you shall say,
     'The LORD is magnified beyond the border of
         Israel.'

Malachi 1:1–5

The theme of Malachi's first message, and of the whole book, is: "*I have loved you, says the LORD*" (v. 1). Like a banner over a Bible Conference, this theme of God's love hangs over every message the prophet delivers. His banner over us is love!

The Hebrew verb "to love" (*ʾāhab*) is used thirty-two times in the Old Testament to describe God's love, twenty-three of which describe God's love of Israel or particular individuals. The noun form of the word, meaning God's love of His people, occurs four times in the Old Testament, making a total of twenty-seven times that God's love for humans is affirmed.

Norman Snaith notes three main characteristics that help us understand God's love. First, God's love is a sovereign love. As lord over all, God is not required to do anything except that which is directed by His own character and being. Love proceeds from His own character and being; thus no definition of God's love can be separated from what He is and does.

The second characteristic of God's love is that it is unconditional. Further, the motivation for God loving us comes entirely from God and is not derived from anything we or Israel are or pretend to be (Deut. 7:7–8).

The third characteristic of God's love is that it is intimately personal. In spite of the fact that our Lord is the one to whom the heavens and earth belong, He has decided to set His love and affection on human beings (Deut. 10:14–15). It is the love of a father taking his infant son by the arms and teaching him how to walk (Hos. 11:4).[8]

One more characteristic can be added to these three. God's love is like the love that exists between a husband and a wife. This is the fourth of four analogies of God's love proposed by C. S. Lewis, and the one that comes closest to Malachi's depiction of what God's love for us is like. In his fourth analogy of God's love, C. S. Lewis compared God's love to "the love between a husband and a wife, wherein each is willing to forgive the most (because that love is willing to love beyond any faults) while condoning the least in the other partner (because that love, while continuing to forgive, nevertheless never ceases to coax, urge, wish and hope for the best in the other partner).[9] In the same way, God continually offers us pardon and acceptance while maintaining the high and holy standards of His righteousness. It is precisely in this tension between forgiving the most and condoning the least that we can understand the uniqueness of God's love. It is this tension that also explains how God can call for justice to be meted out in judgment while at the same time declaring, *"I have loved you."*

This raises the question of how to reconcile the anger of God (*ira dei*) with the love of God. In the history of the Church, this became the question of divine passibility (i.e., whether God was capable of having feelings or emotions) or divine impassibility (i.e., whether God was without the capacity to feel, suffer, or be angry).

Gnosticism took a strong lead in the discussion of this question by denying that God could ever experience anger or other feelings, or suffer at all. A second century heretic named Marcion declared that God was totally free of all affections or feelings—Marcion's god was totally apathetic.

The church father Lactantius (last half of the third century) put the question in a more biblical perspective: "He who loves the good also hates the evil, and he who does not hate the evil does not love the good because, on the one hand, to love the good comes from hatred of evil and to hate the evil rises from the love of the good."[10]

Our difficulty in accepting that anger is part of the character of God is related to our improper association of anger with "the desire for retaliation," or the desire to "get even." Anger, properly defined, however, is the legitimate emotion of a person rising up to resist evil. Anger need not be unchecked or uncontrolled. God's anger is certainly never explosive, unchecked or uncontrolled. In fact, in comparison to His love, His anger passes quickly (Isa. 26:20; 54:7–8; 57:16–19) while His love endures (Jer. 31:3; Hos. 2:19).

Malachi announces three evidences of God's love that constitute in and of themselves sufficient reasons for Israel, and all who love our Lord but have gone astray, to return to Him. These three evidences are:

A. Our God's Election-Love   1:1–3a
B. Our God's Justice-Love   1:3b–4
C. Our God's Universal-Love   1:5

OUR GOD'S ELECTION-LOVE (1:1–3A)

The message of God's love for His people is introduced as *"The burden of the word of the LORD to Israel by Malachi"* (v. 1). While most commentators and modern translations insist on translating "burden" (*maśśāʾ*) as "oracle" or "declaration," there are at least three reasons why "burden" is a superior rendering: (1) The word appears twenty-seven times in the Old Testament, all in prophetic texts of threatened judgment, except Proverbs 30:1; 31:1; (2) The word is never followed by the genitive of the speaker, such as *neʾum* of

Yahweh ("the utterance of the LORD"), but is always connected with a genitive of an object such as the *maśśā'* of Babylon, or Moab, etc. The only exception is where an additional item intervenes, such as "the word of the LORD" (Mal. 1:1; Zech. 9:1); and (3) There is no evidence of a root meaning "to utter" from which *maśśā'* could have come that would also yield the meaning "oracle" or "declaration."[11]

Accordingly, though the prophecy will exalt the love God has for His people, it opens on a threatening note. In spite of God's love for His people, He is going to come to judge the world (cf. Zech. 9:1 and 12:1). The heavy note of judgment was meant to stir up men and women to prepare for that day.

This ominous note was directed towards *"Israel"* (v. 1). During the division of the kingdom from 931 to 722 B.C., the term "Israel" was used to designate the northern ten tribes, but it refers here to the whole Jewish community.

God's Word came by the hand of Malachi. While the Hebrew word for Malachi appears in Malachi 3:1 meaning *"My messenger,"* in Malachi 1:1 it is probably a proper name (contrary to the Septuagint Greek translation and the Jewish Targumim; *see* our discussion of this point in the Introduction (in the section *The Author*).

In verse 2 God says, *"I have loved you"* using in Hebrew a perfect tense of the verb, denoting completed action and making it clear that God had previously announced His love for Israel as the only reason for choosing her (Deut. 7:7; 10:18; Hos. 11:1) and that He continued to love Israel even in her present apostasy. The prophet appeals to God's long-abiding love for Israel in order to raise the sights of the recently returned exiles who had begun to wonder whether God still loved them.

The people's incredible response is *"In what way have You loved us?"* (v. 2). So insensitive were they to God's magnanimous declaration of love, and so hardened had they become through their own sinfulness, that they brashly demanded that God condescend to prove what He so generously claimed.

Amazingly, God condescends to answer their impudent question, thus further illustrating His patient love. God answers the people by reminding them of the election-love He gave to Jacob vis-á-vis His "hatred" of Esau.

But God's answer raises a significant question for modern readers: Does Yahweh "hate?" Yes; we can point in the Bible to some clear objects of God's hatred: hypocritical worship (Isa. 1:14; Amos 5:21) and evils such as pride, lying, evil imaginations, evil deeds, false witnessing, and stirring up dissension among the brethren (Prov. 6:16–19). Further, at the grave of Lazarus, our Lord was angry over the death of His friend (John 11:33, 38). Thus, hate and anger can be proper emotions for disavowing wrong and evil and for differentiating between them and their opposite—love. Only those who have truly loved can understand how it is possible to hate with a burning anger all that is wrong and evil.

However, there is a specialized biblical use of the antonymic pair "to love" and "to hate." A close parallel can be seen in Jacob's response to his two wives Rachel and Leah in Genesis 29:30–33 and Moses' illustration of the two wives in Deuteronomy 21:15–17. The "hated" wife in both these illustrations is the *less-loved* one. This same relationship between love and hate is seen in the Semitism (Hebraic idiom) found in the Greek use of "love" and "hate" in Matthew 6:24 and Luke 16:13. "To love" is, in effect, to *prefer* and to be faithful to one, while "to hate" is *to slight and to think less* of another. Likewise, in Matthew 10:37 Jesus says, "He who loves father or mother *more than Me*," and in the parallel verse in Luke, Jesus says, "If anyone comes to Me and does not hate his father and mother" (14:26).[12]

These illustrations make clear that the Bible does not call for psychological or absolute hatred; rather, it calls for ranking, preferring, or setting priorities. In Jacob's case, God's love signaled his election and call for service. In Esau's case, God's hatred was not a sign of God's disdain, disgust, or desire for unmitigated revenge. Esau too was an object of God's preached word (note the call in Obadiah to the Edomites, descendants of Esau). Esau's descendants would be objects of God's deliverance in the end times (Obad. 19, 21; Amos 9:12). In fact, the act of God's "love" and "hate" (as manifested in His choosing or not choosing people for certain tasks) took place apart from anything the people did or became (God's choice of Jacob, for example, took place before Jacob was born [Gen. 25:23; Rom. 9:11]) and apart from their merits or demerits. His election-love of the one son and His decision not to choose the other for a particular work in His plan was only the sovereign, unconditional, intimately personal, and discriminating love of God (*see* the introduction to this chapter for a discussion of God's emotions and four characteristics of His love for us).

OUR GOD'S JUSTICE-LOVE (1:3B–4)

There was more in Malachi 1:1–5 than just the electing love of God. True, God's election-love had sustained wicked Israel when she deserved to be reduced to rubble. As Malachi says in 3:6, "For I am the LORD, I do not change; therefore you are not consumed, O sons of Jacob."

In contrast, Edom (the nation that descended from Jacob's brother Esau), the subject of God's justice-love, had been *"laid waste"* (v. 3b). It is impossible to say whether this verse refers to Edom's destruction at the hands of Nebuchadnezzar in 587 B.C. (Jer. 49:7–9; 25:9, 21) or, as is more likely, to Edom's destruction at the hands of the Nabateans sometime between 550 and 400 B.C. (1 Macc. 5:25; the Nabateans ransacked Edom, leaving only small pockets of Edomites in the Negev desert).

Edom, of course, could hardly have been surprised at her destruction. Though God had called Jacob, not Esau (Edom), for election-service, both nations were obliged to walk in righteousness before God. Yet Edom had been "immoral" and "godless," as both testaments testify (Gen. 25:32; 36:1–8; Heb. 12:16). God's love demanded that He punish Edom for her sin, for had He abandoned Edom, there would have been no reason to use His justice as a way of calling Edom back to Himself.

Edom exuded confidence in her ability to rebuild her ruins: *"We have been impoverished, but we will return and build the desolate places"* (v. 4). Without God's help, however, she would ultimately fail; Edom might attempt to rebuild, but the Lord would disassemble. The country would be known as *"the Territory of Wickedness."* Sin would leave its mark on both the people and the land. The quiet ruin of Petra (a city in Edom) stands as a mute testimony to the truthfulness of God's word.

God's love for the good meant He had to hate evil; therefore, He exercised His justice-love on Edom.

OUR GOD'S UNIVERSAL-LOVE (1:5)

Had insensitive Israel only looked beyond the provincialism of her own distress, she would have seen a sharp contrast between what happened to Edom and what happened to her. There was a world of difference—God's love had made the difference. But Israel would see the difference one day in the future and confess, *"The LORD is [or will be] magnified beyond the border of Israel."* Since Malachi praises God in verses 11 and 14 of this same chapter as the great king over all nations, he likely means here that God would be exalted in the future beyond the boundaries of the Israeli nation.

God's love exceeds all national, political, geographic, or cultural boundaries. Had not God promised Abraham that through his seed all the nations of the earth would be blessed? (Gen. 12:3). It was that word that Paul called the "good news" (Gal. 3:8).

God brought judgment on Edom and her people just as He had brought judgment on Pharoah and the Egyptians, so that the Edomites and all the world might know that the Lord is God.

The evidence of these two different types of God's love in this text of Malachi is clear. God may have focused His love on Israel, since all the world was to hear through her, but He did not limit His love within Israel's borders. God reached out even to Israel's enemies until tribes and nations far beyond Israel's borders had heard of His love.

CONCLUSION

God's election-love should never be confused with His justice-love or universal-love, His extension of that election-love to all humanity. Neither should those privileged to experience God's great gift of love take that love for granted or act as if it was owed to them. God's love is inscrutably great and is freely given as a gift from His gracious hand.

CHAPTER TWO

A Call to Be Authentic

Malachi 1:6–14

6 "A son honors his father,
And a servant his master.
If then I am the Father,
Where is My honor?
And if I am a Master,
Where is My reverence?
Says the LORD of hosts
To you priests who despise My name.
Yet you say, 'In what way have we despised
Your name?'

7 "You offer defiled food on My altar.
But you say,
'In what way have we defiled You?'
By saying,
'The table of the LORD is contemptible.'

8 And when you offer the blind as a sacrifice,
Is it not evil?
And when you offer the lame and sick,
Is it not evil?
Offer it then to your governor!
Would he be pleased with you?
Would he accept you favorably?"
Says the LORD of hosts.

9 "But now entreat God's favor,
That He may be gracious to us.
While this is being done by your hands,
Will He accept you favorably?"
Says the LORD of hosts.

10 "Who is there even among you who would
shut the doors,

So that you would not kindle fire on
    My altar in vain?
I have no pleasure in you,"
Says the LORD of hosts,
"Nor will I accept an offering from your hands.
11 For from the rising of the sun,
    even to its going down,
My name shall be great among the Gentiles;
In every place incense shall be offered
    to My name,
And a pure offering;
For My name shall be great among
    the nations,"
Says the LORD of hosts.
12 "But you profane it,
In that you say,
'The table of the LORD is defiled;
And its fruit, its food, is contemptible.'
13 You also say,
    'Oh, what a weariness!'
And you sneer at it,"
Says the LORD of hosts.
"And you bring the stolen, the lame,
    and the sick;
Thus you bring an offering!
Should I accept this from your hand?"
Says the LORD.
14 "But cursed be the deceiver
Who has in his flock a male,
And takes a vow,
But sacrifices to the Lord what is blemished—
For I am a great King,"
Says the LORD of hosts,
"And My name is to be feared among
    the nations.

Malachi 1:6–14

Not too long ago it was the fashion to distrust everything and everyone. All institutions, administrators, big businesses, and governments were suspected of being insincere and, generally, "phonies." The search for credible and authentic people was at its height during the sixties and seventies.

We might smile at some of the superciliousness of those searchers now that we are safely beyond those days, but that will not excuse us from heeding the divine call to an authenticity that exceeds the fashions, slogans, and eddies of our day. Not only might the Pentagon, the news media, and the huge institutions of our day lack credibility or authenticity; it may well be that we, too, are of doubtful credibility or authenticity. Malachi's chastisement of men of doubtful authenticity began with the clergy, for as the clergy went, so went the people.

Malachi took dead aim at the priests of his day (1:6) and delivered a stinging indictment of their careless, haphazard, and profane service to the Living God. He then enlarges the scope of his message to include all who worship God in a similarly unacceptable way, saying, *"But cursed be the deceiver who has in his flock a male, and takes a vow, but sacrifices to the Lord what is blemished"* (v. 14). Suddenly, in a context primarily addressed to priests or the clergy, the focus was extended to include any and all who were indulging in the same kind of practices.

The divine love announced in 1:2 was being stifled by the priests' indifferent, careless, and half-hearted spiritual leadership. Their attitude and practices influenced the people and invited a heap of curses from God rather than His blessing.

In the dramatic, conversational style of this book, a protest of innocence is heard from the audience. With a feigned naiveté already seen in 1:2, the audience is depicted as responding to the prophet's charges with the questions: "Who? Us? We did that? We are guilty of that? When did we do that?" Seven times in the small scope of this prophecy that question will occur (1:2,6,7; 2:17; 3:7, 8, 13).

The analysis of the pericope of 1:6–14 utilizes these forms:

> vv. 6–7 an introductory divine proverb
> > a question based on the proverb
> > an innocent protestation as a response
> > a divine answer
>
> vv. 8–9 a probing question from God
> > an ironical suggestion
> > a follow-up question
> > an exposé and reason for clerical ineffectiveness
>
> vv. 10–12 a divine challenge
> > a divine estimation of worship
> > [an evangelical interruption-v. 11]

a divine rebuke
vv. 13–14 a report of a popular conclusion
a report of the sad state of affairs
a divine question filled with reproof
a declaration of the greatness of God

There are four areas in which God calls the priests of that day, and all believers everywhere, to be credible and authentic before the Living God:

A. In Our Profession   1:6–7
B. In Our Gifts   1:8–9
C. In Our Service   1:10–12
D. In Our Time   1:13–14

IN OUR PROFESSION (1:6–7)

While the priests are addressed directly twice (1:6; 2:1), the prophet's indictments carry over to the whole nation in 1:13, 14. Of course, the spiritual leaders were the occasion for causing others to stumble (2:8), and so it happened that "like priests, like people" as well as the reverse of this aphorism, (Hos. 4:9) became more than a proverb.

Malachi begins with another proverb: "*A son honors his father, and a servant his master*" (v. 6a). God had chosen Israel as His "son" (Exod. 4:22; Hos. 11:1; Jer. 31:9) and His "servant" (especially in the shared role of the "Servant of the LORD" in Isaiah 41:8 and following). Unfortunately, the priests' lives apparently did not bear witness to this proverb, for God wanted to know, "*If then I am the Father, where is My honor? And if I am a Master, where is My reverence?*" (v. 6bc). In other words, the priests were giving a lot of lip-service to worshipping God; but their lives did not support their words. It is one thing to say that God is our Lord and Father, but it is another to demonstrate it in our lives. How hypocritical and embarrassing for believers, much less their leaders, to act like this!

The priests' outright refusal to live up to what they claimed was tantamount to treason. They verbally affirmed that God was Lord, but submitted in no area over which He had rightful authority. In effect, they "*despised [God's] name*" (v. 6e).

Never at a loss for words, the priests turned the charge back against God and His prophet, asking, in effect, "How's that? What have we ever done that would lead you to think that we have despised your name?" One can almost see them standing in front of Malachi responding in unison as if it was rehearsed.

Every time I read these responses, I cannot help thinking of an experience I had many years ago. My new bride and I had just moved into a rather large home in a college community as house-parents for thirteen freshmen from the Christian college where I had just begun my teaching career as a junior faculty member in the Bible department. About two o'clock in the morning, I was awakened out of a sound sleep by "such a clatter I sprang to my feet to see what was the matter." Half asleep, but filled with resolve, I trudged out of our bedroom and proceeded up the stairs, wearily pulling myself up each stair on all four limbs. I entered the upstairs hallway just in time to arrive on what appeared to be the final moments of one grand water balloon fight.

In my initial horror, I blurted out, "Gentlemen, who did this?" The question was rhetorical, but the men quickly seized the initiative: "Yes," they responded in mock earnestness, "Who did this?" "Did you?" "Did you?" "Did you?" Knowing that Christians should not lie, they decided to help me ask questions, thereby possibly avoiding admission of what was all too obvious. No one owned up to the deed. I will never forget my deep frustration as I faced those thirteen men who pretended to be just as indignant as I over the results of the damage from some strange event that, for the moment, they could not remember having seen or participated in.

That must have been somewhat how the Lord and Malachi felt when they asked these priests to own up to their deeds. The tack the priests took was to ask repeatedly: "In what way have we" done thus and so. It is maddening, to say the least, to deal on these terms.

"In what way have we defiled You?" (v. 7). The priests were sure they had never done anything like that! But Malachi had a ready illustration. The priests had defiled God when they had said, *"The table of the* LORD *is contemptible"* (v. 7c). They had defiled and belittled God's great name by placing *"defiled food on [His] altar"* (v. 7). The pollution was twofold: (1) polluted men and women cannot offer pure sacrifices to God while they simultaneously reject His lordship and fail to glorify Him; and (2) our gifts are polluted when we offer to God something that is not the best. In doing either we defile *"You,"* i.e, God's person.

Our Lord always inspects the offerer before He inspects the gift. He looks at our hearts first, then He listens to our message or our solo, then He looks at our offering (e.g., Gen. 4:3–4, where God inspected Cain and Abel before He inspected their offerings). If it would not be impossible for the ushers, the Church's motto ought to be, "Put yourself in the offering plate first and then deposit your offering for God." We are teasing, of course; but the level of priorities is correct. Polluted offerers defile the very profession they make with their lips. Their actions belie every high-sounding profession of God's fatherhood and lordship and make the very altar, name, and person of our Lord as despicable and abominable as Antiochus Epiphanes did when he desecrated the altar of God by offering a sow on it in 165 B.C.

IN OUR GIFTS (1:8–9)

"And when you offer the blind as a sacrifice, is it not evil?" (v. 8). Sacrifices, or gifts, offered to our Lord were to be unblemished and whole. In fact, the gifts were judged by what they cost the offerer.

What evidence of inauthenticity is a gift of the blind, the lame, and the sick (v. 8)! With biting irony, Malachi suggests that his people try offering that to their governor or ruler. *"Would he be pleased with you? Would he accept you favorably?"* (v. 8). Chances are that few would have the audacity to demean their leaders in such a way. Therefore, why would they offer such a gift to God? Had not God instructed that sacrificed animals were to be free of any blemish and healthy in every particular? (Exod. 12:5; 29:1; Lev. 1:3, 10; 22:18–25; Num. 6:14; 19:2; Deut. 15:21; 17:1; Ezk. 45:23). To violate such clear instructions not only showed the slight regard the offerer had for his act of giving, but also reflected the offerer's willingness to disobey the commandments of God. His offer was a form of open contempt; it was valueless and, indeed, blasphemous!

Further, the priests, God's delegated ministers, had indulged their people by accepting any kind of sacrifice, even one they knew violated God's instructions.

In verse 9 Malachi relates that the same priests who had so violated God's commands and taught others to do so would *"entreat God's favor."* In this context, the Hebrew word rendered here as "entreat" literally means "to make smooth" or, as we say in the vernacular, "to butter up" someone. Would God be disposed to listen to requests and prayers from these priests?

Of course there is a great deal of authentic sacrificial giving in the body of Christ, but there remains an enormous amount of sacrilegious giving in which men and women give what is left over, what can be spared, what costs little or nothing. This God hates.

Did not our Lord praise the woman in Luke 21:3 who "put in more than all." If you ask, When does a few pence outweigh all the coins from the long stream of givers lined up in the temple treasury? the answer is: when the gift is preceded by the giving of one's self and when it costs something to give.

In Our Service (1:10–12)

God calls us to be authentic in a third area, our service for Him.

So outrageous had the sacrifices been that Malachi now makes an unexpected suggestion: lock the doors of the temple court and block all access to the altar of God (v. 10)! Surely, no worship at all would be preferable to the worthless worship that was taking place. Such a scandalous move of blocking access to God's altar would shock many who would not otherwise be moved.

Malachi made another suggestion along the same lines: do not light the fire on the altar, for it is *"in vain"* (v. 10). The Hebrew word for "in vain" occurs thirty–two times in the Old Testament and generally means "for no reason, without a cause." Thus, while the altar fires and sacrifices were to symbolize the openness of fellowship between God and man, in actuality they were meaningless. Their religion had become vapid, perfunctory, and purposeless. Their gifts and services, based as they were on vacuous activity, were futile and destined only to lull them into a state of false security.

At this point, Malachi (and perhaps the reader) has had enough of this negativism. Despite human failure, God would not be without authentic worship. No wonder, then, that verse 11 explodes with good news. While we may fail in our practice of religion, do not think for one moment that God is going to fail us. *"'For from the rising of the sun, even to its going down, My name shall be great among the Gentiles; in every place incense shall be offered to My name, and a pure offering; for My name shall be great among the nations,' says the* LORD *of hosts."*

The geographic, political, and ethnic scope of this promise is mind-boggling! God's reign would extend from east to west (cf. four other times in the Old Testament where we see similar terminology: Pss. 50:1; 113:3; Isa. 45:6; 59:19). And sacrifices would no longer be offered just at Jerusalem, but in "every place." (What must Malachi's audience have thought about that?) Moreover, the name of God would be "great" among the Gentiles and the nations of the earth. That had been implied in Malachi 1:5, but now it was declared openly.

Israel had been called to be "a kingdom of priests" (Exod. 19:5–6) and a "light to the nations" (Isa. 42:6; 49:6). She had been told that in her seed all the nations of the earth would be blessed (Gen. 12:3) and that it had been God's purpose to bless "all the ends of the earth" (Ps. 67:7) exactly as was stated in the Aaronic benediction (Num. 6:24–26). So in one way, Malachi's audience should not have been surprised by the announcement in verse 11; but in another, given Israel's poor record at being the nations' beacon, they must have been totally overwhelmed by this announcement! Why, even the offerings, offered in every place, would be "pure." It was nothing short of amazing!

As the prophet returns to his main theme he contrasts this marvelous vision of God's triumph over the nations and their pure worship of His name with *"But you profane it"* (v. 12). The local service of God, as Malachi knew it, was impure and given reluctantly following many excuses. People don't go for sacrifices and that type of thing anymore, Malachi hears the people whine. "We find in these changing times that the altar, its fruit and its meat are *'contemptible'*" (v. 12), they complain.

What a pity. The priests and people had retained the traditional form of worship, but they denied the power of God. In situations such as these, God is able to raise up another people to replace those who have grown bored with and perfunctory in their service to Him. After all, God is a great King: service to Him should be a joy and an honor.

In Our Time (1:13–14)

"You also say, 'Oh, what a weariness!'" (v. 13).

Boredom had to be the outcome of the people's hypocritical ministry and worship of God. Bored, the people no doubt came to view their ministry and worship as tedious and empty and began to begrudge the very time they spent in the service and worship of God.

The people's boredom is evident in three areas: (1) their words, (2) their spirit and attitude, and (3) their deeds.

Their words were blunt: "Oh, what a weariness!" All worship and service of the Living God had become a drudgery and a burden. Religious services, the people's words imply, were a bore and a nuisance. Nothing was to be gained from them anymore.

Haughtily, the people sneered at the sacrifices. Their words of contempt knew no bounds. Their acts of sacrifice were similarly offensive; they brought whatever was stolen, lame, and sick. The question was this: Was God obliged to countenance this type of snobbery and to accept this kind of offensive activity? What could be more convincing evidence of spiritual deadness?

Even more disturbing were the people who vowed to God that they would give an unblemished male, but gave instead *"what is blemished"* (v. 14). Why did they engage in such deceit, especially since the offering was voluntary? Did they think they could fool God?

For the third time in this chapter, Malachi announces that God is *"a great King"* (cf. 1 Sam. 12:12; Ps. 10:16; 24:8; 84:3; 95:3; Isa. 33:22; 43:15; 44:6; Jer. 8:19; 10:10; Zeph. 3:15). His *"name is to be feared among the nations"* (v. 14). The people's fearless treatment of God falls far short of recognizing that He is a great King.

CONCLUSION

In the present age, clergy by the scores have concluded that the Church and its ministry are tiresome. Though their own hearts condemn them, some, for unknown reasons, remain in the ministry.

The problem is just as acute in the pew. Members of a church will sit through three–to four–hour operas, lengthy symphonies, or marathon sporting events and rejoice both in the event's length and in its substance. But put those same people in the house of God for just one hour and they fidget; they complain, too, if the Word of God is still being expounded upon for more than the anticipated half–hour.

Shall we continue to reward professional singers and musicians at a rate that is easily many times what we pay those who preach the Word of God? What does this say about our values? Is not this another way of demonstrating our dissatisfaction with God's Word, His service, and our offering to Him?

It is not that God is no longer credible; no, it is we who have lost our credibility. We must become more authentic in the profession of our lips, in the use of our gifts, in the investment of our service, and in the use of our time.

In order to claim to be "sons" and "daughters" of God, we need to do more than profess that God is our Lord, our Master and our Father; we must respond to God's Word by doing what God says. And how can we respond to God's Word if we do not read and listen to that Word? Rejecting God's Word is another form of rejecting His Lordship.

CHAPTER THREE

A Call to Love God Totally

Malachi 2:1–9

2:1 "And now, O priests, this commandment is for
you.

2 If you will not hear,
And if you will not take it to heart,
To give glory to My name,"
Says the LORD of hosts,
"I will send a curse upon you,
And I will curse your blessings.
Yes, I have cursed them already,
Because you do not take it to heart.

3 "Behold, I will rebuke your descendants
And spread refuse on your faces,
The refuse of your solemn feasts;
And one will take you away with it.

4 Then you shall know that I have sent this
commandment to you,
That My covenant with Levi may continue,"
Says the LORD of hosts.

5 "My covenant was with him, one of life and peace,
And I gave them to him that he might fear Me;
So he feared Me
And was reverent before My name.

6 The law of truth was in his mouth,
And injustice was not found on his lips.
He walked with Me in peace and equity,
And turned many away from iniquity.

7 "For the lips of a priest should keep knowledge,
And people should seek the law from his mouth;
For he is the messenger of the LORD of hosts.

8 But you have departed from the way;
  You have caused many to stumble at the law.
  You have corrupted the covenant of Levi,"
  Says the LORD of hosts.
9 "Therefore I also have made you contemptible
    and base
  Before all the people,
  Because you have not kept My ways
  But have shown partiality in the law."

Malachi 2:1–9

In 1:13–14 Malachi had temporarily addressed his challenge to the people, but in 2:1–9 his attention is again on the priests.[13]

Rather than focusing on the priests' motives and attitudes, as he did in 1:6–14, Malachi concerns himself in this text with the glory of God and the Word of God. Anything less than a wholehearted response to the honor, reputation, and status of the Living God and the truth taught in His Word was a type of moral pollution.

In this text Malachi commands the priests to center their thoughts and actions around two things:

A. Love for God's Glory   2:1–3
B. Love for God's Word   2:4–9

LOVE FOR GOD'S GLORY (2:1–3)

Malachi's message is clearly addressed to the priests. Naturally, more is expected from those who have the responsibility of leading and teaching the people. Thus Malachi begins, *"And now, O priests, this commandment is for you."*

The chief end of the priests of Malachi's day was—as it is of the Christian ministry and Christian walk today—to glorify God. The Hebrew word for "glory" denotes first all of the weight, or sheer gravity, of God's presence; the presence that defined His importance and the respect He was owed. Accordingly, "glory" was not so much the renown that had been achieved as the real value a person carried because of who he was and what he had done. Only secondarily did "glory" refer to the effects of God's presence, such as the outshining and effulgence of His person. This, then, is what it meant for the priests *"to give glory to [His] name"* (v. 2).

The "name" of God appears now for the sixth time in the first sixteen verses of this book (1:6, 11 [three times], 14; 2:2). The "name" of God was the summation of all that He was in His person, attributes, reputation, doctrine, and ethical teaching.[14] God's name had been disgraced and made to appear shabby and despised by the way the priests had professed their faith, offered their gifts, entered into their service of God, and thought about the time they had invested for Him. It was now time to reverse that pattern, and to give glory to God's name.

People whose life and ministry did not give glory to God's name practiced merely the "form of godliness," without any of its power (2 Tim. 3:5). They might profess to know God, but their works denied their words (Titus 1:16).

The threat *"I will send a curse upon you, and I will curse your blessings"* (v. 2d) is almost an exact quotation of Deuteronomy 28:20, a passage, together with Leviticus 26, that offered the alternative prospects of blessing or judgment. In fact, the effect of God's judgments had already begun, *"because you do not take it to heart"* (v. 2f; a phrase very similar to one of Haggai's favorites: Hag. 1:5, 7; 2:15, 18). All gifts, goods, production—and even the promise of these (Num. 6:24–26)—would fall under God's judgment.

The penalty for failing to hear and respond to God was strong: three times the text mentions a curse that God would bring on the priests for their disobedience and unbelief. God's name is serious business, and nothing pollutes it more than the misconduct of those whose business is to honor it.

The words *"I will rebuke"* (v. 3) are also reminiscent of Deuteronomy 28:20, where the word "rebuke" occurs in the form of a noun. Once this connection with Deuteronomy is seen, the meaning of the Hebrew word "seed" (or *"descendants,"* v. 3a) seems more likely to be the produce of the ground than it is one's offspring, though either interpretation is acceptable in this context (note Deuteronomy 28:18–19, 21, 23–24). To rebuke the seed is to stop its growth.

The disgrace that the priests' gross sins would bring is described in graphic terms that only those raised on a farm would fully appreciate. To put the matter bluntly, God would spread on the faces of the priests animal dung, and perhaps the entrails that remained after the priests' sacrifices. The poetic justice of God using the remains of sacrifices performed with such hypocrisy can be captured in our more felicitous idiom: the priests were left with egg on their faces!

Even more damaging is the last line of verse 3—*"And one will take you away with it."* The priests would be removed from the presence of the Living God along with the dung, the entrails, and the hide of the sacrificed animal (Lev. 8:17; 16:27)! How dearly must the ancient (and modern) ministers of God have paid for their refusal to bring glory to God's name. The effects of a low regard for the ministry are still being felt; we witness one wave of unbelief and disobedience after another among the clergy in this century. It is no wonder that the "parson" is no longer the "person" in town!

LOVE FOR GOD'S WORD (2:4–9)

The expression in Malachi 2:4 is elliptical. Its general sense is that God sent His commandment to the priests so that, by taking it to heart, the Levitical priesthood might continue. The phrase *"Then you shall know [that I am the LORD]"* regularly occurs in texts where the judgment of God is used as a lever to help men and women face up to the challenge that God has set before them (e.g., the experience of Pharaoh in Exod. 7:10; 9:14, 29–30; 10:2; 14:2, 18 or of others in Ezk. 15:7; 33:29). God's judgment would come if the priests would not respond to His call to change.

Malachi refers to the priesthood as the "sons of Levi" (3:3). Technically, though, they descended from a narrower family within the tribe of Levi, and are more accurately called the "sons of Aaron" (Lev. 8:1–4) or, later, the "sons of Zadok" (Ezk. 44:15). This does not mean that Malachi was confused or mistaken; he deliberately uses the more general term of "Levi" to refer to all who served around the temple, not just to those who ministered at the altar.

God's covenant with Levi included *"life and peace"* (v. 5). "Life and peace" were gifts from God to obedient persons. Repeatedly Deuteronomy and Proverbs taught that these blessings were the result of a total commitment to the commandments of God (e.g., Deut. 4:40; 6:2; 30:15–30; Prov. 3:1,2; 4:10, 22; 6:23).

These words recall those of Numbers 25:12–13, where God gave the same covenant—with many of the same specifications—to Phinehas because he was stirred to action in the presence of evil done by the Simeonite Zimri and the Midianite woman Cozbi. While the whole congregation of Israel was assembled in repentance before God, Zimri and Cozbi brazenly walked across their encampment to

Phinehas's tent to commit fornication in the name of religious prostitution and worship of the dead (Num. 25:6–8; Ps. 106:28–31). But Phinehas "stood up and intervened" (Ps. 106:30) and pierced both of them through while they were in the very act of cohabitation, and "that was accounted to him for righteousness" (Ps. 106:31) "because he was zealous with My zeal" (Num. 25:11). Consequently, God gave him the gift of peace, which would be for him and his descendants after him as "an everlasting priesthood" (Num. 25:13).

But how different were Phinehas's attitude and actions compared to those of the priests of Malachi's day. God says of Levi: *"he feared Me and was reverent before My name. The law of truth was in his mouth, and injustice was not found on his lips. He walked with Me in peace and equity, and turned many away from iniquity"* (vv. 5b–6).

The real task of the true servant of God is set forth in verses 5b–9. He is reverent before God and fears Him. He boldly expounds the Law of God as it is found in His Word. He is not self-seeking or partial and does not engage in any kind of perverseness. The need for a true servant of God who will study and present God's Word thoughtfully and diligently is no less strong in our own day. It is all too easy to play to the gallery and give the pew what it thinks it needs (or to withhold what it thinks it doesn't need). But a true servant of God proclaims and teaches the truth of God's Word—all of it—whether or not it is popular or relevant! The goal of all faithful proclamation of the Word is to lead sinners to repentance—to turn "many away from iniquity" (v. 6d). Faithful proclamation of God's Word will "turn many to righteousness" (Dan. 12:3).

True teachers of God's Word will also "walk" with the Lord in "peace and equity." To "walk with God" means to live in full accord and harmony with what God has taught in His Word (Deut. 8:19; 13:4; 2 Kings 23:3; Jer. 7:9; Hos. 11:10). Enoch "walked with God" (Gen. 5:22, 24) as did Noah (Gen. 6:9). But the expression is used sparingly in the Bible to refer only to those who had an unusually close communion or fellowship with God.

Malachi 2:7 enlarges on the servant's dual mission of proclaiming the Word of God and walking with God. The priests, like contemporary Christians, were to *"keep knowledge."* This was best done by hiding God's Word away in one's heart and mind (Ps. 119:11) out of a fear of God (Prov. 1:7). Audiences should expect to hear sound instruction from the lips of their teachers.

The only time in the book of Malachi when a priest is called a *"messenger of the Lord"* is in verse 7c. Normally this phrase refers to the "angel of the LORD," or an appearance of Christ in the Old Testament, and in Haggai 1:13 the phrase refers to a prophet. Malachi will also use the term "angel" or "messenger" to refer to the forerunner of Christ, i.e., John the Baptist (Mal. 3:1). Here, though, he uses it to refer to the teaching ministry of the priesthood. While God had not made a formal covenant with the Levites, Jeremiah 33:20–21 and Nehemiah 13:29 both seem to allude to some sort of informal covenant. Moreover, Moses did commission the Levites with the responsibility of teaching (Deut. 33:8–11).

Interestingly enough, the apostle Paul seems to draw an analogy between the functions of evangelists and pastor-teachers in Ephesians 4:7–10, and the functions of the Levites in Numbers 8 and 18. The Levites were "taken" (Num. 8:6; 18:6; hence the figure of leading captives) and "given" back to God "to do the service. . . . at the tent of meeting" (Num. 8:19; 18:17), just as God had "led captivity captive" (Ps. 68:18, quoting the Numbers 8 and 18 passages and referring to God's calling of the Levites when He came down on Mount Sinai) and were given as "gifts" to the Heavenly Father so that the "captives" could be prepared to do the work of the ministry. This is Paul's point as well in Ephesians 4:7–10ff.[15]

The priests were also called to exercise a judicial function (Deut. 17:9–11 and 19:17). That is why verse 6 calls for them to exercise justice and impartiality.

God himself was to have been the priests' portion and inheritance (Num. 18:20). Surely that was tantamount to a covenant. But the times had changed, and all Malachi could do was shake his head and say, *"But you have departed from the way"* (v. 8). So far had the priests of that day strayed from their ancestral calling that they had *"stumbl[ed] at the law. . . . [and] corrupted the covenant of Levi"* (v. 8bc).

The priests had engaged in such moral corruption that they had lost all respect in the eyes of the people (v. 9)—and in the eyes of God. They had courted popularity by giving the people what they wanted and by modifying God's requirements so that regard for persons and partiality in justice, not God's Word, were the norms. The priests were now reaping what they had sown. Is it any wonder that so many religious leaders and teachers of our day are similarly held in disrepute? Ironically, the esteem for the ministry could not be lower in a day when we have reached for the stars in mega-movements for the Church. Often our ministers are not true servants of God; they do not give a faithful proclamation of the whole counsel of God (Acts 20:27) and do not walk in communion with God. Neither God nor His Word will be mocked without dreadful consequences.

CONCLUSION

Malachi came down hard on the ministry leaders, but he had every right to do so. The fact remains: as goes the preaching of the word of God, so go the lifestyles of the public at large.

When we do not seek first God's glory and totally love and respond to His Word, then our culture is in desperate trouble. "Like minister, like people" could very well be the proverb raised over our nation as well as Malachi's. It is exceedingly important that those who teach remember that they are accountable not only for themselves, but also for those whom they teach (Jam. 3:1).

CHAPTER FOUR

A Call to Be Faithful

Malachi 2:10–16

10 Have we not all one Father?
   Has not one God created us?
   Why do we deal treacherously with
      one another
   By profaning the covenant of the fathers?
11 Judah has dealt treacherously,
   And an abomination has been committed in
      Israel and in Jerusalem,
   For Judah has profaned
   The LORD's holy institution which He loves:
   He has married the daughter of a foreign god.
12 May the LORD cut off from the tents of Jacob
   The man who does this, being awake
      and aware,
   Yet who brings an offering to the
      LORD of hosts.
13 And this is the second thing you do:
   You cover the altar of the LORD with tears,
   With weeping and crying;
   So He does not regard the offering anymore,
   Nor receive it with good will from your hands.
14 Yet you say, "For what reason?"
   Because the LORD has been witness
   Between you and the wife of your youth,
   With whom you have dealt treacherously;
   Yet she is your companion
   And your wife by covenant.
15 But did He not make them one,
   Having a remnant of the Spirit?

> And why one?
> He seeks godly offspring.
> Therefore take heed to your spirit,
> And let none deal treacherously with the wife
>   of his youth.
> 16 "For the LORD God of Israel says
> That He hates divorce,
> For it covers one's garment with violence,"
> Says the LORD of hosts.
> "Therefore take heed to your spirit,
> That you do not deal treacherously."
>
> *Malachi 2:10–16*

The principle of faithfulness to one's marriage vows was as much under attack in Malachi's day as it is in our own. Few texts of Scripture are as forthright and theological in their handling of the various social consequences of deviation from God's norm for marriage as this text is.

Just as water can only rise to the level of its source, the spiritual level of a people cannot be expected to attain any greater height than that attained by their leaders. Alas, Israel's spiritual leaders had faltered, and thus so had the people.

This led to an outbreak of problems, three of which Malachi addresses here: the people's disloyalty to the spiritual unity of the national family (2:10); the people's disloyalty to their spiritual families (2:11–12); and the people's unfaithfulness to their individual marriages (2:13–16). Included in Malachi's charges are spiritual harlotry, mixed marriages with unbelieving partners, adultery, and divorce. Thus, the priests' failure to teach the truth could be seen in the devastating collapse of marriage and family—in violation of all that God had ordained these blessings to be.

As most commentators do, we consider verses 10–16 to mark a new section of the book of Malachi because Malachi again changes the focus of his address, this time from the priests alone to the priests' congregation. Verses 10–16 contain no indication that the priests were the sole objects of Malachi's charges or even that the priests were being addressed at all. The *"we"* and the *"us"* of verse 10 were fellow Jews, not the whole brotherhood of humanity, or even the tribe of Levi. Malachi's audience was the people that the priests had "caused . . . to stumble" (2:8).

Malachi may well have intended the sins listed in verses 10–16 to constitute a partial catalogue of what happens when the ministry does not keep God's ways, but shows partiality and avoids certain issues on which society has taken the lead. In that regard, Malachi's day may have been no different from our own. Many ministers and teachers are intimidated to the point of silence on issues regarding sexual practices of single people, extra-marital affairs of believers and unbelievers, and divorce. One recent cartoon in *Leadership* magazine showed a pastor appearing before his congregation in a full panoply of knight's armor. As he lifted the hatch over his mouth, he intoned, "My subject today is 'Divorce.'" If that is not a picture of an intimidated pastor, what is?

Malachi issues a call for the renewal of three loyalties:

   A. We Must Be Loyal to the God of the Covenant   2:10
   B. We Must Be Loyal to the People of God   2:11–12
   C. We Must Be Loyal to the Partner of Our Marriage   2:13–16

WE MUST BE LOYAL TO THE GOD OF THE COVENANT (2:10)

Malachi 2:10 picks up the story of 1:6 when it asks, *"Have we not all one Father?"* The "Father" that is intended here is not Abraham, as some scholars (including Jerome and Calvin) have thought, or even Malachi's frequently mentioned patriarch, Jacob (1:2; 2:12; 3:6). Rather, as in 1:6, "Father" refers here to Yahweh. God is the father of Israel, because He is the one who created her (Isa. 43:1).

Since the people of Israel are sons and daughters of the same covenant, the question arises: *"Why do we deal treacherously with one another by profaning the covenant of the fathers?"* (v. 10b). Every form of the people's sins, including marrying foreign women who did not believe in their Lord, divorcing the wives they had married in their youth and joining themselves to foreign gods, was an act of treachery against the whole body—not to mention an act of treachery against God. Where was the instruction from the lips of the Levites? How could people profess to be partners in the covenant of God yet commit spiritual and physical harlotry? God had called His people to be His "special possession," a "holy nation" (Exod. 19:5–6), His "son" and His "firstborn" (Exod. 4:22). But look at them now!

The Hebrew word translated here as to "deal treacherously" (vv. 10,11) is *bāgad*, which is related to the word *beged*, "garment." In effect, what the people were doing in their treacherous dealing was involving themselves in a "cover-up" job. They were masking their covenants with God and their wives. Therein lay the insidious nature of their treachery!

If God were their Father, it was time they started acting like sons. If they abused their relationship to the covenant, were there any loyalties they would not abuse?

WE MUST BE LOYAL TO THE PEOPLE OF GOD (2:11–12)

These verses speak of a second breach of the people's covenant with God: the people had entered into mixed marriages. By mixed marriages we do not mean cross-cultural commitments or marriages to those of different races, but a crossing of spiritual commitments. Some in Malachi's audience had *"married the daughter of a foreign god"* (v. 11e).

Such marriages had been reported in Ezra 9:2–6; 10:18–19 and Nehemiah 10:30; 13:23–27. They had been clearly forbidden in Exodus 34:11–16; Deuteronomy 7:3; and 1 Kings 11:1–2.

As a result of entering into these forbidden marriages, Israel, whom Yahweh called "holy"—the one chosen from all the nations to be His holy people, a royal priesthood, and a special possession (Exod. 19:5–6; Deut. 7:6; 14:2)—had profaned herself. Ezra will likewise bring charges against the priests of his day for allowing intermarriage with pagans (Ezra 9:1–3), just as the apostle Paul will warn believers not to be unequally yoked together with unbelievers in 2 Corinthians 6:15–16. What sort of concord can a believer have with an unbeliever? asks Paul rather pointedly.

God's response to the people who have breached His covenant by entering into mixed marriages is that they will eventually find their families wiped out, for *"the* LORD *[will] cut off from the tents of Jacob the man who does this"* (v. 12a). The idiom that follows—*"being awake and aware"*—is almost impossible to translate. Some have suggested "everyone who awakes and answers"; others suggest "teacher and student," or "watcher and respondent." The general intent of the idiom is clear: the entirety of the transgressor's family—or as we would say today, both "root and branch"—would suffer the "cutting off."

WE MUST BE LOYAL TO THE PARTNER OF OUR MARRIAGE (2:13–16)

The accusations continue. *"And this is the second thing you do"* (v. 13): you have divorced the wives you married when you were young.

The Lord refused to accept the sacrificial gifts of these divorced husbands. Their access to the altar was blocked by the mist of tears shed by the wives they had abandoned (v. 13b). Therefore God was unable to regard their sacrifices any longer. The husbands had dealt treacherously with their wives and God had seen it.

Typical of his conversational style, Malachi records the husbands' rejoinder, *"For what reason?"* (v. 14a). Why does God not pay attention to us or accept our offerings any longer? Malachi's answer is: *"Because the LORD has been a witness between you and the wife of your youth"* (v. 14b).

Broken marriage vows were not solely the concern of the two contracting parties, the husband and wife; God was a "witness" to their "covenant" (v. 14e) as well. Malachi is not the only place in Scripture where marriage is treated as a covenant; Proverbs 2:17 and Ezekiel 16:8 also speak of marriage as a covenant. Thus the nuptial covenant cannot be taken lightly.

To emphasize the seriousness of the husbands' offense against their wives, Malachi uses three graphic phrases to describe the divorced wives: *"wife of your youth," "your companion,"* and *"your wife by covenant"* (v. 14). One Puritan commentator put the matter as sharply as it should be put:

> She whom you thus wronged was the companion of those earlier and brighter days, when in the bloom of her young beauty she left her father's house and shared your early struggles, and rejoiced in your later success; who walked arm in arm with you along the pilgrimage of life, cheering you in its trials by her gentle ministry; and now, when the bloom of her youth has faded and the friends of her youth have gone, when her father and mother whom she left for you are in the grave, then you cruelly cast her off as a worn-out, worthless thing, and insult her holiest affections by putting an idolater and a heathen in her place.[16]

In that magnificent allegory on marital and conjugal fidelity in Proverbs 5:15–21, Solomon had similarly enjoined couples to "rejoice with the wife of your youth" (Prov. 5:18). No doubt when Malachi uses the word "companion" in verse 14, he is calling on the "one flesh" teaching of Genesis 2:24, for the word for "companion" means "united," or "joined together." "Companion" implies harmony and working together to achieve life's goals while sharing all the hardships and pain—and joys!

Verse 15 is regarded by many as one of the most difficult verses in the Bible. The key to understanding it properly is the interpretation of the word *"One"* (v. 15). "One" does not refer to Abraham, which would yield the translation "Did not one [Abraham] do so [take a pagan Egyptian named Hagar as his wife]?" Abraham is never referred to in the Bible as the "one." Moreover, his conduct with Hagar is not what is being discussed here. What is more, Abraham did not divorce Sarah when he took Hagar.

We would argue, rather, that "he," the subject of verse 15a, means God and that "one," the object, means the "one flesh" of Genesis 2:24. Verse 15a could then be paraphrased and explained: Why did God make Adam and Eve only one flesh, when He might have given Adam many wives, for God certainly had more than enough of the Spirit, or creative power, to furnish many partners? However, because God was seeking a godly offspring, He restricted man and woman to a single bonding, for He knew that a plurality of mates for either partner was not conducive to raising children to the glory of God.[17]

Verse 16 contains one of the strongest protests anywhere in Scripture against divorce. God is said in no uncertain terms to loathe the practice and results of divorce. It is important to note that Deuteronomy 24:1 does not contradict this verse. Deuteronomy 24:1 should not be read as approving of divorce; rather, it should be read as discouraging divorce by calling for the husband to provide his wife some protection by declaring in writing his intentions to divorce. A written declaration would make impossible any devious schemes of wife-swapping—wherein the wife's marital status would depend on the whims of her husband—that could have occurred under the prior system, which required only the husband's thrice uttered oral statement of divorce witnessed only by the husband and wife. Of course, Jesus harkened back to the normality of Genesis 2:24 when He spoke in Matthew 19:3–8 on the subject of divorce.

Clearly, the Lord *"hates divorce"* (v. 16). His reference to covering one's garment with violence (v. 16c) recalls the story of Ruth, in which Boaz spread a garment over Ruth (Ruth 3:9; cf. Deut. 22:30; Ezk. 16:8), thereby indicating his intentions to claim her as his wife. The act of spreading a garment over another person had the same idiomatic meaning as our word "bed" has for conjugal relations today. But when the garment was covered with violence the idiom spoke instead of acting unfaithfully and unjustly towards one's conjugal promises.

"*Therefore take heed to your spirit, that you do not deal treacherously*" (v. 16ef). This is the same warning given in verse 15e. Few issues in today's world are more revealing about moral integrity than that of maintaining our covenant with our spouse, with whom we exchanged vows in the presence of God, a witness to the ceremony.

CONCLUSION

God still expects a married couple to work toward the lofty ideal of marriage He originally announced in Genesis 2:24. He disdains and rejects the practice of divorce, as Malachi 2:16 makes clear; divorce earns God's hatred.

Believers must maintain their loyalty to the God who created them, the body of believers to which He has joined them, and the marriage partner He has given them. Anything less than this challenges our claim that He is our Father, Lord and Master.

CHAPTER FIVE

A Call to Trust an Unchanging God

Malachi 2:17–3:12

17 You have wearied the LORD with your words;
Yet you say,
"In what way have we wearied Him?"
In that you say,
"Everyone who does evil
Is good in the sight of the LORD,
And He delights in them,"
Or, "Where is the God of justice?"

3:1 "Behold, I send My messenger,
And he will prepare the way before Me.
And the Lord, whom you seek,
Will suddenly come to His temple,
Even the Messenger of the covenant,
In whom you delight.
Behold, He is coming,"
Says the LORD of hosts.

2 "But who can endure the day of His coming?
And who can stand when He appears?
For He is like a refiner's fire
And like fuller's soap.

3 He will sit as a refiner and a purifier of silver;
He will purify the sons of Levi,
And purge them as gold and silver,
That they may offer to the LORD
An offering in righteousness.

4 "Then the offering of Judah and Jerusalem
Will be pleasant to the LORD,
As in the days of old,
As in former years.

5 And I will come near you for judgment;
  I will be a swift witness
  Against sorcerers,
  Against adulterers,
  Against perjurers,
  Against those who exploit wage earners and
    widows and the fatherless,
  And against those who turn away an alien—
  Because they do not fear Me,"
  Says the LORD of hosts.
6 "For I am the LORD, I do not change;
  Therefore you are not consumed,
    O sons of Jacob.
7 Yet from the days of your fathers
  You have gone away from My ordinances
  And have not kept them.
  Return to Me, and I will return to you,"
  Says the LORD of hosts.
  "But you said,
  'In what way shall we return?'
8 "Will a man rob God?
  Yet you have robbed Me!
  But you say,
  'In what way have we robbed You?'
  In tithes and offerings.
9 You are cursed with a curse,
  For you have robbed Me,
  Even this whole nation.
10 Bring all the tithes into the storehouse,
  That there may be food in My house,
  And prove Me now in this,"
  Says the LORD of hosts,
  "If I will not open for you the windows
    of heaven
  And pour out for you such blessing
  That there will not be room enough to receive it.
11 "And I will rebuke the devourer for
    your sakes,
  So that he will not destroy the fruit of
    your ground,
  Nor shall the vine fail to bear fruit for
    you in the field,"

    Says the LORD of hosts;
12 "And all nations will call you blessed,
    For you will be a delightful land,"
    Says the LORD of hosts.

Malachi 2:17–3:12

Sometimes life can be so harsh and our expectations so far from being met that the ungodly come to deny outright the providence of God in the affairs of men and women. Such seemed to be the mindset of the distraught Jews of Malachi's day. To their way of thinking, the prosperity of the nation and her people were long overdue! As viewed by Malachi's generation, the preaching of Haggai and Zechariah, beginning in 520 B.C., was now a century past, but had not resulted in any long-term dramatic reversals of the fortunes of the struggling Judean colony.

Of course, everyone wanted to have the benefits of God's blessing without making any commitments or taking on any responsibilities. The people had deliberately neglected the more important matter of attaining righteousness and holiness and had instead set out to fulfill less significant ritual and ceremonial duties, hoping thereby to achieve the favor of God on a bargain basis.

But the whole scene was wearying the Lord (2:17). The complaints of Malachi's audience had grown to epic proportions by now. Their words were a direct attack on God's person.

The heart of the text that follows contains the focal point and the subject of our message (which also serves as a joint theme for the whole book of Malachi): *"For I am the LORD, I do not change"* (3:6). This is the doctrine of the immutability, or the unchangeableness of the Living God. While all else might be changing in our age of "future shock" (Alvin Toffler's phrase), one may count on God—His nature, attributes, qualities, being, and person—as a fixed point of reference and as one in whom there is no variableness. Such immutability, of course, must not be confused with immobility; God is not restricted by some blind force or law to which He is bound no matter how much He might wish otherwise to benefit his children. God can change in His actions toward us as much as any other living person can. What He cannot and will not change, however, is the consistency of His own person as the basis of His actions. That is the comforting feature of His immutability.

Two of God's immutable qualities are set forth in Malachi 2:17–3:12.

470

    A.   Our God is Just   2:17–3:6
    B.   Our God is Faithful   3:7–12

Our God is Just (2:17–3:6)

In Malachi 2:17–3:6 we see another example of a very poor chapter division, since the first six verses of what we now call chapter 3 were intended to answer the charges of 2:17; the answer to the question of those who scoffed *"Where is the God of justice?"* (2:17f) is to be found most succinctly in 3:1: *"Behold, I send My messenger, and he will prepare the way before Me."*

With a strong figure of speech involving more than a tinge of sarcasm as he quoted back to them their own words, Malachi allows that the cynics have succeeded in wearying God by their constant complaints about God's partiality to the wicked. At first, they tried to deny that they had wearied the Lord. But Malachi does not let them off easily. He quotes back to them their own charges against God: *"'Everyone who does evil is good in the sight of the* Lord, *and He delights in them,' or, 'Where is the God of justice?'"* (2:17).

In Hebrew the structure of these charges lays emphasis on "everyone who does evil." Like little children caught in the act of doing wrong, Malachi's audience had hastily conducted one of those impromptu polls that showed that "everyone" was doing it. The tactic was an old one: to ask "What about them?"

The charges, of course, were as monstrous as they were wrong. To justify the wicked or their wickedness was "an abomination to the LORD" (Prov. 17:15). And calling evil good and good evil was enough to call down Isaiah's indictment of "woe" (Isa. 5:20).

God did not regard evil-doers as good; neither did He take pleasure in them. What God "delighted in" was seeing His Law kept (Isa. 56:4), seeing mercy and the knowledge of God (Hos. 6:6), acts of justice, gracious love and humility (Mic. 6:8) and truth (Ps. 51:8). But Malachi's mean-spirited audience chided God with their own view of things; they said, in effect, "God must love wicked people since He puts up with so many of them." All the time, what irritated them was that the Lord had not favored them with material prosperity, influence, and benefits.

With more than a hint of sarcasm, the people summarized their case against God with the question, "Where is the God of justice?"

But that only raised another question: according to what standard is justice done or said to have been done? The norm in all of Scripture for justice was nothing less than the character of God himself.

Malachi gives the people an answer to their question—though it was not the answer they were expecting. They would learn firsthand that God was indeed just and that His justice would be observed in His preparation of the path by a forerunner (3:1a), His coming (3:1b–2), His refining work (3:3–4), His judgment (3:5), and His long-suffering (3:6).

Those who were so anxious to see God would get their chance. But His coming would not be a panacea for all the ills of life, as so many unprepared people had imagined. Amos (5:18), too, had sternly warned those in his generation who had thought that the day of the Lord would be some kind of magic cure-all. It would not be that at all; it would be a terrifying day with tragic consequences for all who were not morally and spiritually prepared.

God would send His messenger (v. 1) to prepare the way morally before Him. Obviously, Malachi is drawing on Isaiah 40:3–5, which points to God's messenger, who, we later learned, is John the Baptist. Jesus explained that John was the Elijah who was to come (Matt. 11:14) because he came in "the spirit and the power of Elijah" (Luke 1:17). His work was to call all to repent.

John the Baptist clearly denied that he was Elijah (John 1:21, 23), meaning, no doubt, that he was not the final or complete fulfillment of Elijah who was to come before the second advent of our Lord (Rev. 11). Nevertheless, the scribes all expected that a resurrected Elijah would precede the coming of the Messiah (Mark 9:12). This "yes"/ "no" puzzle can be solved. In one verse, Elijah had come (Mark 9:12) since John the Baptist did come in the spirit and power of Elijah. But the Old Testament Elijah still must come in the future, when he will restore all things (Matt. 17:11) in connection with the second coming of our Lord (Acts 3:21).

God's messenger prepares for Jesus's first and second coming by "clearing the way before the LORD." Levelling the road and straightening out the path are metaphors for the necessary prepatory spiritual work of repentance and faith. The Hebrew idiom for "clearing up" the ground was also used in Psalm 80:9 and Genesis 24:31. But it was a spiritual housecleaning that was needed, not a showing of partiality and unthoughtful favor toward spoiled, demanding backbiters!

Thus the answer to "Where is the God of justice?" was simply *Marantha,* "The Lord comes!" (1 Cor. 16:22). The God of justice whom men claimed they sought was the *"Lord, whom you seek"* (3:1b). He was *"the Messenger of the covenant"* (3:1c), the owner of the temple. He *"will suddenly come to His temple"* (3:1c).

Because the word "Lord" (*hā᾽ādôn*) used in 3:1b is singular and is preceded by the definite article, it is certain that it refers to the divine Lord since *᾽ādôn* preceded by the definite article always denotes divinity (*see,* for example, Exod. 23:17; 34:23; Isa. 1:24; 3:1; 10:16, 33). Adonai is the title borne by Messiah in Psalm 110:1. It signifies ownership; the Lord is Lord of everything.

The Lord is also the "Messenger of the covenant." The covenant referred to here is the single plan of God contained in the succession of covenants beginning with the covenants made with Eve (Gen. 3:15), continuing with the covenants with Shem (Gen. 9:27), Abraham (Gen. 12:1–3), Moses (Exod. 6:2–8), and David (2 Sam. 7:12–19) and concluding with the *renewal* of that same, but progressively enlarged, covenant for the age to come (Jeremiah 31:31–34).

The "Messenger," or "Angel," was the same one God had sent ahead of Israel in the Exodus from Egypt (Exod. 23:20–23). There can be no mistaking his identity, for God's "name is in him" (Exod. 23:21). To equate the "name" of God with this Angel was to call him divine. Since he was sent from God, and yet he was God, then he had to be the second person of the trinity, Christ (cf. John 10:30, 36). Elsewhere in the Old Testament this "Angel" is called the "Angel of the LORD," also understood in those texts to be a pre-incarnate appearance of Christ, or a Christophany (Exod. 33:14, 15; Judg. 6:12; 13:3; Isa. 63:9). Christ is the mediator of the old and new covenants (Heb. 8:8–13; 12:24). He is our Lord and Savior.

Therefore, three persons—not just one or even two—appear in verse one. They are: (1) the speaking Father, (2) the announcing prophet, or John the Baptist, and (3) the sent One, the messenger of the covenant, our Lord Jesus Christ.

He will come *"suddenly"* (3:1), meaning unexpectedly, not immediately. The word "suddenly" appears twenty-five times in the Old Testament and in every case except one (2 Chron. 29:36) is connected with disaster or judgment. Thus, for the wicked, the Lord's "sudden" coming would be "as a thief in the night" (2 Pet. 3:10).

Malachi's sarcastic audience, who professed to "delight" in the coming of the Lord, would not enjoy the day of the Lord's coming. To them the day would be a nightmare rather than a day of restored prosperity. *"But who can endure the day of His coming?"* (3:2). That "day" is the "day of the LORD" mentioned so frequently in Scripture, first in Exodus 32:34 and then in Amos 5:20, Joel 2:11, and Zephaniah 1:15. Malachi 4:5 says it would be a "great and dreadful day of the LORD." Who, then, could stand in that day? Only those who stood with the whole armor of God (Eph. 6:13) and who had "clean hands and a pure heart" (Ps. 24:3–4).

The cleansing work that God would effect in that day is depicted here in two figures: fire and soap. What fire did in separating slag from metal and soap did in separating dirt from clothes, God's cleansing action would do for His people. Only dirt and slag had anything to fear; only the wicked should be frightened by the prospect and experience of that day.

The fire will test every person's work. Human accomplishments—the wood, hay, and stubble (1 Cor. 3:11–15)—will be tried in the fire of God. God, the Refiner of silver, will know by His testing process exactly when we have been purified. "There is a dramatic moment when [the refiner] knows that all dross has gone from [the silver]. Peering over it, the silver suddenly becomes a liquid mirror in which the image of the refiner is reflected. Then he knows that his task is done."[18] So it is with us; when our Lord can observe His image reflected in us, then our trial-by-fire suffering has accomplished its perfect work.

In the day of the Lord, God would *"purify the sons of Levi,"* the very people against whom the charges in 1:6–2:9 had been made. Then they would be able to *"offer to the LORD an offering in righteousness"* (3:3). Such offerings were possible only when both the spiritual condition of the offerer and the quality of the offering were without blemish. That refinement of Israel's Levitical and priestly establishment would only come in the future. What Malachi speaks of here in verse 4 must be the same thing he envisioned in 1:11 (since both are set in the future)—a time when "pure offerings" would be offered in "every place," thus signifying genuine worship of God by all the people everywhere. Thus, just as the prophets described the final battle on earth in the end time in contemporary terms of armament of their own day (e.g., horses, bows, arrows, spears), so Malachi describes future worship using contemporary terms (e.g., offerings, sacrifices, etc.). We conclude, then, that the *form* of worship may change, but the *essence* and the *act* of worship would remain the same. It would center on Christ and include the sacrifice of our lips and praise (Hos. 14:2; Heb. 13:15), which would be a most reasonable service of the living sacrifice of lives dedicated to God (Rom. 12:1–2).

Already in the New Testament we begin to see the firstfruits of such a work among the "sons of Levi," for in Acts 6:7 Luke remarks that "a great many of the priests were obedient to the faith" and believed that Jesus was the promised Messiah.

Since Malachi's audience did not fear God (v. 5h), God would be *"a swift witness against [them]"* (v. 5b). Although they professed that they feared God (1:6), their engagement in the seven sins enumerated in verse 5b belied their professions. With every one of the seven sins they broke God's laws. Sorcery and witchcraft were forbidden in Exodus 22:18, Leviticus 20:27, and Deuteronomy 18:14. Adultery was forbidden in the Ten Commandments (Exod. 20:14), as was perjury, or lying (Exod. 20:7, 16; Lev. 19:12). Likewise, exploiting the poor and cheating the laborer out of his daily wages were serious infractions of God's standards of morality (Lev. 19:13; Deut. 24:14–15). Unprotected widows, orphans, and aliens were not to be cannabalized by the vultures of society (Exod. 22:22–24; Lev. 19:10; Deut. 24:19–32; Zech. 7:10). All such sins—tantamount to offending God himself—earned God's judgment. Engaging in these sins displayed a lack of fear of God—a disregard for His judgments and a failure to believe who He was and what He had said.

But all this time the character and the being of God had not vacillated. In fact, Israel owed her very existence to the Lord's abiding grace, patience, and faithfulness in keeping His promise to her. Even when Israel had "violated" and profaned the covenant of God (Mal. 2:10), God had refused to "violate" His promise to Israel (Ps. 89:34; the same Hebrew word for "violate" is used in both texts). Little wonder, then, that our Lord is celebrated for His justice and judgments even when He is being accused of failing on both points by those who cared little for Him or His works!

OUR GOD IS FAITHFUL (3:7–12)

A second immutable quality of God discussed in Malachi is His faithfulness. In a most gentle way, He continued to deal with all people, even those hardened sinners who continued to oppose Him. In spite of the fact that *"from the days of your fathers you have gone away from My ordinances and have not kept them"* (v. 7), God had not changed in His gracious call to each one of the sinners.

The call of God in verse 7c contains the watchword of all the prophets: *"'Return to Me, and I will return to you,' says the* LORD *of hosts."* The message of all the previous prophets could be summarized in the single word "return" (Zech. 1:3–4), the Old Testament word for repentance. The word invites the listeners to turn 180 degrees, reversing their direction. Instead of heading off toward sin, self, and contemporary idols, Israel is urged to turn around and look in faith to the Man of Promise.

Once again, however, Israel fails to acknowledge her problem; she gives instead a whimper of innocence by saying, in effect, "Who? Us? We need to repent? Why do we need to turn back to God? We never went away from Him, did we?"

God had no other recourse than to point to one glaring example of Israel's refusal to turn to the Lord: Israel's failure to tithe or make offerings. By focusing on Israel's failure to tithe or make offerings, God did not mean to imply that this was Israel's only sin or that this sin had a status greater than others. This was, simply, a readily provable sin. The people's failure to tithe or make offerings, though, was of one piece with their neglect of God's people, their abandonment of the marriage mates of their youth, and their willingness to place any old thing on the altar of God in order to get by as cheaply and quickly as possible.

The people's failure to tithe or make offerings showed conclusively that they were willing to cheat God out of what was due Him. The verb to *"rob"* (v. 8), used in the Old Testament only here and in Proverbs 22:23, means to "rob, defraud, or to overreach" (although in Talmudic literature it means "to take forcibly").[19]

The tithe was generally considered to be a tenth of what a person earned, for that is what Abraham gave the priest Melchizedek even before the Law of Moses was handed down (Gen 14:20). Under the instructions given to Moses, a "tenth" (our "tithe" in Mal. 3:8, *maʾaśēr*) was "holy to the LORD" (Lev. 27:30). From this tithe, or tenth, the Levites paid a "tenth" to the priests (Num. 18:26–28). Others who benefited from the tithe were families entertained at the temple (Deut. 12:18), widows, orphans, and resident aliens (Deut.

14:28–29). The "offerings" were those portions of the animal sacrifices designated for the priests (Exod. 29:27–28; Lev. 9:22; Num. 5:9) or those gifts that were voluntarily given for some special purpose (Exod. 25:2–7). Unfortunately, Israel was robbing God of both of these expressions of His Lordship. (Note, however, that at Israel's revival, the people's joyous giving began again spontaneously [Neh. 10:38ff; 2 Chron. 31:5–19].)

Christians are not governed by any law that commands us to give a tenth of our earnings to God; however, it must be noted that the practice of tithing antedates any provision of the Law of Moses. Another argument often made in favor of Christians tithing is: "If it was appropriate under the law to give a tenth, Christians will want to give no less than a tenth insofar as we have received and known so much more!" How could it be put any more succinctly?

No one robs God without robbing himself at the same time! Therefore, a challenge was issued: *"'Bring all the tithes into the storehouse, that there may be food in My house, and prove Me now in this,' says the LORD of hosts, 'If I will not open for you the windows of heaven and pour out for you such blessing that there will not be room enough to receive it'"* (v. 10).

The "storehouse" is either the "treasury of the temple of the LORD" (1 Kings 7:51) or, in a more figurative sense, the place from which all of God's blessings proceed. The word "treasury" appears eighty times in the Old Testament, but only in a few does it clearly connote a divine storehouse (e.g., Pss. 33:7; 135:7; Job 38:22). Deuteronomy 28:12 and, obliquely, Jeremiah 50:25, do speak of God's treasury-house as in the heavens. Accordingly, we must be careful not to use this verse to insist on the practice known as "storehouse tithing," by which all giving to God's work is channeled through the local church. We must "bring" the tithes to the storehouse, but, in fairness to the text, the "storehouse" does not have to be the local church—good as that practice is as a general principle.

Malachi does call for "all the tithes," or, better translated, "the whole tithe." The emphasis on wholeness must have involved the firstfruits of the crop, the earliest interest off the shekel, and, since God always inspects the giver before He inspects the gift, the entirety of the person (cf. Gen. 4:3–4)—his time, talents, and self.

God's challenge was to *"prove,"* or to *"test, try, or examine"* God. The Hebrew root of to *"prove"* occurs thirty-two times in the Old Testament

477

and is often parallel to the words "to smelt, or refine," or another root meaning "to put to a test." Unlike these other words, though, the word Malachi uses is almost exclusively used in a spiritual or religious sense. So God will allow the people of Israel to determine personally if their obedience to Him makes a difference.

If men will take up the challenge, God will release *"the windows"* or "floodgates" of heaven and send an abundance of rains (cf. Deut. 28:12; 2 Kings 7:2, 19). In fact, God will send so much rain that *"there will not be room enough to receive it"* (v. 10f), or, literally, He will send rain "until [there is] a failure of sufficiency." This suggests either that there will not be enough room to contain all that God would send, or that God would continue to send blessing until the heavenly source actually ran dry—until a heavy run on the bank by believers would exhaust the bank of heaven! The latter suggestion, of course, is a hyperbole, deliberately exaggerating the effect of God's abundant giving in order to make the point more dramatically. The same idiom in verse 10f occurs as well in Psalm 72:7: "until the moon is no more." It is clear, however, that God is promising almost unlimited resources if His people would only put Him to the test.

Moreover, God would *"rebuke the devourer for your sakes"* (v. 11a). He would halt the locusts, and all other devouring mites, if His people turned back to Him. We see in this verse, as we saw in Amos 4:6–12 and Haggai 1:6, the impact human spiritual progress (or the lack of spiritual renewal) has on nature. As we have discussed, the impact was first seen after the fall, and will continue to be seen until the second coming of our Lord, when all of nature will be healed (Rom. 8:18–20).

Further, if Israel turned back to God, all the nations *"will call you blessed, for you will be a delightful land"* (v. 12). The promise that God had originally given to Abraham in Genesis 12:1–3 would be fulfilled. Nations all over the world would rise up and say, "Thank God for those people who have been faithful to Him so that He could be faithful to them and to all of us who have also been blessed as a result of their turning back to Him."

CONCLUSION

We must not infer from the inequalitites of the human condition that God is indifferent to humans or that He has decided to soften

His standards of right and wrong. We must not weary the Lord, as Malachi's audience did (Mal 2:17), with such thinking.

More is required of us than to desire the second coming of Christ; all too many view Christ's coming as a panacea for all our current ills. God is both a fire for the impenitent and a refiner for the believing; therefore, we must say "amen" to all His works, not just to those that particularly please us. Dirt and slag have much to fear from soap and fire, but the believer has no reason to fear either.

We are preserved by the faithful and unchanging God revealed in our Lord Jesus Christ. Our hope must never rest on our love of or service to God, but only on His immutability. What we must do is "turn" and repent of all our sins and offenses against our God and our fellow human beings. For Malachi's audience was wrong; God is not indifferent to the evil and wickedness that surround us.

He will "suddenly" come to this earth one day. No wonder, then, we should be careful in the matter of our tithes, gifts, and offerings. God's challenge to prove and test Him is more than an academic exercise; it is the fabric of life. It is where reality is after all!

CHAPTER SIX

A Call to Take Inventory

Malachi 3:13–4:6

13 "Your words have been harsh against Me,"
Says the LORD,
"Yet you say,
'What have we spoken against You?'
14 You have said,
'It is vain to serve God;
What profit is it that we have kept His
ordinance,
And that we have walked as mourners
Before the LORD of hosts?
15 So now we call the proud blessed,
For those who do wickedness are raised up;
Yes, those who tempt God and go free.'"
16 Then those who feared the LORD spoke
to one another,
And the LORD listened and heard them;
So a book of remembrance was written
before Him
For those who fear the LORD
And who meditate on His name.
17 "They shall be Mine,"
says the LORD of hosts,
"On the day that I make them My jewels.
And I will spare them
As a man spares his own son who serves him."
18 Then you shall again discern
Between the righteous and the wicked,
Between one who serves God
And one who does not serve Him.

4:1 "For behold, the day is coming,
    Burning like an oven,
    And all the proud, yes, all who do wickedly
      will be stubble.
    And the day which is coming shall
      burn them up,"
    Says the LORD of hosts,
    "That will leave them neither root nor branch.
2 But to you who fear My name
    The Sun of Righteousness shall arise
    With healing in His wings;
    And you shall go out
    And grow fat like stall-fed calves.
3 You shall trample the wicked,
    For they shall be ashes under the soles
      of your feet
    On the day that I do this,"
    Says the LORD of hosts.
4 "Remember the Law of Moses, My servant,
    Which I commanded him in Horeb for all
      Israel,
    With the statutes and judgments.
5 Behold, I will send you Elijah the prophet
    Before the coming of the great and dreadful
      day of the LORD.
6 And he will turn
    The hearts of the fathers to the children,
    And the hearts of the children to their fathers,
    Lest I come and strike the earth with a curse."
                 Malachi 3:13–4:6

All too many have wanted to hang a funeral crepe over the work of God worldwide and to say that *"It is useless to serve God"* (3:14). But these contemporary crepehangers had such a mercenary approach to serving God and attending His house that their worldliness was more the root of the problem than any other alleged concern.

This text points to a classic example of worship of God that was not authentic. To those who declared that the Church was finished and now in deep trouble, God responded as He did to the Laodicean Church in Revelation 3:15–17, where He threatened to spit out of His mouth those who were like the lukewarm water for which the region had earned such an infamous reputation: it was neither hot nor cold, just lukewarm.

This final section of Malachi contains three questions designed to call men and women everywhere to take inventory of their lives.

A. Is It Vain to Serve the Lord?   3:13–18
B. Is There No Difference Between the Righteous and the Wicked?   4:1–3
C. Are There No Guides for the Righteous?   4:4–6

IS IT VAIN TO SERVE THE LORD? (3:13–18)

This question is given two sets of answers: one from the arrogant and skeptical members of Malachi's audience (vv. 13–15) and the other from the believing community (vv. 16–18).

The skeptics, ever the aggressors in this argument, had once again managed to offend God with their words (v. 13). They had spoken with strong words and in an impudent and presumptuous way.

God had offered to be put to the test and they had responded, in effect, "The wicked have already put you to the test and have concluded that you are a paper tiger. You threaten, but you never follow up on your threats."

The prophet protested on behalf of God, "But the nations will call you blessed and happy if you will test Him and do what He says."

But Malachi's protest was in vain, for the arrogant only greeted his words with more hooting and jeering while they chorused with unmitigated insolence, as if presenting diplomas to a graduating class, *"So now [by the powers invested in us] we call the proud blessed"* (v. 15a). The situation was almost beyond redemption.

The skeptics' contention was that it did not pay to serve the Lord. They disparaged God's work, saying *"It is vain to serve God"* (3:14), revealing once again their mercenary view of serving God and attending His house. What difference could anyone point to that resulted from keeping God's ordinances and walking humbly like mourners before Him, they blasphemed. All service to God was literally "in vain" (the same word found in the third commandment). It was useless, unsubstantial, unreal, valueless and materially and spiritually worthless to the servant. The skeptics alleged, moreover, that carrying out God's requirements had resulted in no real profit, no increase, no observable return in material prosperity or political influence. The word "profit" occurs thirty-nine times in the Old Testament as a technical term for the weaver's act of cutting a piece of cloth free from the loom. Thus in Malachi it has the negative connotation of men expecting their "cut" or percentage, as a racketeer or gangster would demand his "cut" for his evil work (cf. Gen. 37:26).

The skeptics' last impudent charge was that "mourning" had yielded no profit either. The men had clothed themselves with dark clothing (the word for "mourning" comes from the verb "to be dark"), or perhaps had darkened their faces to convey grief and sorrow for the sin and plight of the nation, but concluded that their acts were useless. It is little wonder that they were useless, for once again the skeptics attributed worth to the acts themselves, though they were devoid of genuine piety (cf. Isa. 58:2–12).

Verse 15 recalls an atrocious statement by the skeptics of precisely the opposite of what God had stated in verse 10! The skeptics have mockingly pronounced the "proud" and arrogant "most happy" or "blessed." Furthermore, they have asserted that it is the proud who *"are raised up,"* or "built up," into families and houses, as Shiphrah and Puah were similarly built into families as a result of obeying and fearing God more than they feared Pharaoh and his command to kill all baby boys (Exod. 1:21). The wicked, they had blasphemously implied, can tempt God and go free; nothing bad ever happens to them. How frequently have we heard that claim in our day!

"Then" (v. 16a), at the same time, another group, the believing community, had an altogether different attitude and response to God. They *"feared the* LORD" (v. 16), for the content of their conversations with one another was focused on Him. We are told twice in verse 16 that the believers feared the Lord. This is most significant, for the primary weakness of the leaders of Israel was their lack of fear of the Lord (1:6).

The "fear of the Lord" is a virtual synonym for the righteous living and holy lifestyle that grow out of this fear (Lev. 19:14; Deut. 17:19; 2 Kings 17:34). Fear is one motivation for holy living and maintaining an attitude of complete trust and obedience to the Lord as one's Master and Savior.

The believing community was distinguished by another characterization as well: they "thought on his name." The NKJV translates this phrase as *"meditate on His name"* (v. 16e). From the somewhat infrequent usage of this verbal form, it is possible to say that what these believers were doing was "setting their value on," or "esteeming as their highest prize," the name of the Lord (cf. Isa. 33:8; 53:3; Ps. 144:3). God's "name" comprises His person, His qualities, His doctrine, and His ethical and moral standards—these were the things the believers judged to be their highest and most prized possessions! If you asked any of these God-fearers what they judged to be their wealth, property, or greatest asset, they would have pointed to the name of God and all that it stands for. This is exactly as our Lord counselled, "For where your treasure is, there your heart will be also" (Matt. 6:21). Solomon said as well, "For as he thinks in his heart, so is he" (Prov. 23:7). The believers thought on the name of the Lord, and as a consequence it was reflected in their character.

God, in turn, *"listened and heard them"* (v. 16). In fact, not only were their prayers answered, but their names and actions were written in *"a book of remembrance"* (v. 16; a book not to be confused with the "book of life," which bears a different designation or title [Ps. 69:28; Rev. 20:12, 15]). Here we see something similar to the Persian custom of entering into a book all acts that should be awarded in the future (e.g., Esther 6:1). The psalmist knew of such a book, for even his tossings on his bed were entered into God's book (Ps. 56:8; cf. Dan. 7:10). God had not forgotten what these men and women had endured. Nor was He unaware that He had been the sole object of their thinking and the center of their values.

In addition to answering their prayers and entering their names into His book of remembrance, God makes two more promises to the believers: *"They shall be Mine"* and they would be God's *"jewels"* (v. 17). In Exodus 19:5–6 Israel had been accorded the status of God's "choice or treasured possession." Unlike real estate, which could not be moved, the believers were possessions that could be moved—God's "jewels." The term "jewels" is used to refer to both Old Testament (Deut. 7:6; 14:2; 26:18; Ps. 135:4) and New Testament believers (Eph. 1:14; 2 Thess. 2:14; Titus 2:14; and 1 Pet. 2:9). Since they had been called God's "son," his "firstborn," and "My people" (Exod. 4:22–23; Hos. 2:23), it is little wonder that He claimed them as His own.

When the day comes for God to carry out His plan for judgment and salvation (v. 18), the believing community will be cared for. God will "spare" the righteous believers, but His punishment will fall on the wicked. Then the distinction between the righteous and the wicked will be clear (v. 18; Ps. 1:1, 4–6; Dan. 12:2). That will end any verbal abuse against heaven.

Is There No Difference Between the Righteous and the Wicked? (4:1–3)

"For behold, the day is coming, burning like an oven, and all the proud, yes, all who do wickedly will be stubble" (4:1). This "day" will be mentioned four times in the closing verses of Malachi's prophecy (3:17; 4:1, 3, 5). It is described in ways reminiscent of Joel 2:11, 31 and Zephaniah 1:14. For five Old Testament prophets, working in four separate centuries, that "day" was "near" and "at hand" (ninth century—Obad. 15; Joel 1:15; 2:1; eighth century—Isa. 13:6; seventh century—Zeph. 1:7, 14; and sixth century—Ezk. 30:3). Each of these prophets saw an immediate event in his own generation as a direct, if only a partial, part of that "day." For example, for Obadiah the event was the destruction of Edom, for Joel it was the locust plague, and for Isaiah it was the pending destruction of Jerusalem. Nevertheless, a group of events would emerge that would surround the second coming of our Lord when He would "destroy the whole earth" (Isa. 13:5) and eventually reign as its King (Zech. 14:1, 8–9).

The view that there are successive fulfillments leading to a single coming at the end of the series does not violate the principle of a single meaning to the prophecy. Says T.V. Moore:

> Every language contains these formulas, which refer not to any one event, but a series of events, all embodying the same principle, or resulting in the same cause. . . .
> We find repeated instances of this species of prediction in the Scriptures. The promise in regard to the "seed of the woman," (Gen 3:15) refers to no one event, but runs along the whole stream of history, and includes every successive conquest of the religion of Christ. . . .
> [This] class of prediction . . . is . . . what the old theologians called the *novissima.*[20]

Thus, the "day of the LORD" is a generic phrase or collective event that gathers together all the antecedent historical episodes manifesting the judgment and salvation of God as they pointed to God's ultimate intervention in human history. Willis J. Beecher defines "generic prophecy" this way:

[It is] one which regards an event as occurring in a series of parts, separated by intervals, and expresses itself in language that may apply indifferently to the nearest part, or to the remoter parts, or to the whole—in other words, a prediction which, in applying to the whole of a complex event, also applies to some of its parts.[21]

On that final day, serialized, as it is described by Moore and Beecher, God would consign the wicked to eternal torment. The image of consuming flames is often employed by the prophets (Joel 2:3, 10; Isa. 10:16; 30:27; Zeph. 1:18; 3:8; Jer. 21:14; Ezk. 21:1–4). God's anger would burn against the wicked (Isa. 13:9) as He came back in "flaming fire" (2 Thess. 1:8).

Some cannot believe what they read here; therefore, they teach that all people will, somehow, be saved. A God of love, they reason, cannot condemn anyone to an eternal punishment. But this reasoning incorrectly pits God's love against His justice. Such universalism cannot be supported by the Scriptures. Rather, Scripture tells us, God's prior judgments are but foretastes of what will come in the final day as the totality of God's wrath will finally be felt. The wicked will all be ignited like dry stubble after a hot summer.

Meanwhile, the righteous God will come as *"the Sun of Righteousness"* (4:2). No doubt Malachi means to point to Christ when He speaks of this one who is the "Light of the world," "the LORD our Righteousness" (Jer. 23:5–6). Did not Zechariah blend together Malachi 4:2 with Isaiah 9:2 in Luke 1:76–79, in that he saw the messianic connotations in the name "Branch," which also had the same root "to sprout, or to spring forth" in it, and thus linked up with the "sunrise" of the Greek translation of Malachi 4:2? Thus righteousness, with all its attending consequences, will arise for those who fear the name of God.

"Healing in His wings" (4:2) no doubt refers to deliverance from destruction, as depicted in Psalm 107:20. When the sun sent forth its rays, like the winged disc so familiar to the ancient Near East, the long winter of suffering for the righteous would come to a glorious end. Those who feared God's name would feel as invigorated as calves released after a long winter boxed in a stall (Mic. 2:13). The wicked, however, would be trampled under foot, just as Genesis 3:15 and Romans 16:20 had promised. God would tread the winepress of His justice (Isa. 63:1–6), and the wine of those bad grapes would flow as He crushed them under His feet.

Are There No Guides for the Righteous? (4:4–6)

The connection between this block of text and the preceding one is difficult to make, but it seems that Malachi wished to remind the righteous that the triumph depicted in 4:2–3 was possible only if they remembered the Law of God's servant Moses.

This was not a call to retreat into formalism or to a ritualistic legalism, but, as E. W. Hengstenberg observes:

> The law is referred to here, . . . not according to its accidental and temporary *form*, but according to its essential character, as expressive of the holiness of God, just as [it is] in Matthew v. 17. In this light, it is eternally the same in the eyes of God and not one jot or title of it can pass away.[22]

God's people and God's Law are inseparable. If God's people did not keep the Law, then they must be subject to the judgments warned of in that Law.

New Testament believers must likewise be careful not to erect a wall of partition between the Law of God and the promises of God, for Paul himself posed the question whether the promises of God had rendered the Law null and void. Paul's answer was swift and clear: by no means whatsoever; instead, by faith the Law had been established, not wiped out (Rom. 3:31). Otherwise, three-fourths of what God had to say to us—the Old Testament—would be obsolete!

Finally, God would *"send . . . Elijah the prophet before the coming of the great and dreadful day of the Lord"* (4:5). There is a clear relationship between this verse and 3:1. They both contain: (1) the word *"Behold,"* (2) the participle "I am sending," (3) the mission of calling the people to "turn," and (4) references to the day of the Lord.

While there have been many forerunners—such as John the Baptist, Augustine, Calvin, Meno Simons, Luther, Zwingli, Moody and Graham—that final day will reveal the one who is the summation of, and more than, each of these. He may well be one of the two witnesses mentioned in Revelation 11:3–12. True, he is not identified there as Elijah, but—in a clear allusion to the work of Elijah—he does have the power to shut up the heavens so that it does not rain during the time he is prophesying (Rev. 11:6.)

Humanity worldwide will turn to the Lord, or God will need to come and smite the earth with a *"curse"* (4:6). The "curse" denotes involuntarily dedicating everything back to God, in contrast to the deliberate act of dedication called for in Romans 12:1–2. After a long pursuit of the wicked, God must ultimately claim everything back to himself, for the earth is the Lord's and the fulness thereof (Ps. 24:1).

Notice, however, that when the hearts of the fathers turn to the Lord the generation gap is bridged, for then it is that the hearts of the fathers are turned to the children and the children's hearts are turned to the fathers (4:6).

CONCLUSION

Is it worthwhile to serve the Lord? Is God a paper tiger not willing to do anything against the wicked? Is there really no difference between the righteous and the wicked? Are there no more guides to direct us?

How flimsy is the case of the arrogant and skeptical. But how vulnerable will they be in that day when God finally decides to act!

Our most valuable possession of all should be God's holy name. And to think, too, that from God's enormous storehouse of wealth in all the cosmos, He should identify the believing community as His "jewels" and most wonderful possession! What a marvelous God is ours, and how enormously and fabulously rich we are as sons and daughters, heirs together with Him.

Malachi is a rich and wonderful book, to say the least. It is one of the most practical and hard-hitting books in the whole canon. What a grand way to conclude the revelatory work of the Old Testament!

NOTES

1. Beth Glazier-McDonald, *Malachi: The Divine Messenger* (Atlanta: Scholars Press, 1987), p. 1.

2. Ibid., p. 2.

3. John Calvin, *The Twelve Minor Prophets* (Edinburgh: T & T Clark, 1849), V:459.

4. Cf. the statements of Dorotheus, Ephraem Syrus, Hesychius, and Isidorus Hisp, as cited by John M. P. Smith, *Book of Malachi: International Critical Commentary* (Edinburgh: T & T Clark, 1912), p. 10.

5. John Irving Lawlor, *The Nabataeans in Historical Perspective* (Grand Rapids: Baker, 1974), and Philip C. Hammond, "New Light on the Nabateans," *Biblical Archaeology Review* 7(1981): 21–41.

6. The most comprehensive analysis of Malachi's form is, Egon Pfeiffer, "Die Disputationsworte im Buche Maleachi (Ein Beitrag zur formgeschtlichen Struktur)," *Evangelische Theologie* 19 (1959): 546–68.

7. James A. Fischer, "Notes on the Literary Form and Message of Malachi," *Catholic Biblical Quarterly* 34 (1972): 315–20.

8. *See* Norman H. Snaith, *The Distinctive Ideas of the Old Testament* (London: Epworth, 1944), p. 132.

9. C. S. Lewis, *The Problem of Pain* (New York: Macmillan, 1953), pp. 30–36. In C. S. Lewis's first three analogies of God's love, His love is compared to: (1) the love of an artist for an artifact he or she has created, (2) the love a master has for a dog or pet, and (3) the love of parents for their child. These provide lesser glimpses of what God's love is like.

10. Lactantius, *The Minor Works: De Ira Dei [The Wrath of God]*, trans. Sister Mary Francis McDonald (Washington, DC: Catholic University of America, 1965), 154:69.

11. These reasons closely follow the arguments of E. W. Hengstenberg, *Christology of the Old Testament*, trans. James Martin, 4 vols (Edinburgh: T. & T. Clark, 1875), III:339–43. *Also see* P. A. H. deBoer, "An Inquiry into the Meaning of the Term *Maśśāʾ*," as cited by Baldwin, *Haggai, Zechariah, and Malachi*, pp. 162–63. Cf. Walter C. Kaiser, Jr., "*Maśśāʾ*," *Theological Wordbook of the Old Testament*, ed. R. Laird Harris, Gleason L. Archer, Jr., and Bruce K. Waltke, 2 vols. (Chicago: Moody, 1980), II:602.

12. *See* J. A. Thompson, "Israel's 'Haters,'" *Vetus Testamentum* 29 (1979): 200–205. The terms "love" and "hate" are used respectively in the religious realm for those who acknowledge Yahweh's lordship and those who do not.

13. The text discussed in this part of our outline, 2:1–9, is, along with 1:6–14, part of the second of the six sections which comprise the book of Malachi (see our discussion above of the six divisions of Malachi). We have chosen to discuss the second section in two parts because it would otherwise be unwieldingly long for the purposes of most sermons.

14. For a fuller discussion of these matters, see Walter C. Kaiser, Jr., "Name," in *The Zondervan Pictorial Encyclopedia of the Bible*, ed. Merrill c. Tenney and Steven Barabas, 5 vols. (Grand Rapids: Zondervan, 1975), IV:360–66.

15. I am indebted for these observations to my former student Gary V. Smith, "Paul's Use of Psalm 68:18 in Ephesians 4:8," *Journal of the Evangelical Theological Society* 18 (1975): 181–89.

16. T. V. Moore, *Haggai, Zechariah and Malachi: A New Translation With Notes* (New York: Robert Carter & Bros., 1856), pp. 362–63.

17. For a more detailed consideration of this significant text with some of the most important recent bibliography, *see* Walter C. Kaiser, Jr., "Divorce in Malachi 2:10–16," *Criswell Theological Review* 2(1987): 73–84.

18. Alan Robinson, "God, the Refiner of Silver," *Catholic Biblical Quarterly* 11 (1949): 190.

19. As noted by Baldwin, *Haggai, Zechariah, and Malachi*, pp. 245–46.

20. Moore, *Haggai, Zechariah*, pp. 397–98.

21. Willis Judson Beecher, *The Prophets and the Promise* (New York: Thomas Y. Crowell, 1905, reprint, Baker Book House [1970]), p. 130.

22. Hengstenberg, *Christology of the Old Testament*, 4 vols. IV: 19.

Bibliography

Micah

Alfaro, Juan I. *Micah: Justice and Loyalty: International Theological Commentary*. Grand Rapids: Eerdmans, 1989.

Allen, Leslie C. *The Books of Joel, Obadiah, Jonah and Micah: The New International Commentary on the Old Testament*. Grand Rapids: Eerdmans, 1976.

Feinberg, Charles Lee. *Minor Prophets*. Chicago: Moody, 1976.

Hagstrom, David Gerald. *The Coherence of the Book of Micah: A Literary Analysis*. Atlanta: Scholars Press, 1988.

Hillers, Delbert R. *Micah. Hermeneia*. Philadelphia: Fortress, 1984.

McComiskey, Thomas Edward. "Micah," in *The Expositor's Bible Commentary*. 12 vols. Grand Rapids: Zondervan, 1985, vol. 7.

Smith, Ralph L. *Micah-Malachi: Word Biblical Commentary*. Waco, Tx.: Word Books, 1984.

Waltke, Bruce K. "Micah," in *Obadiah, Jonah, Micah: Tyndale Old Testament Commentaries*. Eds. Desmond Alexander, David Baker and Bruce Waltke. Downers Grove, Il.: InterVarsity, 1988.

Wolff, Hans Walter. *Micah the Prophet*. Philadelphia: Fortress, 1981.

Nahum

Achtemeier, Elizabeth. *Nahum-Malachi: Interpretation—A Bible Commentary for Teaching and Preaching*. Atlanta: Knox, 1986.

Amerding, Carl, "Nahum," in *The Expositor's Bible Commentary*. 12 vols. Grand Rapids: Zondervan, 1985, vol. 7.

Baker, David W. *Nahum, Habakkuk, Zephaniah: Tyndale Old Testament Commentaries*. Downers Grove, Il.: InterVarsity, 1988.

Bennett, T. Miles. *The Books of Nahum and Zephaniah*. Grand Rapids: Baker, 1968.

Cathcart, Kevin J. *Nahum in the Light of Northwest Semitic*. Rome: Biblical Institute, 1973.

Feinberg, Charles Lee, *Minor Prophets*. Chicago: Moody, 1976.

Freeman, Hobart. *Nahum, Habakkuk, Zephaniah: Minor Prophets of the Seventh Century*. Chicago: Moody, 1973.

Maier, Walter A. *The Book of Nahum: A Commentary*. St. Louis: Concordia, 1959.

Smith, Ralph A. *Micah-Malachi: Word Biblical Commentary*. Waco, Tx.: Word Books, 1984.

Robertson, O. Palmer. *The Books of Nahum, Habakkuk and Zephaniah: The New International Commentary on the Old Testament.* Grand Rapids: Eerdmans, 1990.

Habakkuk

Achtemeier, Elizabeth. *Nahum-Malachi: Interpretation—A Bible Commentary for Teaching and Preaching.* Atlanta: Knox, 1986.

Amerding, Carl. "Habakkuk," in *The Expositor's Bible Commentary.* 12 vols. Grand Rapids: Zondervan, 1985, vol. 7.

Baker, David. *Nahum, Habakkuk and Zephaniah: Tyndale Old Testament Commentaries.* Downers Grove, Il.: InterVarsity, 1988.

Barber, Cyril. *Habakkuk and Zephaniah.* Chicago: Moody, 1985

Craigie, Peter. *Twelve Prophets. Daily Study Bible.* 2 vols. Philadelphia: Westminster, 1985.

Freeman, Hobart E. *Nahum, Zephaniah, Habakkuk: Minor Prophets of the Seventh Century.* Chicago: Moody, 1973.

Gaebelein, Frank. *Four Minor Prophets: Obadiah, Jonah, Habakkuk and Haggai.* Chicago: Moody, 1970.

Gowan, Donald. *The Triumph of Faith in Habakkuk.* Atlanta: Knox, 1976.

Lloyd-Jones, D. Martin. *From Fear to Faith: Studies in the Book of Habakkuk and the Problem of History.* London: InterVarsity, 1953.

Robertson, O. Palmer. *The Books of Nahum, Habakkuk and Zephaniah. The New International Commentaries on the Old Testament.* Grand Rapids: Eerdmans, 1990.

Smith, Ralph L. *Micah-Malachi: Word Biblical Commentary.* Waco, Tx.: Word Books, 1984.

Szeles, Maria Eszenyei. *Habakkuk and Zephaniah: International Theological Commentary.* Grand Rapids: Eerdmans, 1987.

Zephaniah

Achtemeier, Elizabeth. *Nahum-Malachi: Interpretation—A Biblical Commentary for Teaching and Preaching.* Atlanta: Knox, 1986.

Baker, David W. *Nahum, Habakkuk and Zephaniah: Tyndale Old Testament Commentaries.* Downers Grove, Il.: InterVarsity, 1988.

Barber, Cyril. *Habakkuk and Zephaniah.* Chicago; Moody, 1985.

Bennett, T. Miles. *The Books of Nahum and Zephaniah.* Grand Rapids: Baker, 1968.

Feinberg, Charles Lee. *Minor Prophets.* Chicago: Moody, 1976.

Freeman, Hobart. *Nahum, Zephaniah, Habakkuk: Minor Prophets of the Seventh Century.* Chicago; Moody, 1973.

Heflin, J. N. Boo. *Nahum, Habakkuk, Zephaniah and Haggai.* Grand Rapids: Zondervan, 1985.

Robertson, O. Palmer. *The Books of Nahum, Habakkukand Zephaniah: The New International Commentaries on the Old Testament.* Grand Rapids: Eerdmans, 1990.

Szeles, Maria Eszenyei. *Habakkuk and Zephaniah: Wrath and Mercy. International Theological Commentary.* Grand Rapids: Eerdmans, 1987.

Walker, Larry Lee. "Zephaniah," in *The Expositor's Bible Commentary.* 12 vols. Grand Rapids: Zondervan, 1985, vol. 7.

Haggai

Achtemeier, Elizabeth. *Nahum–Malachi: Interpretation—A Bible Commentary for Teaching and Preaching.* Atlanta: Knox, 1986.

Alden, Robert L. "Haggai," in *The Expositor's Bible Commentary.* 12 vols. Grand Rapids: Zondervan, 1985, vol. 7.

Baldwin, Joyce. *Haggai, Zechariah, and Malachi: An Introduction and Commentary.* Downers Grove, Il.: InterVarsity, 1972.

Feinberg, Charles Lee. *Minor Prophets.* Chicago: Moody, 1976.

Gabelein, Frank. *Four Minor Prophets: Obadiah, Jonah, Habakkuk and Haggai.* Chicago: Moody, 1970.

Moore, T. V. *A Commentary on Haggai and Malachi.* Edinburgh: Banner of Truth Trust, 1960.

Smith, Ralph L. *Micah–Malachi: Word Biblical Commentary.* Waco, Tx.: Word Books, 1984.

Stuhlmueller, Carroll. *Haggai and Zechariah: Rebuilding with Hope: International Theological Commentary.* Grand Rapids: Eerdmans, 1988.

Verhoef, Peiter A. *The Books of Haggai and Malachi: The New International Commentaries on the Old Testament.* Grand Rapids: Eerdmans, 1987.

Wolf, Herbert. *Haggai and Malachi: Everyman's Bible Commentary.* Chicago: Moody, 1976.

Zechariah

Achtemeier, Elizabeth. *Nahum–Malachi: Interpretation—A Bible Commentary for Teaching and Preaching.* Atlanta: Knox, 1986.

Baldwin, Joyce G. *Haggai, Zechariah, and Malachi. An Introduction and Commentary.* Downers Grove, Il.: InterVarsity, 1972.

Barker, Kenneth L. "Zechariah," in *The Expositor's Bible Commentary.* 12 vols. Grand Rapids: Zondervan, 1985, vol. 7.

Baron, David. *Commentary on Zechariah: His Visions and Prophecies.* Grand Rapids: Kregel, 1988.

Feinberg, Charles Lee. *God Remembers*. Wheaton, Il.: Van Kampen, 1950.

Laetsch, Theodore. *The Minor Prophets*. St. Louis: Concordia, 1965.

Laney, J. Carl. *Zechariah*. Chicago: Moody, 1984.

Leupold, H. C. *Exposition of Zechariah*. Columbus: Wartburg, 1956.

Luck, G. Coleman. *Zechariah*. Chicago: Moody, 1964.

Smith, Ralph L. *Micah–Malachi: Word Biblical Commentary*. Waco, Tx.: Word Books, 1984.

Unger, Merrill. *Zechariah*. Grand Rapids: Zondervan, 1963.

Wright, C. H. H. *Zechariah and His Prophecies*. London: Hodder and Stoughton, 1879.

Malachi

Achtemeier, Elizabeth. *Nahum–Malachi: Interpretation—A Bible Commentary for Teaching and Preaching*. Atlanta: Knox, 1986.

Alden, Robert L. "Malachi," in *The Expositor's Bible Commentary*. 12 vols. Grand Rapids: Zondervan, 1985, vol. 7.

Baldwin, Joyce. *Haggai, Zechariah, Malachi: Old Testament Guides*. Sheffield: Sheffield Academic, 1987.

Feinberg, Charles Lee. *Minor Prophets*. Chicago: Moody, 1976.

Glazier-McDonald, Beth. *Malachi: The Divine Messenger*. Atlanta: Scholars Press, 1987.

Moore, T. V. *The Prophets of the Restoration: Haggai, Zechariah, Malachi*. London: Banner of Truth Trust, 1968.

Smith, Ralph L. *Micah–Malachi: Word Biblical Commentary*. Waco, Tx.: Word Books, 1984.

Wolf, Herbert. *Haggai–Malachi: Rededication and Renewal*. Chicago: Moody, 1976.